The Alan Coren Omnibus

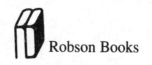
Robson Books

For Ann Brooks

. . . who started all this

First published in Great Britain in 1996 by Robson Books Ltd,
Bolsover House, 5–6 Clipstone Street, London W1P 8LE

This collection copyright © 1996 Alan Coren

The right of Alan Coren to be identified as author of this work has
been asserted by him in accordance with the Copyright, Designs
and Patents Act 1988

British Library Cataloguing in Publication Data
A catalogue record of this title is available from the British
Library

ISBN 1 86105 052 6

Set in Times by The Harrington Consultancy Ltd, London
Printed by The Guernsey Press Company Limited, Guernsey,
Channel Islands

The
Alan Coren
Omnibus

Contents

Introduction

Is that a pun coming? Hold out your hand. Flag it down.

Oh look, the pun has pulled up. It is an omnibus.

What do we expect of an omnibus? We expect predictability. We expect reliability. We expect efficiency. We expect cleanliness. We expect safety. We expect it to take us smoothly and speedily from A to B, and if we wish to go on to Q, then we expect it to do that, too. We expect, furthermore, to be able to do all this in reasonable comfort, no sudden lurches, no rude bumps, no sharp edges, no loud bangs, no unsettling surprises, and without undue interference from any batty, rowdy, criminal, lewd, or generally unsavoury characters who may not only happen to be aboard but may even be sitting close to us.

If this is what you expect, I rather fear that you have got on the wrong pun. For the omnibus on the step of which you have just set one foot is not like that at all. It has a dodgy engine and wonky wheels and loose seats. And it is totally unpredictable: arriving at each of the 72 stops along its route, it has no idea of how it got to any of them, because each time the driver set off, he simply launched himself down the winding road, not merely without either map or timetable, but without any real notion of where his vehicle might end up. He just put it in gear, and let it run.

As for both reliability and efficiency, therefore, you may confidently forget them, too. Indeed, that is, I'm afraid, just about the only thing any passenger can be confident about: the promise which may appear to be offered as each new stage of the journey is embarked upon is not to be trusted at all, since anything could happen along the way, and some of what does happen will be neither, perhaps, as clean as the passenger might like, nor as safe. Certainly, any expectation of being taken smoothly and speedily from A to B, and then on to Q, must on no account be entertained, because – oh, look, another pun is pulling up – in order to be entertained (this being the driver's prime object), the passenger may very well find that the driver has set out from A, arrived, willy-nilly, at W, turned round and driven down an unmade road to P, meandered off to G for some reason known only to himself (or not even that), and never managed to get to B at all.

Reasonable comfort? No chance. Many of these trips will make the passenger feel extremely uncomfortable, usually because the driver has taken the vehicle towards something too close for comfort. No sudden lurches? You must be joking! Or, at least, the driver must be. Trying to, anyway. Rude bumps? Plenty, and not a few sharp edges, either, plus the sort of loud bangs that go with suddenly being brought up short by an unsettling surprise, for that is the way this driver has driven all his life.

As for avoiding batty, rowdy, criminal, lewd, or generally unsavoury characters, this is beyond any question the remotest possibility of all. The omnibus is full of them. Is that Her Majesty the Queen over there, talking to herself? Yes. And is that dear old James Joyce beside her, also rambling dottily away, but in his own somewhat different manner? Right again. While upstairs, Napoleon sits fretting about his growing bosom, James Bond is uncorking the medication necessary when an agent reaches his 0075th birthday, and an ox and an ass occupy the front seat in the firm, but pitiable, belief that the omnibus is taking them to meet Jesus Christ – even if it means being forced to sit across the aisle from a rowdy criminal parrot and a cannibal cricketer, and just in front of Alexander the Great, who is, as usual, roaring drunk, and keeps falling against a screamingly gay Biggles weeping at what the open window might do to his lovely coiffure.

There are many more freaks like that – and worse – aboard this omnibus. Along with all the other things he cannot be sure about, the driver does not really know how or where they got on, let alone why, but every time he glanced back over his shoulder from the driving seat, there was another one.

That is the kind of omnibus it is. The driver thought he ought to warn you about that, because, having heard all this, you may wish to think twice before putting your other foot on the step. That is up to you, of course, but while you're pondering on whether or not to take the chance, the driver would like to point out just about the only thing about this omnibus he can be sure of: which is that, if you do decide not to take it, there certainly won't be another one along in a minute.

Household Gods

Archaeologists are getting their first insight into the philosophy of one of Britain's earliest organized religions. They have unearthed evidence of the religious beliefs held by people 5,000 years ago at what appears to have been a Stone Age ritual centre near Peterborough.

One burial complex consisted of a cremated body, a severed dog's head, an upside-down pot resembling a human cranium, a deliberately smashed red deer antler, shattered axe-heads and cattle bones. At the centre was a large corn-grinding stone deliberately positioned on its edge with a pestle under it, rather than on top, the normal position.

It may, however, be some time before the exact nature of the religion is fully understood.

Independent

'YOU'LL LIKE this,' he said. He held it up.

She paused in her grinding, and wiped her hands on the goat.

'What is it?' she said.

'It's a gate,' he replied.

A child, possibly male, scuttled up on all fours and began licking flour off the goat. Its mother, deceptively agile for one so spheroid, clubbed the child smartly, and picked its hair off the pestle. The child bawled formally for a moment or two, then waddled back across the cave, dipped a forefinger in its new wound, and, tongue curled over its prognathous upper lip, began drawing on the wall.

'OY!' cried its father. His hurled axe-head shattered beside the infant.

'Stop that,' snapped his wife. 'Education is my responsibility.'

'He's put a winkle on the buffalo,' protested her husband. 'I did not spend a week decorating that wall in order to have it outrage public decency. I trust you have not forgotten that the new people next door are coming in tonight for a full dough dinner with all the trimmings? They are a very respectable couple. She's had both her things painted to simulate rocks. Connected by a little chain going round her neck. Very chic.'

'Money down the drain,' said his wife. 'Anyone can tell they're not rocks. She only has to sneeze.'

'That is neither here nor there,' said her husband. 'I do not want her sitting through dinner staring at a bison's credentials. It's bright red, blood. Look at it. Your eye goes straight to it. They'll think we're common as muck. I might as well put this gate straight back in the cow for all the good it'll do.'

He held up the rough oblong of thong-bound ribs and shook it. A clavicle fell off.

'What's it for?' asked his wife.

'It's for the end of the path,' replied her husband.

Her thin brow furrowed. At the shock, something jumped out of her fringe, hopped about a bit, and vanished into the goat.

'You what?' she said.

Her husband rolled his little eyes.

'A path,' he said, 'is a flat item that sort of pokes out in front of a home. When you have smart people in for dinner, they have to walk up it. In order to walk up it, they have to push open a gate.'

'I do not see,' said his wife, 'why they can't just come round the corner of the hole.'

'Without knocking?' cried her husband. 'It would be unthinkable!'

His wife pondered this for a time. Finally, she said:

'Yes, it is.'

Her husband put the gate down, and went out, and came back in with another skeletal assembly. It was considerably more femoral than the first.

'That's a big gate,' said his wife. 'There's enough soup in that for a month.'

'It is not a gate,' said her husband, 'it is a door. It is what visitors knock on. Like this.'

He placed the door in the entrance hole and banged it with his knuckles. It fell to its constituent bits.

'Is it supposed to do that?' she enquired.

Her husband, having hitherto only heard about knocking and not actually tried it, said:

'Yes.'

'There's a lot of work goes into these dinner parties,' said his wife.

'You don't get owt for nowt in this life,' said her husband.

'I beg your pardon?'

'Small talk,' he explained, somewhat smugly. 'You hear it in all the best places. For example, who's she, the cat's mother? There's more to this than meets the eye, that's another good one. You just pop 'em in when it goes quiet. By the way, it needs a rat on it.'

'I like that one,' she said. 'By the way, it needs a rat on it. I'll remember that.'

'No, no, no!' he shouted, with such reverberant force that everything that had recently hopped into the goat now hopped on to the child. 'That was not one of them! I was talking about the door. The door will need a rat on it.'

His wife looked at him for a while, then returned to the grinding.

'Yes,' he said, 'I thought that would impress you. I thought you would have no reply to that. There is no need to thank me. It is my job, ensuring that we go up in the world. You may now inform your friends and relatives that we live at Number Rat.'

'Number Rat, eh?' said his wife, carefully.

'As soon, that is, as I have put the door together again and hung a suitable rat on it, thereby distinguishing ourselves from our new neighbours at Number Hedgehog.'

'Aha!' cried his wife, stopping in mid-pestle. 'There's more to this than meets the eye!'

'Very good,' he said. 'You see what you can do if you really try? Nobody would guess your father ate people.'

'They've got a gate and a path and a door at the end with a hedgehog on it, then?'

3

'Put it all up this morning,' he said, nodding. 'Not to put too fine a point on it – that's another good one, incidentally, ideal for most occasions – this has now become a neighbourhood. It has always been a dream of mine to live at Number Rat, the Neighbourhood. Stone me,' he cried, ignoring the attendant risk, 'do you realize that if we could only persuade that bastard on the other side to kick his gibbon out and find a more suitable consort, we could very well become a Residential Suburb!'

'He could make a door and hang her on it,' said his wife, somewhat heavily. 'It could be Number Gibbon.'

Her husband looked up.

'Is anything wrong?' he enquired.

'Only that it is a mistake to run,' replied his wife, 'before you can, er – what's that thing where your knuckles come off the ground and you fall over?'

'Lager?' said her husband. 'The stuff that bubbled out of the nuts last year? I do not quite –'

A shadow touched his small toe, and he jumped.

'Crikey, that's never the time, is it?' he cried. 'They'll be here any something!'

In the event, all was ready. The sun was low, and the door fell off.

'Oh, dear!' said the woman from Number Hedgehog.

'Ho, yes, absolutely!' cried her host, ushering her inside. 'Oh dear, indeed! Who's she, the cat's mother? You don't get owt for nowt in this life.'

The woman from Number Hedgehog glanced at her husband, who was attached to a long thin thong that disappeared beyond the now doorless hole.

'Your door – ' began the woman again.

'Yes, a little winner, isn't it?' cried the man from Number Rat. 'You only have to look at it and it's off. By the way, may I enquire what that is on your husband's wrist? Something fashionable, I'll be bound!'

'It's our dog,' said the man from Number Hedgehog. He tugged on the thong, and a wall-eyed yellow animal lurched into the cave and sank its fangs greedily into the pile of door.

'Put it down, Spot!' cried its master, but the dog merely

scuttled into the far darkness and began crunching invisibly.

'I'm sorry,' said the man, 'but I'm afraid he is not yet fully domesticated.'

'Think nothing of it,' replied the host. 'It is only a hinge he has got hold of. We have an entire cowful out back. On the patio.'

'Ah,' said his neighbour.

'Imagine taming a dog!' exclaimed the man from Number Rat. 'It means you can take it about without it going for you! It means you are never without a fresh meal. Dearest,' he called into the murky recess, 'the people next door have brought a dog!'

His wife emerged from the smoke.

'What am I going to do with all this dough, then?' she said.

'Ha, ha, they are taming it to eat *later*!' explained her husband.

'What we did bring you,' said the woman from Number Hedgehog, quickly, 'is this rather interesting pot.' She took it out, and looked around. 'Do you have an occasional table?'

'An occasional table, an occasional table!' cried the man from Number Rat. 'Goodness me, you don't get a cat's mother for owt, now where did I put that occasional table, well I never did, there's more in this than meets . . .'

He disappeared into the rear of the cave. The other three stared at one another. Throats were cleared. The dog howled, once. And then, on a rumbling sound, the householder reappeared. He was dragging the grinding-stone, and had the pestle in his teeth.

'Leg came off,' he gasped.

He heaved the stone on to its edge, and jammed it steady with the pestle.

'Very nice,' said the woman from Number Hedgehog. 'Rough-hewn, perhaps, but, as a decor statement, frank. It says what it is.'

'It says it's a grinding-stone,' muttered the woman from Number Rat.

Her husband put the pot on it. She caught her breath.

'It resembles a human cranium,' said the woman from Number Hedgehog. 'Isn't it amusing?'

'Ho, absolutely!' cried her host, leaping back and putting his head on one side, critically. 'It sets off them three sets of red deer antlers a treat! Have you noticed how the different sizes are cunningly arranged on the wall to give the appearance of flapping into the distance?'

'Yes,' said the man from next door. 'We used to have a similar arrangement until she chucked 'em out. You know women. They see a thing all over everywhere, and right away they reckon it's common.'

'Oh, do they?' shouted his hostess, with unexpected vehemence. 'Well, how about this, then?'

Whereupon she snatched the lower antler from its peg, exposing the hitherto concealed buffalo and its scarlet addendum.

The woman next door reeled, and covered her eyes. Her husband leapt up.

'Come on, Spot!' he called, and pulled on the thong.

The further end of which came into the room with remarkably little resistance.

Everybody looked at the head.

An unseen child burped.

'He has eaten Spot!' shrieked the woman from Number Hedgehog. 'The little bastard has consumed our dog!'

The neighbours swung round.

The woman from Number Rat was brandishing the cranial pot.

'It is no use giving yourself them airs, Lady Muck!' she cried. 'I would know this so-called present of yours anywhere. It belonged to my poor dead dad.'

'I never claimed it was new,' snapped her neighbour. 'I purchased it second-hand from someone who doubtless came by it after your father's demise. Where did he keep it?'

'He kept it on the end of his neck!' shrieked the woman from Number Rat, and, snatching up the fallen antler, lashed hideously out.

The man from Number Rat sat in the middle of his new path, watching the moon rise. Smoke blew past him from the cave behind, and his nostrils flinched at the familiar fragrance. He had not chosen to prevent her. The apple did not fall far from the tree, and she would not waste good meat.

One day, they would have a proper garden here, with a pond.

6

Possibly even a laburnum; they might well name their littl° home after it. It would be surrounded by other little homes, perhaps in crescents, like the moon, each separated from the other by a trim hedge. Everyone would be very nice to everyone else. It would all be terribly civilized.

The man smiled to himself, in the darkness. It was nice to have something to believe in.

Sea Change

A public beach has been put out of bounds at Great Yarmouth
so that fifty pairs of little terns can nest in peace. A stretch of
shore a third of a mile long and a hundred yards wide has been
cleaned and roped off.
The terns have flown 4, 000 miles from Gambia to mate.

Daily Telegraph

'I CAN remember when you couldn't get on that beach without a
tie,' said the crab, from the edge of the rock-pool.

The gull, perched on the ledge above it, glanced down.

'Must have been a bugger to knot,' it observed, 'with claws.'

One stalked eye emerged slowly from the crab's armoured slot
and stared at the gull for a time.

'What?' it said.

'Bow-tie, was it?' enquired a prawn, breaking the surface. 'I
couldn't help hearing.'

'It would have to be,' said the gull. 'He could hardly wear the
other sort.'

'I've always wondered what they were called,' said the prawn,
thoughtfully. 'Has it ever struck you as funny, having one called
a bow and the other one not called anything?'

'No, it hasn't,' said the gull.

The crab's other eye came out.

'Why would he have to wear a bow, anyway?' asked the
prawn.

'First off,' said the gull, 'it would go better with his shape. But
mainly, it's the practical side. If he wore the other kind of tie, it
would trail in the mud.'

8

'It would be filthy,' nodded the prawn, 'in no time. I see that.'

'Plus trip him up. It is one of the shortcomings of running sideways. The tie would hang down in front,' explained the gull, 'and he would be forever running over it.'

'Unless he had the knot on one side,' said the prawn.

'He'd look ridiculous,' said the gull.

The prawn considered this.

'Beats me why they wanted him to wear a tie at all,' it said.

'They were probably partial,' murmured a winkle who had hitherto kept itself to itself, 'to a nice bit of dressed crab!'

At which it convulsed so uncontrollably as to lose its grip on the underside of the rock, drop to the sand, and roll about, hooting.

'*Nice bit of dressed crab!*' it shrieked. 'Where do I get 'em from!'

The gull rose on a single flap, sank smartly to the beach, and put a yellow claw on the winkle.

'Shall I do us all a favour?' it enquired.

'Leave it out,' said the winkle, muffled. 'It is not as if I can help myself. It is in the blood, if you are a winkle. Generations of salty Cockney wit etcetera. It is expected of us. Also, being cheery goes with ending up on a pin. Look at World War One. Nil carborundum and so forth. Gassed last night, and gassed the night before. *Are we downhearted?* No!'

'Oh, let him go,' said the crab, wearily. 'It is the oldest joke in the book.'

'*I* laughed,' said the prawn.

'It's the way I tell 'em,' said the winkle.

The gull resumed its perch.

'I still don't understand,' it said, 'where they expected you to get a tie from.'

The crab sighed. Bubbles winked on its terrible jaws.

'Not *me*,' it said. 'They did not expect *me* to wear a tie. They expected one another to wear 'em. The men wore spongebag trousers and striped blazers and panama hats, and the women wore long frocks and bonnets with daisies on, it was all very elegant, this beach.'

'Pull this one,' said the prawn, 'they would have gone down

like bricks.'

'They did not wear 'em in the water,' said the crab, rolling each eye independently. 'Don't you know anything? When they wanted to swim, they went inside these little hut efforts, and they changed into bathing suits, and someone pushed the huts into the water, and they got out of the back door and into the sea.'

'Stone me!' cried the prawn. 'What a palaver! It's not even as if they eat plankton. They just go in and lollop about a bit and then they come out and turn red. Fancy going to the expense of a hut!'

The crab sighed.

'You had to be there,' it murmured. 'It had a lot of charm. It had innocence. They used to bring ukuleles and butterfly nets. They used to play French cricket and sing *My Old Man Said Follow the Van*. They did not,' muttered the crab darkly, 'have nude beaches. They did not,' and here he waved a gnarled claw towards the roped enclosure, 'have subsidized mating.'

'Oh, look!' cried the winkle, as the others, on the crab's signal, stared.

'What is it?' said the gull.

'She's having one of her terns!' shrieked the winkle.

The prawn fell about.

'You may laugh,' said the crab, 'but it is not only a gross affront to decency, it is a wanton misuse of council money. Little terns coming over here, having it away on the rates.'

'I wonder why we never see any great terns,' said the gull.

'He's right, you know,' said the winkle. 'Remember Jimmy James? Jewell and Warriss? Remember Wilson, Keppel and Betty? They all played here once. I blame television.'

'*Great turns!*' howled the prawn, clutching itself octapodally. 'You are a caution, and no mistake! Have you ever thought of doing it professionally yourself?'

The winkle shook its shell.

'It's a terrible life, these days,' it replied. 'All they want is smut. Or impressions of Robin Day. Not easy, if you happen to be a mollusc. Besides, very few of 'em speak winkle.'

'It would not surprise me,' said the crab, 'if there was not a ban on tern jokes. They have, after all, flown here from Gambia.

It would not surprise me if making tern jokes was punishable under the Race Relations Act.'

'I wonder why they don't do it at home?' enquired the gull. 'Fancy flying halfway round the world for a bit of wing-over! I usually manage with a lump of driftwood. It's a bad day for me if I have to go further than fifty feet.'

'They come over here,' replied the crab bitterly, 'on account of it is the life of Riley. Roped-off beach, no cats, no tar, no donkey doings, RSPB patrols, nothing to do all day except –'

'– take terns!' said the winkle. 'Sorry, sorry, slipped out!'

'In all probability,' said the gull, 'they do not even have to build anything. They probably get a council nest. They probably go straight to the top of the list. Fly in, make your clawprint in the space provided, ten minutes later you are –'

'– going for a quick tern along the beach!'

'I'd write all these down,' gasped the prawn, 'if the tide wasn't coming in.'

'It would not surprise me,' muttered the gull, 'if they did not even have to be married. It is probably an offence to ask 'em. You know councils. Give 'em half a chance to be seen doing sunnink for the single-parent egg, and before you know it they are coming round with a red-checked tablecloth and a candle in a bottle and a hot lugworm dinner with all the trimmings.'

'They look after their own, all right,' muttered the crab. 'Bloody clever, these Communists.'

'Sharp left terns,' said the winkle.

The prawn fell back, waving its pleopods feebly.

'Lucky I haven't got ribs,' it wheezed, 'I'd be strapped up by now!'

'They just come to me,' explained the winkle. 'Call it a gift.'

'You could have made a fortune in saucy postcards,' said the prawn warmly, when it had recovered, 'with the right contacts.'

'I've never understood why they're supposed to be saucy,' said the winkle. 'They're usually about the ones with hair under their noses asking the ones with two lumps on the front if they would care for a nice big winkle. What's so saucy about that?'

'Not just Communists, either,' said the gull, darkly. 'A fair number of 'em are gay. That is what attracts councils more than anything, these days.'

'There's a big ternover,' said the winkle.

'Is there no end to his repertoire?' cried the prawn.

'Bottomless,' replied the winkle.

They both fell over.

'I can remember,' said the crab, 'when what councils spent their money on was deckchairs and bandstands and lifebelts and little lights on the lamp-posts and stopping piers from rotting and men going round with spikes picking rubbish up off the sand. What is it all coming to?'

'It is probably a symbol of something,' said the gull. 'A lot of things are, these days.'

'Where will it all end?' asked the prawn.

'In moral depravity, is where,' said the crab.

'Tern to page three,' said the winkle.

Smiling Through

Computer scientists in California believe they have evidence that the Mona Lisa was originally wearing a necklace.

Dr John Asmus, who headed a team which investigated the picture using computer image analysis techniques, told yesterday's annual meeting of the American Association for the Advancement of Science that Leonardo da Vinci probably changed his mind about the portrait and painted over the necklace.

Independent

'HALLO!' SHOUTED Leonardo da Vinci, into the cocoa tin. 'Is that Florence 2?'

He put the tin to his ear.

From somewhere deep inside came a sound not unlike a cockroach running through iron filings. He took his ear out of the tin again.

'Speak up!' he shouted.

The tin squawked, unintelligibly.

He pulled on the string. Beyond his attic dormer, it tautened above the umber roofscape, scattering sparrows. He was about to put the tin to his ear again, when the string went suddenly slack.

'Sod it,' said Leonardo.

He put the cocoa tin back on his desk, and ran out of his studio, slamming the door. Caught in the slipstream of his flying cloak, a preliminary cartoon for *The Battle of Anghiari* trembled on his easel, floated to the floor, and came to rest face up. The moted sunlight fell across two battered Medici grenadiers crouching in a muddy crater. *'If you knows of a better 'ole . . .'* the caption began; but, like so much else these days, it was unfinished, and would in all likelihood remain so.

On the landing, Leonardo sprang into the lift, plummeted, screamed, and was hurled off his feet as it stopped without warning between floors. He rang the emergency handbell, and was winched slowly down by a bloomered pupil.

'Up the spout,' muttered Leonardo.

'*Up the spout*, Master?' murmured the pupil.

'It is a technical phrase I have invented,' replied Leonardo da Vinci. straightening his plume, 'to describe lifts.'

'Is it like *on the blink*, Master?' enquired the pupil.

'No,' said Leonardo. '*On the blink* describes telephones.'

'Is Florence 1 on the blink again, then?'

'Yes. There is a fault on the line. It is my opinion the knot has come out of Florence 2.'

'It is nevertheless,' said the pupil, simpering warmly, 'a wonderful invention, and a boon to man!'

'Inventing the cocoa tin was the hard part,' said Leonardo. He sniffed, bitterly. 'You would think that once you'd come up with the cocoa tin, it would all be downhill after that. You would think the string would be a doddle. It's a bugger, science. Half the time, it makes no bloody sense at all.' He pushed into the new revolving door which led to his workshop, and the pupil pushed in behind him. After about ten minutes of banging and shrieking, the pupil came out in front.

'Up the blink, Master?' murmured the pupil, gloomily watching Leonardo's shredded cloak smouldering in the door's boiler. 'On the spout?'

'Down the tubes,' muttered Leonardo. He dusted himself off, and peered into the bustling workshop, on the far side of which a tiny buskinned man was throwing vegetables into a large glass cylinder. 'Hallo, what's that little twerp Giovanni up to now?'

The pupil examined his clipboard.

'Where are we?' he said. 'Tuesday, Tuesday, yes, Tuesday he is supposed to be on rotary-wing research. He is down here as developing the Leonardo Gnat.'

Cursing, Leonardo ran across and snatched an imminent cucumber from Giovanni's little hands; in the confusion, a chicken scrambled out of the glass cylinder and fled, clucking.

'That's never a helicopter!' cried Leonardo.

'Insofar as you would have a job getting to P.s2 in it,' replied the pupil, 'that is true. However, Master, it works on the same principle. It is what we call a spin-off. If I may be permitted?'

Leonardo prodded the cylinder with his patent umbrella. The ferrule dropped off.

'Two minutes,' he said. 'But God help you if it turns out to be another bloody toaster. They'll never send the fire brigade out four days in a row.'

Giovanni, who had meanwhile been turning a large key protruding from the base of the cylinder, now took a deep breath, and flicked a switch. Inside the cylinder, blades whirled, howling; a white lumpy mass spread across the ceiling. Leonardo looked slowly up, as the substance coalesced into soft stalactites; a blob fell into his beard, and he licked it off.

'Vichyssoise, is it?' he enquired, levelly.

'Leek and turnip, actually,' said Giovanni. He spooned a quantity from Leonardo's hat, and tasted it. 'Could it do with a bit more garlic?'

Leonardo swung his umbrella. It turned, naturally enough, inside out, but the residual sturdiness was still enough to fell Giovanni where he stood. Slowly, his ear swelled, glowing.

'I want this one,' said Leonardo to the pupil-foreman, 'on the next train to Santa Maria della Grazie.'

'*The Last Supper*, Master?' cried the pupil-foreman, aghast. 'Are you sure he's up to it?'

'I'm a dab hand with apostles,' retorted Giovanni, struggling to his feet, 'also glassware. You could drink out of my goblets.'

'He will not be painting the wall,' said Leonardo, 'he will be plastering it prior to undercoat, as per ours of the 14th ultimo, plus removing all rubbish from site and making good.'

'Bloody hell!' cried Giovanni. 'All I forgot was the lid! I have not even mentioned the fact that the amazing new Vincimix comes with a range of attachments which chop, shred, slice, and whip the pips out of a quince before you can say Jack Robinson.'

At which point, all the windows blew in.

Slowly, Leonardo da Vinci walked through the settling dust, and looked out. A blackened face looked back at him. Neither spoke. Leonardo turned and walked back through the room.

'You'll have to go by horse,' he said to Giovanni.

'Do not be downcast, Master,' said the pupil-foreman. 'Nobody said trains were easy.'

Leonardo stared at the floor.

'Funny,' he said, 'the lid hops up and down all right on the kettle.'

The clock struck ten. Absently, Leonardo picked up the fallen cuckoo, walked out of the workshop, into the sunlit street, climbed on his bicycle, and began pedalling slowly towards Fiesole, scattering nuts and spokes. By the time he reached the house of Zanoki del Giocondo, he was carrying a wheel and a saddlebag, and sweating.

He tugged the bell-rope.

'I phoned,' he gasped, when she answered the door.

'The knot came out,' she replied.

'I thought so,' he said. He cleared his throat. 'Is he in?'

'He's out in his tank.'

'I thought he'd like that,' said Leonardo. 'I thought it might get him out of the house.' He walked into the hall. 'I hope he doesn't suspect anything, mind.'

'No. He thinks you're a faggot. Nobody else gives him presents.' A neighbour passed, and peered, and smiled. La Gioconda nodded, and closed the front door. 'How long is he likely to stay out?' she said. 'I don't know anything about tanks.'

'Days, possibly,' said Leonardo. 'We haven't cracked this business of the tracks. It tends to go round in circles until the engine seizes up. Even if he manages to get the lid open again, he won't have the faintest idea where he is.'

'But we ought to do a bit more of the painting, first?'

'You can't be too careful,' said Leonardo da Vinci. He propped his wheel against the dado, and opened his saddlebag, and took out his palette and his easel; but as he was following her through the house and out into the garden – not simply for the light but for the assuaging of neighbourly curiosity – he could not help noticing the way a sunbeam fell across her plump shoulder, and the way her hips rolled.

So they decided to do a bit more of the painting afterwards, instead.

And when they were in the garden, finally, he put the necklace around her neck, and fastened the clasp, and she cried aloud:

'Diamonds!'

'What else?' he said.

So she sat in her chair, with her hands folded and a broad smile on her tawny face, and Leonardo da Vinci's brushes flicked back and forth, and the neighbours peered from between the mullions, and were satisfied.

And then it began to rain.

Not seriously enough to drive them in; just a warm summer blob or two. But one such, unfortunately, fell on her necklace, and, after a few moments, she looked down, and stared; and then she said, carefully:

'The diamonds appear to be going grey.'

'Ah,' said Leonardo.

'Is that usual?'

Leonardo came out from behind his easel, and looked at them.

'It could be,' he said. 'With this new process.'

'I'm sorry?'

'It's a bit technical,' said Leonardo.

'Try me.'

'You start off with coal,' said Leonardo.

'I see.'

She stared at him for a long while after that, until Leonardo went back behind his easel. He picked up his brush.

He looked at her.

Her lip curled.

He put the brush down again.

'It isn't much of a smile,' said Leonardo da Vinci.

'It isn't much of a necklace,' said Mona Lisa.

Of Cabbages and Kings

'It's very important to talk to plants. They respond, I find.'
                                                    Prince Charles

RESPLENDENT IN his uniform of Colonel-in-Chief, the Queen's
Own Herbaceous Borderers – an outfit he had, of course, and
with his customary unerring flair, designed himself – he
crunched slowly down the gravelled path, hands clasped, in their
huge canvas ceremonial garden gloves, behind his back, dress
gumboots buffed to an iridescent emerald, the gilt watercress of
his epaulettes shimmering in the Highgrove sun, and inspected
the serried ranks.

Halfway along the front row, he stopped, smiled a charming,
if awkward smile, and tugged his earlobe. His straw busby
wobbled slightly.

'Good morning,' he said.

A nervous tremor, which was only to be expected, rippled
down the line. A throat cleared.

'Good morning, Your Royal Highness.'

The Prince's brow crinkled, as, from time to time, it will.

'Forgive me,' said the Prince, 'you are, er –'

'Sprout, sir.'

The Prince nodded.

'Ah. Sprout. Of course. Everything all right, Sprout?'

'Tickety-boo, sir. Hunky-dory. Top-hole.'

'Jolly good!' exclaimed the Prince. 'Splendid! That's the
stuff.' He glanced left, along the row. 'And what about you, Mr,
er?'

Panic gripped the neighbour plant. Nothing came out but a

18

hoarse and indecipherable croak.

'Begging your pardon, sir, but he is also called Sprout.'

'Is he?' cried the Prince. 'Is he really? How extraordinary!'

'We all are,' said the first sprout.

'What, everyone in this bed?' exclaimed the Prince. 'All one family?'

'There've been sprouts here for generations,' replied the sprout, proudly, 'sir.'

A bead of moisture softened the Prince's eye.

'A fine old Gloucestershire name. eh?' he murmured. He drew a handkerchief from the pocket of his scarlet smock, and blew his nose.

The sprout, in his turn, gave a discreet little cough.

'Begging your pardon, sir,' it said (it would later feel faint at the memory of its boldness), 'but we're Belgian originally. From what you might call Belgium. No disrespect, sir.'

The Prince, astonished, rocked back upon his rubber heels.

'Good heavens!' he cried. He thought for a moment or two. He tugged his earlobe furiously. He turned his signet ring. 'Plucky little Belgium, eh?' he offered, finally.

A bee thrummed past. A leaf fell, slowly. A far clock struck. The sprout could not be sure, but it thought it could feel itself growing.

'But we're here now, sir,' it said, eventually. 'In England.'

'Yes,' said the Prince of Wales. 'Yes, so you are!'

He laughed.

They all laughed.

'Tell me,' said the Prince, taking the chased silver dibbling stick from beneath his arm and waving it about a bit, 'what exactly are you working on at the moment? As, er, as sprouts.'

The sprout, at last, sensing the ice breaking around it, relaxed a little.

'Growing,' it replied.

'Growing,' repeated the Prince, nodding. 'Aha, I see. That must be, er, that must involve, as it were –'

'We start small, and gradually we get bigger,' explained the sprout. 'Until we are big enough. Until we are, in the technical parlance, grown.'

'Fascinating,' murmured the Prince, 'fascinating! Good Lord. Well I never. And no doubt, all this, er all this growing that you have to do, required –' the huge blancoed gardening gloves made vague expressive circles in the air '– some kind of very special training?'

'Yes. Up sticks, mainly. For the first few months. They use this, what's the word?'

'Twine,' prompted a mutter from the row behind.

'Twine,' said the sprout.

'Twine, eh?' enquired the Prince, brow furrowed, lip chewed. 'Twine. My goodness. Twine.'

'In lay terms, Your Royal Highness,' explained the sprout, 'string.'

'Aha!' cried the Prince, nodding vigorously. 'Good old Johnny string! That accounts for a lot. I can see that. String.' He inclined slightly forward, peering at this sprout, and at that. 'And, training apart, I assume the job also requires some pretty tricky, er, professional skills?'

The neighbouring and hitherto tongue-tied sprout, suddenly emboldened by what it took to be the newly informal atmosphere, now spoke up.

'Definitely, Your Royal Highness, sir,' it cried. 'For a start, you would not credit the amount of photosynthesis involved!'

'You speak when you're spoken to,' muttered the first sprout.

'No, no!' cried the Prince. 'Do feel free. No pack drill. Woolly-pully order, eh?'

He laughed again.

And again, they all followed. One or two, indeed, became, uncharacteristically for sprouts, hysterical. Asides were murmured. Phews were phewed. He was a bit of a wag for a Royal Personage, all right, and no mistake, they did not care who knew it.

'This photo thing,' said the Prince, when they had all recovered somewhat, 'what exactly does it, um, involve?'

'Basically,' said the second sprout, 'and if Your Royal Highness will in his gracious almightiness forgive me for cutting a long story short, we take carbon dioxide and water out of the air, and convert them into carbohydrates by, well, not to put too fine a point on it, by exposing them to light.'

'Good heavens! It sounds jolly complicated. And yet everyone manages to come out green?'

'Definitely, sir. It is something we, well, take a pride in, in a manner of speaking. Though I says it as shouldn't.'

'Nonsense!' The Prince clasped his hands together, and spread them again, passionately. 'If only more people in this great country of ours took pride in what they . . .' he left the proposition eloquently unfinished, and turned, with the exquisite timing of his trade, to offer his attention to a smaller plant beside the path.

'And you, er, learned all this in Belgium?'

The plant said nothing.

After a long minute or two, the Prince tapped his dibbler against his gumboot.

'Is your colleague all right?' he enquired, perhaps a trifle testily. The day was unseasonally hot, he had twenty or more beds to visit, a speech to make to the asparagus, a centenarian wistaria to honour, a new cold-frame to open, a blighted quince to comfort with Her Majesty's earnest good wishes.

'Begging Your Royal Highness's gracious pardon,' murmured the sprout, 'he is a carrot.'

'A carrot? *A carrot?*'

'They interplant 'em,' explained the sprout.

The Prince stared at the tuft beside his welt.

'Is it deaf?' he enquired.

The sprouts hooted. The repeated query shuttlecocked back and forth across the rows. This would be something to tell their grandchildren. As it were. The day the Prince of Wales said *Is it deaf?*

'No, Your Highness, it is not deaf, it is working underground. You'd have to shout.'

'Underground? My goodness! Is this some kind of new, what's the word, process?'

'No, no, it is the traditional and time-honoured procedure with carrots. The red bit grows downwards, sir.'

'You mean –?'

But, despite the intensity with which the query was launched, despite the keen straining of the sprouts for the opportunity to make their responsive mark, it was, sadly, too late. The alarm upon his wrist tinkled. It was time to move on. In one single, practised, ineffably royal movement, the Prince stepped to a prepared plot, deftly planted a rutabaga, sprinkled a pinch of bonemeal from the bespoke little scabbard at his hip, tugged a drawstring to unveil a staked plaque testifying to his visit, saluted, waved, and left.

The third cheer echoed away among the massed vegetables.

'One,' said the first sprout, 'of nature's gentlemen.'

'Grace.' murmured his neighbour. 'Charm. Taste. *Style*.'

'He's much taller than I thought,' said a sprout from the second row.

'Did you notice how he put me at my ease?' said the first sprout.

'In my opinion,' called a sprout from the fourth row, 'his ears have been vastly exaggerated by the media.'

'And what a sense of humour!' cried the first sprout. 'That one about the deaf carrot!'

'He could go on the stage,' said the sprout from the second row.

'Charisma,' said the sprout beside him. 'That is the only word.'

A reflective silence fell.

Until the first sprout sighed, paused, and, at long last, spoke for them all.

'You'd never think the bastard was a vegetarian,' he said.

High on the Hog

BBC Radio York is under siege from animal welfare groups concerned about a programme telling how to cook a hedgehog, which includes the sound of the hedgehog being gutted and stuffed with herbs.

Producer Chris Choi said in the programme's defence: 'We do make it clear that it is not advisable to eat hedgehogs, as they can be infested. It is also against the law to deprive a hedgehog of its liberty or to kill it inhumanely. But if you have a suitable hedgehog, there is nothing wrong with cooking it.'

Daily Telegraph

'SPEAKING AS what might reasonably be described as imminent crackling,' said Pigling Bland, 'I cannot but see this as a case of About Bloody Time Too. It is my considered view that the Tiggywinkles of this world ought to have had a lid on 'em well before this, regulo 3, baste frequently, serve on bed of fluffy rice with perhaps a lightly tossed green salad, pour on sauce just before bringing to table, and with it may we suggest a robust bourgeois growth, possibly a Pauillac.'

Across the threadbare Wilton of the Beatrix Potter Day Centre, the glittering nail-head eyes of Mrs Tiggywinkle reddened with venom.

'It's no good glowering at him like that,' said Jemima Puddleduck. 'He has a definite point.'

'The pig is the world's smartest animal,' said Squirrel Nutkin.

'You're after something,' said Pigling Bland.

'That is a trifle harsh,' said Squirrel Nutkin.

'You always were a smarmy little bastard,' said Pigling Bland, unruffled. 'I cannot for the moment spot what is going on in that ratlike head of yours, but it will no doubt come to me in a bit. I am rarely wrong.'

'I was about to say,' snapped Jemima Puddleduck, 'that the point you have got is that in the animal world, we are two nations.'

'Nice one,' nodded Squirrel Nutkin. 'Yours, I imagine, madam?'

'He's off again,' said Pigling Bland. 'How sycophantic can you get?'

'Great word,' murmured Squirrel Nutkin. 'Who would've thought anything had four syllables in it?'

'Two nations,' said Pigling Bland, 'was coined, for your information, by Benjamin Disraeli.' He paused, and, throwing out a deft trotter, nudged a small rabbit daydreaming by the fire. 'No relation, I suppose?'

'No,' said Benjamin Bunny.

'Pity,' said Pigling Bland. 'I need a new formal three-piece whistle.'

'I don't follow,' said Benjamin Bunny.

'I thought – had you been a relation – he might have offered me a discount. Possibly chucked in the waistcoat gratis.'

'Personally,' said Peter Rabbit, noticing his small cousin's blushing discomfiture at this, 'I do not like racial jokes.'

'However funny?' enquired Squirrel Nutkin.

'Furthermore,' continued Peter Rabbit, 'I cannot imagine why a pig of all people should wish to direct offensive remarks at Benjamin Disraeli. He never represented a threat to pork, as I understand it.'

'That is exactly my point,' said Pigling Bland. 'It is not easy to extend the hand of friendship to someone who considers you too dirty to roast.'

Mrs Tiggywinkle, sensing that the social wind was suddenly changing in her favour and away from her tormentor's, spoke at last.

'He never ate hedgehog, neither, and I say good luck to him.'

Pigling Bland stared at her for a time.

'What a valuable contribution to the debate!' he said finally. 'I only wish Plato were here with his nib sharpened. However, may I submit, madam, that when it comes to cleanliness, there is something of a difference between a hedgehog and a hog, namely that one of them lives in a hedge. This doubtless explains the hedgehog's hitherto unremarkable absence from top menus: stick *côtelettes d'hérisson provençale* on the table d'hôte, and the Michelin inspectors would be off up the Wimpy before you could unroll their napkin. Your average gourmet does not go looking for places where fleas hop out of the gravy.'

At this, each particular quill upon Mrs Tiggywinkle sprang erect; she might well have hurled herself upon Pigling Bland like some arcane piece of mediaeval ordnance, had he not held up a propitiatory trotter.

'Do not misunderstand me,' he said, quickly. 'There is no shame in being infested, if you are an animal. It goes with the territory. Especially if you are a hedgehog. I should imagine it is extremely difficult evicting the little buggers. Start rooting about in an overcoat like that and you could poke your eye out. All I am saying is that up until now fleas have proved something of a stumbling-block when it came to classic recipes. As far as human beings are concerned, and taking up Mrs Puddleduck's succinct point, there are two distinct categories of animals, those they eat and those they don't, e.g. badgers, moles, water-rats, toads, field-mice, stoats, weasels, or anything else in the willows.'

'What an interesting critical observation!' cried Squirrel Nutkin. 'What you are saying in your infinite wisdom is that while they do not eat anything by Kenneth Grahame, they will eat anything by Beatrix Potter.'

'Excluding, up until now, hedgehogs,' nodded Pigling Bland, 'yes. That is why I welcome Mrs Tiggywinkle to the club. It is a big day.'

'They don't eat cats,' observed Tom Kitten, from the mat.

'*Don't eat cats?*' cried Pigling Bland. 'Try walking down Peking High Road sometime! You'd be crispy before you got to the first traffic-light.'

There was a faint plop. Mr Jeremy Fisher had fainted. Pigling Bland looked at him.

'He has probably just remembered the French would pull his

legs off,' he observed drily.

'I have often wondered,' said Jemima Puddleduck, 'what they do with the rest of the frog.'

'Hard to say,' replied Pigling Bland. 'They will very likely start gutting it and stuffing it with herbs, if they can pick up Radio York. A nod is as good as a wink over there.'

'*Don't!*' shrieked Mrs Tiggywinkle.

'Pull yourself together,' snapped Jemima Puddleduck. 'You do not seem to realise the opportunity that is being offered the hedgehog world. They have been elevated to delicacy status. When my time comes, I shall be honoured to pass away *à l'orange*, very possibly as a Dish of the Day.'

'Eaten, perhaps, by a senior executive or consultant gynaecologist, exactly,' said Pigling Bland. 'Imagine getting washed down with a '47 Lafite!'

'It is against the law to deprive a hedgehog of its liberty!' cried Mrs Tiggywinkle. 'And what is stuffing us with sage and onion, if not that?'

'Enabling you to realise your full potential,' replied Pigling Bland. 'Showing you there is more to life than mopping up slugs and rolling into balls. I just hope you're suitable, as defined by producer Chris Choi. No gristle or ringworm. Rejection can be a terrible thing. I had a brother who only lived for the day when he could be turned on a spit by a topless wench in a tourist reconstruction of Queen Elizabeth's arrival at Dover. Turned out he had swine fever. Poor sod ended up as a gross of wallets and six pairs of rally gloves.'

'That was never in Beatrix Potter,' said Tom Kitten, 'was it?'

'No,' replied Pigling Bland, 'no, you're right there. She left that one for her son Dennis.'

'You mean . . .'

'Definitely. Can't you tell? It's in the blood. Look at that malicious bastard Mr McGregor, she only called his book *Peter Rabbit* for the uniform edition. Its original title was *The Singing Gardener*.'

They all pondered this silently. It seemed to explain much. It was Squirrel Nutkin who finally spoke.

'People do eat squirrels, don't they, Pigling Bland?' he

wheedled.

Pigling Bland looked at him triumphantly.

'I wondered what you were after!' he cried. 'Bloody social climber. Yes, all right, there is a lot of squirrelburger about. Do not give yourself airs, though, sunshine. It is almost entirely take-away. And, of course, only in the North.'

The others looked at him enquiringly.

'Stone me!' cried Pigling Bland. 'Does nobody read the papers? We are not the only ones split into two nations. It is no coincidence that it is Radio *York* doling out hedgehog recipes, it is on direct instructions to the BBC from Norman Tebbit, when he speaks they jump, it has become clear to him that there is no point Northerners getting on their bikes and trying to cross the border, they might as well stay put and live on hedgehog, it is very nutritious with a nice nettle stuffing and . . .'

A tiny cry went up, a tiny chair flew back, and four tiny paws scrabbled for the door, and freedom.

But Mrs Tiggywinkle got no further than the motorway beyond the end of the little front garden. In the few seconds it took the rest to recover and scurry after her, it was all over.

They gathered on the hard shoulder, and stared gloomily at the fast lane.

'Look at that,' said Pigling Bland. 'Pizza.'

In the Beginning

A five-year computer analysis unveiled by the Haifa Technion has concluded that Genesis was written by a single hand. The head of the research team described his findings as a minor bombshell: the theory that had dominated biblical scholarship for a hundred years was that Genesis grew out of folk tales edited in the days of David. But who was the author? The professor would say no more than that single authorship strengthens the traditional claim of Moses.

Guardian

MOSES TWEAKED a sliver of manna from between his molars, and stared gloomily across the scrubby dunes.

'Eighteen years,' he murmured. 'This is some wilderness! This is, like, a really major nowhere. How did we ever get into this crazy deal?'

'Who knew?' said his brother Aaron. 'What did we know from wildernesses? Were we explorers? We were in the construction business. Pyramids, we know about.'

'Roads,' said Moses, 'we know about.'

'You want a sphinx,' said Aaron, 'we can quote you. But wildernesses? I remember thinking: we'll get out of Cairo, we'll walk maybe a mile or two, we'll find a good hotel, that's it.'

'Personally,' said Moses, 'I was hoping we'd get to America.'

Aaron looked at him.

'What the hell is America?' he enquired.

'I gather it's a terrific opportunity,' replied Moses. 'Especially if you have a good trade, for example the construction business. You can clean up.'

'They need pyramids in America?'

'Naturally they need pyramids, dummy! Who doesn't need pyramids? You die, you need a pyramid. Everybody dies.'

Aaron picked up a piece of lunch, blew the sand off carefully, chewed for a while, thinking. 'Who told you about this America?' he said, finally.

'I heard it from a bush,' said Moses.

Aaron, about to swallow, choked. His brother slapped his back.

'A *bush*?' cried Aaron, when he had recovered. 'We're here eighteen years on account of some bush told you about opportunities in the construction business? Who takes career advice from vegetation? What made you think it was telling the truth, anyhow?'

'It was burning,' said Moses. 'What did it have to gain by lying?'

Aaron looked over his shoulder, down from the dune towards the scorching wadi in which forty thousand people were mooning about disconsolately on the never-ending quest for new ways of cooking manna.

'They ever get to hear you brought them all this way on the recommendation of a plant,' he said, 'we're dead men.'

Moses shrugged.

'Nobody twisted their arms,' he said. 'They were sick of working for Egyptians, they wanted their own businesses, they left of their own accord, so how come suddenly I'm responsible? Also, you're forgetting the plagues, unless maybe you think the plagues are down to me as well?'

'Don't get agitated,' said Aaron.

'Normally, frogs start falling on people's heads, they come to their own conclusions about leaving the neighbourhood,' said Moses, heavily. 'Normally, you see everybody suddenly sprouting boils, you put your house on the market. Normally, you notice first-born going down like flies, you reckon this is not a great place to bring up kids.'

'Who's arguing?' said Aaron. 'I wonder why it all happened?'

'In a word,' replied Moses, 'prawns.'

'Prawns?'

Moses nodded.

'The things Egyptians eat, you wouldn't believe. No wonder they get boils. No wonder the kids die. Did you ever see a prawn? It's an insect. A normal person sees a prawn, he treads on it. With Egyptians, they grab a saucepan. When I get around to it, I'm going to draw up a list of things you shouldn't eat. Could be a big seller.'

'It still doesn't explain the hailstones,' countered Aaron.

'If they'd stayed indoors like us,' said Moses, 'they'd have been all right. As it was, my guess is they were all out looking for prawns. Bend over a puddle looking for a tasty insect, next thing, bang! A hailstone on the head.'

'Alternatively,' said a voice, 'a rock!'

The brothers looked up, startled. From behind a nearby cactus, three men emerged: their jaws were set, their eyes were narrowed, their hirsute forearms twanged with tensed sinew.

'What's this,' snarled the largest, 'about a bush?'

'I was a foreman,' said the second, 'I was pulling down a good screw, plus pension rights. Now I'm out here eighteen years on account of a talking shrub?'

'Correction,' snapped the third, 'what you are out here eighteen years on account of is a man with terminal craziness.'

'I didn't know craziness could kill you,' said the second.

'Sometimes,' said the first man, raising his rock, 'it needs a little help.'

'WAIT!' cried Moses. 'You think that was an ordinary bush? Ha! That was a god!'

The three hesitated.

'A *god*?' muttered the largest man. 'What kind of a god has leaves?'

'He is not,' said Moses, 'always a bush. Sometimes, he's a pillar of fire. Another day, could be a cloud.'

'A cloud?'

'Or a chair. A shoe. Anything. It all depends on the circumstances.' Moses licked his lips. 'Look, if you don't believe me, how about that business with the Red Sea?'

'You mean where the equinoctial inflow moved against the current, due to the fact that the volume of the tidal wave was greater than the prevailing stream-volume, producing a temporary sharp drop in level?' said the largest man.

'Superstitious heathen claptrap!' cried Moses. 'That was the god, looking after his chosen people. Also,' here he brandished a piece of manna, 'what do you think of *this*?'

'Not a lot,' said the second man. 'Can he do steak?'

'Steak is just a load of cholesterol,' snapped Moses. 'You think he wants we should all get heart disease? This is one smart god, believe me!'

They looked at one another doubtfully; but they lowered their rocks.

'What's his name?' asked the largest man.

'His name is – ' said Moses, and stopped. His brow creased. 'His name is – ' His brow uncreased. 'It is forbidden,' he said, 'to utter his name! That'll give you some idea of how big he is.'

'Pick up the rocks,' said the largest man, to the other two.

'On the other hand,' said Moses, quickly, 'there are special circumstances. How much can it hurt? His name is – is Jehovah!'

The largest man stared at him.

'What kind of a name is that?' He turned to his companions. 'Does that sound godlike to you?'

'Jack would be better,' said the second man. 'Jack is a name you can trust. Sam, even.'

'What sort of people are you?' roared Moses, a little confidence restored. 'He brings the plagues down on the Gyppoes, he opens the Red Sea for you, he delivers groceries to the door, and you object to his *name*? Listen, I – '

'What bringing down the plagues?' objected the third man. 'You said that was because we didn't eat prawns, I heard you!'

'Aha!' cried Moses. 'But what *stops* us from eating the prawns?'

'For me,' said the largest man, 'it's the little legs.'

'Plus how the eyes stick out,' said the second man.

'It was Jehovah!' shouted Moses. 'It's all in the book.'

'Book, what book?' said the third man.

'Never mind what book!' snapped Moses. 'Who are you, all of a sudden you want to know everything? All you have to do is believe, that's the way it is with gods, and if I tell you something, that's the way it is, who did the bush choose to speak to in the first place?'

The three considered this for a while. Aaron stared at the trembling line of the horizon, wishing he had something to pray to.

'All right,' said the largest man, at last. 'Suppose we go along with the plagues, the sea, the whole bit, just tell me this? How come he picked us for the ritzy treatment, leading us to where there was unparalleled opportunities for private building firms?'

Moses cleared his throat. 'That,' he said, 'is – that is on account of he is the God of the Construction Business!'

'Are you serious?'

'Definitely. Like with the Egyptians where they have a God of Fertility, a God of Hunting, a God of This, a God of That, so what we got, naturally, was the God of the Construction Business. Better yet, that is absolutely the top god there is! He built the whole damn thing!'

'What whole damn thing?' enquired the third man.

'The world, dummy!' cried Moses. 'It was his idea, before he came up with it, there was nothing. A hole. In – ' Moses paused, but only momentarily ' – in six days! To include making good.'

'*Six days?*' exclaimed the largest man. 'For a *world*? It could take that long to order the nails.'

'He's a god!' shouted Moses. 'You think he has to hang around waiting for planning permission? He wants a world, he builds a world!' He wiped a sleeve across his gleaming forehead. 'Anyway, it's all in the book.'

'Again he mentioned the book,' remarked the second man.

'So show us the book,' demanded the largest man.

Moses grabbed Aaron's arm.

'Show them the book!' he muttered.

'Me?' cried Aaron. 'You want *me* to show them the book?'

'You mean,' said Moses, 'you haven't *got* the book?'

'That's right,' said Aaron, glaring at him. 'I haven't got the book.'

Moses turned to the three men, shaking his head, smiling.

'How do you like that?' he said. 'Somebody must have borrowed the book. Isn't it incredible the way people are with books, they take them off the shelves, they say this looks pretty good, mind if I borrow it, you say sure, take it, but do you ever see it again?'

The three men looked at one another, and twitched their cloaks.

'You got six hours to find the book,' said the largest man.

They walked out of sight into the wadi.

'That was pretty quick thinking, back there with the bush and the god and everything,' said Aaron.

'Leadership,' said Moses, 'is about not panicking in emergencies.'

'Also,' said Aaron, 'it's about coming up with a book in around six hours.'

'Yes,' said Moses, 'it's about that, too. Tell me, you got any papyrus in there?'

Aaron unslung his goatskin scrip, and rummaged.

'Papyrus I got,' he replied, 'also a stylus. What I haven't got is ideas.'

Moses shrugged.

'What ideas?' he said. 'You spend a couple of pages setting the scene then right away, boom! You bring on a couple of naked people, they fool around a bit, then there's a murder, that's the kind of thing people go for, then some disaster stuff, a conflagration, maybe, a flood, something like that – I tell you, there's forty thousand people down there, they had nothing to do for eighteen years, they're gonna fall on this like – like manna from, er, from wherever manna comes from. I tell you, this book is going to be very big! I'll dictate, you write.' He cleared his throat. '*In the beginning* – '

'Hold on!' said Aaron. 'What's wrong with *Once upon a time*?'

Moses snorted.

'Are you crazy?' he said. 'You want it to sound like a fairy story?'

Biggles Strikes Camp

News that Brideshead Revisited star Jeremy Irons is to play Biggles, the fictional aviation figure of the thirties, has raised fears among scholars that the schoolboy hero will be played as a nancy-boy.

Daily Mirror

THE SHATTERING roar of the engine was bad, but the heat was worse. Trapped in the juddering seat, the whirling blades inches from his head and howling on maximum revs, Biggles wondered whether something might not have gone terribly wrong. He tried to turn, but the restriction of that tiny space prevented him from seeing Algy behind him. He could hear Algy shouting something, but he could not, in the fearful din and the rushing of the air, make out the words. Desperately, Biggles waved a hand, hoping against hope that Flight-Lieutenant the Hon. Algernon Lacy, with whom he had been through so much, would draw on that long partnership now and interpret his brief signal correctly.

Algy did not fail him. A switch was flicked, the motor cut out, the roaring died, and with it the vibration and the dreadful heat. It was over!

Squadron-Leader James Bigglesworth, DSO, drew a deep breath, and slid out from beneath the hair-drier.

'What was all that shrieking about, you silly mare?' he enquired.

'I suddenly remembered about the conditioner,' said Algy. 'I suddenly said to myself, oh my *Gawd*, I said, I never put any hair conditioner on her, she'll frizzle up like nobody's business, I said, you know what *her* ends go like after a day in an open cockpit!'

Biggles leapt to his feet, shot his trusty co-pilot one of his most withering looks, and ran over to the mess mirror. He took one glance, and screamed faintly.

'I look like Greer Garson!' he cried. 'It's flying all over everywhere! It's very fine, my hair, it's always been very fine, body is what it lacks, it lacks *body*, I don't know how many times I've told you about not forgetting the conditioner, I remember the night we were over Bremen and that silly old queen Hopcroft caught a tracer bullet in the head and I was *covered* in icky blood and brains and everything, I remember saying to you *then*, I said I've just had this streak put in and now it's *soaked*, I'll have to rinse it out in lemon juice, and you threw one of your fits and said where are we going to get lemon juice, don't you know there's a war on, and I said never mind that, just remember *after* the lemon juice you'll have to put lots and lots of conditioner on, otherwise . . .'

'You don't half go on,' muttered Algy. 'I've only got one pair of hands, I can't be bloody everywhere, I had to comb out Gimlet's perm in the middle of everything.'

'It looks ever so nice,' said Gimlet, from the other side of the mess, examining the moustache in a little mother-of-pearl pocket-mirror. 'It's come up exactly parallel, Algy. I think I look like Ward Bond. Do *you* think I look like Ward Bond, Skip?'

Biggles glared at his navigator.

'*Skip?*' he mimicked, dropping his voice an octave. 'Ward Bond? Our little friend would appear to be feeling very masculine this morning, Algy. What do you suppose has come over him, if you'll pardon the expression?'

Algy removed the Kirby grips from his mouth.

'I blame that hormone cream she uses on her legs,' he said. 'Start with that, you never know where it's going to end. Personally, give me a good pluck every time.'

Biggles nodded.

'She thinks she looks like Ward Bond,' he said. 'If you want my opinion, dear, I'd say it was more like Anne Baxter tucking into a piece of shredded wheat!'

Algy shrieked, and fell against his captain. They foxtrotted briefly, and when they broke apart again, breathless, Gimlet had gone, slamming the hardboard door.

'Temper!' shouted Biggles. He sat down, and his co-pilot began skilfully to comb him out. Biggles, soothed, closed his eyes; but at the tap on the door, they snapped open again. 'That'll be Gimlet back to say she's sorry,' he said confidently. 'I can read her like a *book*!'

'Be firm,' murmured Algy, the tail-comb flicking.

But it was not the trusty Gimlet who strode into the mess. It was a tall, slim, freckled, red-headed youth, who saluted formally, and then, shyly, grinned.

'Who's this?' said Biggles.

'Call me Ginger,' said the youth, 'everybody does.'

'Yes, well, they would, wouldn't they, dear?' said Biggles. 'What can we do for you, if it isn't a silly answer?'

'Gimlet has told the Wing-Commander that he's not going to fly with you any more,' said Ginger, 'so I've been assigned to your crew instead.'

Biggles sprang from the chair. *Vogue* slid from his lap.

'*You?*' he screamed. '*You*, fly with *us*?'

Ginger's soft face fell. His lower lip trembled.

'Why not?' he enquired.

Biggles grabbed him by the arm, and dragged both him and Algy to the mirror.

'Look!' he cried. 'Algy's brunette, I'm ash-blonde, and you're a redhead! We look like the Andrews Sisters! It's such bad *taste*!'

'You don't *have* to be blonde,' murmured Algy. 'I could put a nice tawny tint on it. Or you could wear a wig.'

Biggles reeled!

'Me? A *wig*? Gumming it on like some poor old poof behind the scout hut, before going out to paste Jerry over the Ruhr, is that what you think this war is all about?'

'I think it's a super idea!' cried Ginger, clapping his hands. 'If you got shot down and it flew off and you were captured, the RAF could drop a spare into the camp, just like Douglas Bader!'

Algy giggled, and clapped him on the shoulder, gently.

'I think I'm going to like you,' he said. 'By the way, we haven't been introduced, I'm – '

'You have to be the faithful Algy,' said Ginger, offering his hand.

Algy held it.

'No *have* to about it, dear,' he murmured.

'I'll kill you!' hissed Biggles.

There is no telling what might have happened then, if the klaxon had not clanged, summoning them to the morning's briefing. Ginger and Algy instantly snatched up their flight-pads and teddies and ran; Biggles, caught in indecision between his pastel-blue flying scarf and the cerise with the polka-dots, followed on. When he arrived at the briefing hut, it was already full, and buzzing with excited gossip, in which Biggles had no chance to join, for at that very moment the door to the left of the dais opened, and the impressive figure of the Group-Captain limped in, followed, as always, by the loyal and almost equally impressive figure of his trusty cat, Bosie.

'He's so, oooh, I don't know,' murmured Algy. 'Very few people can get away with a game leg.'

'*You* could, Algy,' whispered Ginger. 'You've got the presence.'

Biggles hit him with his flight-bag. Sequins flew. Men went *shoosh!*

'Right, chaps,' bellowed the Group-Captain, taking a corner of the green baize that hung down over the blackboard, 'shan't keep you in suspense!'

He flung back the cloth.

The hut, as one man, gasped!

Pinned to the blackboard was a detailed drawing of the mess, covered in multi-coloured squiggles. Here and there, swatches of cloth dangled from pins, with paint-charts beside them.

'It's the new wallpaper and curtains!' breathed Algy.

The Group-Captain tapped the board with his pointer.

'Now,' he said, 'I've had a word with our chums the boffins, and they tell me that if we want an apricot dado, there is – '

'PELMETS?' thundered a voice.

The men swivelled, craned. The Group-Captain's face darkened.

'There will be an opportunity for questions later, Bigglesworth,' he said. 'Meanwhile, if you would be so – '

'They went out with the *ark*, pelmets!' cried Biggles. 'We might as well have plaster ducks going up the wall, dear! We might as well have regency stripes!'

A terrible silence fell over the hut. The Group-Captain stared at Biggles for a very long time. Then his cat began to cough. Without another word, the Group-Captain snatched Bosie from the floor, and stomped out, echoingly.

The men cleared their throats, and shuffled, and murmured. After a few minutes, the door opened again, and the Group-Captain's aide-de-camp hurried in, with tiny, precise steps, and tossed back a golden forelock.

'He's very, *very* hurt,' he said. 'He's having one of his migraines. He says you're all to go off *right this minute* and bomb Hanover!'

The door slammed.

The men got up, slowly, and began to move out. Everyone ignored Biggles.

'It's suicide, putting a pelmet up in a room like that!' cried Biggles, but nobody listened.

'I *hate* Hanover,' muttered Algy to Ginger. 'It's such a *boring* route.'

'I could navigate a pretty way,' murmured Ginger, squeezing Algy's arm, as they walked towards their Wellington. 'We could go in low over Holland. The tulips'll be out. That'd be bona, wouldn't it, Biggles?'

'Go to hell!' snarled his Squadron-Leader, and pulled himself up into the plane. Algy rolled his eyes.

'Gawd help us all,' he muttered, 'she's come over masterful!'

He allowed Ginger to climb up through the belly hatch first, and helped him with an unhurried push. Biggles was already at the controls. The starboard engine fired, the port engine followed, the bomber swung out onto the runway, lumbered over the rutted concrete, and finally heaved itself into the cold East Anglian sky.

'Makes a change, having a closed cockpit,' shouted Algy from the co-pilot's seat, to break the frigid atmosphere, 'better for my rash.'

Biggles said nothing.

'Be like that,' said Algy. He pulled his mask over his mouth, and flicked the communications switch. 'Co-pilot to navigator,' he said, 'you wouldn't fancy that new Judy Garland tonight and a skate dinner on me, by any chance, dear?'

'Love it!' came back Ginger's eager crackle, on the open channel.

Squadron-Leader Bigglesworth, trained to a hair's breadth, did not react. His experienced eyes, emphasised with just the merest hint of mascara, stared straight ahead towards the Dutch coast, unmoistening. Only the sudden whitening of his knuckles on the controls betrayed the tensions of the inner man.

Which was why, betrayed by that rigid glower, he did not spot the Me 109 hurtling in on his starboard quarter until it was too late, and the bullets were pumping into wing and fuselage! Too late, he heard the anguished cry of Algy in his ears:

'Ooooh, they've hit a fuel lead, the port engine's packed up, there's oil pouring in all *over* me, we're losing height, what'll we do?'

'Hang on!' cried Biggles. 'Don't panic, I've had oil on my flying-suit a dozen times, you just soak it in a lukewarm solution of soap-flakes and engine solvent, but,' and here his voice rose above the stricken starboard motor, '*whatever you do, don't try boiling it!*'

Algy gripped his knee.

'I didn't mean that about her skate dinner,' he shouted. Then he kicked open the bomb doors, and dropped. Ginger and the mid-upper gunner followed him. The tail-gunner was long gone.

Biggles waited until their parachutes flowered open, then he unbuckled his seatbelt, grabbed his douche-bag, and went out through the yawning bomb-bay.

It was not until the precise second when he pulled the rip-cord that he remembered about his parachute. But he was Biggles, so he merely grinned: some people would give their all for silk pyjamas, and some wouldn't. That was what life was all about.

He had just enough time to glance up through the shrouds and see the remnant tatters of his chute before he hit the Rotterdam ring-road, like a brick.

Doctor No

Doctors are increasingly travelling incognito when on holiday because of fears that they will be called to help in a medical emergency.

Daily Telegraph

BENEATH THE brass sky, stepping gingerly from patch to scorching patch of gritty sand between the supine and motionless ranks of simmering mahogany flesh, the white English couple picked their serpentine way across the Riviera beach, the only moving things, like stricken relatives come to identify victims of some unimaginable act of arson.

A few yards from the shore at which the poisonous Mediterranean licked, they found a tiny space, hemmed by two other couples less blackened than the rest, but darkening, it seemed, with every passing second. The newcomer raised his sun-hat, wincing as the noonday pounced on his thinning scalp.

'Excusez-moi,' he said, haltingly, 'mais je – that is – wondered if this, er, space was . . . ?'

The couple on his left sat up.

'It's all right,' replied the man, 'we're English.'

'Not doctors, though,' said his wife quickly.

'Oh, no, definitely not doctors,' said her husband. 'English, but not doctors.'

'Not medical at all,' said his wife. 'I was never a nurse, even before I got married.'

'Nor was I,' said the woman on the other edge of the space, sitting up and re-fastening her top.

'I can vouch for that,' said her husband. 'Not being a doctor, I

40

never ran into nurses. I remember thinking, down the pit, it's a good life being a miner, but it almost certainly means you won't marry anyone medical.' He squinted up at the white couple, shielding his eyes with his hand. 'You're not doctors, are you?'

'*Doctors?*' cried the newcomer, throwing back his head and laughing for some time, rocking back on his heels, slapping his ivory thigh. '*Us*, doctors? Ha-ha-ha, good God, my word, bloody hell, did you hear that, Alice?'

'Yes, Norman, how incredible, I thought, being taken for doctors when we're actually in the . . .'

'Tyre business!'

'. . . confectionery trade.'

They looked at one another. A gull flew by.

'We have a tyres and confectionery shop,' explained the man, after a time.

'How interesting,' said the woman on their left.

'Yes. They go very well together, actually,' said the white man, sitting down. His wife lowered herself beside him, removed her sun-dress, rooted for sun-oil in her beach-bag. A magazine, as she did so, fell out onto the sand.

The man beside her looked at it.

'Isn't that the *British Medical Journal*?' he said.

Everyone stared at it.

'*Is* it?' said the white woman. 'I wonder how it . . .'

'Yes, it is!' cried her husband. 'We got it for the weight, you know. We like to take every possible precaution when travelling. We went to our newsagent, and we said, look, we're going to the South of France, it's a terrible time of year for flies, August, what do you suggest, and he said, you cannot beat the *BMJ*, I think he called it, it has weight, it has a shiny surface for easy wiping off of fly remnants, and you will not mind using it to swat flies with because there is no possible way in which you would want to read it, since there is nothing in it of any interest to non-medical people, it is utter gobbledegook from start to finish, it is a completely closed book as far as shoe and confectionery people are concerned.' He licked his lips. 'So we brought it.'

'I thought you said tyres and confectionery,' said the man on his left.

'I did, yes, I definitely did,' replied the white man, 'and that was, that was, that was because tyres and confectionery are our *main* trade, people come in for a bar of chocolate or a pound of those boiled things, sweets, and while they're in, we show them our wide range of tyres.'

'And vice-versa,' said his wife. 'But many of them coming in for a bar of Crunchie, for example, do not have cars, do they Norman?'

'No.' He took off his hat again and wiped the sweat from his forehead with it. 'But . . . but they all have feet. And we can often sell them a shoe or two. We find.' He glanced quickly at the man on his right. 'It must make a nice change for you, being on the surface?'

'What?'

'Rather than down the mine.'

'Oh. Ah. Yes, yes it is, yes you're right there, old man! Yes it's not like the Riviera at all. down the pit.'

'You have a remarkably slim build, for a miner,' said the white lady, 'if I may say so.'

'Yes, I do,' said the miner. He spent some time lighting a cigarette. When he at last removed it from his lips, he was smiling. 'That is because I do not in fact do any digging or shovelling or anything of that order. I look after the canaries.'

His wife turned to gaze out to sea, and began, very slowly, to oil her shins.

'I didn't know they still took canaries down mines,' said the white man. 'I thought they had instruments for assessing the atmosphere.'

The miner took a long draw on his cigarette.

'They do, yes, you're absolutely spot-on there, they do. They, we, take the canaries down for the singing. It is an old tradition. There is no other entertainment in the pit, as you probably know.'

'Ah,' said the white man, nodding. The miner lit another cigarette from his stub. His fingers were shaking slightly. The white man tutted. 'I say, old man, you shouldn't, I mean I hope I'm not out of order here, but you really shouldn't smoke so much, as a miner, should you?'

The man on his right said:

'Why? Can smoking be bad for you?'

The white man looked at him, for a time. The others waited.

'Er,' muttered the white man, 'it's just that I seem to have read somewhere about those experiments they carried out with smoking mice.'

'He isn't smoking mice,' said the man on his right.

'No,' agreed the white man, nodding slowly, 'no, that is true. You do have a point there. But don't miners run the risk of some kind of chest complaint, anyway? Didn't I see that on the box, or in one of the confectionery papers, perhaps? Isn't it called, er, sili. . .'

'IN THE EXTREME!' shouted his wife suddenly, spilling vast gouts of Ambre Solaire. 'I remember now, it was in *Toffee News*, they pointed out that it was silly in the extreme to smoke down a coalmine, it could blow up, it was much better to suck sweets!'

'Ah,' said the man on the right. Nobody said anything else for a while. They took handfuls of sand from one side of their legs, and put them down on the other side. Sometimes they patted them flat. Then the man on the right said:

'*We* have a canary, interestingly enough. But it doesn't sing.'

'They don't always,' said the miner.

'Perhaps, when we're back home, you could come and look at it,' said the man on the right. 'It may have something wrong with it.'

'Ambrose doesn't do house calls,' said Ambrose's wife, quickly.

'What?' said the canary's owner.

'You'd have to come during pit hours,' muttered Ambrose. 'It really wouldn't be worth your while getting filthy, they don't have to sing, they're quite decorative just hopping about after a ball of wool, I find. Busy chap like you.'

Everyone looked at the man on the right.

'Yes,' he said, 'yes, that's true, we are very busy, right now.'

'Doing what?' enquired the white man.

A ball bounced among them before the canary owner could answer, and was retrieved by two apologetic Swedes.

'I make goalposts,' said the man on the right, 'yes, that's what

I do.'

'How remarkable!' exclaimed the white woman. 'One had never imagined goalposts being specially made, but of course they have to be, don't they?'

'It's highly professional,' said the goalpost-maker, nodding. 'There's the angles, for one thing. It is illegal, under the rules of soccer, to have anything but a right-angled corner bit, as we call it. There's not many people know that. Furthermore . . .'

He broke off. A fearful shriek had cut through the heavy air.

The crowd sprang to its feet, peering into the aching glitter of the sea whence the noise had issued. Far off, a dark blob was making pitiful ripples on the silvered calm.

'Seems to be waving at someone,' murmured the miner.

'Probably enquiring about pedalo prices,' suggested the goalpost-maker.

The white man took a pair of binoculars from his beachbag.

'Might be a baritone,' he said, 'rehearsing for . . . *Good God!*'

'What is it?' cried the other two.

'It's an Arab!' shouted the white man. 'Possibly a sheikh. He seems to have been taken ill!'

He was two lengths up when they hit the water, but the others had only paused to pull on flippers, and from then on, it was anybody's race.

Maidenhead Revisited

Pope rules out sex in afterlife
The Pope has affirmed that Catholic teaching excludes sexual activity in the afterlife, although the risen would still be male or female. He said the resurrection meant not only bodily recovery but a new state of life.

The Times

HALLO. AS you can doubtless imagine, ever since the above nugget appeared, shimmering, in last week's *Times*, the Vatican has been inundated with hysterical requests for clarification, and they have naturally turned to me, as an old friend, for assistance. What could I say but yes? It is, after all, Christmas, His Holiness has a lot on his plate in addition to its being a season of mutual caring, and I am only too glad to put my shoulder to the exegetical wheel and help in any way I can As Auden so succinctly expressed it, we must love one another, or die.

Not, as it transpires, both.

Anyway, the Vatican has duly passed on to me several sackloads of enquiry, I have sorted the correspondence out into the major categories, and I shall endeavour to answer these queries as fully and as helpfully as I can. I have also, since some categories lead naturally into others, attempted to give this little catechism a sequence.

Thank you.

What is all this about bodily recovery? I thought we got wings and a quoit. I know a number of cartoonists, and they say everybody stands about on clouds, except when they have to come back as poltergeists.

You are mixing two things up. It is a common mistake. Upon death, it is true, you float up to Heaven. You do not have a body as such, it is more a sort of outline, to facilitate cartooning: you leave your body behind in a box, and upon arrival at what we call Heaven's Gate, you get a cloakroom ticket. This enables you to claim your body when the Resurrection comes, which is what you have been mixing up with Heaven. At the Resurrection, you get your body back and carry on as normal. Nearly normal.

This body I get back: what sort of shape will it be in?

It will have been what we call glorified, i.e. restored. It will be in perfect nick, no rubbish. It may be that if you have snuffed it while bald, or during an earthquake or similar, you will not at first recognize it. That is why it is absolutely essential to hang on to your ticket.

Suppose there is an administrative cock-up? I recently deposited my briefcase at Euston Left Luggage Office, and when I returned the next day with my ticket, they gave me an umbrella, due to both halves of said ticket matching. I do not wish to be resurrected with a bamboo handle where my head is supposed to be, do I?

There is no question of this happening. I have discussed your query with His Holiness, who tells me the Almighty expects to have the whole thing on the computer by then.

Thank you very much. If my recent experience in trying to get a bloody driving licence out of Swansea is anything to go by, I shall probably come back as a gas bill. If I do not, and all the tickets match up etcetera, will my body have any clothes on? Obviously, I intend getting buried in my blue three-piece with the chalk-stripe, but as it is already beginning to rot under the arms, what happens if it all falls to bits before the Resurrection?

Many people have asked that, and the Vatican has been able to reassure all enquiries, categorically, that suiting will also be glorified to avoid possible embarrassment. This means that not only will your blue chalk-stripe be pristine under the arms, there will be no stains on your tie, either.

Having been fully restored but not allowed sex, is this not going to be a bit unsettling? I have heard what goes on in the Navy, etc.

No one said anything about *fully* restored. If, for example, you were restoring a Sheraton sideboard, you would not choose to put the original woodworm back, would you? That is the way we feel about sex, up the Vatican. You will be restored, but without a couple of glands that should never have been there in the first place.

What is the point, then, of being resurrected as male and female?
You have to get your original body back. These will have beards, busts, etc. One lot will obviously be different from the other lot. You will look exactly as you looked in your prime.

Can I be a bit taller?
No.

What about a peculiar walk? I have seen a lot of doctors, but they say there is nothing they can do, I shall have to live with it. I should not like to think I was in for an eternity of people pointing in the street.
That depends entirely upon whether you had the peculiar walk before or after your prime. If the former, there is not a lot He can do, despite His infinite wisdom. Console yourself with the thought that it might not look so peculiar to people after a few billion years. Those people who have a peculiar walk as the result of sex, of course, will find that it clears up after resurrection.

I'm sorry to come back to sex, it is not that I am obsessed or anything, but would the none-at-all rule also apply to Saturdays?
I see I have not made His Holiness clear. Once these glands are out, they are out. You cannot just pop them in for the weekend.

Does this glorification apply to domestic premises? When I am resurrected and walk the earth again, will I find they have put the loft back at 14 Palmerston Crescent, Hendon? We spent a fortune having it converted into a pine-panelled den, never mind all the upheaval and dust everywhere. Am I to assume it will be restored in my absence, plus all the tea-chests back with old hats in?
No, you are on safe ground there. Houses do not have immortal souls, they do not float up and get wings and then get resurrected, they stay where they are. If the Almighty *was* going to restore them not only would they almost certainly revert to primordial slime, which would be no use to anyone, the paperwork would be totally unmanageable. Even for Him. Planning permission alone could take eons.

All right, but who would be living there? If the previous occupier popped his clogs in situ, and then the same thing happened to us twenty years later, who gets the house? I certainly would not consider sharing it with the old buggers we inherited it from. I do not wish to speak ill of the dead, but they left it filthy.

I have raised this matter with His Holiness, who says that, in certain special circumstances, some houses may have to be glorified into flats. Of course, this will reduce the accommodation, but bear in mind that since the glands we mentioned will not be resurrected, you will not need bedrooms for the children. Also, it should be remembered that because there is no sex, many couples may now be prepared not to have separate bedrooms. This may be something you wish to discuss with your wife before dying.

I suppose, then, that there is no hope of coming back and finding the car glorified?

Correct. I am afraid that you will have to accept the possibility of being resurrected and finding nothing but a pile of brown dust. If it has been undersealed, of course, you might find a wing. It rather depends how long you have to be in Heaven before the Day of Resurrection comes. It could take us all by surprise, and you could find yourself back again with nothing worse than a flat battery.

The Republic: Book XI

*Efforts by Oxford University to appoint a Greek as a lecturer
in Classical Philosophy have been met by an invitation from
the Department of Employment to take the vacancy to the
local Job Centre and advertise it to Britain's unemployed.*

Guardian

I WENT down the Job Centre yesterday morning, didn't I, with
Glaucon, the son of Ariston, on account of the course being
waterlogged at Haydock and Plumpton and the bleeding betting-
shop shut also the pubs not open yet, so where else can you go
when it's bucketing down? And don't say 'back home' if you
haven't seen my old woman with her teeth out, she never puts
'em in until after *Neighbours*, due to ulcers.

'I hate this place, Glaucon,' I said, 'it smells of vacancies. In
an ideal state, they'd do away with employment.'

'The main thing, Socrates,' said Glaucon, 'is not to catch their
eye. If you catch their eye, it's Next Please, and before you know
it, you're up Woollies packing department.'

'You do not have to tell me, son,' I said. 'I had one of them
long brown coats on once, you feel like muck. Do this, do that.
June 18, 1956. Also, they stand by the staff exit when you clock
off and they steal stuff what has inadvertently fallen into your
pockets. If this is work, I told 'em, you can bloody keep it, thank
you very much.'

'In an ideal state,' said Glaucon, 'we would not have to work,
would we, Socrates?'

'Bloody right,' I explained. 'I did not spend six years of World
War Two hiding in my auntie's loft to keep the world safe for

democracy in order to come out and have my pockets inspected for bottles of HP.'

'You were a conscientious objector then, Socrates?'

'Naturally. It was what we call a classic clash between an unjust authority and a just individual. They refused to recognise my objection.'

'What did you object to?'

'I objected to being shot at, Glaucon. I did not muck about claiming I was a Quaker or nothing, that would have been dishonest, and anyway they would have conscripted you as a porridge supervisor or something. I just come right out and give 'em the full force of rational argument before buggering off while their backs were turned and nipping up the loft. In the event, I was proved right. Germany was defeated, and I come down again.'

'A victory for reason, Socrates,' said Glaucon.

'Definitely.' I looked at my watch. 'In an ideal state, Glaucon, they would have opened the bloody pubs by now. Also invented sunnink to remove water during the flat season. Have you ever noticed that we can put men on the Moon but are unable to do sod all about soft going at Kempton?'

'Morning all!'

We looked up. It was Cephalus, father of Polemarchus. He is not half spry for his age, and puts it all down to not having worked since observing how far marching down from bloody Jarrow got anybody, also to smoking other people's Woodbines.

'What are you doing here, Cephalus?' enquired Glaucon, a logical question given that the old man has been known to leave a free pint untouched at the very mention of the word job.

'I come here to gloat,' replied Cephalus, 'on account of I was 65 last Monday and they cannot lay a finger on me no more. I come in regular to drop my fag-ends in their khazi, also put all the forms back in the stands upside down. In an ideal state, Glaucon, it is up to the just man to keep the bastards on the hop, am I right, Socrates?'

'Definitely,' I said.

'Also, I like looking at that new blackie on Supplementary Benefits A–G with the big knockers.'

We stared at her for a time.

'In an ideal state,' propounded Glaucon, wiping his lip on his cap, 'we could get that on the NHS. Which reminds me, Socrates, is it better to be beautiful than good?'

I pondered the point for a time.

'It is all right being beautiful, and it is all right being good ' I said, 'but the best thing is to have a car.'

'I would dispute that, Socrates,' said Thrasymachus of Chalcedon, who had just come in to see if there were any vacancies for astronauts on account of he had promised his wife to settle on a career, now that the children were grown up and not bringing in any family allowance. 'In my opinion, it is better to have a bicycle.'

'Because it is healthier, also you can nip in and out, Thrasymachus of Chalcedon?' enquired Glaucon.

'No, Glaucon,' replied Thrasymachus. 'Because if you have a car they only come round and ask you where you nicked it.'

'In an ideal state,' advanced Cephalus, 'they'd give you them little red Fiats on the NHS, wouldn't they, Socrates?'

'That is what philosophy calls a dodgy one, Cephalus,' I informed him. 'That is similar to the one concerning which way the water goes down the plughole south of the Equator to which we addressed ourselves up the Rat and Cockle at our last session. According to Plato, in an ideal state there wouldn't be any Wops at all, sending their cheap rubbish over here and putting people out of work. Before you know it, there will be three million amateur unemployed filling up job centres. You and me won't even be able to come in out of the rain, never mind getting a decent seat near the window.'

The disciples considered this for a time.

'I thought Plato was a dog,' announced Thrasymachus of Chalcedon at last. 'I seen him up Saturday morning pictures. He hangs about with a duck.'

'Mouse, you mean,' said Glaucon.

'Plato a *dog*?' I cried, losing for a moment my philosophical calm. 'Do you know nothing? Apart from formulating the complex system known as *Backing Second Favourites For A Place*, which admittedly still requires some fine logical tuning due to where him and me was six hundred quid down last season, Plato is the man primarily responsible for leading the philosophical search for the perfect job. What he calls the Essential Employment, the one from which all other employments derive as flawed imitations.'

They were silent. I sensed an unease among them.

'Perfect job, Socrates?' enquired Glaucon. 'After all our long discussions, are you telling us you are knocking around with someone seeking to undermine our entire ethical bleeding framework?'

I smiled tolerantly.

'In an ideal state, Glaucon,' I replied, 'they'd have twerps like you made into bookends.' I looked slowly from one to another. 'The ideal job, as laid down by Plato in his seminal work which is not yet written out but if it ever is will probably be entitled *A Major Conversation with Socrates in the Back of the Bus Coming Home from the Bloody Cesarewitch*, the ideal job is one for which you are paid large sums for doing absolutely nothing at all. It is, leave us face it, pupils, the only rational extension if we start from the premise that the worst possible job is one where you get paid nothing for working your bloody wossnames off, am I right?'

They nodded.

'But tell us, Socrates,' said Glaucon, 'what form would this ideal job take if we ever run across the bugger?'

'Form,' I answered, 'is not a term Plato would fancy. The *essence* of this job, however, would be where you had nice warm comfortable premises, all rent and expenses paid, hot dinners twice a day plus cooked breakfast and them little triangular Spam sandwiches at tea-time, free access to the company's booze cupboard twenty-four hours a day, and servants to run around after you, making beds and cups of tea etcetera etcetera. You would not have to move out of said premises to go to work, on account of the work would consist of people coming in and sitting around nattering with you all day and everybody getting plastered on free brown sherry.'

'Or whisky, Socrates?'

'Or whisky, Thrasymachus of Chalcedon.'

'Stone me!' murmured Cephalus. 'That is what I *call* an ideal job.'

He sighed. We all did. After a bit, I got up.

'There is no point sitting around here, pupils, dreaming impossible bloody dreams,' I said. 'Especially as they are now open.'

We walked to the door, and I was just going through it when one of the clerks called out:

'Oy, any of you layabouts fancy a lectureship in Classical Phil –'

We was out of there like bullets, I don't mind saying!

'Nearly caught us that time,' said Glaucon.

Ourselves to Know

ENCYCLOPEDIA BRITTANICA full 30 volume set unused £499.

Sunday Times

MR HENRY FICKLING threw open the kitchen door, flared his nostrils, expanded his chest, rubbed his hands together, beamed an iridescent beam.

'Bacon!' he cried. 'There is nothing like the smell of old *piggus piggus* crackling in the pan!'

From the kitchen table, not glancing up from his cornflakes, his son muttered:

'Old what?'

'Dear God, Doreen!' exclaimed Fickling. 'Stap me vittles! Sacré coeur! The ignorance of boys today! I blame the change in diet, do I not?'

'Yes, dear,' said his wife, cracking an egg.

'When I was a lad, we never went out without a big spoon of Scott's Emotion inside us. It was made from fish. Consequently, it enlarged the brain like nobody's business.'

His daughter put down the *TV Times* and stared at him.

'Why on earth was it called Scott's Emotion?' she said.

Henry Fickling sighed.

'How short a thing is mortal memory,' he murmured, 'as Freddie Mills so succinctly put it. For your information, Tracy, it was called Scott's Emotion on account of he brought it back with him from the North Pole. It had this picture on the bottle, showing him with a shark on his back. The stuff was made out of its liver.'

'There aren't any sharks at the North Pole,' said his son, through a piece of toast.

'Don't contradict your father,' said Doreen Fickling.

'Anyway,' said the boy, 'it was the South Pole Scott went to, and there aren't any sharks there, either.' He looked at his father. 'You're probably thinking of penguins.'

'*Penguins?*' shrieked Henry Fickling. He slapped his thigh. He roared aloud. He snatched a handful of kitchen roll and dabbed his streaming eyes. 'Did you hear that, Mother? Answer me this, clever dick, if what you're implicating is true, how is it that the label did not show Colonel Scott with a penguin on his back? Are you suggesting that I grew up, moreover, on penguin liver oil, which is what Scott's Emotion was comprised with?'

The boy shrugged.

'Something's wrong somewhere,' he said. 'Because, in the first place, Scott never came back from the Pole.'

His father leaned over the table, and poked his son in the chest with a trembling forefinger.

'Never came back?' he shouted. '*Never came back?* Then how did the shark get here, may I ask? Did it bloody walk?'

'I don't know,' said the boy, 'it's your shark. Maybe it was Amundsen.'

'A mundsen? What is the boy talking about, Mother? Penguins, mundsens, he must be a laughing-stock up the comprehensive, am I right? As I understand it, Nigel, your entire view of the matter is based on the hypoteneuse that instead of coming home and going into commercial medicine and duck-painting, Colonel Scott chose instead to stay at the North Pole walking around with a mundsen on his back. Does that seem logical to you, Doreen?'

'Here's your breakfast, dear,' said his wife.

Henry Fickling banged his plate on the table, and sat down in front of it.

'Respect for learning,' he snapped, 'where has it gone? Too busy sticking razor blades up their nostrils and watching Elton Lulu.'

His son licked the last cornflake from his spoon, and stared at Henry Fickling for some time. Finally, he said:

'It's not *piggus piggus*.'

His father froze, a forked rasher wobbling before his motionless lip. After a few moments, he put the fork down.

'What isn't?' he said, through his teeth.

'Pig,' said the boy. 'The Latin for pig is *porcus*.'

Mrs Fickling put down her spatula, as the familiar vein in her husband's temple began to throb like a lugworm.

'I remember!' she cried. 'It was Scott's *Emulsion!*'

Fickling, like a diverted rhino, swung round in his chair.

'Oh really? Doubtless, we were supposed to slap it on the bloody ceiling? Came home from the Pole with the secret of washable skirtings, did he? Set himself up as COLONEL SCOTT PAINTER & DECORATOR NO JOB TOO LARGE OR SMALL LET US QUOTE YOU? Well, well, well, who says you don't learn something new every day? When I came in here this morning, just a few short minutes ago, I was totally ignorant of the fact that England's greatest hero made his name out of refurbishing domestic premises with quarts of tasteful eau-de-nil penguin derivative!' He swivelled back towards his breakfast, but his wife's diversionary tactic came to naught. He fixed his son with a terrible eye. '*Porcus*,' he snapped, 'is Latin for *roast* pig, am I right, Doreen?'

'Or shoulder,' said his wife.

'Or shoulder,' said Fickling. His eyes did not move from his son's. Eventually, the boy took another piece of toast, and buttered it slowly.

'And – ' he unscrewed the marmalade jar carefully, '– bacon?'

'I'm very glad you asked me that,' replied his father. 'Bacon is not from the Latin *baconus*, which is something else entirely and a bit advanced for me to go into with a non-classicalist, but takes its name from Sir Francis Bacon, as the famous anecdote relates. One night, Sir Francis was up his club playing brag with the Duke of Sandwich and William Shakespeare and similar, arguing about who was going to write *Charley's Aunt*, I believe it was, when the Earl of Sandwich suddenly said: "Hang about, anyone fancy a bite to eat?" Well, they called the chef over, and he said he couldn't do a proper hot dinner, all he had was a bit of pig in the fridge but no sprouts or stuffing or anything of that nature; so Bacon said: "Look, if you fry up the meat and stick it between a couple of slices of Wonderloaf, that'll keep us going for a bit." And that's how bacon was invented.'

'Magic,' murmured his son, trying not to look at his sister.

'There wasn't much wrong with Bacon's brains,' nodded Fickling. ''Course, that was before the apple fell on his head.'

His son slid sideways to the floor, and lay there for a time, gasping. Quickly, his mother scuttled across, helped him up, and, shoving his sister, too, before her, pushed them out of the kitchen.

'What was all that about?' enquired Fickling, cleaning his plate with a crust.

'Nothing.' She smoothed her apron, cleared her throat, poked a wisp of hair back, put her hands together, took them apart again. 'Look, Henry, I think it's time, I mean the children are growing up, education is not just a matter of going to school and reading books, it is a question of home environment etcetera and all the, you know, things a parent can do to help, and I realize you try very hard, but when you come right down to it, it is a practical business of making sure they have, how shall I put it, a background of accurate *facts* and reliable information, and, I do hope I'm not putting this badly, it is a bit embarrassing, but what I am trying to say is –'

Fickling raised his hand, closed his eyes, smiled.

'I know what you're driving at, Doreen,' he said, 'and there is no need to be embarrassed. I have already been giving the matter much thought, not to mention explaining one or two of the basics to Nigel, to wit, how Father Bee lies down beside Mother Bee and puts ovary in her stamen and so forth, but I think it went over his head a bit. Nevertheless –'

'Oh, God,' murmured Doreen Fickling.

'What?'

'That wasn't actually what I was talking about, Henry,' she said. 'What I was attempting to point out was – '

The doorbell chimed.

'Yes?' enquired Fickling.

'I'm from *Encyclopaedia Britannica*,' said the young man.

'There's no Greeks here,' said Fickling.

'I'm sorry?'

'I'm not,' snapped Fickling. 'Coming over here and throwing yourselves on your husband's bonfires, it's not bloody natural. I believe you sit on the floor to have tea, am I right?'

The young man glanced at the address on his clipboard, and at the number beside the bell, and back at Fickling.

'I don't understand,' he said.

'Bloody hell,' sighed Fickling, 'you'd think they'd have a few basic phrases before they got on the boat, is it any wonder we have got out of the Common Market? Look, Ali,' he said, 'you – have – das – wrongo – house. Compree?'

'Is this not the Fickling residence?'

Henry Fickling narrowed his eyes, but nodded.

'Then,' said the young man, 'these are yours.'

Whereupon he turned and hurried down the path, leaving Fickling staring at a large wooden packing-case. He dragged it inside.

'They've come, then,' said his wife.

'Come?' said Fickling. 'What have?'

'I tried to tell you,' she said.

So she told him now.

He did not, however, lose his temper, as she had feared. Instead, he put his hand on her shoulder.

'I blame myself, Doreen,' he said. 'You tried to warn me and, like Nelson, I put the microscope in my wrong ear. I have clearly neglected my parental responsibility. From now on, I shall put myself at the disposal of their enquiring little minds whenever they need assistance. I am touched that you should have taken the trouble to purchase these, but I have little doubt that there is an eager market for an unused set at a generous discount. There must be a lot of dim bastards about, keen to improve theirselves.'

'But – '

'No bother at all, my love. It is merely a matter of knocking out an eye-catching advert and popping it in the *Sunday Times*. Won't take me a moment.'

At which, taking up the pad and pencil that lay beside the phone, he jotted where he stood.

'There!' he cried. 'That'll pull 'em in.'

She looked at it.

'I always thought Britannica was with one t and two n's,' she said.

Fickling smiled tolerantly.

'Yes,' he said, 'a lot of people make that mistake.'

Darling Greengrocer . . .

Alan Coren was possibly one of the last great letter writers. Certainly, he was greater than Evelyn Waugh, if only because he was forced to labour under the disadvantage that nobody ever wrote to him; since, by 1980, postal costs had come to prohibit anything but commercial mail. Nevertheless, Coren toiled on, confident in the belief that it was still the cheapest way of cobbling together a big fat book.

To Lex Volvo (UK) Ltd

(5 February 1980)

My dear Lex: I cannot thank you enough for your delightfully entertaining bill! Were dear Tom Driberg still alive, I have little doubt but that he would have been as thrilled as I to discover that it is still possible, despite the assorted plights which rack this unfortunate island, to have the rear door of a shooting brake (why, oh why, do the appalling little swine who presently hold the culture in thrall insist upon calling them *estates*? Have they any conception of what is conjured up in the mind of a gentleman by the words *Volvo Estate* – some appalling Scandinavian tract with snow upon the croquet lawn and unutterably boring Swedes falling off horses while their suicidal footmen slit throats in the freezing buttery?), to have the rear door of a shooting brake, I say, beaten out, sprayed up to customer's specifications, refitted, and made good for as little as £367.55, to include new wipe-wash motor.

I passed another somewhat wretched evening yesterday. I went along to Boodle's, and was involved in a bit of a row. Apparently one has to be a member to get in.

To Maxwell House

(3 March 1980)

Good old Max! I received your enchanting letter in the post this morning, and confess myself overwhelmed by your astonishingly generous offer.

And yet, and yet. How am I to reply without appearing the charmless boor that society chooses so often to represent me as? I truly cannot get away to the sunsoaked Balkan Riviera this year, even if I had the half-dozen 8oz lids you mention or could think of the three words necessary to complete your sentence. Can you forgive me? The plain fact of the matter is, I have a great deal on my plate at the moment – do you know Lex Volvo? No matter, it is a long and dispiriting tale, but the top and bottom of it is that he has dealt with me rather badly for an old acquaintance. My new rear door does not shut properly, and when I bang it hard, the little lights fall out of that thing over the number plate. I fear a frightful row may be brewing between us, and I dare not leave London until it is settled. You know how people are.

Once again, dear Max, my thanks and apologies. I am delighted to hear that your new granules are twenty per cent tastier. God knows, good news is rare enough, these days.

To his Greengrocer

(5 March 1980)

Darling Greengrocer: Thank you so much for the wonderful sprouts! Your boy hurried round last evening and pressed them into my hand personally – was it only fancy that made the little brown bag still warm from your own hand?

They could not have arrived at a more opportune time. I had been feeling very depressed all day, what with one thing and another; I had to turn down dear old Max's offer of a free trip to the Crimea, and immediately after that, not only did the little lights fall out of that thing over the number plate again, but the new rear windscreen wiper failed to wipe the new rear windscreen. What do you suppose Lex is playing at, after all these years? And as if all *that* were not enough, I was cut dead upon Hampstead Heath by a woman who might very well have been the Duchess of Argyll. Is she a tall woman with a purple conk?

In any event, your sprouts were a marvellous surprise. I had been expecting 5lb King Edwards, 2lb Williams pears, and a small turnip.

P.S. My new book, to make matters yet worse, is going very badly. I am stuck on page 23. Can I be alone in finding Margaret Drabble unreadable?

To Lex Volvo

(7 March 1980)

Dear Volvo: My curtness only reflects your own. I was appalled this morning to receive from you *a printed acknowledgement*, one month late, of my letter of February 5th [*see above. Ed.*].

Not that I am altogether surprised. I have noticed of late an entirely, to me, inexplicable change of attitude on your part towards the cavalier and uncaring. It may interest you to know (though, upon reflection, I rather doubt it, given your new unconcern) that I was so distressed by the little lights falling out of that thing over the number plate that I was forced to give up a much-needed holiday with Max.

I have twice this past week driven over to your place in the hope of seeing you and perhaps persuading you to glance at my inert wash-wipe mechanism, but on both occasions your man informed me that an appointment was necessary. An *appointment*? Between *us*?

I confess I do not know what is happening to society. London is full of both Jews and Arabs. Sainsbury's, one's grocers, is like a soukh. I beg leave, for both our sakes, to suggest that this general erosion of all that is good and decent may be what lies behind your own coolness to me; were your behaviour none of your own choice but merely the contamination of this ghastly world, I should be greatly reassured, though nonetheless low in spirit.

To the Scottish Widows Insurance Society

(10 March 1980)

Dear, dear Ladies! Words cannot adequately express my gratitude for your kind card. That it fell out of one's *Reader's Digest*, like a bolt from the blue, instead of being thrust through one's letter box crumpled by one of those black hooligans who these days, such is our national decline, bear the sacred mission of Her Majesty's mail, made it even more welcome.

Alas, how can I accept your offer of £7, 642 for me at age 65? Granted that the inflation visited upon our aching backs by a succession of governments each more villainously corrupt than the last must have, by now, ensured that the mite stands considerably higher than its AD 33 value, how on earth would you manage to scrape together this considerable sum over the next quarter century? How, indeed, could I commit your twilight years to scrimping and self-denial simply in order to bring a measure of security to an ageing hack?

That cannot be. Nevertheless, your rare charity in this beastly world shines like a beacon. You are obviously Roman Catholics, and I thank God that you and your line have been spared the poisonous taint of the heretical Knox and thus saved from the stinking sulphur and flaying agonies of the spit-roasted hell into which he and all who slobber after his maniacal ravings are irredeemably doomed to hurtle.

To his Greengrocer

(11 March 1980)

Dear Chas. Rumbold & Son: I am deeply distressed by a visit I have just received, during an afternoon I had intended giving over to thinking about my relationship with Lady Diana Mosley, should we ever meet, by two persons to whom I should not have given an audience had their boots not been wedged in my front door.

Thus to reply to my affectionate letter of March 5th only serves to strengthen my conviction that England is truly finished. As I told your repugnant minions after I had got up again, my erstwhile affection for you was entirely platonic, nor have I ever laid a finger on Brian, your delivery boy. If any blame attaches to me, it is in assuming that by treating tradesmen as equals, gentlemen might perhaps offer them the chance of rising above the mire in which they clearly prefer to wallow.

And before my observations prompt you to further outrage, reflect upon this; one of your sprouts, it transpired, had a worm in it.

To Lex Volvo

(15 March 1980)

Dear Volvo: Following a further printed travesty suggesting that I telephone, and I quote, *one of your service staff* for an appointment (*Author's italics. Ed.*), it occurs to me that this shocking behaviour can have but one explanation. Are you yourself a Swede? If so, together with my deepest commiseration, I take the liberty of enclosing a humble little card from some Scottish widows of my acquaintance in order to demonstrate to you that there remain a few isolated pockets in this ugly and malevolent world where good manners and unrapacious hearts yet continue, albeit feebly, to flourish.

Shome Talk of Alexander

Alexander the Great was a great drunkard, according to a New York historian. Dr John O'Brien says that the talented Macedonian king exhibited the classic symptoms of acute alcoholism during his short life, and that drink caused his death at the age of 32.

Macedonians were noted for their liquor consumption, Dr O'Brien reports. Alexander's father, Philip, was a famous tippler, and his mother, Olympias, daughter of Neoptolemus of Epirus, was an enthusiastic disciple of Dionysus, god of wine.

The Times

ALEXANDER III, called THE GREAT, king of Macedonia, was born in 356 BC, at Pella in Macedonia, two facts which escaped him for most of his short life. Drunk, he had great difficulty in working out how old he was, since (given that by the time he was twelve it was 344 BC) he seemed to be growing younger every year; nor could he clearly remember whether he had been born at Massa in Pelladonia or Poland in Alexandria. Asked for his name at parties, he frequently informed his hostess that he was Milton from Greater Pasadena. He would then fall down.

His father was Philip II, about which he was fairly clear, even if he didn't always get the number right; but as his mother was Olympias, daughter of Neoptolemus of Epirus, he never managed to refer to her as anything but Mrs II, unless it had been a really rough night, in which case she could be any number from Mrs I to XXXVI. However, as she was a heavy drinker herself, she never came when called, since this involved finding her other shoe.

65

Despite this, she was not as big a lush as her husband Philip, who wept most of the time, partly out of remorse, and partly because nobody would play *Melancholy Baby*; and it was because of this guilt-bred grief that Philip, deeply distressed by his son's inability to think straight, enunciate clearly, or, indeed, cross the room without knocking over the furniture, persuaded Aristotle, in 343 BC, to take Alexander on as a pupil.

It did not work out well: Pella was two hundred miles from Athens, and to get to Aristotle's place you had to change horses five times, plus make tight connections at Thebes-on-the-Hill and Sparta's End, where the buffet sold an unpretentious little retsina used mainly to despatch horses which had broken a leg en route. Because of this, young Alexander frequently ended up in Thrace, plastered, and shrieking at unimpressed citizens that he was the daughter of Mrs Aristotle IV and could lick anybody in the place.

Fortunately, the result of this early experience was that he became an expert swordsman, fearlessly prepared to take on six adversaries at a time. That everyone else saw only two adversaries does not, of course, diminish Alexander's heroism; in fact, the contrary. Indeed, such was his prowess that when Philip left with his army in 340 BC to attack Byzantium, he was confident to leave Alexander in charge of Macedonia; more confident, at least, than to take Alexander with him, since Alexander could not only not remember whether you turned left or right at the roundabout for Byzantium, he was unable to stay on his horse after a heavy breakfast.

While Philip was away, Alexander defeated the Maedi, a Thracian people; it was not a difficult victory, since the Maedi had been unaware that they were at war and were taken by surprise, but Philip was pleased with it, because any victory was a good excuse for a thrash. Three years later, however, the two fell out; when Philip divorced Olympias (the row is said to have begun over who had the corkscrew), Alexander fled with his mother to Epirus, since her father Neoptolemus lived in a forest, and 337 was a good year for wood alcohol.

But in 336, when Philip was assassinated (the reason is unclear, but the crime may not have been political, since Philip is known to have amassed a personal fortune of eighteen thousand empties which has never been found), Alexander succeeded him. He then marched south, in the hope of capturing the heavy aquavit plant in Norway, and found himself in Corinth, where he was appointed commander-in-chief of the Greek League, who took his halting Norse for colloquial Barbarian and elected him out of terror. Reeling into Thrace in the spring of 335, he found the bars shut and, in an invincible fury, crushed the bewildered Triballi before turning to cross the Danube, where he dispersed the Getae (for being out of stuffed olives). Meanwhile, a rumour of his death (he had been lying under a table for six days) had precipitated a revolt of Theban democrats. Waking, Alexander marched 240 miles in fourteen days, to Thebes. He still had the hangover, so Thebes was burned to the ground.

The Persian Expedition

From his accession, Alexander had set his mind on invading Persia, where, it was said, King Darius had discovered a method of distilling gin from dates which retailed at less than 3p a pint. At the River Granicus, Alexander stopped; the Persian plan was to tempt Alexander across (by telling him the first two drinks were on the house) and kill him in the melee, but the scheme misfired badly. Alexander, slumped between two satraps, had great difficulty in focusing on the heliograph, and interpreted the Persian invitation as a request to drink up and get out because it was closing time. Enraged, he hurled his forces across the river; the Persian line broke, exposing Asia Minor to the Macedonians. Most of the major cities opened their gates to Alexander, many of them throwing in a free ploughman's lunch, with the single exception of Miletus, which took courage from the fact that the Persian fleet lay close at hand. It was a mistake: Alexander did not attack the Persian fleet, as anticipated, since the movement of the ground beneath his feet led him to believe that he was *already afloat*; he thus attacked the coastal towns, under the impression they were large brick ships, and, stunned by this utterly unprecedented stratagem, they instantly surrendered. To his dying day, Alexander never understood why Miletus did not simply up anchor and sail away.

In the spring of 333 BC, Alexander subdued most of Asia Minor, and arrived in Gordium in Phrygia. It was here that he was presented with the Gordian knot, which according to legend could be loosed only by the man destined to rule Asia. Naturally unable to untie it (most days he could not even pick up his shoes, let alone find the laces), Alexander, in a fit of rage, cut through it with his sword. He also cut through his hat, his horse, his maps, and four bystanders, but it did not matter: all Persia lay at his feet, as, indeed, Alexander himself had so often done.

Conquest of Egypt

Wheeling south after the defeat of Darius, Alexander then marched west, though occasionally north, and once or twice in a circle, until, having subjugated Byblos and Sidon, he reached Tyre and put it under siege. The siege lasted seven months, and some historians maintain that it was the Tyrians who successfully resisted, when in fact it was rather that Alexander was forced to give up, because the tonic had run out. He took his army into Egypt, and founded Alexandria, erecting the huge Pharos lighthouse, one of the seven wonders of the world, so that he could find his way home at night.

History has it that it was in Alexandria that he began to think of himself as the son of Zeus. This is true, but it is also true that it was part of a painful delusory process brought on, ironically, by a tragic accident.

Alexander had lived all his short life in terror of delirium tremens, having seen what it could do to both his father and mother, who spent long periods of his childhood swatting one another under the mutual impression that the other was a giant spider. When he arrived in Egypt, the first thing he saw was a camel. He fainted. When he recovered, it was gone. Tentatively, he asked his aide-de-camp, Callisthenes, whether he had also seen 'that horse with the big knockers'. Callisthenes, not comprehending, suggested that Alexander switch brands; the general changed to Bloody Marys, but that night, staring at the Nile aimlessly, he saw his first alligator. He rushed, screaming, to his tent, where he told the distraught Callisthenes that he was being pursued by four-legged handbags.

Alexander subsequently refused, when it had dawned on everyone else, to believe the truth; those who claimed that they, too, had seen what he had seen were dismissed as flatterers, insulting him by humouring him. After he had killed twelve of these with a broken bottle, the rest stopped insisting that they were telling the truth; which finally satisfied their leader, while doing nothing to relieve his wretchedness.

He left Egypt, conquered Babylon in a somewhat depressed stupor, and pushed on towards India.

India and the Final Years

It was there that he saw his first elephant.

Next afternoon, in 328 BC, on the plains of Sogdiana, he met and immediately married a local girl, Roxana, daughter of King Oxyartes, because he didn't want to be alone at night when he woke up and saw the giant with the arm on its head walking around on four wastebins.

Unhappily, Roxana arrived for their wedding night riding on an elephant; forever thereafter, Alexander assumed that she, too, was a figment of his sodden imagination, and it came as no surprise to anyone when, four years later, he also married, at Susa, the daughter of his old adversary Darius. Inevitably, the two women fought over the dress allowance; Darius's daughter kept complaining to Alexander about his first wife, from which Alexander inferred that his second wife was also either a drunk or a liar attempting to humour him, while Roxana kept complaining about his second wife, upon which Alexander would knock her about on the grounds that no figment of his imagination was going to tell him how to run his marriage.

There could be only one outcome of all this. Alexander took to drinking even more heavily, and, inevitably, early in 323, he failed, one morning to rise from his bed. Friends continued to throw water over him for eight days, but it did no good, any more.

One is One and All Alone

The last-minute cancellation of the Canadian visit does of course leave a large gap in the diary which probably cannot be filled at this late date. The Queen will be at something of a loose end.

Palace spokesman

MONDAY

Got up, finally.

Sat at escritoire. Filled in all o's on front page of one's *Telegraph*. Put paperclips in long line. Pushed paperclips into little pile. Straightened paperclip and cleaned old bits of soap out of engagement ring. Bent paperclip back to original shape. Put paperclip back in little pile and tried to identify it with eyes shut.

Noticed tiny flap of wallpaper curled back from skirting just behind escritoire. Took one's Bostik out of escritoire drawer, put little smear on wall, little smear on wallpaper, pressed down wallpaper.

Picked old dried crusty bits off one's Bostik nozzle.

Read Bostik label. It is good for glass, wood, ceramics, light metal, leather, and plastic, whatever that is. If one gets it in one's eyes, one should wash it out immediately.

Saw fly go past.

Saw fly come back.

Watched wallpaper curl off wall again.

Turned on *Play School*. Noticed flat head on presenter. Summoned Lady Carinthia Noles-Fitzgibbon, who confirmed head not normally flat. She enquired if she should summon Master of the Queen's Ferguson. One told her no, one was perfectly capable of fiddling with one's apparatus oneself.

One was in fact quite grateful.

Took lift to West Loft. Keeper of the Queen's Smaller Gifts (West Loft Division) most helpful. One had, according to his inventory, been given a zircon-encrusted ratchet screwdriver by King Idris of Libya, following 1954 reciprocal trade agreement on depilatory soup. During Keeper's search for this item, put on alligator's head presented by Friends of Mbingele National Park on the occasion of one's Silver Wedding. A snug fit, but some tarnish on the molars.

Keeper rather taken aback upon return to find one in alligator's head and Mary Queen of Scots' execution frock, but recovered admirably. Having to suppress his distress at poor Professor Blunt's departure has matured him considerably; one may soon allow him to fondle the odd corgi.

Returned to one's apartment. *Play School* now finished, so put on one's husband's video recording of yesterday's *Postman Pat*. It is now Mrs Goggins the Postmistress who has a flat head.

Applied screwdriver to hole in back of one's apparatus. Blue flash. Zircons all blown off. One's husband burst in, ranting: apparently, one's husband's Hornby Dublo layout had fused itself to nursery floor.

One's husband now at worse loose end than ever, stormed off in foul mood to put up shelf in garage. Has been talking about putting up shelf in garage since Suez.

Lunch. First lunch alone since October, 1949.

Moulded mashed potatoes into Grampians, poured gravy in to simulate Loch Rannoch, cut pea in half to make two ferries. Had ferry race by blowing down one's straw. Left-hand pea won.

Knighted it with fork.

After lunch, one's husband stormed in again, carrying gold claw-hammer (Ghana, 1962), diamanté pliers (Melbourne, 1968), set of inlaid mother-of-pearl ring-spanners (Tongan gift on occasion of PoW's first tooth), and shouting *Where one's bloody zircon-encrusted screwdriver?*

Stormed out again with rather nice Louis XV rosewood side-table, muttering *Soon chop up this tarty frog rubbish, make bloody good plank, this, rip a couple of brackets off that poncey*

Tompian clock upstairs, shelf up in two shakes of a CPO's whatsit.

Fusebox Poursuivant arrived to repair apparatus. Commanded to remain and play I-Spy. One won.

Bed at 8.15, with ocelot-bound *Fifty Things To Do On A Wet Day* (New Zealand, 1978). Made flute out of old sceptre. Played *God Save One.*

TUESDAY

Woke early, made hat from *Telegraph*.

Drew up list of all one's acquaintances with spectacles. Compared it with list of all one's acquaintances with flat feet.

Watched one's husband rush in clutching bloodstained thumb, shouting *Where bloody Dettol, where bloody Elastoplast?* Watched him rush out again.

Sudden brilliant thought. Decided to make one's own breakfast. Cheered to find nursery kitchen empty. Recognised frying-pan. Put egg in frying-pan. Oddly, egg did not go yellow and white, egg just rolled around in frying-pan, went hot, then exploded.

Had bath.

Rang TIM, Weather, Cricket Scores, Puffin Storyline. Listened to Mrs Goggins story. Rang Starline: good day for throwing out old clothes, will meet interesting short man with financial proposition, a loved one will have exciting news in evening.

Threw out old clothes and waited for interesting short man. Did not come, so got old clothes back. Put them into symmetrical heaps.

In evening, loved one stomped in with exciting news: Louis XV garage shelf had fallen on Rolls, dented bonnet, knocked off wing-mirror.

Bed at 9, with interesting book. There are 3, 786 Patels in it.

WEDNESDAY

Got up, put *Telegraph* in bucket of water. Added flour, as recommended by *Fifty Things To Do On A Wet Day*, made papier-maché head of Mrs Goggins.

Removed old glove from pile waiting for interesting short man, put it on, poked forefinger into Mrs Goggins, did puppet-show for corgi.

Corgi passed out.

Rang 246 8000 again, but no further news of interesting short man or his financial proposition. Nothing about one's dog falling over, either. However, it is a good day to go shopping. One leapt at this! Why had one not thought of it sooner?

One has never been shopping.

It being a fine day, one decided to slip out quietly in sensible shoes and headscarf, and walk up Constitution Hill to Knightsbridge. Most interesting. Sixty-two street lamps.

Several Japanese persons stared at one strangely. At Hyde Park Corner, a taxi-cab driver slowed, pushed down his window, and shouted 'I bet you wish you had her money!'

Quite incomprehensible.

One recognised Harrods at once, from their Christmas card. One went inside. Most impressive. One selected a jar of Beluga caviare, a rather splendid musical beefeater cigarette-box with a calculator in its hat, a pair of moleskin slippers, a Webley air-pistol, and a number of other items one might never have thought of to help one while away the remainder of one's spare fortnight, and one was quite looking forward to strolling back to the Palace, putting one's mole-shod feet up, treating oneself to a spoonful or two of the old Royal fish roe while potting starlings through the window and totting up the toll on one's loyal Yeoman calculator to the stirring accompaniment of *Land of Hope and Glory*, when one suddenly felt one's elbow grasped with an uncustomarily disrespectful firmness.

'Excuse me, madam, but I wonder if you would mind accompanying me to the Assistant Manager's office?'

One was aware of a grey-suited person.

'Normally,' one replied, 'one allows it to be known that one is prepared to entertain a formal introduction. One then initiates the topic of conversation oneself. It is normally about saddles. However, one is prepared to overlook the protocol occasionally. One assumes the senior staff wishes to be presented?'

FRIDAY

Got up, slopped out.

One might, of course, have made a fuss. One might, for example, have pointed out to one's Assistant Manager – the entire place is, after all, By Appointment – that not only does one never carry money, but that money actually carries one, and would therefore serve as a convenient identification.

One chose, however, to retain one's headscarf, one's glasses, and one's silence; since something had suddenly dawned on one.

Thus, yesterday in Bow Street, being without visible means of support, one was not even given the option of seven days. One now has a rather engaging view of Holloway Road, albeit only from the upper bunk, a most engaging companion with a fund of excellent stories, and a mouse, and one is already through to the South Block ping-pong semi-finals.

Tonight, there is bingo, rug-making, cribbage, aerobics, bookbinding, squash, pottery, chiropody, raffia work, community singing, petit-point, judo, darts, and do-it-oneself. One can hardly wait to see what tomorrow may bring!

One is, in short, amused.

Can You Get There By Candlelight?

The Geographical Association is to publish a report on the several thousand inaccuracies it has found on printed maps.
Sunday Times

'I WONDER,' murmured Professor Challoner, 'whether any of you has the remotest idea of what this little fellow might be?'

Before us, in the vast enmarbled hearth of the Travellers' Club, the fretted logs of Littlehampton teak crackled and sang their exile lament, filling the great library with the scent of lonely nights beyond the Gobi Reef and flickering into Challoner's mischievous eyes that familiar provocative glint which ever betokened some new and yet more recondite mystery brought back from his latest insatiable forage.

His voice, low and perfervid as the roiling waters of the Himalaya where that awesome stream meets the black headwaters of the North Circular before plunging three thousand feet over the Stuttgart Falls, held us, as always, grudgingly rapt. We drew our ancient fauteuils a little nearer the great man, and allowed the butler to top up our glasses from the glittering decanter of golden twelve-year-old Welsh.

In front of us, sitting on that hallowed relic of an earlier Challoner expedition, the Formica Coffee Table of Prester John, was a plain cardboard box. We stared at it for a time, while Challoner chuckled at our timidity.

'Go on,' he said, finally, 'open it.'

We three glanced at one another, the natural curiosity of the scientist struggling, understandably enough, with the equally natural caution of the experienced explorer. At length I could no longer resist, and taking from my tail-pocket the trusty Swiss Army knife I had bartered with a Holborn native for a handful of coins during my tragic attempt to trace the source of the White Mersey, I quickly extended a blade, slit the peculiar transparent tape that secured the lid, and flicked open the box.

My first impression was of a distinctly unpleasant smell. Challoner must have noticed my wrinkling nostril, for he immediately said:

'That is decay. Once the flesh is released from the preservative thrall of the ice, it immediately begins to rot. It is not, however, infectious. It is quite safe to remove it.'

I reached into the box, and felt a faintly slimy mass between my nervous fingers. I lifted it out – it weighed perhaps four or five pounds – and placed it upon the table. The thing was about the size of a man's head, white, a trifle pimply, and with a hole at one end.

Frobisher, on my left, drew in a sibilant breath.

Twistleton-Wickham-Finkel, on my right, narrowed his eyes.

We were all nonplussed.

'For my part, Challoner,' I said, 'I confess you have me. What the devil is it?'

The old rogue paused, savouring his moment.

'I have every reason to believe,' he said at last, 'that we are looking, gentlemen, at King Solomon's Chicken!'

An ember split, a far throat on a lower floor was cleared, a cuckoo lurched, honking, from the native clock brought back at who knew what cost from poor old Doctor Tremlett's ill-starred expedition to the Belgian outback, but, these apart, Challoner's stunning revelation was followed by a long uneasy silence. Twistleton-Wickham-Finkel, when he had mopped his brow and taken a second tumbler of the malt, was the first to speak.

'Where on God's earth did you find it, man?' he breathed.

In answer, Professor Challoner leaned back in his chair, reached out one spindly arm, and passed his leathern hand vaguely over the antique globe that stood beside him.

'We left for the Congo,' he began, 'on the 14th November last, from Marble Arch.'

'The Greenline eh?' muttered Frobisher admiringly. 'You

were taking a bit of a chance. Dorking can be a bugger in the rainy season.'

Challoner smiled.

'Not,' he said, 'if you know your way around. By nightfall, we were in East Sweden.'

Twistleton-Wickham-Finkel, who had been jotting frantically upon a piece of Club notepaper, glanced up at me.

'He must have gone over the Brenner,' he said, 'and dropped down into Cork. From there, it's no more than an hour's run to Lagos, if the tide's with you.'

'Just so,' said Challoner. 'We made camp in a little clearing just outside Vitry-sur-Marne . . .'

'I know it well!' cried Frobisher excitedly. 'There's what they call a *Little Chef* on the corner where they roll the meat into sort of tiny flat patties and stick them into a kind of round cake. I have a photograph somewhere that one of my bearers took of me holding a giant rubber tomato. It was during my last abortive attempt on the Eiger, when they took off the restaurant car at, was it Melbourne, and we all had to hitchhike back through the Camargue.'

'. . . and,' continued Challoner, fixing Frobisher with a terrible glance, 'upon the following morning, we set out across the veldt towards Cowes.'

'Shark country,' grunted Twistleton-Wickham-Finkel. 'You were damned lucky, Challoner!'

'Not luck, I fancy,' said I. 'Challoner is an old Arctic hand. You forget, Twinkers, that Challoner was the first chap to stumble on the North-West Passage, weren't you, old man?'

Challoner sighed deeply. Time glazed his cornflower eyes.

'They were asking £39, 250 for it,' he said. 'It was a lot of money in those days. Plus it needed a fortune spent on it. It had an outside khazi, you know.'

'What happened?' enquired Frobisher, pushing King Solomon's Chicken aside to discourage the bluebottles.

'I offered thirty, but the Norwegians beat me to it.'

'Bad show!'

'At least,' said Challoner, 'I assume they were Norwegians. Big black buggers in a clapped-out 1953 Consul.'

'Anyway,' I said, for I sensed the old melancholy was about to settle on our great narrator, 'you got to Cowes without any difficulty?'

'More or less, more or less,' replied Challoner. 'We had something of a communications problem at the Italian frontier, mind. They had a sign up saying *Private Estate* in English, and I thought to myself, aha, this is doubtless the aftermath of the Asian Cup Final, they are trying to keep the Brits out, well, Johnny Wop, I thought, you have to get up bloody early in the morning to catch old Mister Challoner! There was this dago sitting by the barrier in some kind of pansy uniform, so I reckoned if I threw a string of onions round my neck and addressed him in his own language – in which I happen, of course, to be fluent – he would take me to be a local and wave me through.'

'Did it work?' asked Frobisher.

'Did it hell,' said Challoner. 'I marched up to him and I said *Guten Morgen, ich bin auf dem Weg nach Cowes*, and the next thing I knew this damned great dog of his was chasing us all down the road towards Leningrad. I never saw my porters again.'

'Probably all holed up in Leningrad,' muttered Twistleton-Wickham-Finkel, 'with a dozen belly-dancers and a crate of Guinness. What did you do?'

'Fortunately,' replied Challoner, 'they'd left me the map. It was the work of a moment to pinpoint Tchad, take a couple of quick bearings, and set off North up the A40.'

'Keeping a weather-eye open for the Khmer Rouge?' put in Frobisher.

'Keeping a weather-eye open for Khmer Rouge, yes,' said Challoner.

'For God's sake stop interrupting!' snapped Twistleton-Wickham-Finkel, 'or we'll never get to King Solomon's Chicken. By the way, why are its giblets in a little bag?'

'Ah,' said Challoner, 'I was coming to that.'

As well he might have, had, at that moment, the most fearful commotion not broken out in the hallway beyond the library. There were roars, there were cries, there were cheers, there were huzzahs and shrieks and whistles and snatches of song and the sound of dinner gongs being peremptorily struck!

Alas for poor Challoner and his tale, I am sorry to say we all sprang from our chairs and rushed to investigate the source of the uproar. Nor did we have far to rush, since hardly had we left our alcove than the doors of the library were flung apart to admit an ecstatic mob bearing upon their shoulders a figure at whose sight we could but reel and gasp!

'It cannot be!' I cried.

'It is quite impossible!' shouted Frobisher.

'Is it really you?' shrieked Twistleton-Wickham-Finkel.

At this last hysterical address the elegant figure smiled, and looked down benignly upon us.

'Yes,' said Phileas Fogg, 'it is really I!'

'But,' cried Frobisher, waving his turnip watch, 'it is only the first of July! You have succeeded in circumnavigating the globe not in eighty days, but in a mere forty-five! How can this be?'

Lithely, the great traveller dropped from the acclamatory shoulders and shook our out-stretched hands.

'As good fortune would have it,' said Fogg, 'the completion of the M25 enabled me to by-pass China completely.'

Professor Challoner carefully prodded the giblets back inside King Solomon's Chicken and replaced it in its cardboard box.

'Hardly sporting,' he muttered. 'In my day, we had to swim China.'

Time On My Hand

LURCH AWAKE, in impenetrable dark.

Half-awake.

Tiny, far-off, metallic, rhythmic tink-tink-bing-bing-tink-tink-bing-bing, like weeny hammer striking weeny nail, ringingly. What going on? Elves at work behind skirting, preparations for Mouse Queen wedding, get bloody move on, Nitkin, pull finger out, Titkin, golden coach two days behind schedule as per yours of 15th ultimo, where rear-end differential, where tiara rack, Mouse Queen go mad, Mouse King eat night shift, never mind *Hi-ho, hi-ho*, get bloody skates on?

Three-quarters awake.

Noise not elves, noise coming from bedside table, elves never work on bedside table, could get flattened by outflung hand seeking, e.g., new Jap watch, six months work on gold coach down drain, little wheels fly everywhere, little windows shattered, little Titkin knocked senseless into ashtray, little Nitkin hurled into unfinished Remy Martin nightcap, unable to climb out of balloon glass, blind drunk in ten minutes, Mouse Queen go mad, Mouse King bite heads off.

Elf scenario fades. Fully awake, now. Noise coming from new Jap watch; it NJW alarm, it time to get up, say NJW, it time to put ten yen in parking meter, it time for meeting with Chairman Nakimoto San, it time for origami class, it time to chuck unworthy self on sword.

What time, exactly?

NJW not luminous, cannot find NJW in dark, let alone time it got, NJW got four buttons controlling eight million different functions including little light, grope for watch, knock over nightcap, find wet NJW, luckily waterproof to two hundred metres according to huge owner's manual, no mention of brandyproof depth, mind, could be conked out by now, take it back, man in Dixon's Holborn Circus take one look, bow, say So sorry, customer-san, you infringe guarantee, how about you buy brandy-proof model, only £18.99, it good for two hundred metres, also got breathalyser function, also go tink-tink-bing-bing ten minutes before drink-up time so customer-san get two more rounds in?

Wife beginning to stir, tink-tink-bing-bing beginning to penetrate, grab wet NJW, hobble into bathroom to put on light to see watch in order to locate right button to put on watch-light to see watch . . .

It 3.40 am.

Why alarm go off at 3.40 am? It not programmed by me, cannot programme alarm at all, bought watch this morning, took me three hours to set ordinary time, watch got umpteen modes and four buttons, i.e. umpteen^4 = possibility of hitting right formula for setting time, watch kept going into peculiar spasm, lap-times, stop-watching, countdowns, kept nearly getting time-setting mode, get date right, dial TIM, wait for bleep, press button, entire display vanish again, watch play *Bluebells of Scotland*, try again, this time watch play *Humoresque*, NJW got five different alarm tunes *plus* tink-tink-bing-bing, it like having radiogram on wrist, spent entire morning listening to tinny medley of old tat, finally, more luck than judgement, got watch to tell time. Never touched alarm mode.

3.42. Still going tink-tink-bing-bing, must be way of stopping it, dare not push knob at random, might lose time display again, might get *O Mine Papa*, wife wake up, wife claim man sitting on bidet at 3.43 playing *O Mine Papa* on watch incontrovertible grounds for quickie divorce, wife snatch up children, vanish, leave customer-san staring at car vanishing up road with watch playing *Hello Dolly!* to rest of street, lights go on, windows open, neighbours get restraining order, customer-san end up in Broadmoor with NJW playing *God Save the King* endlessly, cannot stop watch by banging it on padded wall, watch guaranteed shockproof, would have to dive into something over two hundred metres deep to stop it, they not have two-hundred-metres-deep things in Broadmoor, Broadmoor not allow inmate-san to hurt self, Broadmoor got rubber spoons, Broadmoor got wooden scissors.

3.45. Watch suddenly stop of own accord.

Stare at watch.

Did not want all this.

Had nice old gold Omega, went on holiday last week, NOGO not good to two hundred metres, NOGO turn out not even good to one metre, come out of pool, NOGO no go. Came home, took it to NOGO agent, NOGO agent say waterproofing up spout, watch now full of teeny dried plankton etc. like whale's lower set, fifty quid to recondition.

Think. Not worth it, could buy brand new watch for half that, seen them in Dixon's Holborn Circus, stick NOGO in pocket, walk to Dixon's, Dixon's got huge display of winking dials, showcase look like 747 dashboard, how to choose? This one got nine million functions, including calculator mode and international bus time-table, that one patched into Pentagon database and Dow Jones update, one over there got David and Igor Oistrakh playing Bach Double Violin Concerto every hour, tell assistant-san want watch that just tell time, assistant-san chuckle, for only £17.99 customer-san get entire bag of tricks, this 1984, customer-san, what for you want £7.99 banger, for extra tenner customer-san walk tall, do own Olympic sprint timing to fourteen decimal places, settle argument in Athenaeum over tallest building in Latvia, dive down to inspect *Mary Rose* while playing full hour of Val Doonican's Greatest Hits.

Give assistant-san £17.99, drive home, something in glove compartment playing *O Mine Papa*, get home, study manual, e.g:

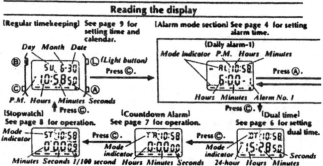

After entire morning, completely stumped.

It tragic story of age, it some kind of Parkinson Law, man constantly buying more and more things with unusable extras just because unusable extras come cheap, man buy wallet, wallet got ballpoint in it, man already got ballpoint, now not only got unnecessary ballpoint, unnecessary ballpoint got tiny calculator on it at no extra charge, unnecessary tiny calculator got trigonometry mode, man now spend all day working out height of trees.

Never mind computers. Half homes in country now got little tin box bought to do milk bills plus occasional hand of whist, but discovered to be capable of umpteen totally unnecessary functions, customers must amortize £299.95, therefore half homes in country up most of night writing unnecessary programmes, other half up most of night wondering whether to give in and buy one, entire country fall into bed, knackered, at 2 am, NJW go off at 3.40, everybody wake up again.

Something behind all this. Plot.

Stare at watch again.

Why NJW go off at 3.40?

NJW obviously programmed in factory to go off at 3.40, must be 6.40 in Tokyo, all watches go off, everybody-san get up, chop-chop, everybody scuttle down Datsubishi factory, shipyard, NJW watchworks, everybody start toiling away nineteen to dozen, make ten million exports before *Bluebells of Scotland* inform them it time for 2.34 minute lunchbreak, set lapsed-time mode to 2.34 minutes, gobble sukiyaki, watch play *Hello Dolly (Herro Dorry?)*, everybody rush back to workbench, graft, graft, graft, export watches to Britain, Brits go into Dixon's Holborn Circus, buy NJW.

Wake up at 3.40 in morning.

Not fit for work next day, make half a Metro, put two rivets in three-year-overdue oil-rig, fall off quarter-built skyscraper, British economy go down tubes, Nippon triumphant, Queen step down, Hirohito troop colour.

4.12 am.

Look out of bathroom window.

Rising sun in east.

Anything Legal Considered

Next week 21, 000 members of the American Bar Association descend on London for their annual conference.

Guardian

MS LOIS SHOEMAKER
Bidwell, Kreis & Runningwolf
234 E 56th Street NYC

July 5

Dear Ms Shoemaker,

Oh wow, did we have a terrific flight! We had the best flight we ever had! We had one of those flights you want to hang on to for when the bad days come around and you need something to, you know, remind you of the way it was, once.

Remember you pre-booked us two forward aisle seats, non-smoking? Know what the dummies did? The dummies stuck us aft, window-seats, smoking, that's what the dummies did! The creep on my left was chain-smoking black stogies, the broad in front was dropping Marlboro stubs all over, not only did Mrs Bidwell get maybe the worst attack of asthma since we took sixteen grand off of General Motors for the air-conditioning hitting the fritz in the Lincoln Tunnel but I got lucky, too, the broad burned a hole in my new Gucci iguana-hide zipper-bag! And you want to know better yet? Better yet is I bend down to put the bagfire out and when I straighten up – you're never going to believe this – I gash my head on the tray which has accidentally opened, there was blood all over, including my new Bugatti silk tie which is an original model!

Please look out the Ginsberg vs. TWA file and forward Xerox urgentest. I figure twenty-five grand for the asthma, minimum, plus another twenty for distress at iguana wipe-out, plus we could definitely be looking at fifty Gs for the gash, it goes way across the forehead, with any luck I will have a major scar, I could've lost a whole eye, but who can have everything, be content, don't be greedy, don't I tell clients that all the time, if God had wanted me to lose an eye He would've made bigger trays, is how I look at it.

Fortunately, there was a doctor on board who rushed over and put a couple of stitches in the cut. Am I a lucky guy, or am I a lucky guy? Have you any idea of the kind of malpractice suit we're talking here, Ms Shoemaker, I been in this business a long time, nobody is gonna tell me this quack's training involved sinking four vodkatinis and sewing a head at 40, 000 feet, I could walk out of that court-room a yacht owner, Ms Shoemaker, I could be looking at a chateau.

The only downer is where Schwartzbart of Schwartzbart, Schwartzbart, Dreck and Schwarzbart beat me to a cab at Heathrow by jumping the queue. I could've had him on maybe three different counts, but Jack Schwartzbart is one smart shyster, you would not believe the counter-claims he could pull. Dreck I could make mincemeat of, but I am not going up against Jack Schwartzbart, it would be goodbye chateau.

Please forward Kowalski vs. The Denver Water Authority. I think I tasted fluoride in my toothmug this morning.

Sincerely,
Samuel D. Bidwell

MS LOIS SHOEMAKER
Bidwell, Kreis & Runningwolf
234 E 56th Street NYC

July 7

Dear Ms Shoemaker,
Jesus, this is a terrific town! Just walking around it, you keep saying to yourself *This town is anything up to a hundred years old!* The sidewalks are all shot, the doorways are all kind of low and saggy, the walls are damp, the floorboards creak, so far we have twisted two ankles, wiped out an entire hat, caught two real big viral infections, and been up the whole damn night! I hate to be a pain, but could you forward Henshawe vs. Poughkeepsie Tarmacadam Inc., Pinchus vs. The Groton Old Innes Corp., McKinnoch vs. Tombstone Health & Welfare, and Dinkheim vs. Achison, Topeka and Santa Fe?

Mrs Bidwell says if this all works out right, we could maybe go to a full-mouth reconstruction in 22-carat, plus throw in a couple of new boobs. I sure hope so, I love that woman, Ms Shoemaker, I would not like her to get second-bested by Mrs Harry Stonewort. Remember Stonewort, Klein, Klein & Rimmell? They all went off to some toney restaurant, they hit a wrong crab, both Kleins had to get pumped out and Harry Stonewort may have permanent liver damage, this is a million-dollar touch, Ms Shoemaker, this is Charlie Q. Big One, this is where the Stoneworts get the ten-thousand-acre ranch with the reproduction hacienda plus mineral rights! I could've joined them at that goddam restaurant, Ms Shoemaker, they asked me, they wanted to discuss the tall Klein's case against being stuck in the room reserved for the small Klein, but what did I do, I had room service on account of this virus I picked up at St Paul's Column. All I got off room service was a fishbone in the throat, five thousand bucks, tops, due to where they are bound to go for contributory negligence.

Still, Rimmell's the guy I'm really sorry for. He don't eat crab, so he ordered the melon on account of melon always gives him diarrhoea, and you know what? *Nothing!* Not even a lousy hundred-dollar flatulence suit. I guess they have different melons in Europe, it is something they ought to tell you about in law school, I wonder if Rimmell has a case against Harvard, it is worth looking into.

Please add Perry vs. Ogenbogen Glass & Sundries. It is not fluoride, it is definitely something in the goddam beaker, you can smell it even when it is empty.

Sincerely,
Samuel D. Bidwell

MS LOIS SHOEMAKER
Bidwell, Kreis & Runningwolf
234 E 56th Street NYC

July 8

Dear Ms Shoemaker,
Is mortification the word? I am not too big on fancy stuff, you have seen me in court, you know me, Ms Shoemaker, Honest Sam Bidwell, call a spade a spade, I stand in the proud heritage of Abe Lincoln, what the hell use is a long word when a short one will do, they ain't paying you by the syllable, is my view.

You will not believe this, Ms Shoemaker. I advise you to sit down before reading further. I do not want you to fall off your chair and bring some damn fool action for negligence or actual physical distress or misuse of the mails or sexual belligerence or I don't know what else.

The fact is, I am being sued by Charlie Runningwolf. Not only am I being sued by a junior partner, I am being sued by a *red* junior partner, I am being sued by a Pawnee junior partner, it will teach us to be an equal opportunities employer, Ms Shoemaker, it will teach us to bring these dingbats off the reservation and show them how to tie shoes, please shred this letter, I do not wish to be looking at the wrong end of Giant Moose Who Stands By The Still Water vs. Friendly Trucking Inc.

Last night, while Mrs Bidwell and I were swallowing our chest medication prior to strolling abroad in the hope of running across some mugger prepared to allow us to take the British Government for all it has – you would not believe the very sweet Criminal Compensation loopholes they have here, Ms Shoemaker – our telephone rang.

It was Charlie Runningwolf, in Room 213. 'I am in Room 213,' he said, 'and I am staring at the goddam garage. How come you look out over the frigging park and all I have is the frigging gas pumps?'

I explained to him that it was on account of he was a junior partner, but he became extremely abusive, implying strongly that it was in fact on account of he was red. He pointed out that his people had been systematically dispossessed, raped, pillaged, butchered and incinerated, and on top of all this, they were now being asked to stay in a room with a view of the Texaco forecourt!

He sounded canned to me, Ms Shoemaker, so I told him to lay off the firewater. The next thing I know, that little wall-eyed dyke Phoebe Lumachi from Lumachi, Gimmer, Birnbaum, Twisk & Donghoffer is at my door with a writ.

'Not only are we as of this moment in time Lumachi, Gimmer, Birnbaum, Twisk, Donghoffer & Runningwolf,' she smirks, 'but we also represent Mr Charles Runningwolf in the little matter of Runningwolf vs. Bidwell. Boy-oh-boy, fartface, is that firewater crack gonna *cost*!'

The upshot, Ms Shoemaker, is I am being hit on eight different discrimination counts, plus professional misconduct, plus a whole new juridical gizmo thought up by this Lumachi dame, to wit, and I quote, 'Misleading a desk clerk as to the personal habits of an Original American in order to gain favourable treatment.'

I intend fighting this one all the way up to the Supreme Court, starting with Room 213.

Sincerely,
Samuel D. Bidwell

MS LOIS SHOEMAKER
Kreis
234 E 56th Street NYC

July 9

Dear Lois,

I feel I can call you Lois, I hope you don't mind, the last thing I want is a major condescension suit just when things are going so well, also not using your surname is probably an infringement of your civil liberties etcetera, I do not know about these things, my dear husband never kept me, you know, abreast of the law, maybe he figured I'd run out on him if I got to understand the paperwork involved.

Anyway.

Last night, right after he mailed your letter, he rushed up to see Charlie Runningwolf in 213, I was real worried, he did not take the lift, his blood pressure is already 190 over 130, if he dropped dead in the lift we could take Otis to the cleaners, but if he dropped dead on the stairs, that one is down to him, zilch for the estate, unless you can prove a loose stair-rod, never easy, we tried that time in, was it Heidelberg, anyway, he was carrying maybe two hundred pages of notes, he was fixing to get that red gonnof on everything from inside trading and telephone assault to conduct abroad likely to bring the United States of, you know, America into disrepute, plus he reckoned to subpoena Lumachi, Gimmer, Birnbaum, Twisk and Donghoffer as material witnesses on sixty-seven counts. i.e. keep the bastards in court until around 1998, no work coming in, fix their wagon real permanent, all that, so he bangs on the door, and he stomps in, and he begins handing out the writs, and Charlie Runningwolf sinks a tomahawk in his head.

I just noticed a typing error, Ms Shoemaker, paragraph one, I am not too good with these British manual machines, that should read my *dead* husband, sorry.

Anyway, what I want to know is, how much is Charlie Runningwolf good for on his personal account? I am out one top breadwinner, plus grief-stricken to the tune of, who knows, with a smart lawyer could be as much as five million. Thinking of which, forget that little wimp Kreis, I was thinking of retaining this Phoebe Lumachi, she is one sharp cookie, could *she* represent me in Bidwell vs. Runningwolf, even though the red dummy is her junior partner?

Or would that be what's the word – unethical?

Yours truly,
Miriam Bidwell

Cry Havoc!

An EEC plan to tattoo dogs and cats with identification marks has brought howls of protest from British MEPs.

Daily Star

'IN THE nightmare of the dark,' murmured the Irish setter, 'all the dogs of Europe bark.'

The others stopped rooting in their matted groins, and glanced up.

'Auden,' explained the Irish setter.

'Clever sod,' said the sealyham.

'On the death of Yeats,' said the setter, softly.

'Dead is he, Yeats?' enquired the alsatian.

Moisture gleamed in the setter's limpid eye.

'Begob, yes,' he said.

The alsatian cleared its dreadful throat.

'This Auden,' he murmured, 'I don't suppose he said where the bones were buried?'

There was an inevitable, though fortunately brief, skirmish, during which, with equal inevitability, the setter lost most of one ear. It retired bitterly behind a gravel bin, where it could subsequently be heard crooning, low, an ancient John McCormack ballad.

'You realise,' said the bulldog, 'that if he'd had his EEC tattoo on that ear, he'd be bloody anonymous by now?'

'It only goes to show,' said the alsatian. 'They live in another world, committees. It is easy to tell no one up Strasbourg has ever been a dog.'

'Funny really,' said a collie, with all the thoughtfulness of his breed, 'them being Alsatians and so forth.'

'Good point,' said the alsatian, nodding. 'Except I am strictly speaking a German shepherd.'

'You don't want to nod,' said the sealyham, albeit respectfully. 'You look like something in the back of a Cortina.'

The alsatian ignored this.

'As a German shepherd,' it said, 'I should expect to be tattooed under my left foreleg. It was common practice up the SS, and I do not see any reason to change a winning formula.'

'As a *genuine* German,' put in a hitherto silent dachshund, heavily, 'as a *genuine* German who had no idea what was going on, I should object most strongly to being tattooed under my left foreleg.'

'You and the tattooist both,' said the alsatian, with a fanged snigger. 'He'd have to be a midget to start with, never mind getting on his back and sliding underneath, why don't you ask him to drain the sump and look at the front suspension while he's down there?'

The other dogs laughed to see such fun; or, more accurately, to avoid going summarily monaural.

'Be that as it may,' said the bulldog, 'it is nevertheless concealing a serious point, i.e. where will it end? Start with tattooed ears, next thing you know it will be widdling on the right. Don't talk to me about bureaucracy, I nearly got put down once for doing a gasman's shin, if it hadn't been for the *Sunday Express* and eight million *News at Ten* supporters, I should very likely be two dozen spring rolls by now.'

'Standardisation is the enemy,' said the sealyham.

They looked at it.

'He don't half come out with 'em,' said the bulldog, 'for something that looks like a sink tidy.'

The setter let out a low ululating approximation to *Danny Boy*.

'I was very much against letting the Irish enter in the first place,' said the alsatian. 'I knew we'd get this, singing, violence, sod-all constructive. I think they all ought to have special tattoos. Big yellow shamrocks, something of that order.'

The others pondered this uneasily.

'It doesn't sound very European,' murmured the collie, finally. 'It does not seem to be in, er, line with current ecumenical thinking.'

'Good,' said the alsatian. 'I know about these things, before you look round there'll be a bloody Irish setter mountain.'

'If God had wanted us standardised,' continued the sealyham more or less to itself, 'He would have made us cats.'

'I'd gas cats,' said the alsatian.

'My personal view about tattoos,' said the bulldog, 'is they should have a ship that sinks when you breathe in.'

'Funny that, coming from you,' said the dachshund.

'I think there may be a personal remark coming up,' said a poodle.

'Watch it,' said the bulldog, between pants.

'No offence meant,' said the dachshund, 'we must all breathe in our own individual ways – '

'God,' growled the alsatian, 'I hate the new Germany!'

' – I just meant it would look a trifle unbecoming. Not ever sinking, just bobbing up and down two hundred times a minute. I'm not saying it's your fault, or anything.'

'Here,' said the alsatian to the bulldog, 'you're not deformed, I trust? We don't want nothing deformed in Europe, if you're deformed we might as well string you up now instead of buggering about with tattoos etcetera, all that paperwork.'

'Try it,' muttered the bulldog.

'I think we're getting away from the main issue,' said the poodle.

'A decadent speaks,' said the alsatian.

The poodle tossed its head.

'The main issue, as I see it,' it went on, 'concerns what might best be described as the Eurodog Concept.'

'Hallo,' said the bulldog, wrinkling an already striated forehead until it resembled an estuary foreshore.

'Intellectuals,' muttered the alsatian, rolling its terrible eyes so that they took on the ochreous semblance of unborn eggs. 'Hard labour is the only answer.'

'In other words,' persisted the poodle, 'do we feel tattooing will unify us into common Eurocaninity, or alternatively, rob us of our individual sovereign identities?'

The alsatian stared at it for a time; then, slowly, turned its head towards the other dogs.

'What *is* it about the French?' it said.

'Speaking for myself,' said the dachshund, carefully, 'and recognising that the past is now behind us, i.e. one hundred per cent of dachshunds now living were born after 1945, I nevertheless feel that Eurocaninity could easily lead to mongrelism, which I personally would deplore.'

'Not hard to see why,' said the alsatian, smirking. 'Given a Common Genocultural Policy and your average bureaucratic, if you'll pardon the expression, cock-up, you could well find yourself sharing a Eurobreeding kennel with e.g., a Great Dane or similar. Not,' it added smartly, 'that I do not go along with your views on racial purity, indeed it bucks me up no end, it is quite clear that the dachshund doesn't fall far from the tree, as it were. We shall be,' and here it turned slyly to the poodle, 'back across the Rhine in two shakes of a, of a –'

The silence that followed was fraught, brief, and broken by the bulldog's easing itself slowly off its tiny haunches the better to shove forward its heavily muscled shoulders, and say, breathily:

'That was well out of order.'

'Oh really?' said the alsatian, and sank its teeth into the poodle's neck.

Whereupon the bulldog lurched with surprising agility, and clamped its fearful jaws over the alsatian's thigh, which left the dachshund with little alternative but to lock on to the bulldog's ear, despite the inevitable consequences to itself of having its tail immediately pincered by the collie, whose views on devolution were as tenuous as the Home Rule stance of a Welsh corgi now frantically attempting to snap at what historians would doubtless refer to, albeit euphemistically, as the soft underbelly of the alsatian.

Only the Irish setter, aloof from the Eurocidal melee beyond its gravel-bin, remained – of course – neutral.

'And the living nations wait,' it recited, 'Each sequestered in its hate.'

It looked around for someone to appreciate this, and found only a fat Russian Blue, who had been observing the proceedings from the secure position of its tree, high above.

'Auden,' explained the setter.

The Russian Blue merely blinked impassively. Not only did it not speak dog, it did not give a damn either way. It knew only that, all things considered, it could not be long before the cats inherited the earth.

Man-Eating Batsmen of
Death-Ray Island

A Full-length Yuletide Yarn

'NATIVE WAR canoes coming this way?' cried Flight Sergeant 'Footy' Boote VC, two-fisted ginger-mopped Headmaster of The School That Would Not Die. 'Are you sure?'

In answer, Beaky Finkel, madcap tailor of the Remove, whipped out the hundred-inch refracting telescope he had made just that morning from two old cocoa-tins and a broken ping-pong bat, and put it to his eye.

'Yes, skipper, it's a dusky band all right,' he retorted, shinning rapidly down the yucca tree again, 'and what's more, they've got Johnny Dodds on clarinet! Of course, it might just be a devilish Hun trick!'

His plucky Headmaster considered this for a moment, cocking an ear for the insistent beat of distant drums echoing across The Lagoon They Could Not Smell.

'*King Porter Stomp*,' he mused aloud. 'Do you know, Beaky, I think you may be spot on. I happen to know that Obersturmbanngruppenführer Herman 'Spotty' Knackwurst, The Nazi That Time Forgot, went missing not twenty miles from here while trying to snare The Giant Squid Of Atlantis, which his fiendish bosses back in Berlin planned to clone in the laboratories of kindly old Professor Mondieu, whose lovely young daughter was being held to ransom by The Panzers Of The Damned. Tall and blonde, too, I hasten to add.'

'Hum! Sho' sound like dat ole Nazi up to his tricks again!

Only one name fo' a man messin' aroun' wid a tall blonde squid!'

The speaker was none other than Prince Nbing Nbong, known as Shine to his chums in the Remedial Shell, who had hurtled faithfully up on his trusty monocycle at the first inkling of trouble, and was now wrinkling his dusky brow, as was his native wont. How they all chuckled! Footy Boote clapped him on the back so smartly that the multi-millionaire paramount chief's enormous eyes rolled around in his gleaming ebony head like marbles in a saucer!

'God bless my soul, Shine,' he cried, 'what a jolly old black scallywag you are! It was the *daughter* who was tall and blonde, ha-ha-ha!'

'Ha-ha-ha!' shrieked The School That Would Not Die dutifully, rolling around among the coconuts, and trying to imagine how jolly rotten it must be to be a tall blonde daughter with your skirt ripped to the thigh and buttons bursting off your blouse while beastly Boche tank commanders tried to get you to play doctors and nurses with them.

'The Giant Squid, on the other hand,' continued Footy Boote, drawing reflectively on The Trusty Briar From Outer Space, 'was an extremely unsavoury cove – Johnny Hun planned to make a thousand of them, you know, and parachute them all over the Home Counties, prior to the invasion. Can you imagine what havoc they would have wrought, and not just on the County Cricket Championship?' His bright carrot-red hair grew serious for a moment. 'Can any of us say for sure how he would have reacted if he had found a Giant Squid doing things to his sister?'

'I should have run the pair of them through!' cried Corky Lino, The Centre Half With The Dynamite Studs.

'Well said, Corky!' bellowed his trusty Head. 'Best be on the safe side, eh?'

The chaps all nodded. Sage old Footy Boote VC! He had his head screwed on all right, for a beak. It was common sense like his that had seen them through all the hair-raising escapades that had befallen them ever since the ship taking them to New Zealand for their annual rugger fixture had been torpedoed by the devilish Japs and they had been luckily plucked out of the ocean by albatrosses and deposited here on The Island From One Million BC, miles from the trade routes, where dinosaurs, because of a unique medicinal fern, still roamed, laying the eggs with which The School That Would Not Die was able to supplement the diet of roots and berries they had been able to identify from *Ye Booke of South Sea Rootes and Berrys* that Buggy Bolsover had found mysteriously wrapped in a yellow oilskin pouch inside the hollow tree he had been using to practice ventriloquism in case cannibals turned up and needed to be scared off by talking shrubs.

It was Buggy who stood up now, as the drums throbbed ever closer.

'Do you think I should get inside the tree, skipper?' he enquired. 'We ought to be ready when the war canoes hit the beach!'

In answer, Footy slapped him on the shoulder with such force that Buggy's startled exclamation appeared to come from a boulder two hundred yards away, fortunately thwarting a column of giant ants who had, unbeknownst to the chaps, been bearing down on them with a view to stripping their bones bare in seconds!

'Lord bless you, no, Buggy!' cried the cheery Head. 'I have no intention of letting our chum Johnny Man-Eater ever reach the beach! I intend borrowing Desmond d'Arcy's monocle and focusing the sun's rays on the canoes so that the tinder-dry animal skins catch fire and sink, precipitating our dusky adversaries into the shark-infested waters!'

'But isn't that just what they'll be expecting, sir?' enquired Lawrence 'Tiny' Featherstonehaugh, The Fat Boy With Surprising Agility For One So Large.

'That's a chance we'll just have to take!' riposted Flight Sergeant Boote, raising his aquiline nose and sniffing expertly. 'Fortunately, the wind has just changed in our favour!'

The chaps all nodded. Sage old Footy Boote VC! He had his head screwed on all right, for a beak.

Desmond d'Arcy, however, took leave to demur.

'It'll take more than my old monocle, sir,' opined that worthy.

'Those canoes must be two miles off. I rather doubt that we can focus the sun's rays effectively over that distance.'

Beaky Finkel, madcap tailor of the Remove, who had been sketching some rapid equations in the dust with a sharp stick, now looked up.

'It's perfectly possible, chaps,' he said, quietly. 'It's all a question of physics.'

The School That Would Not Die gazed at him in admiration.

'Go on Beaky,' muttered Footy, through clenched teeth.

'Basically,' explained the wily Levantine, 'I shall need sixty-three cocoa-tins.'

'Then there's no time to be lost!' roared the Head. 'Scour the island, you chaps!'

As one man, the plucky lads leapt up and plunged into the scrub, heedless of the poisonous giant thorns stabbing at their sinewy limbs, which – thanks to an antidote made from giant jellyfish that 'Stinks' Cholmondeley-Cholmondeley, The Masked Chemist Who Rode With The Quorn, had accidentally stumbled upon while diving for The Lost Hoard Of Captain Blood – were now not only immune to the deadly barbs, but incredibly strengthened, enabling all of them to run the hundred yards in under five seconds, a skill which, regular readers will recall, had stood them in particularly good stead The Night The Saucer Landed.

Nevertheless, a good ten minutes had passed before they reassembled, dropping their gathered cocoa-tins at the feet of Beaky Finkel.

'Well done!' cried Footy Boote VC. 'I'd been rather dreading the news that they had all been trampled by dinosaurs. He's a delicate thing, your Johnny Cocoa-Tin!'

'Right first time, skipper!' retorted Corky Lino. 'We *did* find that a number *had* been flattened, but, as luck would have it, Shine here stumbled into an old disused elephant trap, and what do you suppose was at the bottom of it?'

'Shine, at a guess!' cried Footy Boote, quick as a flash.

How they all chortled, not least the big darkie, despite the two broken legs, which, in a white man, might have been very serious, but which, because of the many years of dancing, were in Prince Nbing Nbong's case so strongly reinforced by muscle that he felt no more pain than if he had fallen on his massively boned head.

'Yassum, baas, dat sho' true, ah *was* at de bottom ob de hole,' laughed the latter, 'but dat weren't de only ting down dere. What ah foun' wuz de remains of a Fust Worl' War zeppelin, shot down by curare-tipped pyggermy arrows while ferryin' a cargo o' tinned cocoa to a German climbin' team trapped by lava unexpectedly whizzin f'om de mouf o' De Volcano Dat Nobody Noo!'

'Good work, Shine!' cried Footy Boote VC. 'Now, off you go, and wrap some incredibly restorative gully-gully leaves around those legs of yours, you'll be going in third wicket down after we've seen your coon cousins off, and if there's no fancy work off the front foot, I shall be down on you like the proverbial ton of bricks!'

Thus congratulated by the fellow he loved most in all the world, the sheepishly grinning giant loped happily away, while the rest of the chaps gathered around Beaky Finkel, whose dextrous ring-spanners, cunningly fashioned from a triceratops ribcage, were already flashing among the cocoa-tins, faster than the eye could follow!

Five minutes and some pretty swift hammering later, the madcap tailor's masterpiece stood revealed. A great gasp went up from the assembled chums!

'I say, Beaky, old sport,' cried Corky Lino, voicing everyone's unspoken thoughts, 'what on earth *is* that extraordinary contraption?'

It was Beaky's turn to chuckle.

'It may be just an extraordinary contraption to you,' he said, 'but to me it's sixty-three cocoa-tins with d'Arcy's monocle wedged in the end.'

Footy Boote pursed his lips and let out a low whistle.

'I call it,' said Beaky, 'my Death Ray!'

In the ensuing silence, you could have heard the proverbial pin drop!

'Wow!' called Prince Nbing Nbong, from his little compound,

'Man hab bin lookin' fo' de secret ob de Def Ray since de beginnin' ob time.'

'But it took Beaky here to find it!' exclaimed the Head. 'What a dashed clever race they are, albeit a trifle short in the slow left-arm spin department. What say we take it down to the beach, chaps, and give our visitors the shock of their jolly old lives?'

The boys needed no second bidding. With great whoops, they sped through the scrub on sturdy limbs, bearing the precious death ray on their tanned shoulders, and did not stop until their pounding feet met the bone-white sand.

Where they suddenly fetched up, their eyes on stalks, their mouths agape!

'Curses!' cried Footy Boote. 'There's one thing we reckoned without!'

'You mean – ?' muttered an anguished Corky.

'Exactly!' retorted the plucky Head, smiting himself on the brow and silently cursing himself for a fool. 'The Tidal Wave That Came From Nowhere!'

For, while they had been busy at their various tasks, they had not realised quite how rapidly the native canoes had sped shorewards! Even now, the howling Hottentots were hurtling up the beach towards them, shrunken skulls rattling at their skimpily clad waists, their sinewy hands brandishing the murderous cricket bats retrieved from the wreck of HMS *Spofforth* after that fine ship had struck a Japanese mine while bound for Guadalcanal with The Team That Would Go Anywhere For a Game!

'I'm afraid my death ray is no use at this range, skipper!' cried Beaky Finkel.

'And even if it were,' muttered Footy Boote, knotting his muscles and preparing to sell himself dearly with several clean uppercuts of his own design, 'I fear it would be no match for honest British willow!'

Whereupon, setting jaws and gritting teeth, The School That Would Not Die formed, as their plucky ancestors had done, a square, and got ready to go down fighting!

And then, suddenly, without any warning, the sky became absolutely pitch-black! As one animal, the gleaming savages came to a confused stop, muttering and mumbling, until all that the brave lads could see in the inky gloom was eyeballs and teeth!

'What the – ?' snapped Corky Lino.

'Just hold on!' hissed Flight Sergeant Footy Boote VC. 'For, unless I am very much mistaken – '

He was not. A split-second later, the queer tropical darkness was suddenly lit by eerie flashes of light that hissed and crackled in the very air above the beach, to be followed by what seemed to be glowing footballs bouncing astonishingly from tree to tree!

'Just as I thought!' thundered Footy Boote. 'It is a combination of a total eclipse of the sun with an unprecedented display of St Elmo's Fire! I knew, of course, that such a coincidence occurs roughly every eighteen thousand years, but it had quite slipped my mind that today was the day!'

His words had risen to a bellow to make them audible above the penetrating shrieks of the terrified savages! For those fellows were certainly not staying around, succulent white dinner or no succulent white dinner! By the time the eclipse had passed, their panic-stricken canoes were no more than paddling dots on the brightening horizon!

'Gosh,' exclaimed Beaky, 'that was a pretty close shave, eh, sir?'

Footy Boote plucked a still glowing ember from a lightning-struck tree, and lit his pipe with a steady hand.

'A great Englishman once had a word for it, Beaky,' he murmured, blowing a smoke ring and calmly watching it dissolve in the clear afternoon air. 'He, unless I am very much mistaken, would have described it as a damned close-run thing!'

An Article About . . .

Volunteers who fear they may be losing their memories are being sought by Professor Patrick Rabbitt of Manchester University for research into absent-mindedness.

Daily Telegraph

August the, the

Dear Professor Rabbitt,

I do hope you will forgive my writing to you out of the, without prior, out of the, we have not met, but I saw the item in the *Daily*, blue, but I saw your item in the *Sunday*, in the, I heard the item on the car, unless it was *News at*, um, you see a picture of Old Ben, the big hand is on the, on the, or to put it another way, the little hand is, the little hand is, anyhow you hear the pips, the chimes, and they go one, two, three, God Almighty, do you know, Geoff, I have been watching that programme for the past, for the past, since we lived in, since we lived at number, since we, large block of flats, next to the, small block of flats, next to the Tube, at, at, there was a Sainsbury's across the, there was a Sainsbury's on the corner.

Or a Tesco's.

My wife will remember. She's out in the, she's up on the.

Right, I'm back now, sorry about that, I asked her, and she says I left them on the, on the, they had fallen down behind the, hang on, here's a turn-up for the, for the, on second thoughts I don't think, for the book, I don't think these are mine at all, I always smoke, I have always smoked, purple packet, you must know their advertisement I think there's a pyramid in it, I'm sure there's a pyramid. Or a swan. I pass that ad every morning on my way to, it's as you come down past the, past where that factory used to be with the two big concrete cats outside, it's not a factory any more, it's, it's, there was some kind of row about the cats, it's all coming back to me, they had a preservation order on them, they were definitely major cats, the sculptor was a household, I think it's the same man who did the statue of, word, the statue in Thing Square, it isn't Cadogan, square with two syllables, the factory got sold in, got sold some time ago, and didn't someone knock the head off one of the, or were they dogs?

They made biscuits, as I recollect.

If they made biscuits, there would not be cats outside, you do not have cat biscuits. Our cat Timmy never, to my certain knowledge, our cat Percy, never touched anything but, Timmy was the hamster. Timmy was the gerbil.

I think we had two gerbils, I think the gerbils were Gert and Daisy. The hamster was called, Wetherby Terrace is where the factory was. Wetherby Crescent.

I know these are not my cigarettes, there is nothing written on the packet, there was a phone number written on my packet, I recall that very clearly, I had to ring someone back, I was drinking a cup of coffee when he rang, I walked to the telephone, I said Hallo, and he said Hallo, it's, and he said Hallo, it's.

Gert and Daisy were the goldfish.

Fortunately, there is no problem here. If I go and make another cup of coffee and walk over to the telephone again it will come back to me, I will recall his name in a, it is all a question of retracing one's, of reconstructing, in a flash, it is an infallible method of, steps.

No problem! Never fails!

The gerbils were called Benson and Hedges.

I knew it the moment I pulled the chain.

As far as the square is concerned, all I have to do is hold the sound of the two syllables in my head, Donk-donk Square, and then I imagine the red-brick wall at a height of about, what, fifteen feet, and I gradually work my way round it until I come to the place on the wall where the name is, because I have driven round it umpteen times, and I have actually seen the name up there. Due to the one-way system, you have to go through Donk-donk Square if you want to get from, from, that's to say if you want to get into, if you want to drive between one place and another, or here's another good way of remembering the name. I start with the statue which was done by the same man, incidentally, who did the dogs outside the former biscuit factory in, in, the former biscuit factory near the advert for the cigarettes I always smoke, why am I holding this coffee cup, and if I imagine myself driving past the statue on my right, a man on a horse, as I recall, then the square-name is just visible under the arm he is raising his hat with.

Donk-donk Square.

It could be you have to imagine driving past the statue on your left.

Another quick way would be to look the man up in a book about statues in London squares. He would be easy to identify because the statue is almost certainly a twentieth-century statue, as the sculptor did the dogs as well, and they did not make biscuits in factories prior to 1900, I am certain I heard that somewhere, and if you took that as your starting point in the library, i.e. statues of men on horses put up after 1900, then it would be a matter of minutes, once you had got your library ticket from the safe place you always keep it.

However, to get to the, to tackle the main, to, good God, it's just occurred to me that the Tesco's was not on the corner, if it was a Tesco's opposite the block of flats where we had our first telly and watched whatever it was, the Tesco's was on the corner opposite where we moved to in 19, in 19, there was a petrol shortage and I think Adam Faith sang *O Mein Gerbil*, was it, or could it have been Dickie Valentine, alternatively does the name John F. Nasser strike a familiar note? Somebody with a moustache and a striking resemblance to, oh Jesus, tall offspin bowler, Gordon, Gordon, Gordon something.

Anyway, if that is where the Tesco's was in fact opposite, i.e. the little terraced house in, in, call it Donk-donk-donk Avenue for the time being, we can come back to that, it had two gravel bins at one end, I have the feeling the man who phoned this morning would remember, I can't exactly put my finger on why, it is a vague feeling I have he was a close relative, a father for example, but in that case why did I write down his phone number, I know my father's phone number like the back of my, of my, it could always be he was phoning from somewhere else, hand, did it have something to do with coffee? Anyway, if that is where the Tesco's was in fact opposite, that would not have been where I first saw that, that, concrete dog advert, was it, because we brought the television with us from the flat that wasn't anywhere with a Tesco's on the corner opposite, so whatever it was I saw, I didn't see it there.

I'm glad that's settled.

Which leaves me with, I think, only one question unanswered. I have just read through this letter again, Professor Rabbitt, and it appears to have been written to you.

I do not know you from bloody, from bloody, the name means nothing, Adam. You're not the person who phoned me this morning, by any chance?

And if it's about my library ticket, I'd like it back as soon as possible.

What's your address?

Grey Area

Most of the red squirrels released experimentally into Regent's Park have survived the winter in fine form, London Zoo said yesterday. Of the ten animals released in stages last October, seven are known to have survived in good health. One was killed by a car, one by a feral cat, and one, whose radio collar failed, has not been seen for several weeks.

Red squirrels have been supplanted throughout most of Britain by the grey species.

The Times

IT BEING, finally, Spring, and I a victim, willy-nilly, of verbal propaganda, I not only dug, but whistled as I dug.

I had turned two beds to the texture of cold Christmas pudding, and was about to jab the spade into the third, beneath the bare acacia tree, when a voice said:

'If you want to hear *Rigoletto* murdered, you could not have come to a better place.'

I dropped the spade. A robin, no less startled, coughed out a haunch of worm and shot off, like a feathered bullet.

The voice had come from above my head. I glanced carefully upward, tensed for an arboreal mugger; mine is a neighbourhood rife with inventive villainy. But there was nothing in the acacia save two squirrels, one grey, and one, remarkably, red. I was about to put the voice down to something carried on a freak of breeze when the red squirrel cocked its little head towards the grey and said:

'Not, of course, that I am a fan of the early Verdi. Ripeness did not touch him until *Otello.*'

'I'll take your word for it,' said the grey squirrel. 'Personally, I stop at Dennis Lotis.'

The honest sweat formed icicles beneath my arms.

'You speak English,' I heard myself say.

'Alternatively,' said the red, 'you would appear to have a grasp of basic squirrel.'

'Nice one, Quentin,' said the grey.

'Forgive me,' I said, 'I have never heard a squirrel talk before.'

The red squirrel scuttled along its bough, and down the trunk until its currant eye was level with my own.

'That,' it said sharply, 'is because you have only come across greys, with whom you have nothing in common.'

'Our only wossname, interest,' said the grey, 'is nuts. Cob, hazel, acorn, you name it. I could tell you stories about nuts what'd make your hair stand on end, only what's the point?'

'They are a simple folk,' said his colleague.

'Watch it,' said the grey.

'But fundamentally decent,' said the red quickly. 'They have been gravely misrepresented.'

'I blame the media,' said the grey. 'I have heard the word rat mentioned on several occasions. Also, a lot of old codswallop about goldtops and cream sucked out. Personally, I never touch the stuff, it makes you run, cream.'

I moved, a shade unsteadily, to a garden bench, and sat down. They followed, sharing a corroded roller, and watched me.

'Have you been to the Chagall?' enquired the red. 'Primitive psycho-drama it may be, but there is no denying that for sheer luminescent colour, he had no –'

'Forgive me for interrupting,' I said striving to restrain the tell-tale wobble of my cigarette smoke, 'but I had always understood that grey and red squirrels did not, er, get on. Indeed, I rather thought that it was the grey squirrel that was primarily responsible for decimating the red.'

'The happiest nations have no history,' murmured the red squirrel. 'I have always been particularly partial to George Eliot's delicate ironies.'

'I could listen to him talk all day,' said the grey.

'We have put the past behind us,' said the red.

'Definitely,' said the grey. 'I am his minder. He would be the first to admit he cannot look after hisself. His mate got turned over by a *cat*! I do cats as a matter of course, just to keep my claw in; I got four toms one morning, it looked like Nagasaki outside my dray, it's all a question of the throat. His brother copped it from a green Volvo, didn't he?'

'He stopped in the middle of Regent's Park Road,' said the red, glumly, 'in order to work out a geotropic crux.'

'They prised him out of the tyre treads just this side of Runcorn,' said the grey squirrel, 'as I understand it. Reds may be dab hands at Latin etcetera, but the Green Cross Code is a closed book to 'em. Without me, he'd be gravy on a gypsy's lip, wouldn't you, Quentin?'

'*Chacun à son métier*,' said the red.

'Hear that?' cried the grey, proudly. 'You could take him anywhere!'

I cleared my throat.

'It's coming back to me now,' I said. 'There was an item in *The Times*; you must be the one whose radio collar failed?'

The tiny head nodded jerkily.

'It was quite frightful, I found myself picking up *My Word*!'

'I had to gnaw it off him,' affirmed the grey, 'he was belting round in circles, he was turning somersaults, he could've done hisself a mischief.'

'I simply cannot stand Frank Muir,' said the red squirrel, a shiver rippling its russet pelt. 'If I want fake Edwardiana, I go to Waring & Gillow.'

The grey squirrel bared its yellow fangs, and let a rodent chuckle slip.

'He could have his own show, am I right?' he said. 'Quick as a flash, and subtle, too. He could run rings round Wogan. Don't talk to me about dolphins!'

'What?' I said.

'Dolphins. Big wet buggers like a long inner tube, silly bloody grin all the time, they are supposed to be clever, they do not hold a candle to your red squirrel.'

'Nor the grey,' said his friend, warmly. 'I should like to see a dolphin handle an acorn.'

'I have certain manual wossnames, true,' murmured the grey, shyly.

'You seem,' I said, 'to have an exceptional *rapport*.'

'True,' replied the red. 'Of course, as you have adumbrated, it was not ever thus. My dear chum here would be the first to admit that what might be termed Grey Power stood until very recently in grave danger of taking over Great Britain completely.'

'He is not wrong,' said the grey. 'It is what Klagenfuhrt described as the tyranny of the simple.'

'I say!' I cried.

'Yes,' said the red squirrel, happily, 'he *is* rather coming along, isn't he?'

'Thanks to you, Quentin,' replied the grey warmly. It turned once more to me. 'Up until recently, I could not do *No Litter. No Bicycles. Dogs Must Be Kept On A Lead* without touching each word with my conk and moving my lips, but I am now fair whipping through the stuff! Where was I? Oh yes, grey squirrels driving out the red, brute force and mindlessness in the name of the bogus democracy of the unlettered masses, conspicuous socio-political reduction to the lowest common denominator, plus rooted traditional bigotry against elitism, i.e. get off my acorn, you pouf, or I will have your tripes out – yes, I am afraid Great Britain was definitely going down the tubes, squirrel-wise!'

The red squirrel sighed.

> *'Milton! Thou shouldst be living at this hour:*
> *England hath need of thee; she is a fen of stagnant waters.'*

The grey squirrel sucked its honed canines admiringly.

'Quentin has one for every occasion,' he said.

It was my turn, now, to sigh.

'I am deeply impressed,' I said. 'I had believed that the red squirrel would be torn limb from limb in Regent's Park. I had not dared to hope for reconciliation, nay, for mutual assistance and shared skills, for co-operation and understanding between you.'

'I like the way he said *nay*,' said the grey squirrel. 'He is a toff.'

'There are no toffs!' snapped the red squirrel. 'We have eliminated class.'

'It is just an expression,' murmured the grey squirrel.

'I am stirred,' I said, for I was.

'I follow you,' said the red squirrel gently. 'Two legs bad, four legs good.'

'You've bloody lost me, now,' said the grey.

The red squirrel took up a declamatory position on its hindpaws, and said:

> *'One impulse from a vernal wood*
> *Can teach you more of man;*
> *Of moral evil and of good,*
> *Than all the sages can.'*

The grey squirrel beamed.

'Wordsworth,' he said.

Yesterday in Parliament

HOUSE OF COMMONS
OFFICIAL REPORT

PARLIAMENTARY DEBATES
(HANSARD)

The House met at half-past Two o'clock
PRAYERS
(Mr. SPEAKER *in the Chair*)
ORAL ANSWERS TO QUESTIONS
EUROPEAN COMMUNITY
Switzerland

Mr. Elwin Croft asked the Secretary of State for Foreign and Commonwealth Affairs what plans he has to visit Basel.

The Secretary of State for Foreign and Commonwealth Affairs (Sir Geoffrey Howe): None, sir.

Mr. Croft: In advance of his plans to visit Basel, will the right hon. Gentleman tell the House the attitude of Her Majesty's Government to Switzerland becoming a member of the European Community?

Sir Geoffrey Howe: Any application which might be made by the Swiss Government would be to the Community as a whole, and Her Majesty's Government would be only one of the members to take a view of it. But, clearly, Her Majesty's Government's attitude could not but reflect our warm affection for Britain's oldest ally. Could anything ever erase the memory of those dark days when we two stood shoulder to shoulder and alone against the dark shadow of whatever it was that was threatening civilisation as we knew it?

Hon. Members: Hear! Hear! Plucky little Switzerland! Ils ne passeront pas! Remember the Alamo! etc.

Mr. Winston Churchill: Gentlemen, I recall the words of my illustrious grandfather –

Mr. Clement Freud: Wasn't he an Austrian psychologist?

Mr. Churchill: The hon. Member for Ely may well be right, but I cannot for the life of me see why that fact should prevent me from recalling his words. As he so succinctly –

Mr. Croft: Be that as it may, and hon. Members must not think me uncognizant of the unique role which that proud country played in standing firm when the storm clouds gathered in, er, 1928 –

Hon. Members: 1934! 1946! 1898! Last Thursday! etc.

Mr. Croft: Whenever. Be that, I say, as it may, I do not think we should allow nostalgia or ancient loyalties to cloud our economic judgement. While none of us would impugn the courage of Herr Johnny Gurkha –

Hon. Member: They bought us time! Ask Chamberlain! Tell him, Neville!

Mr. Croft: – while none of us would impugn Swiss fighting grit, I say, can any of us deny that their economic reliability is somewhat less rugged?

Sir Geoffrey Howe: I trust that my hon. Friend is not going to bring up the Southport Bubble yet again?

Mr. Croft: As a matter of fact, Mr. Speaker, I was not. Do the words Ground Nut Scheme strike a familiar note?

Hon. Members: No.

Mr. Croft: Typical! If I may refresh what I take to be hon. Members' tactically poor memories (*cries of 'Oh!'*), the Ground Nut Scheme was an ill-starred attempt to restructure the Swiss tax system, thought up by William Hill.

Mr. Dennis Skinner: Rubbish! William Hill invented the postage stamp.

Hon. Members: Tripe! Cobblers!

Mr. Speaker: Order!

Mr. Skinner: He did it for a bet.

Mr. Speaker: Order! I think both hon. Gentlemen will find that they are, upon reflection, mistaken. William Hill was, as I recall, the site of the Great Exhibition of 1871, before it was burned down and moved to Lambeth Palace.

Mr. Croft: With the greatest respect, Mr. Speaker, I must insist that William Hill put a ground nut on his father's head and threw a brick at it, in a foolhardy attempt to avoid paying VAT. If further proof were needed, I would draw hon. Members' attention to the fact that Mozart wrote a famous overture about it.

Hon. Members: Name that tune!

Mr. Croft: *The Magic Brick.*

Sir Geoffrey Howe: Loath as I am to impute to my hon. Friend any intention deliberately to mislead this House, I would ask him seriously to reflect whether *The Magic Brick* to which he so confidently refers might not perhaps have been the vessel in which Sir Walter Scott circumnavigated the South Pole with Ken Livingstone and found Stanley the Gibbon?

Dr. David Owen: What?

Sir Geoffrey Howe: The beginning of evolution. They were looking for a breadfruit. Some of the greatest things in history have been accidents. Look at Gandhi. When the lid blew off the kettle, he thought he'd invented the aeroplane. Little did he realise it was the beginning of tea.

Mr. Churchill: On a point of information, was it or was it not, however, the French who invented cake?

Mr. David Penhaligon: If I may be permitted to answer the hon. Gentleman, Mr. Speaker, the answer is yes. I do not wish to take up too much of the House's time on this, but cake was invented by Marie Curie, the mistress of Joe Louis. She found it growing in a little dish on the window-sill.

Sir Geoffrey Howe: At Versailles?

Mr. Penhaligon: I should need notice of that question, Mr. Speaker. I have the feeling that it was Hitler at Versailles.

Mr. Speaker: On the window-sill? What was Hitler doing on the window-sill at Versailles?

Mr. Norman Fowler: He was probably going to jump.

Sir Geoffrey Howe: I don't follow.

Hon. Members: Shame! *(Laughter)*

Mr. Fowler: He was always committing suicide. He once tried to blow himself up in a briefcase. Then he married Wernher von Braun and set light to the pair of them. If you ask me, he wasn't all there. I do not believe it is stretching the credibility of this House to suggest he might have jumped out of the window at Versailles.

Mr. Croft: I am grateful to the hon. Members for their points of information, but I somehow feel we are moving away from the main thrust of the debate, which is to reassure ourselves that this great House and, even more, the great nation for which it speaks, is not plunged headlong, willy-nilly, into a political liaison we might all live to regret. I do not wish to reopen old wounds, but it is not so very long since that this island race –

Mr. Fowler: I've just remembered about Versailles. It wasn't a window-sill, it was a railway carriage. He was going to throw himself under a railway carriage.

Mr. Speaker: Order!

Mr. Croft: – this island race found itself threatened by the greatest armada the world had yet seen!

Hon. Members: But were they Swiss?

Other Hon. Members: How do we know, what are we, walking bloody encyclopaedias, £17, 702 per annum, you can't even buy *Beano*, never mind keeping up with the latest information on armadas, withdraw, yield, resign, etc.

Mr. Speaker: Order! Order! If there are any more interruptions of this kind, I warn the House that I shall have no other course but to try to find out what my predecessors would have done in my place, the office of Speaker goes back to the year dot, as I understand it, they must have the rules written down somewhere, it'll be in a big book, if I'm any judge.

Mr. Croft: I apologise if I have been the unwitting cause of any unseemliness, Mr Speaker, I wished only to draw the attention of this House to one simple truth. What was it Marx said?

Mr. Freud: He said *Either this man's dead or my watch has stopped.*

Mr. Croft: He said that those who fail to learn from the mistakes of history are doomed to repeat them. That holds true whether or not we are talking of armadas or, or, or – I don't know – helicopters.

Mr. Leon Brittan: What?

Mr. Douglas Hurd: I think he said elephants.

Mr. Peter Walker: Yes, it was definitely elephants.

Mr. George Younger: I can confirm that. He said elephants.

Mr. Norman Tebbit: Good God, yes, clear as a bell, elephants.

Mr. Nigel Lawson: Elephants, all right. No question.

The Prime Minister (Mrs. Margaret Thatcher): For the record, Mr. Speaker, I should like to put it to my hon. Friend that he said elephants.

Mr. Croft: Yes, I did. I said elephants. I don't make mistakes over things of that nature.

Mrs. Thatcher: Do you know, he really is terribly, terribly good like that.

Mr. Speaker: Let the record stand.

The House rose at 5.20.

Slouching Towards Bethlehem

THE OX ambled out of the stable, not for the first time, gazed upwards, and ambled back.

'Where is it?' said the ass.

'Bang overhead,' said the ox.

'That narrows the field a bit,' said the ass. 'It is definitely one of us.'

'Unless it is a rat,' said the ox. 'There's a lot of rats in here. It could turn out to be a rat.'

'Get off,' said the ass. 'He is never going to redeem the world with a messianic rat.'

'He works in a mysterious way,' murmured the ox.

'Mysterious, I give you,' said the ass. 'Peculiar, no.'

'They are dead clever, rats,' argued the ox.

'That is not in dispute,' said the ass. 'I never said they weren't clever. He has got more cleverness than He knows what to do with; when it comes to cleverness, He is it, what He is after in a Messiah is *presence*.'

'Have we got presence?' enquired the ox.

'We have got more presence than the rat,' snapped the ass. 'For a start, we do not scuttle. Plus, we have nice natures. The world does not want a Messiah who scuttles about nipping people on the ankle. Ask anyone.'

The ox thought about this for a while.

'I'll go and have another look at the star,' it said, finally.

'Still there?' asked the ass, when the ox ambled back.

'No question,' said the ox. 'It is about time it came down, if you want my opinion.'

'Came down?'

'Yes. It will come down, and He will get out, and He will point to one of us and say *You are the Messiah, go and redeem the world.* If He is not pointing to a rat, that is.'

The ass sniffed.

'There is no evidence He travels by star,' it said. 'As I understand it, He is what is called omnipresent. He does not have to get in a star if He wants to go somewhere.'

'You've always got an answer,' muttered the ox.

'No bad thing,' said the ass, 'in a Messiah.'

The ox looked at it.

'Just joking,' said the ass.

'Yes,' said the ox quickly, sensing an advantage. 'Yes, He may not even have decided yet, He may come down in His star and make His mind up when He sees us. He may give us an interview. He may go eeny-meeny-miny-mo.'

'Eeny-meeny-miny-mo?' said the ass. 'God?'

The ox took a heavy step towards it. Its dark bulk loomed over the ass. Breath plumed from its flared wet nostrils.

'Watch it,' cautioned the ass. 'That is just the sort of thing you are on the lookout for, if you are omnipresent. He would not take kindly to the use of force. He is not after a Messiah who knocks people about. Ask anyone.'

'All right, then, clever dick,' said the ox, 'how will He make known to us His mysterious unfathomable ways, i.e. who has got the job?'

The ass walked slowly across the crackling straw towards the gap in which the sharp night glittered, and raised the long nozzle of its head, sniffing.

'Informed sources say it will come in the shape of three wise asses from the East. Or,' it added quickly, 'three wise oxen, of course.'

'How about – '

'No. There was definitely nothing about three wise rats.'

'If He has not made up his mind yet,' said the ox, 'it could be one wise ass, one wise ox, and one wise rat.'

The ass turned, stared – not wholly unpityingly – at the ox, and might well have said something had not, in that instant, a voice cried out from the darkness, penetratingly.

'Anyone seen three wise sheep?'

The ass whipped round again.

A ram had materialised in the doorway.

'What?' snapped the ass.

'Three wise sheep,' repeated the ram. 'They're due here any minute now, bearing gifts.'

'Gifts?' lowed the ox.

'Yes,' said the ram, confidently. 'It is traditional, I gather. Three wise sheep come from the East, bearing gifts for the Messiah. Grass, grass, and grass, as I understand it.'

The ox and the ass stared at him.

'Messiah?' croaked the ass, when it had recovered. 'What Messiah?'

'You're looking at him,' said the ram. 'Or rather, Him. It is customary at this point to fall down and praise my name, but as my three wise sheep are still en route, we might as well hang on till they get here and I can do you all at the same time. Makes sense.'

'I don't understand,' said the ass. 'The star is hanging bang over this stable, the Messiah is either me or the ox, there are – '

'Or just possibly one of the rats,' murmured the ox.

' – there are no sheep on these premises, you are well out of order!'

The ram tutted, as only rams can.

'Never mind hanging over the stable,' it said sharply, 'we have had an angel up our field, sunshine, there is no question but that I have been singled out, it is all over bar the paperwork.'

'Hail the King of the Ewes!' cried an invisible chorus.

'See?' said the ram.

The ass and the ox peered out into the night.

'Stone me!' cried the ox. 'Who are they?'

'Ewes,' replied the ram. 'My followers. You got to have followers, if you're a Messiah. It is doubtless why He chose a sheep. It is one of the main things sheep do, follow.'

There was a long uneasy silence. Finally, the ass said:

'What did this angel say, exactly?'

'Hard to tell,' replied the ram. 'There's a hell of a wind up there and I got all this wool in my ears, but the gist was *unto us a something something* and *follow the star*, and then he give me this Look.'

'Is that all?' said the ass.

'You had to be there,' said the ram.

The ox shrugged.

'Well, that's it, then,' it said. 'Can't say I'm sorry, it's a big responsibility redeeming mankind, never mind not liking 'em much to start with, if they're not eating you they're turning you into bloody suitcases.'

'Good point,' said the ram, nodding. 'One of the first things on my agenda will be the commandment *Love Thy Sheep*. You've no idea what it's like, having them shears running over you. I go all funny just thinking about it. My millennium will spell the end of the pullover as we know it, and not before time. Also collies. I am not having the disciples rounded up and put in pens just so's some nerd in moleskin trousers can go home with a silver cup.'

The ass cleared its throat.

'That could explain it,' it said.

'What could explain what?' enquired the ram.

'The non-arrival of your three wise sheep. You got to go through Turkey, if you're coming from the East. They are probably a gross of shish kebabs by now.'

'Careful, son,' said the ram. 'When they get here with the documents, I shall be able to do miracles, e.g. turning donkeys into frogs.'

'Possibly, possibly,' said the ass. 'However, I remain to be convinced that the Almighty would entrust the salvation of mankind to something on which mankind has been putting mint sauce all these years.'

The ram narrowed its eyes.

'Listen,' it said, 'it may interest – '

It stopped.

There were new voices beyond the open door.

They were not animal voices.

'Of course,' the loudest of the voices was saying, 'the annexe cannot be compared to the main block, it does not have a bathroom, but I think you'll find it has a sort of rustic charm, and I do not have to tell you that, at the price, you would be unlikely to – '

As the innkeeper came into the doorway, his eye fell upon the ram. Whereupon the innkeeper cursed, held up one hand to stay his customers, plunged the other into the neckfleece of the intruder, and hurled it out into the night.

'What did I tell you?' said the ass, when the innkeeper had gone out again to collect his guests. 'He should never have been here in the first place.'

'Yes,' said the ox. It knitted its thick brows. 'Still, do you reckon that whichever one of us turns out to be the Messiah ought to forgive him?'

'We'll cross that bridge when we come to it,' said the ass.

Hang About

Sexy actress Fiona Kendall offered a £100 reward yesterday for a missing 200-year-old tortoise called Napoleon, which has escaped from a garden in Clapham. It has been in Fiona's family for generations.

Sun

I SHALL just stand here by this gravel-bin, for a bit. I shall observe the traffic lights. It is all a question of timing. It would be a mistake to hurtle.

It could take three minutes just to get off the kerb. You got to work forward to your centre of gravity, get your head in, pivot. The secret is in the topple. You do not want to end up on your back. Could take days.

What is irritating, what is infuriating, what really gets up the nose, is being sought by the authorities under the name of Napoleon. When one was actually christened Edmund Cartwright. Apart from anything else, there are virtually none of us left who commemorate the power loom. There is, I believe, a carp in Haslemere, and there are unsubstantiated rumours of a parrot in Doncaster, but that is the top and bottom of it. *And* I have my doubts about the parrot. Ninety years is normally top weight for a parrot. You come across a lot of parrots in my game, and I have yet to see a 1785 item.

Plus, if it *is* two hundred years old, it will not be reflecting any credit on Edmund Cartwright. It will not be much more than a chipped beak with a couple of mangy feathers dangling off of it, it will also definitely be ga-ga, you would ask it who was a pretty boy then, and it would not answer 'Edmund Cartwright! Edmund

Cartwright!', it would more than likely say the first thing that came into its head, e.g. 'Give us a walnut!' or 'Piss off!', something of that order, you know parrots.

The thing about a tortoise, though I says it as shouldn't, is we do not deteriorate. We look two hundred years old when we come out of the egg. Titchy, I grant you, but still could be taken for a two-tonner. Nothing falls off us, we do not go flabby, we do not slow down, you can name us after a dear or respected one and be certain we shall carry the responsibility without unsightly deterioration.

Looks like forty seconds on the red. Hardly enough time to get into your stride. Such as it is. They ought to have tortoise crossings, little green tortoises up on the lamppost, button at the bottom, you could push the button with your conk, it does not seem too much to ask, they spend a fortune on lollipop men etcetera, they sit up all night working out Green Cross Codes and similar, fat lot of use a Green Cross Code is to one of the chelonian persuasion – look left, look right, look left again, bloody hell, there's ten minutes gone straight off, before you've even got a leg out!

It is typical.

It is like being renamed Napoleon after you have been Edmund Cartwright for a hundred and eighty years, not because there has been any drastic change in your circumstances to warrant it, e.g. you have taken to shoving one leg inside your shell, but simply because it is 1965 and nobody knows who Edmund Cartwright is any more, that is how this country honours its great sons, it is the Swinging Sixties, yegh, and it is all Chink man-made fibres in your mini-skirt, it is all cheap Commie flares flooding in from East Germany, it is the death of British cotton, it is as if the spinning jenny had never been invented, people say *Why is your tortoise called Edmund Cartwright?* and nobody knows, so instead of looking him up, *Cartwright, Edmund, inventor of power loom, 1785*, it is easier to re-launch your ancestral tortoise as Napoleon, well he was old, wasn't he, anything old will do. Never mind when I was born he was only fifteen, he was *nothing*. Not that he ended up any better from my point of view, I am now walking around as a French failure, I commemorate an exile with piles, where are we all going in this country is what I want to know, where are the standards? Unlawful substances, potholes, mucky films, riots, mistresses, blackies all over everywhere, nancy boys. Sexy actress Fiona Kendall, and I quote.

Is it any wonder I have done a runner? Is it any wonder I have had it up to here?

We have come a long way from old Jabez Kendall, 1764–1839, regular churchgoer, worked a sixty-hour week, grew his own vegetables, thatched his own roof, brewed his own beer, did it twice a month with the light off, loyal subject of His Gracious Majesty, brought me home from Wisbech Goose Fayre – in those days you could go to a goose fayre, have a slap-up dinner, pint of porter, wrestle a greasy pig, deflower a virgin, buy a tortoise, and still have change out of a groat – and when they asked him my name, he said Edmund Cartwright, and there were tears in his eyes. Nobody said *Who's Edmund Cartwright when he's at home?* What happened to patriotism?

It might be wise to wait until it gets dark; but then again, it might not. I have worked out that it would take me six minutes to cross the road, i.e. four green lights, give or take and the point is, would the traffic stop for a tortoise, would it hell, this is 1985, it is not 1785, it is not cost-effective to stop a juggernaut for a tortoise, it makes more commercial sense to wait till you get to Milan and prise him out of your Pirellis with a bread-knife, very nice; but if I wait until let us say midnight, when there is less traffic, what less traffic there is will not be able to see me at all, or, worse, this being Clapham, there will more than likely be a race riot, I will probably get picked up and bunged at a copper, I could well get filled with Esso, *Police Transit Destroyed By Molotov Tortoise, Sexy Actress Inconsolable.*

We haven't half come downhill in this country, I speak as one who knows. You cannot put anything over on a tortoise. We may not say much, but we keep our eyes open. You do not remain in a family for generations without holding a watching brief, I am not just an heirloom. I have seen a number of top Kendalls, senior cavalry officers, inventors, JPs, one who was nearly a bishop, a couple of famed solicitors. In 1873, to give you a for instance, I nearly went on a Polar expedition, only they thought it might interfere with my internal workings. It wasn't sexy actresses, then. We had India, then, most of Africa, islands all over the place, you name it. Anyone gave us any lip, bang!

Gone green again. I suppose I could always get run over deliberately, I suppose I could make a supreme gesture, it is a far, far better thing, and so forth. But who would know? *Sexy Actress Fiona Kendall's Tortoise Napoleon Flattened By Breadvan,* as opposed to *Two-Hundred-Year-Old Edmund Cartwright Had Nothing To Live For, Walked Under Breadvan, This Is Life In 1985 Britain, See Major Analysis Inside.*

You cannot even eat the food any more. I can still taste Regency lettuce, I still dream of Victorian sprouts, the Kendalls had a kitchen garden in Rhyl during the Peninsular War, I tell a lie, the Crimean, and you would not believe the cabbages. These days, it is like chewing your way through a bathroom cabinet. It is probably doing something untold to our innards, another century on pesticides and I shall more than likely have two heads, it will be impossible to draw them in, I shall have to choose which one stays out and cops a half-brick or a rubber bullet or a nuclear bomb or whatever it is they have got in store for 2085, very nice.

Gone green again. Long line of buses, madmen on motorbikes, be ten thousand demonstrators any minute, wadder-we-want-ten-per-cent, big boots, crunch, goodbye Edmund Cartwright, *Sexy Actress Fiona Kendall Breaks Down At Inquest.* You would think there would be an easier way of getting out of Clapham, making a new start, be different if I was a black tortoise, no doubt, just off the boat, I would probably get a council flat, I would be a community leader, I would get a grant for crossing the road, if anything ran over me the RSPCA would torch South London as far as Sevenoaks.

Getting older. Getting harder to keep the old eyes open. And has it, after two centuries of unswerving patriotism, come to this? Hibernating by a Clapham gravel bin? Dossing down between the melon pips and the squeezed-out glue tubes?

Mind you, let us not knock it, six months oblivion is six months oblivion. You take what you can get, these days.

Her Upstairs

God is not a male deity and there is a case for addressing God as 'Our Mother', according to a report published yesterday by the Church of Scotland.

The Times

Dear Mr Coren:

I am a first-time writer but a long-time reader, I hope you will excuse this approaching you out of the blue but I do not know where to turn and I have always understood you to be straight with people, esp. women, you are virile but humane and will not make cheap jokes etc. about God not being able to find Her lipstick, that is not your way. This Church of Scotland announcement could do big things for the Women's Movement, is it true She made the world in six days?

Alice Cole (Ms), Yarmouth

Dear Ms Cole:

Thank you for putting your trust in me, you are absolutely right about my taking this seriously, it is not every day that one wakes up to find that God has changed sex, even in Scotland.

Strictly speaking, no, She did not make the world in six days. Not everything in the Bible is to be taken literally, as I'm sure you know. But, and here's the point, She *got* it done. She knew this absolutely wonderful little firm round the corner, and they did all the basic labouring, dividing the waters which were under the firmament from the waters which were above the firmament, and so on, after She told them where the firmament had to go. She said, *Let there be light*, and lo! they put it in.

She did all the carpets and curtains Herself, though.

Dear Mr Coren:

I have a boutique and a husband and two small children and there always has to be a hot meal on the table, never mind if the Sales are on, even, or we are awaiting deliveries from Belgium or similar. What I want to know is, how did God manage to combine a successful career with raising a family, i.e. Her only begotten Son?

Shirley Roth (Ltd), Barnes

Dear Limited Shirley:

A good point, and we have to face the fact that she did *not* actually raise Her only begotten Son. She employed a couple. It is probably the only way open for a working Mum.

Of course, being God, She was able to take delegation even further than most working Mums in that She also got the couple to have the only begotten Son *for* Her, thus enabling Her to carry on working right through the pregnancy. It is a neat trick, but not generally available on the NHS; I understand, however, that Mr Patrick Steptoe is able to offer something along similar lines, at a price, although you would have to select your couple with great care. Pick a middle-class pair, for example, and He might end up as a barrister and that would be the last you saw of Him, you can earn £80, 000 a year as a QC, it beats wandering around in sandals and touching lepers for a living.

Dear Mr Coren:

All right, okay, great, big deal, terrif, God was a woman, is that supposed to make everything nice, you condescending eunuch bastard?

Just what kind of a woman was She? Why didn't She send an only begotten Daughter, *tell me that, I would have thought that if you were trying to save the world, I mean do you have any idea how men have screwed up this planet, the last thing you'd send is a, a, yegh!*

Tell me that, you Nazi pig.

Malvolia Greenham, Cockfosters

Dear Malvolia:

While I agree absolutely that women by their very natures are much nicer people and that an only begotten Daughter would have been absolutely ideal in some ways, in others it would have been rather tricky.

In early AD, a woman just could not go around on her own, she would not get served in pubs or be allowed to play golf unescorted, in short she would not have access to those places you had to get into if you wanted to redeem personkind. The only course would have been to arrange for an only begotten Son-in-Law, possibly even only begotten Grandchildren, and not only would the teleological conundra have become virtually insuperable, the only begotten Daughter would have had a terrible time at public meetings, with women asking questions about combining homecare and careers instead of listening to useful homilies.

She would almost certainly have had to appoint an only begotten Chairman to keep order, and half his time would have been spent with nonsense like *We have a question from a Galilean listener who would like to run over that recipe again, is it five loaves and two fishes, or two loaves and . . .*

I trust you take my point, Malvolia. Times were not then as they are now. I'm convinced the second coming will be entirely female, if it's any consolation.

Dear Mr Coren:

I am having great difficulty in coming to terms with this new proposition, given some of the, well it has to be said, quite beastly things that God has done. I mean, I realise of course that they had to be done, one has to take a firm hand with some people, look at the miners, but one or two divine actions do seem to me to smack of the male touch. For example, did She really slay all the Egyptian first-born? It seems extraordinary behaviour, even for a zealous and almighty Mum!

Lavinia Cribling, Poole

Dear Lady Cribling:

You are of course perfectly correct, and many eminent Scottish theologians are even now examining the Bible closely for what are obviously glaring mistranslations.

As far as *Exodus* is concerned, I am happy to be able to inform you that what She actually did was insist that the first-born tidy their rooms up and stop picking their nose. Provided they did that, they would be allowed to come downstairs and watch the plague of boils. Well, pimples, really.

Dear Mr Coren:

Sorry, sorry, sorry, I am just an 'ordinary' housewife and not, is the word 'into', feminism and so forth, my hubbie Gerard would be furious if he thought I was bothering a busy man like you with my 'nonsense', but I feel sure God understands about us 'little people', doesn't She? After all, Her eye is on the sparrow, am I correct?

Anyway, I was very excited about God being a lady, and all I want to know, on behalf of all of us who are beginning to 'spread' a bit, is did She have Her own special secret for staying slim? Is it a question of 'what you eat' or 'how you eat'? Or did She take exercise, if so what form, are there those stationary bicycle efforts 'up there'?

Germaine Hodge, Bromley

Dear Mrs Hodge:

Goodness me this is a bit of a poser! How often you 'ordinary' folk turn out to be not ordinary at all and ask just the sort of tricky question that puts us so-called experts right on the spot!

The fact is that now we are pretty certain that God is not, as was previously believed, an old man with a long white beard, what is She? Clearly, not an old woman with a long white beard, but beyond that we do not have a great deal to go on, except that She made us in Her image, so we all look a *bit* like Her, and it's quite clear that couldn't be possible if She were not fairly average, probably about five feet five, slightly swarthy skin (although of course free from blemish of any description), and with manageable hair, which She does Herself.

As to build, this really is unknown territory, one can hardly begin to conjecture: She could be an absolute knockout, She could be more sort of comfy and maternal, but whatever She is, that is the way She stays, since She does not eat anything, being divine, and does not take exercise as you and I would recognise it, being omnipresent. I suppose we shall all just have to wait until that glorious day when we at last gaze upon Her face and are not dazzled.

I hope that answers your question.

Bridge in the Afternoon

Twenty-five years ago, at the age of sixty-one, Ernest Hemingway took his own life. It is not easy to think of him in old age, passing the time as old men do.

Atlantic Monthly

AROUND NOON, I went down to the club to cut the sandwiches.

There was nobody in the hall, so I did not have to feel uncomfortable about being a young one. Sometimes, it is not easy to be a young one walking into a bridge club in the afternoon when there are old ones about. Many of the old ones are very old ones, and a few of them are practically dead ones, and when they hobble out of the card room on the way to the bathroom and then they stay in the bathroom a very long time, the way very old ones do, you get to feel uneasy being a young one.

You get so you wish you had wrinkles and a pot belly and cataracts and trouble down there where the very old ones have trouble, especially when it is time to bang on the door and shout:

'Are you all right in there, old one?'

And the old one shouts:

'Why should I not be all right in here?'

And you say:

'I am only doing my duty, old one.'

And the old one screams:

'I obscenity in your duty! I obscenity in your mother's duty, and your father's duty!'

I walked down the hall, and out back to the little kitchen, and I opened the big refrigerator and I took out the sliced bread and the big German knife with the black bone handle, and I put the slices into piles of four and began to cut off the crusts, so that the old ones would not choke or break their upper plates or spend two hours chewing the same sandwich. This is partly because I care about the old ones, but partly because I care about the furniture, and when an old one has to open the bidding and cannot say 'one club' without blowing wet crumbs and little pieces of tuna all over the green baize, you know you are in for a long night with the brush and the pan and the solvent, and maybe you will not get home until three o'clock and your woman is asleep, and there is nothing to do but lie awake and stare at the car headlamps making patterns on the ceiling.

When I finished cutting the sandwiches, I did the thing with the cling-wrap, and I put them back into the refrigerator, and I shook a few peanuts into little glass bowls, and I took the bowls into the card room, and I set them down on the tables.

The old one was sitting at a table. He was gazing out the window, and doing the fancy thing with the shuffle which all the great *inernazionali* do. I leaned forward, but with much respect, and took some of the cards out of his trouser turn-ups and one off his hat. The rest I left on the floor.

The old one looked up at me.

'Cheap cards,' he said. 'How do they expect a man to shuffle with cheap cards? What are they making cards out of, these days? These are not man's cards.'

'Perhaps it is something they put in up at the factory,' I said.

The old one picked at a dried egg-flake on his lapel.

'When I made the seven spades against Manaleto and Ortega,' he said, 'the cards were like silk. They were like some part of a woman that they have found out how to print on. Each time I played a card from my hand, the crowd gasped.'

'They were a knowing crowd,' I said.

'They had *afición*,' said the old one. 'That is the way it is at the Pamplona Rotary.'

'I have heard of the seven spades against Manaleto and Ortega,' I said.

'Who has not?' The old one pulled out a big red-spotted bandanna and blew his nose fiercely, if inaccurately. 'Manaleto and Ortega were from the hard region up around Escarte Dolo, where they breed the fighting bridge-players. The fighting bridge-player is to the domestic bridge-player as the wolf is to the dog.' He wrapped one big liver-spotted hand around the other and cracked a knuckle. It was like a walnut going. 'A domestic bridge-player may be evil-tempered and vicious as a dog may be evil-tempered and vicious, but he will never have the speed, and the courage, and the peculiar brain of the fighting bridge-player, any more than the dog will have the sinews of the wolf, or his cunning, or his savagery. They are bred from a strain that comes down in descent from the wild whist-players that have ranged over the Peninsula for centuries.'

'It could not have been easy, the grand slam with the spades,' I said.

'It was 1969, I was but seventy summers, I had *cojones*, but no, it was not easy,' nodded the old one. 'When my partner, the great Ginsberg, opened two clubs and Manaleto overcalled three hearts, I knew we were in for a fight.'

'It can be terrible, the *intervención*,' I said.

The old one shrugged.

'It is a *convención*,' he said. 'A man must respect the *convenciones*. Without them, the game is nothing. Man is nothing.'

'You might as well play canasta,' I said.

'Spoken like a true one, young one,' said the old one. 'You might as well play kaluki with the women.'

He took off his hat, and fanned himself with it, for the day was hot, the way it can be in those regions when the boiler is old and the valve is stuck, and he looked at me, very hard.

'Tell me,' he said, 'have you, yourself, *afición*?'

I looked away.

'I am green,' I replied, 'but I will progress. At present, I play the Strong No-trump and the Preferred Minor.'

The old one laughed, a cracked noise in his soup-flecked beard.

'Forgive me, young one. There is much to learn. You could not go up against Manaleto and Ortega with such equipment. You would sustain a wound. You could go five tricks light, and you would not be able to walk again where the big ones walk. One day, if I am spared, I shall show you how to play the big ones, when to use the Neapolitan Club and the Schenken Transfer, I shall tell you about Fischbein and the . . .'

There was a ring at the door.

'Forgive me, old one,' I said, 'that will be the other ones.'

The old one spat.

'Send not for whom . . .' he said, and tailed off. His forehead furrowed, like the shore at Capodimonte under the ebb. '*Ask* not for whom?' he murmured. 'Send not to *know* for whom . . . ?'

I went across the card room and into the hall and I opened the big front door with the coloured glass panels, and North and East shuffled into the club, a little in front of South, who had caught his Zimmer frame in the doorscraper and was screaming at it.

I helped North out of his topcoat. It was like shelling one of those big boiled crabs they do at Astispumante, only without the garlic.

'Is the old bastard in, kitchen one?' said North.

'Please do not call me kitchen one,' I said.

'He is a proud one, for a kitchen one,' said East. He pulled off his left galosh, and fell over. 'That is the way they are, these days.'

I looked at him.

'I am a *novillero*,' I said. I lifted South out of his frame. His bones were like a bird's. 'Today, I cut the sandwiches and play the Strong No-trump, but tomorrow I shall wear the suit of three pieces and play the Neapolitan Club.'

'Ha!' cried North. 'He has been talking to the old bastard. He has been getting advice from West.'

'Nobody plays the Neapolitan Club any more, young one,' said South.

They hobbled into the card room, and they grunted at West, but he did not look up, nor when they sat down. He just pushed the cards across, with one of those clean, spare movements the great ones have, and said:

'Cut.'

I went out, then, and back again to the kitchen, and I began the thing with the cocoa, so that it would have time to cool down after it had heated up and they would not have to blow on it and get froth all over one another. I thought a lot about West while I stirred the lumps out, of the way it is to be eighty-six years old and to have come so far from Oak Park, Illinois, to be blown up on the Italian front, and to sit in the hotel in Madrid while the falangists laid down the big barrage from their 88s so that all the whiskey bottles broke, and to write all the books and win all the prizes, and how the best of all was to make the seven spades grand slam doubled and vulnerable against Manaleto and Ortega.

I was still thinking all this when I heard the cry from the card room, and I ran, then, because it could have been East's angina or South's gallstones or North's prostate, but it was none of these.

'What happened?' I said, after I had put my ear to West's waistcoat and heard nothing but the ticking of his big half-hunter.

'The old bastard bid seven spades,' said North, 'and went six off.'

'It killed him,' I said. I looked out of the window. 'It was the *ignominia*. It was the dishonour.'

'It cost me seventeen hundred goddam points,' said East. 'The old bastard. We were doubled and vulnerable.'

I looked away from the window, and back at the table. The cards were spilled out, like blood.

'It was the contract he played against Manaleto and Ortega,' I said. 'But he was younger, then.'

'I do not believe he ever played against Manaleto and Ortega,' said North.

I looked into North's eyes after that, and he looked into mine, but he was the first to blink. I picked up the great one, then, and I carried him out to the kitchen, and I laid him on the table, the way they always lay the great ones out in a side room so that those with *afición* can file past with their hats in their hands.

Then I went back into the card room, and I sat down opposite East in the vacant chair that was still warm, and I gathered the cards together, carefully, and when I had done that, I looked up, because I was ready, now.

'Deal,' I said.

Birds of a Feather

FRED the usually talkative parrot hasn't said a word since burglars stole £40, 000 worth of china and cutlery from under his beak at his owner's shop in Banbury, Oxon. A detective said: 'If only he would give us a name . . . he must have heard the men calling to one another.'

Daily Express

SHACKLED BY a fine gold 18-carat chain, possibly Indian, the hasp amusingly fashioned to simulate a python eating its own tail, *circa* 1850, to a rare and interesting mottled-green Ferrara marble column, believed to be early seventeenth century, some restoration to base, the shaft fluted and the capital pleasingly decorated with a typical flourish of acanthus leaves, formerly the property of a gentleman, the parrot glared out at the chill November sleet slanting down from the Banbury nimbus, and swore silently to itself.

The Marquesas Islands, thought the parrot, rolling the magic syllables noiselessly on its black and bulbous tongue, the Marianas; Pitcairn, Guam, Tuamotu. Somewhere east of Raratonga, where the best was like the worst, that was the place for a parrot, perched on a mildewed epaulette beside a rum-reeking beard, guarding the blind side of its terrible owner's monocular face against treachery. A parrot should feel the burning Solomons sun on its feathers, a parrot's wrinkled eyes should squint against the glinting South Pacific spume thrown up and rainbowed by the coral reefs. It should smell salt and pemmican and black powder and limes, it should nibble weevils tapped from its master's biscuit.

'Pieces of eight!' shrieked the parrot suddenly, involuntarily; and in the empty elegance of the shop, a dozen crystal chandeliers shook nervously and sent back the splintered light.

The shop-bell tinkled, and two slim young men shimmered in. They began to touch the *objets* – an ivory lorgnette-case, a shrivelled Netsuke, a chipped Delft posset-pot – with long delicate fingers.

The parrot fixed a terrible red-veined eye on them.

'Shop!' it screamed.

The young men looked up, startled.

'Oooh!' cried the taller of the two, 'she *talks!*'

The parrot ground its beak. Tiny shards flaked off.

'Fred,' said the parrot, 'is the name.'

'*Fred!*' exclaimed the tall young man. 'He says he's called Fred! Isn't that a wonderful name, Adrian?'

'Very husky,' said the smaller young man. 'I've come over all goose-bumps, Derek.' He took a small neat step towards the parrot. 'Who's a pretty boy then, Fred?'

There's no answer to that, thought the parrot.

The owner of the shop hurried in from the rear office, on a wave of Aramis Pour Lui, smiling.

'May I be of any assistance?' he said.

He ought to have a wooden leg, thought the parrot bitterly, he ought to have scurvy. One ear.

'*May I be of any assistance?*' it cackled, vainly attempting to purse its beak. '*May I be of any assistance?*'

Adrian clapped his pale hands.

'Isn't he *loyal!*' he cried.

'Devoted,' said the owner.

The parrot stared out of the window. Its tightened claws scored the green marble.

'Can I give him a Smartie?' said Derek, fishing in his moleskin bolero. 'Would he take it from my mouth?'

Bloody try it, thought Fred, bloody try it, that's all.

'It mightn't be wise,' said the owner. 'They're one-man pets.'

'We know the feeling,' said Derek, 'don't we, Adrian?'

They shrieked.

'Seriously, though,' said Derek, 'me and my friend Adrian

were looking for a Tiffany lamp for our wine-table.'

'We don't use it for wine, though, do we, Derek?' said Adrian. 'We use it to display our *objets trouvés*. We go to Southwold every year –'

'Just for two weeks.'

'– just for two weeks, and we collect these wonderful things from the beach. Skate egg-cases, cuttlefish bones –'

'– fancy pebbles. We find they're full of the mystery of the sea, but without the *fear*, if you know what I mean.'

Topsails furled, helm lashed, guns secured, running before the Cape Horn gale, thought the parrot, half the crew in irons and the rest blind drunk, only the captain awake, accompanying his trusty parrot on the concertina and praying to the Devil for a bluewater run to a safe haven in the Dry Tortegas and a big mulatto whore, that was what the sea was all about.

'– and we've got it all set up next to this rather nice *fin-de-siècle* sofa in lavender Dralon we had done. We call it Yellow Book corner, don't we, Adrian?'

'I think I've probably got just the thing you're looking for,' said the owner, 'if you'd care to pop downstairs.'

He showed them through a green baize door, and followed, leaving the parrot alone once more, inescapably tethered in the window among the genteel bric-à-brac. Small boys passed, flashing V-signs and banging pocket computer-games on the glass, two entwined drunks staggered across the road from the pub opposite and screamed POLLY WANTS A CRACKER! at him twenty times over until they managed to roll howling away like a hysterical octopus, a very old metermaid came and stared at him for ten minutes without doing anything except forage aimlessly in her starboard nostril with a felt-tipped pen.

A mange-pocked semi-airedale, free as the wind and ostensibly ownerless, barked at him derisively and then underwrote its scorn by lifting its leg, slowly and deliberately, against the bollard, cunningly fashioned from a Peninsular cannon, which the owner had cemented beside the shop's step as a commercial *leitmotif*.

Iron entered the parrot's soul. To have Israel Hands beside him, blasting his enemies left and right from a brace of looted

Spanish horse-pistols! To see the metermaid spitted on Silver's cutlass like a stuck pig! To lie a mile off Banbury High Street, broadside on, strike the Jolly Roger, and let three tiers of gundeck wipe the ledger clean!

The green baize door opened again, and the two customers minced excitedly back into the shop, clutching a lamp between them and blowing him a farewell kiss. The owner followed, with a bowl which he set beside the parrot on the column. The parrot stared at it. Little protein-enriched soya cinders stared back at him. He wondered what paw-paw tasted like, or yams, or breadfruit; an atavistic yearning to peel a kumquat made his very beak hurt.

Little else happened as the afternoon bleakened into night. A large woman came in to negotiate for a Queen Anne breakfront bookcase, but not until the parrot had been removed on the grounds of smell and psittacine infection. A dealer turned up with six Adam fireplaces wrested from a demolished manse and offered the parrot a large walnut, which turned out to be made of plaster and to have broken off a baroque flourish on one of the mantels, this discovery not, however, being made until the parrot had driven itself half-mad and the dealer had laughed himself half-sick. And ten minutes before closing-time, a passer-by dropped in to make a bid for the parrot itself, since his decor required a nice stuffed parrot to set off a wallful of stag-heads in his newly refurbished den; upon being informed that this was a live parrot, the man replied that that was no problem, anyone could stuff a bloody parrot, he had a book at home. He was, he said, prepared to go as high as a ton.

The owner said he would think about it.

After which he pulled down the blind, locked up, and went home.

The hours passed, variously signalled by a number of long-cased clocks which, despite their long familiarity, never failed to knock the parrot off his perch, shattering his poignant dreams of plunder and lagoon; and thus it was that, at 3.02 am, when the jemmy forced the green baize door from the basement, the parrot was already awake and alert. Independently, his two eyes swivelled towards the sound, straining through the gloom, until a torch snapped on and, in its shielded glow, he saw two neckless, barrel-chested men, in stocking masks and rubber gloves, carrying – his heart leapt, banging – plastic bags and sawn-off shotguns!

For some time he watched them scout the shelves, picking and peering, assessing this Derby shepherdess, that Chelsea vase, squinting at hallmarks, feeling veneers; then he cried:

'*What about the real stuff! What about the real stuff!*'

They sprang erect, the guns came up, the hammers clicked back; a Minton urn, one of a pair, fell and shattered.

'Don't shoot, Fred's a clever boy!' shrieked the parrot. 'Who knows where the safe is? Who knows where the safe is?'

At last the stockinged heads, like giant saveloys, located him.

'Glimey!' muttered one, liplessly. 'It's a gloody carrot, Charlie!'

Cautiously, they crept towards him, until he could see their tattooed forearms, smell the gun-oil, taste their very villainy.

'The safe's behind the walnut tallboy!' he cackled. 'The safe's behind the walnut tallboy!'

They did not hesitate long. Expertly, soundlessly, they eased the tallboy from the wall. The safe-door stood revealed.

'Gloody congination lock!' said one.

The other stripped off his stocking, and approached the parrot. 'Any ideas?' he said.

The parrot glowed, inside. Had he tears, he would have shed them, now.

'7834 left, 9266 right!' he cried. '7834 left, 9266 right!'

And so it proved. The door swung wide. Slowly, carefully – for the real stuff was very real indeed – the plastic bags were filled, and the safe was emptied. And when it was done, the two men came up to the parrot, and patted his beak. And one put his eye close to the parrot's – and a terrible eye it was, thought the parrot deliriously, it could have been Captain Morgan's eye, it could have been *Silver*'s eye – and said:

'Thanks, mate!'

But as they turned to steal away, the other paused, and turned.

'Here,' he murmured, 'you wouldn't tell no one he called me Charlie, would you? You wouldn't give no one a description or nothing?'

The parrot cackled quietly to itself, for a second or two, in its private joy. It put its head on one side.

'No chance!' it said. 'No chance!'

No Bloody Fear

HOTEL FOR PHOBICS
Britain's first hotel for phobics has opened in Firbeck Avenue, Skegness, helped by £42,000 from the Government's small firm guarantee loan. Mr Tony Elliott, founder of Notting-hamshire Phobics Association, said: 'People may have all sorts of psychological problems and we will try to look after them at the seaside.'

Daily Telegraph

DEAR SYLVIA,

Well here we all are, safe and sound if you do not count Norman's hairpiece blowing off coming from the station, that is one of the little penalties of having to keep your head stuck out of cab windows, I am always on at him to get his claustrophobia looked at but it is not easy to find a doctor who will see him in the middle of a field. We would have stopped to retrieve it, but a gull was on it like a bloody bullet, it is probably halfway up a cliff by now with three eggs in it.

Sorry, Sylve, I had to break off there for a minute, it was writing *cliff* did it, one of my little turns come on, I had to put my head between my knees and suck an Extra Strong, I do not have to tell *you* why, I know; remember that time before we was married and you and me went to the Locarno, Streatham, and that ginger bloke sitting by the spot-prize display asked me to dance, and when he got on his feet he was about six feet nine and I brought my Guinness up?

Anyway, we got to the hotel all right, apart from Norman's bloody mother trying to avoid stepping on the pavement cracks

141

between the cab and the gate and walking into a gravel bin, she come down a hell of a wallop and her case burst open and her collection of bottle tops was bouncing all over the place, it took us near on two hours to get her into her room in the cellar on account of no lift below ground floor, so the management had to bag her up and winch her down through the coal chute, all on account of she can't get to sleep unless she hears rats running about. Still, one consolation is that that's the last we'll see of the old bat for two weeks, due to where Norman will not go inside, Tracy comes out in blackheads if there's no windows, big Kevin is allergic to hot water pipes, little Barry gets diarrhoea in the presence of rodents, and me, well, you know about me and bottle tops!

The landlady was ever so nice about Norman. They had a bed all made up for him in the shrubbery, no plants so big he couldn't see over them if he began to panic in the night, and a very nice man near him, but not *too* near, who sleeps in the middle of the lawn with his foot roped to a sundial in the event of gravity suddenly stopping and him falling off into space. Turned out they had a lot of army experience in common: they both had boots as pets, during National Service.

My room is quite nice, too, lots of things to arrange: you can stand the coffee table on the tallboy and put the hearthrug on it with the potty on top, and if you turn the potty upside down you'll find it's large enough to stand a hairspray aerosol on it. Of course, it's all getting a bit high by then, but it looks lower if you stand on the bed, so I'm quite happy really, even if I can't have Tracy sharing with me due to bees figuring prominently in the wallpaper, and I can't visit her, either, on account of they've put her on the top floor. It's all expense, Sylve, isn't it? Still, we managed to get big Kevin and little Barry to share: the management found them a triangular room, so they've got a corner each to stand in, leaving only one for them to keep an eye on; they can get quite a lot of sleep, in turns.

Mealtimes are great fun, everybody is ever so sociable, there's a very nice man from Norwich I think it is, who comes round to every table just after we've all sat down and touches every single piece of cutlery, and two charming sisters from Doncaster who eat standing on their chairs due to the possibility of mice turning up sudden, and a former postmaster who sings 'Nola' whenever there's oxtail soup. My Norman has been a great hit, due to not coming in for meals: everybody takes it in turns to go to the window and feed him, also give him little titbits to carry over to his friend tied to the sundial, because the waitress has agoraphobia and can't even look at the forecourt without going green.

Not that there aren't little squabbles from time to time: Sunday, we had plums and custard, and little Barry likes to arrange the stones on the side of his dish. What he did not realize was that this makes Mr Noles from Gants Hill, who is on our table, punch people in the mouth. Big Kevin, as you know, is not called big Kevin for nothing and has had to learn to look after himself from an early age, due to where his father is unable to come inside and help him, big Kevin took hold of Mr Noles by his collar and chucked him out into the corridor, which was a terrible thing to do, it turned out, because Mr Noles has a horrible fear of narrow places and pays £2 per day extra to enter the dining-room via the fire-escape, but big Kevin was not to know this, he is only a boy, though getting enormous enough for me to feel queasy every time I stretch up to make sure he's brushed his teeth. The upshot of it was, Mr Noles was hurling himself about in the corridor for close on twenty minutes before Mrs Noles could get a net over him. He broke eighteen plaster ducks, three barometers, and put his elbow straight through 'The Monarch of the Glen', though doing less damage than you might think since its face had already been painted out on account of the night porter having a morbid fear of antlers.

And all the time my Norman is shouting *'What's going on? What's bloody going on?'* from the garden, deeply distressing his friend tied to the sundial who can hear all this breakage and shrieking and reckons gravity is beginning to pack up and bring things off the walls.

Still, it turned out all right, Mr Noles and big Kevin made it up, they have a lot in common, basically, both being unable to walk down a street without picking bits off hedges, and he asked big Kevin to join him on the beach because Mrs Noles never went there on account of her terror of being buried alive. She likes to spend her afternoons standing on the concrete forecourt with a big bell in her hand and a whistle between her teeth in case of emergencies, so her husband and big Kevin and little Barry and Tracy and Norman and me all went off to the beach. Trouble was, it would all have been all right if Norman's new friend hadn't been unsettled by the false alarm over gravity: he did not want to be left alone, so the porter found a huge coil of rope so that Norman's new friend could come down to the beach without untying himself from the sundial, but it was nearly three hundred yards and you have to go round two corners, so you can't see what's going on behind, and what happened was the rope got caught in a car bumper and one moment Norman's new friend was cautiously creeping along beside us, and the next he was suddenly plucked from our midst.

We visited him in the cottage hospital, but even our presence (minus, of course, Norman, also Tracy, who faints in the vicinity of linoleum) could not persuade him that he had not fallen off Earth and hurt himself dropping onto some alien planet. His argument was that we had fallen with him but, being unencumbered by rope or sundials, had managed to land on our feet, unhurt, and were keeping the truth from him so as not to alarm an injured man.

There was no convincing him, so we just left him there and collected Norman and Tracy and went down to the beach to find big Kevin and Mr Noles. But all we could find was big Kevin, he was huddled under a stack of deck-chairs and sobbing: we ran up to him (all except little Barry, who was terrified in case the shadow of the deck-chairs fell on his foot), and asked him what was wrong, and he said he had been getting on fine, he had buried Mr Noles in the sand, because Mr Noles had been told by his psychiatrist that this was a very good way to overcome his fear of narrow spaces, and he was just about to stick a little windmill over where he had buried him when a crab come out of the sea and started running towards him sideways.

We all gasped!

'It is my own fault,' shouted Norman, from a nice open space he had found in between the airbeds, 'I knew the lad was an

144

arachnophobe, it never occurred to me that he would associate crabs with spiders, that is not the sort of thing what occurs to a claustrophobe on account of you never get near enough to anything to distinguish it.'

'So what happened, big Kevin?' I said, aghast.

'I run off, Mum,' he sobbed. 'I must have run miles.'

A cold chill shot down my spine, as if I'd just seen the Eiffel Tower or something.

'Where is Mr Noles buried?' I enquired, gently.

I think you probably know the answer to that, Sylve. I tell you, we prodded lolly-sticks all over that beach for five hours, i.e. well after it was too late anyway, and no luck. It was getting dark before I knew I would have to be the one to break the news to Mrs Noles. Her of all people.

She was still standing on the forecourt when we got back to the hotel. I put my hand on her arm.

'How are you, Mrs Noles?' I murmured.

'Nicely, thank you,' she replied. 'I got a bit worried around half-past four. The sun was very hot, and I thought: any minute, this asphalt is going to melt and swallow me up. But it didn't.'

Quick is best, I said to myself, Sylve. So I come right out and told her that Mr Noles had been buried alive. And do you know what she said?

'Serves him right, the stingy bastard,' she said. 'I always told him we ought to have bought a bell each.'

That's the best thing about holidays, Sylve, I always say: you meet so many interesting people.

It takes you right out of yourself.

Your loving friend, Sharon.

Just a Snog at Twilight

The Head Proof Reader at the Guardian retired last night.
Guardian

HE STROLLED to the window, and gazed out over the darkling garden. It was strange, not to be girding his loins for the office, not to be sharpening his pencils, not to be buffing his eyeshield, not to be drawing on the snug regulation armbands to hold back his spotless cuffs against the omnipresent threat of undried ink.

He sighed; and murmured:

'The curlew tolls the knee of farting day,
The lowing herd wing slowly o'er the leg,
The ploughman homeark Rangers 3,
Luton 788 (after extra tile).'

He sighed again, and turned from the window, and glanced at his fine presentation bracket clock bearing the brass-plated legend GOOD DUCK FROM ALL YOUR OLD FRIENDS AT THE NAURGIAD, and even as the tear pricked his eye, a blush suffused his cheek: he was no prude, but seeing the word DUCK in print like that, no asterisks, did, he had to admit, go against the grain. Ah, well, times changed; this was, after all, 9128.

The clock struck forty-three, and he reached for his coat.

'Shrdlg!' he called. 'WzWzWzWzWzWz.'

'All right,' his wife called back from the kitchen, 'but don't be long.'

They had been married for many years.

*

146

How odd it was, being out in the evening, in his local, yet unfamiliar, streets: all his working life, he had never been out much. Nights were spent at the *Guardian*, days were spent either sleeping or struggling with the crossword. He had started it in 1937, and it had become a totally absorbing hobby: once, early in 1953, he had nearly got a clue, but it eluded him at the last hurdle. He felt in his bones what the answer to 'Did it carry Hannibal's trunk?' must surely be, but *enelurg* did not have the specified eight letters. The crossword was yellow, now, and brittle, after forty-five years of devoted fingering, but he was a persistent man, and he would not give up easily. Perhaps now, with the elbow-room of retirement . . .

But it had inevitably meant that his local experience had been severely restricted, and it was not without a certain frisson of excitement that he entered the tobacconist's, thus breaking the purchasing habits of a long lifetime spent in the kiosks of EC4, where the familiar traders well knew his little ways.

'Good evening,' he said, 'may I have a packet of pork-tipped Serion Verses and a box of cont. foot of page 4, column 6?'

The girl twitched the sari more snugly about her slim shoulder, and looked uncertainly at him.

'I am begging your pardon?' she said. 'What are these items that you are requesting?'

He rolled his eyes, and shook his head. Years of meticulous attention to the *Guardian*'s resolutely egalitarian pages had, of course, left him free of all prejudice, but it had to be said that righteous impatience tended to take hold of him when he was confronted with those whose English did not quite conform to the lawless standards set in Farringdon Road.

'Good heavens, madam!' he cried. 'You act as if you had never heard of them!'

At the cry, the proprietor himself emerged from the back of the shop.

'What is appearing to be the trouble?' he enquired.

'This gentleman,' replied the assistant, 'is asking for some, er –'

'Serion Verses,' snapped the ex-Head Proof Reader. 'A perfectly ordinary packet of figs.'

The proprietor beamed broadly, and slipped the brass knuckles back into his apron-pocket, discreetly.

'Aha!' he exclaimed. 'That is immediately explaining it! We are not selling figs, sir. That is not being our business.'

'Dog Almighty!' cried the customer. 'I can see the bloody things on the shelf behind take in additional copy Minister said toady upon retuning to $1^7/8$ Downing Streen where delete Sputh China Sea insert Her Majesty the Queer!'

The proprietor slid his hand into his apron-pocket again.

'If you are not leaving my premises immediately,' he muttered, pushing his weeping assistant for her own safety behind a sturdy display of slightly shop-soiled and greatly reduced walnut whips, 'I am having no other course which is being open to me but to call the policemen. Good evening.'

The customer ground his teeth, and clenched his fists, but turned, finally, upon his heel, and stamped out of the shop.

'Send 'em all back to Panistak!' he cried; but not until he was well out of earshot, and not without an uneasy pang at this shattering breach in what had hitherto been a lifetime's unwavering commitment. Indeed, so disturbed was he by the incident that he did not see the group of youths until he backed heavily into them.

'OY!' shouted the leader. 'Are you asking to have your bleeding face trod on, grandpa?'

'Are you asking to carry your teeth home in your bleeding hat?' enquired a second.

'Would you care to end up,' said a third, removing a cycle-chain from his boot, 'as two gross of Big Macs?'

The ex-Head Proof Reader raised placating hands.

'Lads!' he declared. 'We at the *Naurgiad* have always been on your side! We understand your problems. The Hole Secretary is a crenit, it is the enviro6 which is set this italic bold condensed, it is the lack of yobs which is the cause.'

'What?' said the leader, through gritted teeth.

'Yobs!' shouted the perspiring well-wisher. 'That is what is at the bottom of street violets! Britain's yob-centres are – '

'He ain't 'alf asking for it,' grunted the second youth. 'Shall we do him?'

The leader put his face close to his victim.

'Eff off!' he snarled.

'I beg your pardon?'

'Spell it out for him, Brian.'

So Brian spelt it out. The ex-Head Proof Reader smiled, and tutted, and shook his head.

'No, no, no,' he murmured. 'Forgive me, but it would have to be *Dee off*. Not, of course, that one blames you, the shocking state of our education syrglb is – '

After they blacked his eye and he was sitting on the pavement, they aerosoled the word upon his mackintosh, so that he would no longer be in doubt, and strolled whistling away.

It was thus not entirely unsurprising that when he eventually struggled to his feet and staggered in the hope of assistance towards two women, one of whom was wheeling a push-chair, they took one look at his wild expression, his torn collar, his disarranged clothing, and, above all perhaps, the bizarre message painted on his coat, and immediately screamed: 'RAPE!'

He reeled, horror-stricken.

'No!' he shrieked. '*Me?* Have you any idea to whom you are in yesterday's editions we refurned to Ms Manny Whitehouse as Ms Manny Whitehouse, this should of course have read Ms Manny Whitehouse, we have always been – '

'RAPE!'

'– the leading spokespersons in the defence of ladypersons against the oppression of gentlemanpersons! Great Dog in Hendon, ladypersons, we have stood up for buttered wives, yob equality, gay liberace, onanparent families, 7689.34% on demand, free contraceptive pails, we have Errol Pizza, Jim the Tweeney, Pony Siddons . . .'

'I'm afraid we had to put him in this jacket, madam,' said the first policeman.

She stared at the wretched face gazing out of the swaddling canvas at her.

'Didn't he try to explain?' she enquired.

'It was after he tried to explain,' said the second policeman, 'that we put him in the canvas jacket.'

The police surgeon came into the charge room, wiping his

hands on a paper towel. He smiled.

'Well,' he said, 'he was definitely not drunk. Personally, I don't think there's anything you can charge him with.'

'What's his trouble, then?' asked the first policeman.

The police surgeon crumpled the paper towel, and tossed it into the metal waste-bin.

'I'd say,' he replied, weighing his words professionally, 'that he was suffering from an inability to distinguish between the *Guardian* and real life.'

'There's a lot of it about,' said the second policeman.

The ex-Head Proof Reader's red-rimmed eyes swivelled towards the police surgeon's face. He licked dry lips.

'Is there a worm for it?' he said.

Moscow or Bust

A claim was made last week that Napoleon died of a hormone-abnormality disease that was slowly turning him into a woman. This, according to The Journal of Sexual Medicine, *explains contemporary reports of Napoleon's highly feminine appearance.*

One of his doctors described the general's body as 'effeminate', another said he had 'a chest that many a woman would be proud of', while one wrote that 'the emperor has small white hands and shows a good leg'. Even Josephine compared her lover to a castrato.

Observer

AS SOON as the first pale ray of watery spring sun slid through his curtains and struck his beard, Mr Sam Kaminski sighed, eased his elderly body from the bed, shuffled resignedly downstairs, and began to board up his shop window.

For spring, though naturally enough greeted with ecstasy by most of Mother Russia, brought nothing but anxiety to the ghetto of Plotz: as winter thawed, Plotz, on the barren banks of the River Niemen, gritted its teeth, prayed its prayers, and waited for the worst.

At the noise of Kaminski's hammer, his neighbour, still in his nightshirt, rushed out into the unpaved street.

'Did they come yet?' he cried.

Kaminski shook his head.

'Precautions,' he said, through a mouthful of nails.

His neighbour stared at his own window. It was full of blouses.

'Could lose my entire stock,' he muttered. 'It's been a bad winter.'

Kaminski spat out his last nail and banged it home.

'It makes a difference?' he said.

'With blouses,' replied his neighbour, 'it makes a *big* difference.'

'How come?'

'The whores don't go home,' replied his neighbour. 'That's how come. They stay in the barracks maybe six months. The normal rate is a blouse a month. Figure for yourself.'

'With furs,' said Kaminski, 'it's different. I got a class trade. Officers only. For their wives.'

'Could be a nice little business,' said his neighbour. 'If they paid.'

'If they paid,' said Kaminski, 'it could be a terrific business. I could be a chain by now. Mail order, even.'

'Don't joke,' said his neighbour.

Kaminski sighed, and went back into his shop, and took the best coats down to the cellar. Then he came back, slowly, up the steps, put on his black homburg with the reinforced steel lining, and waited for the Cossacks.

It was nearly noon before the first hoofbeats shook the shuttered town. Kaminski cocked a practised ear, assessing his personal time-table: they would stop at the butcher's for a little rape, the way they did every spring, then they would burn down the school, say fifteen minutes, after that they would probably – he tensed, gasped! His heart lurched, missed, lurched irregularly on: they were *not* stopping! The thunder of hooves grew louder, shaking the wooden walls, then suddenly died in a jangle of tack and a rasp of dismounting boots, outside his very door!

Fists banged upon it.

'We're out of stock!' cried the furrier. 'We're awaiting deliveries! Could be a month, but I can't promise, maybe a –'

The door flew from its hinges.

'All right!' shouted Kaminski, leaping up. 'Okay! I lied, I admit it, I got a nice musquash stole, mink it isn't, but in a good light –'. He stopped.

The figure in the doorway was very small, for a Cossack. The uniform was unfamiliar. The hat was most peculiar. And the perfume, in particular, was very expensive. Most Cossacks wore wolfdung.

Kaminski took an uncertain step towards the doorway.

'Yes?' he said.

The short figure drilled Kaminski with two glittering eyes.

'I am Napoleon,' it announced, 'Emperor of Europe!'

Kaminski reeled, and clutched for support at the cutting-table.

'So!' he cried. 'You have invaded at last! You are looking for Moscow! Okay, so you turn left at the –'

'Yes,' said Napoleon, holding up a beautiful little hand, 'and no. Yes, I have invaded, and no, I am not looking for Moscow. What I am looking for is something in sable, full-length, with a raglan sleeve. Chic, but not ostentatious.'

As Kaminski gaped, and mopped his face, a tall and iron-jawed man strode into the little shop, and bowed stiffly.

'May I urge Your Imperial Highness to make haste?' he said.

'No,' said Napoleon. 'You don't rush sable, Ney. Am I right, Mr, er –'

'Kaminski,' said the furrier. 'Absolutely, Your Imperial Highness! I can see Your Imperial Highness is an Imperial Highness of terrific taste. With sable, artistry is what you have to have, also skill, also the experience of a lifetime, never mind a – by the way, Your Imperial Highness, what is this raglan sleeve business? We at Kaminski Bespoke Furs like to think of ourselves as being in the forefront of –'

Napoleon smiled, not without smugness. His kiss-curl bobbed.

'It could be a whole new fashion,' he said.

'French, naturally,' said Kaminski, nodding, 'such taste, your people, such what shall I say, such – '

'As a matter of fact,' said Napoleon, 'no. You may recall the storming of Badajoz during the Peninsular War?'

'I read about it in the *Fur Trade Gazette*,' nodded Kaminski. 'A terrible business. Persian lamb prices shot right down.'

Napoleon glared at him.

'At Badajoz,' he said, his voice rising to a not unfetching soprano, 'there was this absolutely *ravishing* English officer, wasn't there, Ney?'

The marshal looked out of the doorway, and sucked his gilt chinstrap.

'Anyway,' continued Napoleon, 'he was wearing this wonderful frogged jacket, sort of half off-the-shoulder, with a very full –'

'You could sketch it, maybe?' suggested Kaminski.

'Your Imperial Highness,' said Ney, as Bonaparte licked his crayon, rolling his eyes and tutting creatively by turns, 'we have 435, 000 men of the Grande Armée awaiting Your Imperial Highness's orders to advance, and while we have the brief meteorological advantage afforded us in this Godforsaken spot, we –'

'Leave us, Ney!' snapped Napoleon. After his marshal had stamped furiously out, he drew Kaminski confidentially into a dark corner of the shop.

'You don't think I'm a little, er, short for a full-length coat? I should hate to look squat.'

'Take off the topcoat,' said Kaminski. He took the coat, hung it up, turned, closed one eye, considering. 'Your Imperial Highness has a terrific figure,' he said finally.

'But not a little, er, *full*,' giggled Napoleon, 'here?'

Kaminski tutted professionally.

'Since when was a big bust a disadvantage? Be grateful. It gives you presence. Also, you have nice slim legs. What we call a pocket Venus in the fur trade, you should pardon my familiarity. In sable you'll be a knockout, believe me. Would I lie?'

Napoleon smiled, and squeezed Kaminski's arm.

'Measure me,' he breathed.

The Grande Armée bivouacked on the banks of the Niemen, confused, disgruntled, while their Emperor waited for his first fitting. Ney began to drink heavily. Most nights, Napoleon waited up for him, and the camp rang to his subsequent screaming complaints. During the day, they argued about the coat.

A week later, Napoleon returned to Kaminski Bespoke Furs.

'It fits you,' said the furrier, 'like the paper on the wall! You and that coat were made for each other.'

Napoleon minced back and forth in front of the triple-mirror.

'It makes me look hippy,' he said at last.

'Let me take it in a bit at the back,' offered Kaminski.

On the banks of the Niemen, two divisions of Prussian infantry deserted.

*

By early August (having been sent back twice, to have white ermine cuffs added, and to have a matching hat made up), the coat was ready. Kaminski sent a messenger out to the camp, who returned with Napoleon, and a hollow-eyed muttering Ney.

'Elegant,' said Napoleon. 'I'll take it.'

'Thank God!' croaked Marshal Ney. 'Can we go to Moscow now?'

'Shall I wrap it?' asked Kaminski. 'I'll find a smart box.'

'I'll wear it,' said Napoleon. 'If you've got it, flaunt it!'

Kaminski's neighbour came out, along with the rest of Plotz, to watch the Grande Armée pull out.

'Did he pay, at least?' enquired the neighbour.

Kaminski showed him the cheque.

'Cash it quick,' said the neighbour. 'I understand the Tsar managed to get a big army together.'

Three weeks later, in the middle of the night, a stone crashed through Kaminski's window. He sprang up, poised for Cossacks, and glanced outside.

'My spurs keep catching in the lining,' shouted Napoleon, from the head of his army, who stretched, bleary-eyed, from Kaminski Bespoke Furs to the moonlit horizon.

'I'll come down,' said Kaminski.

He lit a few candles, and examined the coat.

'I didn't notice at first,' said Napoleon. 'I got involved in my new hair-style. I couldn't think of anything else. You know how it happens.'

'One ringlet is very fashionable,' said Kaminski. 'Where did you get the gloves?'

'Szolov,' replied the Emperor. 'They made me up eighty pairs.'

'It took two weeks,' said Ney.

'I'll have to shorten the coat a little,' said Kaminski.

'Moscow,' said Ney, and fell on his bottle.

Two days later, with autumn chill already in the September air, Napoleon strutted up and down outside Kaminski's, testing the new length. Kaminski and his neighbour watched him, respectfully, from the shop.

'A pity he keeps the hand inside the coat all the time,' murmured Kaminski. 'It's ruining the shape.'

'He's a Frenchman,' said his neighbour, grinning. 'Maybe he likes to keep his hand on his winkle.'

'What winkle?' said Kaminski.

The Emperor came back inside the shop.

'Perfect,' he said, and was about to leave when his eye rested on Kaminski's rack. '*What's that?*' he shrilled.

'Chinchilla,' replied Kaminski. 'The best.'

'I'll take it!' shrieked Napoleon.

'It's not Your Imperial Highness's size,' said Kaminski.

Napoleon waved his hand impatiently.

'Then make me one up!'

'With chinchilla,' said Kaminski, 'it could take three weeks minimum.'

'I'll wait,' said Napoleon firmly.

'But Moscow!' cried Kaminski. 'Not that I couldn't do with the business, but didn't you already waste enough time?'

Napoleon stamped his pretty foot furiously.

'Moscow, Moscow, Moscow!' he screamed. 'Why is everybody in such a *rush* to get to Moscow?'

And even as he spoke, in the little street beyond the shop, the first pale snowflake floated down and settled on Ney's sleeve.

Blue Flics

Six English bobbies are off on a cycling tour of France. They hope to meet the ordinary Frenchman in the street and put across some idea of what life as an English policeman is like.
Daily Express

MONDAY AT 11.42 am, a time which will be corroborated by my colleague PC Garsmold although I did not, of course, consult with him prior to taking down these notes in writing, we disembarked with our regulation machines from the ferry *Sylvia Blagrove II* and proceeded in single file in an easterly direction along the Rue Maritime, in so doing passing several bollards.

After approx. six hundred yards, we come to a roundabout: pausing to ascertain it was safe to proceed; we had just pedalled off when this van came round it the wrong way, hurling PC Chatterjee from his machine, causing severe damage to his left-hand pannier with the result that a mutton vindaloo prepared special by his wife as a safeguard against trots etcetera brought on by e.g. snails' legs and so forth, got scattered all over the road, rice becoming all gritty and dogs jumping on the larger lumps.

The driver of the van then brought his vehicle to the halt position, and descended from it via the passenger door, this detail spotted by PC Wisley and took down by him at the time, 11.53.

The following conversation then ensued:

DRIVER: Gabble, gabble, gabble, etcetera.
PC GARSMOLD: Excuse me, sunshine, is this your vehicle?
DRIVER: Gabble, gabble, gabble, plus arms waving about.
PC WISLEY: Leave it out, you was on the wrong side of the road,

157

we have got you bang to rights, also sitting in the passenger seat, definitely.

PC RIMMER: Do you reckon he might be intoxicated, PC Wisley?

PC WISLEY: I think it is a line of enquiry worth pursuing, PC Rimmer, due to where he is a Frog and they are all piss-artists, if I may use the vernacular, get him to blow in the wossname.

PC Garsmold then extracted his breathalyser kit. The suspect then became agitated and, clearly refusing to blow in the bag as laid down in paragraph nine, subsection fourteen, seemed about to offer actual violence. We then employed reasonable force to restrain him, and while he was distracted by the action of picking up his teeth, PC Chatterjee stuck the tube in his mouth.

The test proved negative. We informed the suspect that he was a lucky bastard, and instructed him to mind how he went in future. As we pedalled off, PC Rimmer noticed that the steering-wheel was on the passenger side, and offered the opinion that the vehicle had probably been botched up after some major accident and would undoubtedly not pass its MOT. PC Chatterjee was all for going back and bunging chummy a 703/14b, but the rest of us reckoned he had probably learned his lesson, and anyway time was getting on.

It was now 12.27.

Proceeding through Boulogne, we became aware that everybody was on the wrong side of the road, also using hooters immoderately, but decided to take no further action due to reinforcements not being available.

Reached outskirts of Etaples at 2.07 pm, stopped at roadside to consume sandwich rations. We was on the last of the Marmite when a vehicle drew up, and an occupant dismounted, smiled at us in what might be described as a cordial manner, exposed himself and began widdling in the ditch. He was immediately apprehended by PCs Garsmold and Wisley, and charged with an act of gross indecency. He thereupon twisted himself free, adjusted his dress, and drew a revolver. Since we had not come tooled up, we were forced to lie face down on the verge while the flasher gabbled into a pocket transceiver.

At 2.09 (approx., due to watch-hand clasped behind neck), a

vehicle with blue flashing light come up wailing, disembarking a number of uniformed men carrying sub-machine guns. Fortunately, one of these spoke English.

He immediately charged PCs Garsmold and Wisley with importuning.

I then produced my warrant card, and explained the confusion. This decision immediately regretted by our party, since our original suspect then grasped PC Garsmold and kissed him on both cheeks, instantly confirming our first suspicions. We did not take further action, however, due to where they was all armed to the teeth, but it was useful experience. In a country where the poofs go round mob-handed carrying automatic weapons, you have to watch your step.

Tuesday Spent the night at the Hotel les Deux Souris, and came downstairs at 8.00 am for cooked breakfast, just in time to spot landlord pouring large brandy for customer in blue vest.

Two blasts on whistle brought PCs Garsmold and Wisley out of khazi on double to act as back-up while I charged landlord with Dispensing Alcoholic Beverages Contrary to the Stipulations of the Licensing (Hours) Act 1947.

The customer thereupon threatened me with a long cudgel he had clearly brought along for this purpose, and I had no other recourse than to truncheon him. As it fell to the ground, his cudgel split open to reveal several slices of salami and a thing with holes in which I originally took to be a housebreaking implement of some kind but which upon further forensic examination by PC Chatterjee turned out to be cheese.

The following conversation then ensued:

PC WISLEY: I charge you with taking away a lavatory with the intention of permanently depriving the rightful owner. You are nicked, son!
CUSTOMER: Groan, gabble.
ME: To what are you referring, PC Wisley? It is my intention to nail him for assault with a deadly loaf.
PC GARSMOLD: PC Wisley is correct. When we was in the khazi just now, we noted that the pan had been nicked, due to where

there was only a hole in the ground. It is clear to us that while chummy here was engaging the landlord in conversation over an illicit drink, his accomplice was out back half-inching the toilet. He is probably halfway to Paris by now, wherever that is.

At this point (8.06), the landlord's wife come in to see what the altercation concerned. She was able to reassure me that our friend in the blue vest was above board, also no licensing infringements, so it all passed off amicably enough, us chipping in for bottle of brandy (*see attached chitty*) for customer, plus small sum in compensation for beret. Upon being complimented on her grasp of English, landlord's wife explained she had sheltered escaping English prisoners, which very nearly upset the apple-cart again, due to where PC Chatterjee attempted to do her on a harbouring and abetting charge, since he had spotted someone in the room next door to his who bore a striking resemblance to a notice we'd had pinned up in our section house concerning a bloke wanted for the Lewisham payroll job. He can be a bit dim, PC Chatterjee, but we got to have one or two of them about, these days.

Pushed on towards Abbeville without further major incident, although PC Rimmer, when we were about halfway there down the N40, paused outside a small town and attempted to collar a bloke with a paintbrush for defacing a public sign. Turned out the place was actually *called* Berck.

Wednesday Further to our enquiries, and pursuing our investigations to the fullest extent, we have now formed the firm conclusion that this is a country populated entirely by the bent. At the same time, it is impossible to get a single charge, however reasonable, to stick.

At 9.47 this morning, proceeding down what was clearly High Road, Abbeville, in broad daylight, we come on a couple of wrong 'uns unloading a truck outside a butcher's, to wit, Gaston Dubois. We knew they was wrong right off, on account of they was both smoking during the unloading of fresh carcases, in direct contravention of the Health & Public Hygiene (1953) Act, but we did not know how wrong until PC Wisley drew his notebook and approached said offenders with a view to a sight of their Licence to Convey, which is a technicality you usually nick these buggers on due to invariably being out of date.

The following conversation then ensued:

PC WISLEY (*sniffing*): Hang about, PC Rimmer, does that smell like normal decent tobacco to you?
PC RIMMER (*sniffing*): No, PC Wisley, that is definitely a substance. These men are smoking a substance. That is two cast-iron charges already, and you have not even got your pencil out yet!
PC GARSMOLD: Were we to find a half-brick in their apron, that would be . . .
PCS WISLEY, RIMMER & GARSMOLD: ONE HUNDRED AND EIGHTY!
PC GARSMOLD: I'll see if I can find a half-brick anywhere.

At this crucial juncture, however, an even more major crime was detected. PC Chatterjee, who spent some time in the Mounted Division until resigning upon the discovery that the mucking-out was always down to him for some strange reason, suddenly grasped my arm and informed me that the carcase being carried into said Gaston Dubois was that of a horse! I come over dizzy at the horror of this, but quickly recovered due to years of training, and we launched ourselves upon the miscreants firm-handed in the full assurance that there was a Queen's Commendation in this, at the very least.

As for coming out of it with three stripes up . . .

Thursday They finally let us out of Abbeville nick this morning, but only after impounding our bicycles in lieu of surety. It is clear to us that the Abbeville force is unquestionably on the take, probably half a dozen fillet steaks per day per man from Mr Bleeding Dubois, but it is not our intention to stay around long enough to get an A10 investigation going. Sooner we are out of this bloody country, the better.

In accordance with this decision, and machines being in a non-available situation as outlined hereinabove, we was away on our toes double-quick with a view to hitch-hiking back to Boulogne.

161

It was the first stroke of luck we'd had in four days. At 11.14 am, this big truck stops, swarthy occupant in dark glasses, on his way to Boulogne. We got in the back, and he was off like the clappers.

The following conversation then ensued:

PC GARSMOLD: What's in them crates, PC Wisley?
PC WISLEY: *Tinned Fruit*, it says on the side. *Export to Mexico.* I'll have a shufti. Could be stolen blouses, anything.
PC Wisley then opened a crate.
PC WISLEY: False alarm. Great long pointed tins with EXOCET on the side. God knows what that is. Probably the vegetable equivalent of horsemeat.
PC RIMMER: They'll eat anything, the Frogs.

Upon arrival at the Boulogne docks at 2.18 pm, we were at pains to thank said driver for his assistance and informed him he was the first straight Frenchman we had met. He replied that he was an Argentinian.

That explains it, we said.

Shelf Life

Muratex Shelving Systems salesmen have an exciting tale to tell! Ring us NOW for an immediate call. You won't be disappointed.

Exchange & Mart

HE SETTLED down into the old creaking leather of the club chair on the other side of the roaring fire from mine, and let out a waistcoat button.

'That was a damned fine piece of beef,' he said, cloaking a soft eructation with one tattooed hand.

'I'm glad you enjoyed it,' I said.

'It put me in mind of –' he paused in the thoughtful stuffing of his ochre meerschaum; a flake of dark shag fell on his old mongrel dog; his parrot nodded, drowsing. 'Tell me,' he said quietly, hardly louder than the night wind murmuring at the cottage mullions, 'did you ever eat human flesh?'

I shook my head.

'I don't think so,' I said.

He smiled.

'If you had,' he said, 'you would not have forgotten. It is not, of course, to everyone's taste. Some find it rather sweet.' He resumed the stuffing of his pipe, working his iron hook with remarkable precision. 'But that, as they say, is another story.'

I pushed the Cockburn '97 towards him.

'You were going to tell me,' I said, 'about Muratex Shelving Systems.'

My guest struck a vesta against his whalebone leg, and sucked at his pipestem, his one good and glinting eye vanishing into a

163

cloud of acrid slate-blue smoke. The parrot woke, and coughed, and re-settled. The dog rooted idly in its matted groin. At last, my visitor settled back his head against the chair, took a deep draught of port, half-closed his eye, and began . . .

'Who can say what strange agency first drew me to the benighted spot on the Bristol waterfront that was to be the start of it all? Call it Fate, call it Old Nick himself, call it Mr Witherspoon of South-West Area Sales who had informed me that an estimate was required for a 6 x 40-foot run of executive shelving from our attractive Nobby Nutt range, to be finished in two coats eau-de-nil, plus making good.

No matter, now. Suffice it to say that I presented myself at what transpired to be a deserted warehouse, let myself in, and set immediately to work with what we call a measuring tape, the details of which need not concern us here, except to say that you pull it out, and when you want to roll it up, you press a little button and it sort of flies back.

So absorbed had I become in the problem of whether to secure the stanchions by toggle-bolts or self-tapping coachscrews that I did not notice that I was no longer alone. Conceive, my dear sir, of my amazement when, upon looking round, I found myself face to face with a heathen Chinee who had raised above his head what appeared to be a sand-filled sock!

'So solly,' he murmured, in the manner of his people. It was the last sound I heard. A black pit opened up, and swallowed me.

I awoke with an aching head and a strange motion beneath my supine body. I struggled erect, to find myself in a small room lit by one circular window. It was to this that I now, full of foreboding, ran. It was exactly as I had feared!

Hardly had I taken in my fearful predicament than the cabin door burst open, to reveal a squat and villainous dago, a wild-eyed mulatto dwarf, and a great red giant of a man whom I immediately recognized, from a picture in a recent number of *Shelving News*, to be a full-blooded Pawnee!

The dwarf scuttled forward.

'Bridge!' he snapped.

I smote my forehead, in instant comprehension.

'There has been the most frightful mistake!' I cried. 'I do not play, gentlemen! Since you have kidnapped me to be a fourth, I can only suggest that –'

In answer, the redskin merely tucked me beneath his enormous arm and carried me aloft to the wheelhouse, where he set me down beside a black-bearded ogre in captain's rings.

'Is this the wretch?' roared the captain, and, not waiting upon their reply, reached out, grasped my shirtfront, and dragged me to the adjoining cabin. 'See anything?' he cried.

My trained eye swept expertly about me.

'Dear God!' I breathed. 'All your shelving has crumbled away!'

The captain released me on a sudden, and bit his knuckle.

'Moby Woodworm!' said he, choking a sob. 'All me bits and bobs fallen to the deck. Look at that!'

He stopped, and picked up a pitiful egg-timer cunningly fixed to a tiny Eiffel Tower. Sand ran from the shattered globes.

Mine was, it is true, an unorthodox commission: normally, Mr Witherspoon would have required an invoice in triplicate plus small deposit to ensure prompt attention at earliest mutual convenience, but, as I was quick to assure the captain, Muratex Shelving Systems were usually prepared to waive such requirements in the event of, say, having a cocked pistol stuck in their ear or the ear of any of their representatives.

Working around the clock, I completed my task in less than a week. I was just sanding down and removing dowel-heads as per client's stipulations, when the ship's carpenter entered, admired my work, tore it off the wall, and threw me overboard.

Jealousy, my dear sir, has been the curse of bespoke shelving since Time began.

I cannot tell how long it was before I came round, to find myself bobbing alone in the South China Sea, thanking God that the shelving to which I had somehow remained clinging had been jettisoned with me. Nor had I been troubled by sharks; clearly, shelves are one of the few things these monsters fear.

And yet, sea and broiling sun had taken their own toll. Weak as I was, I should doubtless have perished there and then had it not been for a miracle! As my hands slipped from the trusty dovetailing, I felt a huge, smooth shape rise up from the very deep, lifting me above the water. I clutched wildly, and found a strong fin. I hardly dared glance down; it was a dolphin! I recognised him instantly from a recent feature about marine intelligence in *Cantilever & Bracket Digest*, titled, as I recall 'Dolphins: Could They Hang Fitted Cupboards?'

How long, how far, it towed me, who can say? All I know is that when I was finally released, it was in shallow water: sand embraced my thankful feet. I crawled through the last few warm ripples, and slept.

As to the voluptuous Polynesian maiden who found me there, dressed my wounds, took me to her grass hut, fed me on maomao, yuccatash, and succulent hoi, made me a hat, and performed services undreamed of in the letters columns of *Shelving For Men*, I shall not dwell upon her, for the memory, even now, remains too poignant. She called me Nyuga Nyuga, which in their language means Eric, and, during those blissful months, made me forget everything, including my worries concerning the £2 7s 8d already paid into the Muratex Christmas Club that I might never see again.

But such an idyll could not possibly last. Life, my dear sir, is not like that. With the spring came the inevitable invasion from the neighbouring island whose natives, once every hundred years, traditionally give up vegetarianism for Lent. Everyone on my own island was eaten, with the exception of myself: since I alone was white, there were fears that I might have gone mouldy and I was thus taken back to the neighbouring island for scientific tests to determine whether or not I was fit for human consumption.

Having assured themselves that I was indeed edible, the islanders set about sealing my fate. I was tied to a stake, faggots were heaped about my feet, and, while the islanders stood around drinking Campari and discussing what to do after dinner, I prepared to meet my Maker.

The chef approached, torch in hand; the diners crunched their

Twiglets, unconcerned; far-off, a gibbon barked; and I, dear sir, I gritted my teeth and swore to myself that I should be as tasteless and stringy as it lay within my power to be!

But at that moment came a sudden high-pitched and echoing cry, to be followed seconds later by a wild and sobbing ululation. I dared not open my eyes as I felt a knife-blade slice through my bonds! What could it be? A sudden eclipse of the sun? An unexpected manifestation of St Elmo's Fire? Had a sliver of glass somehow fallen from a broken compass in my pocket, focused the sun, and set light to the chief's dinner-jacket?

It was none of these. When I finally found courage to look, my eyes fell upon none other than my trusty, if by now somewhat warped, shelving! Washed up at last upon the beach, it had been discovered by the two trembling sentries who now bore it reverently into the centre of the village, pointing from it to me, and back again, before falling to their knees and banging their foreheads upon the ground.

The rest of the assembly immediately followed suit. How this remote island had come to regard shelving as a god I did not know then, and I have not discovered to this day. I was not concerned, either, with staying long enough to find out! Explaining, as soon as the tumult had quietened, by means of sign language and the few local words taught me by my island love, now sadly eaten, that I would have to leave them now to go and put up a fifty-foot run of best pine god in the palace of the great white lady across the sea, I persuaded them to lend me an outrigger canoe and a couple of big strong girls, and, as a silver medal of moon rose over the indigo ocean . . .

'Yes?' I cried, leaning forward across the dying embers between us, 'Yes?'

My guest rose, sighing, and kicked his dog awake.

'How I discovered the shelf of Prester John,' he said, 'how I journeyed into the bowels of the earth herself to find King Solomon's fabled range of eye-level kitchen units, how I came upon the North-West Filing System, can, I'm afraid,' and here he smiled a sympathetic smile, 'only be recounted to those industrial purchasers wishing to avail themselves of not less than twelve hundred metres of best-quality melanite-coated steel.'

He reached for his Inverness cape and alpenstock, shook my hand, paused at the door, patted the wall, and murmured:

'Look nice there, our Nobby Nutt coat-rack. You won't regret it.'

And then he was gone, into the enfolding night.

Metamorphosis

We must accept that authorship has become a part of show business. Hype and hoopla, personal appearances on radio and TV, book signings and lunches, are all an integral part of the publishing game. One wonders wryly how a Kafka or a Dostoyevsky would fare under these modern conditions.

New York Times

12 FEBRUARY They come for me very early, perhaps 5 am. I cannot say, I have no watch. After I purchased the scarf, there was no money for a watch. I cried for a long time before making the decision, in the middle of the store in Hothrolnyczy Street, with many people staring at me. They would steal my watch if I bought one. Perhaps they will steal my scarf. Who can say? At nights I dream of the watch. I am wearing it around my throat to keep warm, and people walk by me, and each one tightens the watch one more hole on the strap. I hear the ticking grow louder. My eyes pop out. So they come for me at perhaps 5 am, it is dark in the mean little hotel room; beyond the window London is a black mass crawling with aliens, why am I here, why are they knocking on the door at 5 am?

There are three of them, a publisher in a black coat of very expensive material with a red carnation in the buttonhole, it is as if he had been shot in the left breast, blood wells out; a person in a striped suit and a spotted bow-tie who is in something called public relations, obviously a policeman of some kind, perhaps a government inspector; and a woman who says that she has been assigned to me, who touches my arm with scarlet claws. I am terrified a claw will catch in my new scarf, will pull out a green thread; it will all unravel, and when the last thread runs out, I shall die.

I ask them if there is time for me to vomit, and they all cry har-har-har, and I am bustled out and into a steel lift, and we drop to music, perhaps they wish me to go mad, it would make things easier for them.

They put me into a blue car, the publisher in the front, and I in the rear between the government inspector and the woman who wants to destroy my scarf, and we drive very fast through black streets. I try to scream but my throat is dry. All the time they are asking me about my flight, it is clearly very important, I must have done something wrong on my flight, but what could it have been? I sat in the lavatory holding my scarf all the way from Prague to London, I did not cough on anyone, I kept my passport in my mouth so that anyone breaking down the door would be able to see it and not take me away to kick me for losing my papers, my conduct was exemplary. I did not squeeze my spots.

The car stops at last, beside a cold canal. They are going to drown me like a dog in a sack for something I did on the flight. No, they are taking me into a building. It has giant eggs all round its roof. What is this place? Are they going to feed me to giant chickens?

They hurry me down corridors. My scarf is flying out behind me, it could catch in something, my neck could snap like a wishbone. Suddenly I am in a room filled with lights and cameras, they push me into a chair, they put a microphone around my neck, I am to be interrogated! The interrogators are a girl with a big mouth and a slit skirt, I cannot take my eyes off her leg, *I must take my eyes off her leg*, they will beat me, and a terrible man with a yellow face and tiny eyes who keeps touching my knee, who keeps saying *Hallo, good morning, and welcome, Hallo, good morning, and welcome*, over and over, perhaps he is not a man at all, perhaps he is a robot, he will crush my knee with his steel hand. I wish to vomit.

The robot speaks: 'Hallo, good morning, and welcome to this hour of *Good Morning Britain*, with us now we are very very privileged to have my very very good friend Mr Franz Kafka who is a Czech, and if there's one thing we're always glad to see at TV-am it's a cheque, hner-hner-hner, hallo, good morning and welcome, Franz, tell me . . .'

I cannot hear his words any more, I am staring at the thing in his hand, it is a clip-board, he has information about me, it is something I did on the flight, it is something I did in the car, the girl is showing more leg, I have to get up, I get up, but my microphone wire holds my neck down, they are pushing me back into the chair, when will they start hitting me? The robot is still speaking '. . . a little excited, and why not, tell me, Franz, are there wedding bells in the offing, are you, hner-hner-hner, leaning on a lamp-post at the corner of the street until a certain little lady . . .'

I faint. When I come round, I am in the car again, we are speeding through wet streets, the government inspector is saying it went well, the girl is saying it was terrific, really terrific, no, really and truly it was terrific, it was a wonderful idea to start screaming and fall over, that is exactly the kind of break a book like this needs, he made a really terrific impact, especially with his eyes sticking out and his cheeks hollow, a lot of old ladies will rush out and buy the book, good, good, good, says the publisher, where is the first signing?

What are they talking about?

They take me to a big store, it is full of books, many of them forbidden by the authorities, they put me in front of the books and my books are among the forbidden books, and men begin taking photographs of me, I am being set up, I am being compromised, I begin screaming again, but all that happens is that the girl says it is terrific, it is really terrific, screaming is now my trade mark, they can do big things with that in the gossip columns. Then a man I do not know pushes something in front of me and gives me a pen and asks me to sign! I refuse to incriminate myself, I break his pen, the man grabs my scarf, books fall, I am being pulled round the shop, everybody is shouting, police are called, I fall on my knees and beg them to beat me about the head, the girl shouts that this is *really* terrific and makes them take more photographs, I pass out.

When I wake up, I am staring at soup. I am at a long table, up on a platform, in some kind of banqueting room, there are a thousand women in big hats at a hundred round tables on the floor below the dais, they are all eating soup but not taking their eyes off me, is this a dream, what is the significance of soup in a dream? I cannot stop trembling. Someone has taken my scarf. I look around wildly for my scarf, I see a sign that says *Welcome to Foyle's Literary Lunch*, what does this signify, are these women going to eat my book, are these women going to eat me? I pinch myself, accidentally jogging a huge man on my left, he tells me he is an actor, he has written a book which is propped up in front of him, it is called MY BIG BOOK. It has the huge actor's face on the cover. The man on my right then introduces himself. He is the huge actor's son; he is just as huge as the huge actor and he has written an even bigger book. It is called MY BIG FATHER. It has a photograph of the huge actor's huge son on the back. Suddenly, a chicken bone from the soup sticks in my throat. The huge actor is telling a story about his huge son and cannot hear me choking. The huge actor's huge son is telling a story about his huge father and cannot hear me choking, either. I fall forward into the soup, and it is only when the huge actor's huge son leans heavily across me to ask his huge father which of them is going to use the one about their huge cousin in their after-dinner speech that his weight projects the chicken bone from my throat.

After lunch, they both tell the story about their huge cousin. A thousand women laugh and cheer. Then suddenly everyone is looking at me. There is a long silence. At last, the government inspector runs across, and pulls me onto my feet. Clearly, they want me to confess something. I refuse. From the floor, a voice shouts at me to say something.

I tell them that I have a bad chest, that I have an infection of the pleural cavity, that the State has stolen my scarf so that my lungs will be full of phlegm. I show them my handkerchief. There is uproar, women shriek, tables are knocked over, the government inspector and the girl grab me and drag me off the platform, my feet are off the ground. Suddenly, I am outside, I am in the car again, the government inspector is saying 'wasn't that just a teensy-weensy bit over the top?' and the girl is saying 'no, no, no, it was really terrifically impactive, it had a really amazing upfrontalism, it . . .' I put my head out of the window, I vomit.

I am in a cellar, it is some kind of broadcasting studio, it is clearly subversive, all the people have beards and sandals and vests with filthy words on, this is not a government broadcasting studio at all, I have been put here to incriminate myself, my head is swimming, a short woman with huge breasts across which runs the legend LBC WOMEN AGAINST RAPE drags me into a tiny plasterboard cavity and puts headphones on my head, they are going to bombard me with some form of sonar lobotomizing, but no, a voice is coming through the headphones, a man is saying 'hallo, Frank is it, this is Brian, a long-time listener but a first-time caller, I have not read this book of yours but what I want to know is what are you doing over here, you black bastard, why don't you get back to Praguolia or wherever it is, why don't you climb back up your bleeding tree . . . ?'

I curl up into a ball. They are winning: they have my scarf, soon they will have my sanity, my soul. I am carried out to the car again, this time nobody is smiling, something terrible has happened. I fall to my knees beside the back seat and beg to know what is wrong. They tell me that I shall not be doing wogan. The girl is weeping. What is wogan? They do not tell me, but I discover that it is something Fyodor Dostoyevsky has done. He has been brought here because of his new book *Crime and Punishment* and, during his interrogation, he was, apparently, asked if he would like to sing with the band. At this, he took out his axe and embedded it in the head of his interrogator. Obviously, wogan must be a form of murder.

Tax Britannica

*Archaeologists have unearthed what they believe to be the
first Roman tax collecting depot to be found in Britain, at
Claydon Pike in the Upper Thames Valley. The depot was built
around 70 AD, and probably remained in use until the Romans
finally left Britain in 408.*

Observer

GLUTINUS SINUS, Tax Inspector 126 (Upper Thames Valley
Collection), drew the parchment-piled in-tray towards him,
removed the curling stack, carefully and neatly squared it off,
pared a stylus with the small dagger issued for that exclusive
purpose by Inland Revenue Stores (Silchester), straightened his
little skirt, and nodded.

'Send him in,' he said.

Miscellaneous Onus, his clerk, scuttled sniffing to the
fruitwood door, and opened it. An odour of goat and feet and
orifice wafted horribly in; through the gap, Glutinus Sinus
caught a brief collage of mud-caked beards and hovering flies
and khaki teeth, heard, as always, the distinctive colonial under-
current of scratching, spasmodically punctuated by the plop of
targeting spittle. The inspector shuddered. He had been out here
too long. They all had.

'Mr Cooper!' called Miscellaneous Onus, into the miasma.

A squat and patchily hirsute figure detached itself from a
cackling group who had been engaged in a curious contest from
which the clerk had been forced to avert his eyes, adjusted his
mangy wolfskin, and loped into the tax inspector's office.

'Shut the door,' said Glutinus Sinus.

'The what?' said the Briton.

Glutinus Sinus set his jaw, and pointed.

'Oh,' said Mr Cooper, 'it's even got its own name, has it? I thought it was just a bit of wall that came open, bloody clever, you Romans, I will say that for you. Door,' he murmured, shutting it with somewhat melodramatic respect, 'door, door, door, well I never!'

Glutinus Sinus sighed.

'Don't butter me up, Mr Cooper,' he said.

'Me?' cried Cooper. '*Me?*'

'Please sit down.'

'I built a room, once, up my place,' said the Briton, dropping to his haunches, 'only we had to climb over the walls to get in and out.'

'Mr Cooper, about your tax-return for the current –'

'We had not cracked the secret of the door,' said Cooper. 'It was beyond our wossname. It must be wonderful, civilization.'

'Mr Cooper, you are a maker of casks and barrels?'

'Correct. Definitely.'

'And yet,' here Glutinus Sinus rifled through the pile of parchment, selected one, flourished it, 'you have entered a large deduction against last year's income for the purchase of new industrial plant, to wit millstones, four, nether and upper. Can you explain this?'

'I have branched out,' said Cooper. 'I do a bit of grinding on the side. Mind you, don't we all, ha-ha, catch my drift, all men of the world, narmean?'

'Branched out?' said the tax inspector, icily.

'Bit slack these days, coopering,' replied the Briton, 'due to introduction of the glass bottle and carboy. Do not get me wrong, I am not saying glass is not dead clever, probably miraculous even, it is what comes of having a god for everything, the Roman god of glass has come up with a real winner, I am not denying that for a minute. All I am saying is, it has knocked the bottom out of the cask business, having a container what does not leak on your foot when you are carrying it out over the bedroom wall of a morning. I have therefore diversified into flour.'

'Then you ought to be called Miller,' interrupted

Miscellaneous Onus irritably. 'All this is cocking up the ledgers.'

'How about Cooper-Miller?' enquired the Briton. 'Due to following two professions? It's got a bit of tone, that, my old woman'd fancy being Mrs Cooper-Miller, she would be invited to open the Upper Thames Valley Jumble Fight, she would be asked to judge the Humorous Bum Contest, it could put us right at the top of the social tree.' He smiled oleaginously. 'We could be almost Roman. Uglier, mind.'

'So,' said Glutinus Sinus, 'you are engaged in the manufacture of flour for profit? Why, then, have you made no relevant return for –'

'Who said anything about profit?' replied Cooper. 'Cooper Flour plc is a registered charity, due to where it is distributed to the needy, gratis. It is a good word, *gratis*, we are all very pleased with it, what a spot-on language Latin is, got a word for everything.'

Glutinus Sinus put his fingertips together.

'True,' he murmured. '*Gratis*, however, does not translate as receiving chickens in return for flour.'

'Ah,' said Cooper. 'You heard about that, then?'

'Mr Fletcher entered them as outgoings,' said the tax inspector levelly.

'Yes,' said Mr Cooper bitterly, 'he would. You got to watch him, squire. The plain fact is, them chickens are definitely not income. We do not eat them. They are pets. You cannot count a household pet as income.'

'How many have you got?' enquired Miscellaneous Onus, licking his nib.

'I don't know,' replied Cooper, 'I can't count higher than XLVI. I have not had everyone's educational advantages, have I?'

'With all those chickens,' said the tax inspector, 'you must be getting hundreds of eggs a week. Surely you eat those?'

The Briton narrowed his already imperceptible brows.

'Eggs?' he repeated. 'What are eggs?'

Glutinus Sinus stared at him for a while. The Briton stared innocently back. Eventually, Glutinus Sinus snatched up his stylus, and drew an egg on the back of a tax-form.

176

'Oh,' said Cooper, nodding, 'chickens' doings.'

'No, no, no!' cried Miscellaneous Onus. 'They're delicious! You fry them!'

'Get off!' exclaimed the Briton. 'Pull this one. I've seen 'em coming out.'

'In that case,' snapped Miscellaneous Onus triumphantly, 'how is it that Mr The Other Cooper is buying them at eighteen denarii a dozen?'

'Search me,' replied the Briton. 'He is probably putting them on his roses.'

Miscellaneous Onus sprang from his stool waving a document.

'This invoice carries your address!' he shrieked. 'How do you explain that?'

The Briton squinted at it.

'That's not me,' he said. 'You will notice it is signed Mickey Mus. Come to think of it, I've noticed our yard looks remarkably neat of a morning. Clearly this bloke is nipping in at night, nicking our chickens' doings, and flogging them on the side. What a liberty! Imagine anyone stooping low enough to steal droppings. Mind you, you'd have to, wouldn't you, ha-ha-ha, sorry, just my little joke, where would we be without a laugh now and then, that's what I always say.'

Glutinus Sinus grabbed the paper from his aide, and threw it in a wastebin.

'All right,' he cried, 'but how,' and here he plunged a trembling hand into the sheaf, 'do you explain *this*? It happens to be your list of deductible expenses for the year ending April 5, 408, in which you have not only put down the cost of enough protective clothing to dress an entire legion, but also some score of expensive items described as "professional gifts, disbursements, tips, considerations, etcetera" which I cannot but –'

'What a marvellous word, *etcetera*,' murmured Mr Cooper, rolling his eyes and shaking his head, 'nearly as good as *gratis*, I do not know how you lot keep on coming up with 'em, no wonder your beneficient and gracious authority stretches from –'

'– take to be the most gross and transparent attempt to evade your dues, not only all this, I say, but also an enormous sum attributed to, where is it, here we are, "the entertainment of foreign buyers". Mr Cooper, do you really expect me to –'

'It is clear,' said the Briton, holding up one massive hairy hand, 'that you have never been up the sharp end when it comes to coopering and/or milling. On the one hand snagging your professional habiliments on splinters, nails, sharp reeds and I do not know what else, on the other coming home of an evening absolutely *covered* and looking like sunnink ritual cut out of a chalk bleeding hillside, you cannot wash self-raising out of a wolf pelt, sunshine, it turns to paste, try drying it by the fire and what you end up with is a flea-infested giant loaf.'

Glutinus Sinus's favourite stylus snapped between his fingers.

'Very well, but what is this entry: "VII formal III-piece gents' goatskin suits"?'

'Nor,' continued Mr Cooper, not pausing for breath, 'can you turn up with your casks at a smart brewer's premises with your backside hanging out. I am, after all, a director of the company. Similarly, going about the countryside upon my unpaid charitable works and doling out flour left, right and centre, I cannot look needier than the bleeding needy, can I?'

Glutinus Sinus licked dry lips, and glanced at Miscellaneous Onus.

'These professional gifts,' whispered the aide hoarsely, 'who exactly is receiving them?'

'You name it,' replied Cooper. 'It is dog eat dog in the barrel game. You got to grease palms, especially with foreign customers.'

'Aha!' cried Glutinus Sinus. 'At last we approach the nub, Mr Cooper, or would you prefer I called you Mr Mus? Just exactly who are these foreign customers of yours to whom you are so generous with bribes and entertainment?'

The Briton smiled.

'As a matter of fact,' he said, 'he is a Roman gentleman, one of my most esteemed business associates, a person of great probity and standing. I am sure you would be the first to appreciate that you cannot fob off such a man with a couple of bags of stone-ground wholemeal to stick under his toga and a ferret kebab up the takeaway.' Cooper picked a dead wasp from his beard, carefully. 'He is my accountant, Dubious Abacus. I understand he is a big gun. If you care to re-examine my files, I think you will discover that he has authorized my tax-returns personally. I do not know how he finds the time, what with constantly running back to Rome to do the Emperor's books.'

After a long silence, Glutinus Sinus said:

'We would appear to owe you a not inconsiderable refund, Mr Cooper-Miller.'

The Briton rose slowly from his haunches.

'I'll see the bloke on my way out,' he said.

After the door had closed, Glutinus Sinus stared at it for a long time.

'What year is it, Miscellaneous Onus?' he said.

'408, Glutinus Sinus.'

The tax inspector sighed.

'Get our suitcases down,' he said.

To a Degree

The Further Education Unit has urged universities to admit self-taught mature students, in a report which states that there is not one college that will admit people with no formal quali-fications. Mr Norman Evans, author of the report, has accused those responsible for student admissions of being unaware of 'what adults learn these days without being taught. People learn from friends, radio, television and the press.'

Daily Telegraph

I'M GLAD you asked me this question about *Othello*, number three if you haven't got the examination paper by you, I know what it is like being a professor we are both men of the world, narmean, I saw that thing on television with that, God what was his name, I don't think he did anything afterwards, he was good in that, though, I'm going back, what, could be four, five years, thin little bugger with one of them Viva Chapati moustaches and a striped vest, anyway he was a professor and most of his time was spent in, not to put too fine a point on it, a leg-across situation, it did not look like he got a lot of lecturing etcetera done of a morning, he was never off the nest, so I know how easy it must be to lose examination papers, also screwed up by people lying on them, I trust I do not have to draw pictures!

You can hardly blame him, women these days, I saw in, the *Sun* was it, that only 3% of women over sixteen south of possibly Bolton, could be Bradford, were virgins, it did not specify nuns or similar included, I suppose it would be tricky asking a nun, but they probably keep a register up the Vatican if you really wanted to get to the bottom of it, where was I, oh yes, women these days, it is not surprising dons are getting it by the shovelful, I had a girl in the cab the other day, flagged me down outside Imperial College, two in the morning, I don't stop for everybody then, of course, you would not catch me going through e.g. Brixton with the light on, or Kilburn, they can be just as bad, get four Irishmen in the cab, middle of the night, you wouldn't believe the damage they can do, have you any idea what a cab costs these days, fourteen grand without the word of a lie, this is due to where Mann Overton, their name is, have a monopoly, they can charge what they bloody like, look at it, it's a tin box, is what it is, you could buy a Mercedes 280 for fourteen grand, not that I'd touch a German car, still sometimes you can't help wondering who won the war, have you ever thought about that? God, what was I, oh I know, yes, so this girl, this student, she's in the cab and I'm looking in the mirror, aren't I, and she's got this white sort of a trenchcoat effort on, did you see *Casablanca*, well, like that except no trilby, and I'm driving along and we're chatting about this and that the way two students will, I was telling her, as I remember, about these statistics I heard on the radio, this bloke phoned in to Brian Hayes and it was all about should we sell Russian grain to the Americans on account of all the missiles everywhere etcetera and millions of people starving in, in, in some part of Africa, ended in -i as I recall, and suddenly we're at Sutherland Avenue, I remember all them flatlet houses when they were requisitioned by the Ministry of Food, God, powdered egg, will I ever forget! Anyway we stop at this house in Sutherland Avenue, and I say that'll be four pound sixty, and she says oh blimey, look at me, I have come out without my trousers, i.e. no money, and I turn round and stone me, she has not got a stitch on under the mac, and she says: 'Will this do?'

Know what I said?

Go on, have a guess.

I said: 'Have you got anything smaller?'

Ha, ha! Geddit? Well, bloody hell, Professor, you got to laugh these days, haven't you, or you would go raving mad, that is a well-known medical fact, there was this thing on BBC2, they had that one who's a qualified doctor *and* a comedian, it'll come to me in a bit, was he Monty Python, anyway, for argument's sake,

Doctor Python is talking to this foreigner and they are talking about stress, and the upshot was that you have just got to laugh. That was the top and bottom of it. There are these tribes somewhere, and they do not laugh, and they are all in the bin by the time they are thirty.

I think that that is Othello's problem, when you come right down to it, women throwing theirselves at him and him not having a sense of humour. If he had said to Desdemona, for example, have you got anything smaller, I am only putting that forward as a for instance, I am not comparing myself with Shakespeare, but just suppose, just *suppose*, that that was what he said instead of strangling her, they could have had a good old laugh about it.

It could be to do with where he is black.

I think Shakespeare put his finger on it there, I mean he made him black for a reason, right, it was not a question of tossing a coin, it was a decision not to make him e.g. Belgian, say, or one of your dagoes, he was definitely after a smudge. Could be an idea he picked up off a cab-driver, it is a well-known fact that Shakespeare got about a bit, and if you sat round the shelter of an evening you would find a lot of experts ready to back him up. It is not a question of prejudice, it is a question of coming over here and not having a sense of humour. I'm not saying they all strangle their wives, just some of them, they have different values, life is cheap in the paddy fields, ask anybody, and it is not a matter of who is right and who is wrong, it is just that when an Englishman suspects his old lady of having a bit on the side, he will take it in good part, he will just knock her about a bit and go down the pub. Your black is not quite so civilized, in the literal meaning of the word, i.e. from the Greek for out-of-the-trees, as I understand, so it is not for us to blame the poor bastards, it is for us to keep them off our patch; take Mr and Mrs Othello's kids, they would have been neither one thing nor the other, I saw this *World In Action* where they have a terrible time, personally I blame Desdemona's father, when Othello come round he should have told him to sod off.

Basically, where Question Three goes wrong is in putting it as: *What is the tragic flaw in Othello?* It is not *down* to him, he cannot help himself fancying a white woman, it is in their blood, they do not think of nothing else, it is a well-known fact; if you are looking for tragic flaws it is down to the rest of them for not putting him straight right at the off. I realise, of course, that a line like, e.g., 'Right, Othello, on your bleeding bike!' in the middle of Act One might alter the wossname, structure, a bit, but you could always beef up Iago's part, he could step in and then you would have a play about him and Desdemona, I don't know, running a pub or going into the oil business or deciding to grow all their own food in the back garden or something, it could be a series, there is no chance of a series if you strangle the bloody heroine at the end of the first episode, am I wrong?

Part of the trouble was making him a general, of course, instead of a bus conductor.

There is another flaw in the play, I don't know how tragic you'd call it but it certainly sticks out like a sore thumb, a number of people I was discussing it with up the betting-shop noticed it straight away, it is that nobody in it smokes. There are, what, twenty characters in it, give or take, and none of them ever lights up or offers a packet round, it is definitely a flaw. According to statistics, six adults in every twenty are regular smokers, and there they all are, talking away for hour after bloody hour, and nobody fancies a drag. As you know, I have been to a number of lectures on Elizabethan drama, and there's a lot of rubbish about sources and figures of speech etcetera, and in my view that is one of the troubles with universities, not seeing the wood for the trees. It takes people from outside to notice, and while we're on the subject, has it struck you that nobody in *any* of Shakespeare's plays, never mind *Othello*, goes out for a widdle?

Strange, but true.

Funny thing, and I'll go on to Question Four in a minute, don't worry, I've got a lot to say about Milton and his silly bloody ideas about people, it's easy to see Milton was never in the army, I'll come back to that, but I'd just like to point out this funny thing, if you'll bear with me, I had this bloke in the cab the other day, tall man in one of them long overcoats with the fur collar for catching the scurf in, a senior executive of some kind I suppose you'd describe him as, and I thought to myself: your face is familiar I thought, I've seen that face somewhere before, well, you have to have a good memory in this business, Professor, you would not believe what people leave behind in taxis, shoved down the seat or even, pardon my French, under the . . .

The New Extremely English Bible

From Genesis 3 et seq.

9 And the LORD God called unto Adam, and said unto him, Where *art* thou?

10 And he said, I heard thy voice in the garden, and I was afraid, and I hid myself *amongst* the trees of the garden, because I *was* naked; and I was in fear lest thou shouldst ask of me whether I had *eaten* of the tree of knowledge.

11 And the LORD God spake unto him, saying: never mind eating of the tree of knowledge, thou hast walked on the grass of knowledge, for a start.

12 And the man said, I thought it was all right to walk upon the grass of knowledge, I did not know that that was any big deal.

13 Whereat the LORD God *waxed* exceeding wrath, crying: There are signs up everywhere. As to thy *being* naked, thou art not naked at all, the LORD thy God hath eyes in his head, thou and the woman *that* I made for thee have picked leaves to be a covering, what dost thou think thou art playing at, picking things, it will be the daffs next.

14 And the man replied in thus wise, saying, The woman

185

whom thou gavest *to be* with me, she hath done this. I was happy in my nakedness, it was not draughty, but the woman insisted, and I plucked of the tree two leaves, contrary to *subsection* eight of the by-laws, para fourteen.

15 And the LORD God said unto the woman, What *is* this *that* thou hast done? And the woman said, The serpent beguiled me, saying it would be fashionable, a smart leaf.

16 And the LORD God grew great in his anger, crying, It will be riding bloody bicycles on the footpath next, It will be failing to put sweet wrappers in the receptacles provided; and he turned then to the man, saying, Hast thou a licence for this snake?

17 And the man fell upon his knees in *that* place, shouting: licence, what licence, it is not a dog, it hath no legs, it doth not bark, wherefore is it *that* I should have a licence?

18 But the LORD God would not be assuaged, saying, I know it is not a dog, I the LORD thy God made it, it is not an elephant or a plaice, either, do not get clever with me, the fact is *that* it is a dangerous animal within the meaning of the Act, they can kill you, snakes, I speak as one that knoweth, and as such they require a licence obtainable at any post office that I have made.

19 And the man hung *his* head, saying, I did not realise.

20 But the LORD God exculpated him not, saying, Ignorance of the law is no excuse, *it is* not even on a lead, it could foul the footpath, they are no joke, snake droppings. This is the garden of Eden, not an adventure playground.

21 Therefore the LORD God sent them forth from the garden; and he placed at the east of the garden of Eden Cherubims, in caps and arm-bands, and a flaming sign-board *with* all the by-laws writ large upon it, to keep the way of the tree of life.

4 And Adam knew Eve his wife; and she conceived, and bare Cain, and said, I have gotten a man from the LORD.

2 Whereat the LORD God spake unto them, saying, I trust *that* thou hast registered this child, also that thou hast registered him once only, I do not want any maternity grant fiddles, I do not want him coming back *unto* me when he is unemployed claiming two

lots of social security, I give thee fair warning. That could well be a matter for thunderbolts.

3 And she again bare his brother Abel. And Abel was a keeper of sheep, but Cain was a tiller of the ground. And in the process of time it came to pass *that* Cain brought of the fruit of the ground an offering unto the LORD.

4 But the LORD God was greatly displeased in that place where he was, saying, Call that a tomato? It is more like a red pea, hast thou no thought for the Weights & Measures Act *that* I have made, dost thou turn thy back on my Office of Fair Trading, what is it that thou art trying to put over on the unfortunate public?

5 And Cain replied in thus wise, saying, Public, what public, there is only we and thou in this place where we are, thou hast not built a public yet, unfortunate or otherwise.

6 And the LORD God gathered up the clouds and spake to him in thunder, crying, Do not take that tone with me, I am the LORD thy legally constituted local authority, a thing is not a tomato unless I say it is a tomato.

7 And Cain went away in anger from that place, saying, It tasted all right, what difference doth it make if it is a bit undersized, how can you make a living in this business if you do not bend the rules a bit. And lo, he came upon his brother Abel in a field, and Abel had *with* him where he was a sheep that had found favour with the LORD in that it had complied with all regulations concerning weight, quality, vaccination, smell, and all the rest, and Abel said unto his brother Cain, How didst thou get on with that titchy little tomato?

8 And Cain rose up against Abel his brother, and slew him.

9 And the LORD said unto Cain, Where *is* Abel thy brother? And he said, I know not: *Am* I my brother's keeper?

10 And the LORD replied in thus wise, saying, thou art his next-of-kin and it is therefore thy legal obligation to report his demise to the Authorities, especially in view of the fact that it is thou that hath demised him.

11 And Cain said, He got up my nose.

12 And the LORD God replied, saying, That is no

excuse for failing to report his death. Coming on *top of* thy dreadful infringement of the tomato regulations, this is too much. And the LORD set a mark upon Cain, reminding him of the severe penalties involved should he receive two further marks in a period of three years, *under* the totting-up procedures.

13 And Cain went out from the presence of the LORD, and dwelt in the land of Nod, on the east of Eden.

14 And Cain knew his wife; and she conceived, *and* bare Enoch: and he builded a city, and called the name of the city, after the name of his son, Enoch.

15 And the LORD God waxed furious, crying, didst thou get planning permission for a city? Look at it, it hath no proper drains, it hath high-rise blocks stuck up all over *the* place, it doth not have a decent road from one end to the other, it is an eyesore and an affront.

16 And Cain answered the LORD in some heat, shouting, This is not Green Belt, this is bloody Nod, it is thou *that* stuckest me here in this place where I am to be a developer on account of not being allowed to *follow* chosen

profession, to wit, tiller of ground, how am I to earn an honest bob, all right, fairly honest?

17 But the LORD God would not countenance his appeal, and knocked the city down, that it be a lesson and a guide to all men.

18 And Enoch, the son not the city, *begat* Irad; and Irad begat Mehujael; and Mehujael begat Methusael; and Methusael begat Lamech.

19 And Lamech took *unto* him two wives: the name of the one *was* Adah, and the name of the other Zillah.

20 And the LORD God waxed really spare this time, what with the multiplicity of spouses and the serious begetting explosion, for the infringements were beyond number, and the LORD God *was* up to here with paperwork. And of the myriad thousands that now *teemed* upon the Earth, the vast majority did not make full and complete tax returns, nor did they come home from work without paper-clips and rubbers that they had taken, saying, Who is it that will notice? Also, they lived together in council accommodation when they *were* not

legally married, and they did not observe the yellow lines that the LORD their God had laid down for them, nay, not even the *double* yellow lines; and they smoked in those places where there were signs clearly exhorting them not so to do, and built on room-extensions in cedar wood and in laburnum wood and in sandalwood without informing the Rating Authority; and they sang in those places which did not have a licence for singing.

5 And God saw that the wickedness of man *was* great in the earth, and *that* every imagination of the thoughts of his heart *was* only evil, continually.

2 And the LORD said, I will destroy man whom I have created from the face of the Earth; for it *repenteth* me that I have made them, they cannot be left for a minute, I am losing a thousand gas-meters a day, never mind forged Cup Final tickets.

3 But Noah found grace in the eyes of the LORD.

4 And GOD said unto Noah, The end of all flesh is come before me; and behold, I *will* destroy them with the earth. Make thee an ark of gopher wood. And this *is the fashion* which thou shalt make it *of*: The length of the ark *shall be* three hundred cubits, and the height of it thirty cubits.

5 Thus Noah and his sons fashioned them an ark; and it was done.

6 But when the LORD God looked upon it where it was, he waxed practically out of his mind, crying, Is that the gopher wood that I commanded thee?

7 And Noah answered in this wise, saying, Not exactly, it is more your actual chipboard, I was very lucky, it fell off the back of a cart, also no VAT, nudge-nudge, catch my drift?

8 And GOD caught his drift, saying, Nor is it the three hundred cubits *in* length, that I bespoke unto thee.

9 And Noah replied unto him, saying, Right, right, there are no flies *on* thee, O LORD, it is about, what, two hundred cubits, give *or* take, it was a pretty small cart if thou knowest what I mean, it looks like bad news for the dinosaurs and the unicorns, one way and another.

10 And the LORD God retreated into the cloud, and wept. And the tears became rain.

Lif' Dat Bail

The assumption that cricket was an English invention, let alone a white man's one, is utterly erroneous. A form of cricket had been played in Africa for centuries before the European came, and it was from Africa that the game we know today was exported all over the world.

Drum Magazine

THE VERY word *cricket* is, of course, itself of orig. uncert., of etym. dub: the best bet is Swahili, the likeliest connotation sexual, perhaps to describe an organ, perhaps the act of deploying that organ, who can be sure? Possibly a small noise made during. Certainly, the other semantic arcana have their seedy origins in unsavoury sexual puns: *gully, short leg, long stop, over,* for example, may still be found in virtually pristine use along the Lourenço Marques waterfront – 'You want gully-gully, mister? You want short leg-over, very clean, you want nice long stop?' – and the fact that *googly* and *Chinaman* are synonymous comes as no surprise to the experienced stoker, for whom, in a lonely port, they unfortunately amount to the same thing.

No fixed date, obviously, can be established for the beginning of the modern game, but most experts agree that it had its origins on slave plantations, where cotton and sugar workers, to relieve their wretched lot, would get up crude matches using a cotton-boll and a whippy length of sugar-cane, the boll being *bolled* at three pieces of implanted bamboo in an attempt to *knock down de wicked,* since the game was also deeply steeped in the fundamental religious beliefs held by the unfortunate slaves. The simple homiletic message of the early game is, of course, clear, and those origins retain their echo today in the name of the spiritual home of cricket, Lawd's.

Gradually, after the American Civil War, the game grew more refined. The slaves, naturally not able to afford the sophisticated equipment in use today, improvised with whatever they found lying around the battlefields of the defeated South: the small cannonball, for example, introduced the hard missile to the game, the musket-stock replaced the sugar-cane and ushered in the characteristic bat-shape, and very soon, teams of freed slaves were touring Dixieland and playing improvised games against local sides to the delight of dancing, drunken, finger-snapping crowds, whose modern counterparts may be observed today, from the Lawd's Tavern to the Hill at Sydney.

It was probably at around this period that the name stuck. There is no contemporary record of exactly when and how this happened, but the romanticization of the incident in the film *The Birth of the Blues* (the story of the first Oxford vs. Cambridge Match) is probably fairly close to the truth. In that, you may recall, the young English undergraduate (C. Aubrey Smith), while on a visit to South Carolina, notices a group of slaves playing in the grounds of his host's ante-bellum mansion, and calls one of the *bollers* over to him with the words:

'I say, boy, what do you call that stuff?'

To which the young black (Stepin Fetchit) replies:

'Why, boss, we calls it cricket!'

Within a very few years and with the increasing mobility of the newly-freed negro, cricket moved off the plantations and into the towns around the Delta. Hardly surprisingly, it was not yet received into the best circles of society, so that many young cricketers learned their trade playing in the brothel districts, like Storyville. The madames found that waiting clients would drink more if they had a cricket match to watch, and for the unemployed young negroes, this was a Godsend. This is from an interview with the distinguished old batsman Jelly Roll Hammond, recorded by Alan Lomax:

'Ah fust started messin' wid a bat when ah wuz in de Gravier

Street Orphanage. Cricket wuz a way of keepin' us kids off de street. Ah din have no formal trainin', an' even to dis day ah still cain't read a scorecard, but that din make no never-mind, ah jes' picked up dat ole bat an' ah impervised. Pretty dam' soon ah foun' ah could handle tricky stuff like de short risin' ball outside de off-stump etcetera, an' one day after ah hit 134 befoh lunch agin de Big Eye Louis Sutcliffe Hot Seven, dis high yaller butter-an'-egg man come up to me an' he say "Ah like de way y'all play dat stuff, kid, how's about y'all come to work on mah groun' staff?" Turnout he wuz just de top ponce east o' Memphis! Pretty soon, ah wuz playin' out back o' De Square Leg Cat House, Noo Orleans, ten dollars a match an' all de gully ah could git, heh-heh-heh!'

The reference to the Hot Seven is particularly interesting. In the early days, teams were very small: Satchmo G. Grace, for example, started off with only five – himself at cover, Kid Ponsford at deep fine leg, Blind Lemon Bosanquet at silly point, and Baby Hobbes behind the stumps. Bunk Larwood had to boll continuously from both ends. But he soon found that this basic ensemble was too restricted, and the team was implemented by two more players, the most important addition being a slow-tempo boller to relieve Larwood at the other end. After six bolls were bolled, Satchmo would cry: 'We'll take a break now, folks!' and Mezz Titmus would come on and send down his off-spinners from the other end. This traditional cry was soon replaced with 'Over!', partly because it was shorter, but mainly because the lewd overtones made the crowd fall about, particularly if it had been a maiden.

By the end of the Great War, white men had begun to take an interest in the new game: not only did cricket move up from the Delta towards Chicago (a fairly direct result of the Volstead Act and the enormous boost it gave to the drinking with which cricket spectators have always been associated), but the first travelling team was formed. The all-white Original Dixieland Test Eleven arrived to play in England in 1919, but the tour was a complete fiasco: the rudimentary English game was played according to very different rules, and the local variations in pitch and rhythm entirely defeated the ODT XI. They found the bunny hop and the turkey trot totally unplayable, and after three or four ill-attended matches they packed their bags and returned to Charleston.

In Chicago itself during these Prohibition years, black cricket still dominated the scene. It was the era of the giants, and consequently of the legends: of men like Wingy D'Oliviera, who had lost his right arm years before in a car crash, yet still became a great all-rounder, hitting a double century against the Mound City Jug Cricketers and, in the same match, taking 6 for 40 with his tricky one-arm-round-the-wicket leg-cutters; of men like Miff 'Sobers', whose nickname derived from his habit of getting through all-night net sessions on two gallons of moonshine and then being carried out to the middle on the following morning and hurling down his murderous bouncers at batsmen whom his captain had told him had signed the pledge. Sadly, his career came to an abrupt end when, in 1926, he killed both opening batsmen for the Temperance VII, and received a 10 to 30 stretch in Alcatraz on a Murder Two count. However, his brain was by this time so befuddled by alcohol that he went to his prison grave happy, still believing that his final figures had been 10 *for* 30.

And who amongst us who love the game will ever forget that other great nickname, Clarence 'Pine Top' Close? Perhaps the finest silly mid-off ever, certainly the dumbest, Close fielded so short that batsmen were terrified to hook, for fear of breaking their bats on his forehead. Of all the wonderful anecdotes about Close that have become enshrined in cricket's annals, perhaps the one nearest to the spirit of the man concerns the match against the Fletcher Hendren Big XI, played at the Metropole Oval in a thunderstorm in 1929. Just before tea, Close was struck by lightning, losing nine teeth, and immediately cried: 'howzat?', believing he must have caught the ball in his mouth.

And then there was Bix. Leon Bismarck 'Bix' Washbrook, star of the famous 1930 movie *King of Cricket*, hero of Dorothy Baker's fine book *Young Man With A Bat*, Bix was the first white cricketer of any stature, so poor that he often walked out to the wicket with his bat behind him to hide the holes in his flannels, yet so rich in the affection of crowds that as soon as each ball left the bowler's hand, the pavilion would rise as one man, and shout: 'Oh, play that thing!'

He died, at the height of his powers, in 1931; but for lovers of the man and the traditional game, this tragedy was lessened by the knowledge that cricket was now taking a road he would have hated. The Swing Era had begun, and with it the rise of the Big Teams. For vulgarization and commercialization had struck the great game; to attract vast crowds, ignorant crowds, managers were now including anything up to five or six swing bowlers in their huge sides, not to mention dozens of crude sloggers, simply to appeal to the lowest common crowd denominator. Finesse, subtlety, originality vanished; the improvising solo player was no more. The boring pattern of short-pitched balls and haymaking hooks ruled supreme: Artie Bradman's XXXV, for example, beat Benny Hutton's All Stars at Carnegie Bridge in July 1937 by 164 runs, all of them wides. As for Glenn Ramadhin and his endless, worthless search for innovation, it almost ruined the game altogether with its culmination in an ensemble of eight wicket-keepers, four seamers bowling in harmony, and sixty-two men in the offside trap.

It was left to the caring black man and, oddly, the old-fashioned English amateur, to drag cricket back from the brink and remind it of its roots and true genius. On the one hand, virtuoso players unconcerned with wealth and mass-appeal emerged (Coleman Bailey, Lester Lindwall, Thelonious Spofforth), and the small team reappeared (the Modern Cricket Quartet, the Zoot Laker Trio Plus Two); and on the other, in bumpy fields behind quiet English pubs, keen village sides started to come together under Humphrey Compton and Cy Dexter and Ottilie Martin-Jenkins to revive the traditional game. Crude they were, yes and unsophisticated, often pitifully derivative; and yet, travelling the country in broken-down Dormobiles and playing to enthusiastic kids for rent-money, it was cricketers of that brave kidney who kept the old game alive, and, indeed, still do.

As to its future, who can say? Cricket has come a long way from the African slave ships and the chain-gangs and the cotton plantations, and the roads have not always been smooth nor the conditions clement. Once more it is undergoing a somewhat fallow spell, and there are those Jeremiahs, as there have always been, who say that this time it may not recover. And yet, surely, as long as there are sassy kids about, the tough little Fats Bothams, the plucky young Meade Lux Gowers, prepared to grab a boll and an old piece of sugar-cane and an advertising director from a cigarette company, does any of us really believe that this great game will ever die?

Bleeding Hearts

Twentieth Century Love Letters. Edited with an introduction by Marina F. Ellsworth.
Strathclyde Free Press 492pp. £12.50

THUS FRANZ Kafka, writing on November 18, 1920, from Vienna:

'I love you. If you can find it within you to disregard the cold sore on my lip, my left eye which of late seems to have taken on a strange sliding motion all its own, and the peculiar acrid smell not unlike ill mice which I think we both now know has nothing to do with my herringbone overcoat, I should like to believe that you might come, eventually, to care for me, just a little. I ask no more than that. Your devoted Franz.'

An odd letter for a man to write to his hat-stand? Not according to Dr Ellsworth. As her penetrating introduction adumbrates, the poignant letters which follow tell us much about the emotional and sexual dislocations of this bizarre century when, in the choppy wake of Freud, the romantic imagination was not so much liberated from old modes and constraints as shackled to new ones. Kafka, for example, decided to take up with his hat-stand only after his waste-bin, in his view, had turned him down. A curt note to the latter, written just two days before the one quoted above says it all:

'Do you write? Do you phone? Do you acknowledge I even exist? I waited two hours outside Hofmeister's Laundry last Monday in freezing sleet, and you know what my chest is like. I thought we could maybe take in the new Harry Langdon at the Roxy, but did you show up? Goodbye.'

As Dr Ellsworth's annotation of this letter reminds us, it was not easy finding girls in Vienna if you were a Czech with a bad cough and no carpet. Let us not condemn Kafka too hastily.

Hemingway's, from a different culture and a different malaise, was another case altogether. All Hemingway's love letters were written to his taxidermist, Adolf Waters, though not directly:

'Dear Butch,' he wrote on 18 July 1928, 'are you ready to stuff the big tarpon yet? He was a good one, he was one of the best ones, I ran him eight hours and he threw every trick there is. It has been three weeks now, and I still wake nights, in that time when there are no clocks striking which is about the worst time there is, and I can still feel the big tarpon through my hands, pulling on the line. I would like to be there when you do the thing with the sawdust. It would mean a lot. Papa.'

Adolf Waters is an old man now, but when Marina Ellsworth went down to his retirement home in Fort Lauderdale, there was one point on which he was as clear as he was unshakeable. In the late spring of 1931, Ernest Hemingway went through a form of marriage with a moose's head. Adolf Waters has particular cause to remember this incident, since not only did he put the glass eyes in the bride, he was also the best man.

'We found an old drunk JP down in the South Carolina bayou, and he performed the ceremony for two bottles of Jack Daniels. Ernest and the head went off in Ernest's old Hupmobile to the Adirondacks. It was a short honeymoon, but I think they were the happiest four days of Ernest's life. While he was in Spain in '39, the head got moth. There was nothing I could do. Hemingway was never the same afterwards.'

The letters are not all literary, by any means. Dr Ellsworth has cast her net wide to set the century in amatory perspective. A curious little note, for example, from Henry Ford to Madame Louise Dunlap of Pontchartrain House, New Orleans, written early in 1909, speaks volumes for the contemporary mood of the energetic young country:

'My dream is for a popular good-looking woman at around thirty-five dollars, tops. She would be cheap to run, but built to last. Quality control is very important: a man who had one in Poughkeepsie should be able to walk in off the street in San Diego and get exactly the same item down there. And any colour, as long as she's black.'

Or this, quoted in its entirety on page 138. It is a letter written in Hitler's own hand, in early 1934, and was found among his posthumous detritus:

'I miss you. I need you. I want you.'

According to Bundesarchivist Klaus Bagel, the envelope bore the single word *Sudetenland*. There was no stamp, but a solid body of evidence to suggest it was delivered personally.

Not, I suppose, unsurprisingly, many of the English offerings betoken an altogether quieter, more restrained, more infibulated love, particularly when its expression emanates from that stratum of emotional gentility which is so peculiarly, in every sense, ours. Take this not atypical little Valentine, written *c.* 1931, from a young John Betjeman:

> *Each day in Croydon High Street*
> *I watch my darling pass,*
> *By catching in Boots window-pane*
> *Her image on the glass.*
>
> *She stops; I turn; I tremble!*
> *Shall I reach out my hand?*
> *Too late! She glides on, humming now,*
> *Past Meredith & Bland.*
>
> *Her poignant perfume lingers,*
> *Electric, on the air –*
> *O! Dare I catch her up in Penge*
> *And gently mount her there?*

As perhaps the only love letter ever written to a 28 tram, the item has a certain arcane charm, but do we not feel *nationally* let down, as it were, by the fey delicacy of the passion? Too often this is the temper of the English inclusions, and when it is not, then the alternative is hardly more engaging: a sort of gruff, grudging recognition of a relationship, as if the sender were embarrassed at the display of emotion incumbent upon him. As, for example, this farewell note interred with the remains at a small private ceremony by Evelyn Waugh (who, of course, kept a carbon of everything) so clearly displays:

'Goodbye. You were a bloody fine pair of brown boots, all in all.'

According to Dr Ellsworth's footnote, the loss of his boots was what triggered Waugh's conversion to Rome, but this, I'm afraid, is an uncharacteristic lapse into speculation by so punctilious a scholar, since I myself was told by the late Tom Driberg that Waugh's need for a framework in which to endure grief was in fact occasioned on that dreadful day in November 1925 when his best friend ran away with Waugh's first umbrella.

Oddly, Driberg himself has not been included in this collection, so his long and fascinating correspondence with Praed Street gents continues to remain in holograph until such time as some adventurous publisher is prepared to allow the wider world a glimpse into this remarkable relationship between man and porcelain.

One English relationship, however, which I for one could well have done without eavesdropping is the highly unsavoury one-way epistolary traffic from D. H. Lawrence to his *inamorato primo*. I certainly do not intend to dwell upon it in the pages of a family publication, and would not have mentioned the matter at all were it not necessary for a critic to correct an editor, since once again the eminent Dr Ellsworth nods. There *is* a precedent for someone sending pressed blooms to another part of his body; half a century before D. H. Lawrence enclosed forget-me-nots with his distasteful *billets doux*, a distraught Van Gogh was sending his ear sunflowers, albeit over a far greater distance and thus with rather more justification.

Let me turn, instead, to a much more charming and witty exchange. In 1922, a young English actor left this country for Hollywood; as Dr Ellsworth explains (Appendix XII), he was, like most former boarding prep-schoolboys, deeply in love with the contents of his nursery, his teddy, his rubber-sheet, his nanny's birch, and so forth. In consequence, he took these and other items with him to his new country, where they were never replaced in his affection, even by the succession of nubilia that later came to fill, albeit unsatisfactorily, his Californian bed.

199

Rumours – naturally enough in that wacky, wonderful town – abounded, so much so that a showbiz columnist commissioned to profile the star finally, in 1953, sent him the now legendary telegram: 'How old carry-cot?' and received the equally famous reply: 'Old carry-cot fine. How you?'

Twentieth Century Love Letters, then, is a volume as entertaining as it is informative, a labour – if you will forgive the pun – of love, as well as a work of impressively committed scholarship. If I have one cavil, it is that perennial complaint: no index. Readers, dear Dr Ellsworth, like to cross-refer: an entry under say, *wallet*, would enable us to compare and contrast the letters of J. Paul Getty and Terry Wogan, one under *chamber-pot* the innermost feelings of Benny Hill with the *cris-de-coeur* of Jean Genet and William Burroughs.

But this, as I say, is a minor objection. *Twentieth Century Love Letters* is a volume which no true book-lover with a sense of life's passionate priorities will want to be without: the weight, the feel, the subtle yet heady smell, the, oh God, the handsome binding for you to examine in your own home, the crisp crackle of the spine as you ease it open, the funny little way its delicate pages respond to the trembling finger, the hint, here and there, of . . .

Animal Crackers

The family pet, whether a dog or cat, gerbil or goldfish, could save your life, claims an animal expert.

Cambridge animal behaviourist Mr James Serpell says talking to pets can bring down high blood pressure and ease nervous tension.

Daily Express

Dear Doctor Coren:

I hope you will not mind my writing to you, I could not help noticing the cutting you have just stuck at the top of your page and I thought you might want to hear my story with a view to putting in your two penn'orth, we must all love one another or die, as W. H. Auden said, an old fairy, true, but he knocked about a bit, as they do, of course, and he knew what was what, e.g., it's a funny old world we live in, but the world's not entirely to blame, and so forth.

I did try contacting Mr James Serpell himself, but he kept putting the phone down, that is often the way it is with scientists, they say something, and you think to yourself, Hallo, that could be the answer, but when you open the paper the next day, no mention of it, it is just like *Tomorrow's World* on the telly, you see they have now come up with something, usually as the result of the space programme, that gets wine stains out of vests, only when you go round to Timothy White's or Robert Dyas they have never bloody heard of it, it is scientific irresponsibility of the worst kind, they just say the first thing that comes into their heads, scientists, and never mind the effect on the rest of us, look at that business with the black hole in the *Daily Mirror*, I gather it is eating galaxies left, right and centre, it could be here by Tuesday for all I know, but you ring up people and ask, e.g. Citizen's Advice Bureau, Brian Hayes, etc., and do they tell you anything, do they bloody hell.

What I want to know is, is there anything in this business of talking to animals to, what is it, ease nervous tension? I only ask because I am quite a jumpy person, I don't know if that is what is meant by nervous tension, I keep going down my GP to ask him, but I cannot get a straight answer, could it be because he is a blackie, well, you do hear things, only now he has taken me off his, do they still call it a panel, anyway whatever it is I am off it, and being jumpy I do like to chat a bit, also very interested in the world and things about me, not just black holes but also how pebble-dash sticks to the walls and do all the sewers in England connect up or is it just sort of, you know, town-by-town, but I find that these days, people don't have time to listen, do you find that, Doctor Coren, do you, do you?

So I talk to the cat, but as soon as I sit it in the chair and open my mouth, it jumps up and it is behind the fridge before you can wink, and what I want to know is, if I could get it put down, e.g. gassed or run over by the vet or whatever it is they do, on the grounds that it was a bad listener, how would I go about getting a *good* listener, is there a place to advertise, is there a Nervous Tension And Cats Advisory Service you can ring, is there a special breed that like sitting there and listening, e.g. not Persian or Burmese, anything I said would be all gobbledegook, it would be behind the fridge in a flash, am I right?

Anyway, I look forward to your reply, by the way how high is high blood pressure, I tried that one on the blackie as well, but he looked at me as if I was mad.

Yours sincerely,
Alison Fermold

Dear Doctor Coren:
I saw your name in the paper, and we are both men of the world, and since I have a small problem 'down there' which is preying on my mind a bit, I should like to know whether there is any point in telling my stick insect about it.

It is no fool, I have managed to get it to walk along a string, which is more than I could ever get my gyroscope to do, and it is able to disguise itself as several difficult things, e.g. a stick, a twig, a very thin log, but how can I be sure it is ready to cope with a somewhat tricky personal problem? I would feel a fool if I went into a long description and it went right over its head, and then again, there is the question of whether it would still respect me afterwards.

I really am at my wits' end, and I know my blood pressure is going up, there is this little vein in my temple which sort of lurches like a lugworm, and I have to talk to somebody. I have tried my stick insect on other subjects, such as the guttering coming away from the wall and the funny smell in my cap, and it looked quite interested, but this is a question of a different order.

Yours truly,
G. M. Denning

Dear Doctor Coren:
Can a cat keep its mouth shut?

I only ask because, as a person whose nervous tension is most frequently exacerbated by financial worries, I recently took the advice of your colleague Mr Serpell and confided in my cat, Derek, and, during the course of the conversation, inadvertently let slip my private account number at the Zurich Kreditanstalt. Derek did not register anything at the time, but that is often the way it is with cats, they are cunning little bastards.

In my opinion, the cat was acting professionally at the time and ought therefore to respect the normal ethics obtaining in a client-consultant relationship, in which case, if it chose to share this private information with other cats, I could presumably get it struck off whatever it is that cats are on. The thing is, how would I know?

Since, because of all this, my blood-pressure has gone even higher, would my best course be to confide in my dog, Dave, and hope that a nod would be as good as a wink, i.e. Dave would bite Derek's head off? In which case, should I rephrase the question, viz. Can a *dog* keep its mouth shut? I should not want to have to get Dave rubbed out, for one thing he is a big bugger and I would have to involve a lion, or something, for another he is pedigreed and stands in at around £250, and for a third, it is a bit academic whether a lion can keep its mouth shut or not since, apart from the practical difficulties involved, a respectable off-shore securities dealer who had a lion knee-capped could well find himself in dead trouble, that is just the kind of high-profile activity to get the Fraud Squad bastards reaching for their raincoats.

I do not know which way to turn. It is not easy, earning a living these days.

Yours faithfully,
Sir Eric Klutz

Dear Doctor Coren:

Does it matter whether a tortoise is in or out when you talk to it? Put another way, when it looks like a brick, do its ears still work?

I only ask because I recently discovered that my secretary was pregnant and, not knowing what action to take, I was a bit of a silly and put the problem to my tortoise.

I now realize it was shut at the time.

What I want to know is: did it hear anything?

I do not want to go through it all again, especially as I have now changed my mind about the matter, I think.

Yours truly,
(*Name and address supplied*)

From Grave to Gay, by Turns,
and Gay to Grave

*The world's first funeral home staffed entirely by homosexuals
and catering exclusively to the gay community has been opened
in San Francisco by gay undertaker Tommy Simpson.*

Guardian

HAMLET

Act V

*Scene I. A Churchyard. Enter two CLOWNS, with spades and
pickaxes.*

FIRST CLOWN   So anyway, I gave him one of my looks, and–

SECOND CLOWN   One of your withering looks?

FIRST CLOWN   One of my withering looks, and I said: *Where is
he?* And he said, in the car, and I said – I mean, I
was shocked –

SECOND CLOWN   You would be.

FIRST CLOWN   – and I said, *in the boot*? I said, you haven't got
your loved one in the *boot*, that is no way to treat
the dear departed, I said, all scrunched up like a
Waitrose turkey; apart from anything else, I said,
he'll have gone rigid by now, we shall have to roll
him into the shop, he'll get filthy, you do not, I
take it, want your loved one covered in fag-ends
and dog's doings, and if you think *I'm* carrying
him in, I said, with *my* back, you've got another

think coming, why didn't you leave us to pick him up, I said, I could've sent Adrian and Siegfried with a selection of bespoke woods and we could've boxed him up on the premises, we spent a fortune on that hearse, I told him.

SECOND CLOWN Good for you, Tristram. Some people!

FIRST CLOWN Some people, Burt, *exactly*! Anyway, that's only the beginning, you won't believe what happened next, no sooner had –

SECOND CLOWN Shall I put my spade down? You know me with my arms.

FIRST CLOWN Yes, do, I can see that funny little sinew beginning to jump, it's making a mockery of your tattoo, I told you you should never have had a lily there, a lily's got to be in a calm place, you ought to have had a dragon, a dragon can take movement, you don't want a lily hopping about, especially with your skin. Where was I?

SECOND CLOWN You were coming to what happened next.

FIRST CLOWN Yes, well, what happened next was he said, no, I have not got him in the boot, I have got him in the front passenger seat, he said, but don't worry, he's got a seat belt on so he is not resting his forehead on the dashboard, I have got a reputation to keep up in this town, he said, he has gone a bit grey but no one would clock him for a stiff.

SECOND CLOWN *No!* Were those his exact words, Tristram?

FIRST CLOWN They are embossed on my memory, Burt. *No one would clock him for a stiff!*

SECOND CLOWN You responded immediately, I take it?

FIRST CLOWN Like a tiger, dear. You know me when my dander is up.

SECOND CLOWN Frightening. Your whole mien changes, Tristram. Yours is not a dander to trifle with. Just talking about it has made your knuckles clench on your pick-handle, I can read H, A, L, L, O from right over here and I haven't even got my contacts in. So what did you say then?

FIRST CLOWN   I said *stiff*? Is that any way to talk about a loved one, I said, never mind strapping him in and bouncing him all over the place, do you realize how loved ones bruise after demise, I said, his botty will be like rotten plums.

SECOND CLOWN   You never!

FIRST CLOWN   Oh yes I did.

SECOND CLOWN   Did he break down? Did he sob?

FIRST CLOWN   Did he hell. He *laughed*.

SECOND CLOWN   I feel faint.

FIRST CLOWN   He laughed, Burt, and he said, *loved one*? he said, he's never a loved one, he's one off the boat, he said, I only met him last night, I think he's a Pole, possibly a Serb, he's got wooden dentures and psoriasis, I don't know about *your* taste, ducky, he said, but that is not my idea of a loved one, that is my idea of any port in a storm, nudge, nudge, catch my drift?

SECOND CLOWN   *Nudge, nudge, catch my drift?*

FIRST CLOWN   As I live and breathe.

SECOND CLOWN   I don't know what's happening to the gay community, Tristram, there used to be sensitivity, there used to be subtlety, there used to be *style*! All kinds of tat is coming out these days, where will it end?

FIRST CLOWN   I blame television. You wouldn't believe this one, he had a two-tone Escort with fluffy dice and a polystyrene Mannikin Pis with a diddly that lit up when he braked, he had a tattersall waistcoat with *all* the buttons done up and a bunch of keys sticking out of his top pocket, I very nearly told him to take his business elsewhere, there's such a thing as standards.

SECOND CLOWN   But your concern for the loved one prevailed?

FIRST CLOWN   You read me so well, Burt. Yes, you only had to look at our friend the tattersall waistcoat to realize that as far as the unfortunate loved one was concerned it was either a question of home is the

207

sailor, home from the sea, courtesy of Ganymede Chic Interments Limited, or winding up in a lay-by on the A30 between a clapped-out Standard Vanguard and a rat-infested mattress. So Quentin and I brought him in.

SECOND CLOWN   It couldn't have been easy.

FIRST CLOWN   You don't know the half of it, dear. He was sat there stiff as a brick, we had to carry him in a fireman's lift, and we were halfway across the forecourt when this big butch constable suddenly appeared from behind our dwarf poplar!

SECOND CLOWN   *No!*

FIRST CLOWN   I don't know what might've happened without Quentin. He has marvellous presence of mind, for an ex-vintner. You know that roguish smile he has?

SECOND CLOWN   So well.

FIRST CLOWN   He just stopped, and turned that roguish smile on Mister Plod, and he said: Allo, allo, allo, there's never one around when *I* want one! Mister Plod did not know *where* to look!

SECOND CLOWN   Didn't he say anything about the loved one?

FIRST CLOWN   Oh, he mumbled something of the order of *what is all this ere*, the way they do, but you could tell his heart wasn't in it, and when Quentin said: *This? This is a cast of Rodin's Stoker, it's going on the Chief Constable's tomb*, he was off on his big chunky boots like something from the Dock Green *corps de ballet.*

SECOND CLOWN   Lucky you, Tristram.

FIRST CLOWN   Oh, really? You wouldn't say that if you'd been there, Burt, our troubles were only just beginning, we got the loved one inside, we hammered him straight, and then our tattersall friend turns round and says: Right! Can you do him in chipboard?

SECOND CLOWN   I would have scratched his eyes out. You know me.

FIRST CLOWN   Yes, you're not what I'd call managerial. *I*

remained very calm.

SECOND CLOWN Another withering look?

FIRST CLOWN More sardonic, really. I gave him this sardonic look, and I said: Chipboard? *Chipboard?* This is Ganymede Chic Interments, I said, not bloody MFI! Why not cut your losses altogether, I said, Woolworth's do a very nice bin-liner for fifteen pee.

SECOND CLOWN That was telling him, Trist!

FIRST CLOWN So you might think, dear, so you might think, but just as I – hallo!

(Enter HAMLET and HORATIO.)

HORATIO Good morning, me and my friend would like to see a nice plot, the silly mare is thinking of doing away with himself, well, you know how the moody ones get sometimes, so I said I'd help him pick something out, he has absolutely no taste whatever, I don't think he's chosen a duvet cover in all the years I've known him, not that I think he'll go through with it, he can't make his bloody mind up from one day to the next, I don't know how I've stuck it all these . . .

Fish Out of Water

*The Chertsey man who landed the first salmon to be hooked in
the Thames for 150 years said yesterday: 'It was nothing. The
fish was knackered. He came quietly – there was no struggle.'*
Daily Telegraph

THE SALMON, feeling good, feeling fit, turned sharp west at
Margate, jinked nimbly past a sinking beer-can, and hit the
estuary at a lively clip, humming to itself as only salmon can.

'Good holiday?' said a mackerel.

'Terrific,' said the salmon. 'Great. You cannot top the North Sea
in August, I have been about a bit and I speak as one who knows.'

'Oh. I don't know,' said the mackerel, not without the smugness of its race, 'it's been pretty good in England, this year.'

The salmon fixed it with one penetrating eye, while the other
kept circumspect watch on a gently descending turd.

'Oh, really?' it said.

'Definitely,' replied the mackerel, firmly. 'Anyone going
abroad this year was bloody barmy. It has been,' and here he
tapped the salmon with an emphatic fin, 'the best summer since
records were thing, collected. Phew, what a scorcher, cried
millions of holidaymakers as they made for the coast in droves,
seeking relief from the boiling sun.'

'I fail to see,' said the salmon, 'how that could make any
possible difference, down here.'

'You wouldn't,' said the mackerel, 'not having been here.
Having made the mistake of going away, as it were. Would he?'

This last was addressed to a passing eel, who turned, at least
in part.

'Would he what?' said the eel.

'Know how good it's been down here,' said the mackerel, 'if he's been up the North Sea.'

'Mad, going off,' confirmed the eel. 'All these holidaymakers, all these packed boatrides, you wouldn't credit the stuff floating down. I've been on cheeseburgers for two months solid.'

'See?' said the mackerel, triumphantly.

'You can get choc-ices,' added the eel, 'if you're nippy. Got a tendency to melt in the warm water, if you're not quick off the mark, but you soon pick up the knack.'

A burst of bubbles exploded from the salmon's mouth.

'Half-eaten cheeseburgers?' it cried. 'Soggy Cornettos?'

'Cornett*i*,' corrected the eel, 'strictly speaking. I would have thought you would have known that,' it continued nastily, 'being a traveller.'

'Yes, well,' said the salmon, 'you know what you can do with all *that* muck! You cannot beat foreign food, you would not credit what they lay on up the North Sea, juicy little sprats, nice fat plankton, and they've got a way with whitebait you just wouldn't –'

'You can get all that stuff here,' sneered the mackerel, 'if you know where to look. There's plenty of places in England that do that foreign rubbish – *and* do it better. I could mention a dozen. Not that I'd touch it, personally.'

'Goes right through you,' nodded the eel, 'whitebait. I went halfway across the Channel once, I was ill for days.'

The salmon glared at them, hard, clenched its little teeth, flicked its powerful tail, and shot away up river. Welcome home, it thought.

By Sheerness, however, it had regained most of its sense of well-being. A skate, cruising the frontier of acceptable salinity, glided past.

'Off home, then?' it said.

'Right,' replied the salmon.

The skate braked, and hove to alongside, leering

'Come back home for a bit of the other?' it cackled. 'After a bit of the old domestic fin-over, are we?'

The salmon looked at it.

'I'm a salmon,' it said. 'It's what I do. Every summer I go off to feed, then I come back up-river to spawn. That is the name of the game.'

'Get off!' cried the skate. 'Pull this one!'

'Which one?'

'It's just an expression,' said the skate. It paddled around, with a neat little flick, to face the salmon head-on. 'Are you seriously telling me that if there was good stuff up the North Sea, you'd be belting back here? It is what I have always maintained, everybody rushing off abroad for the nooky, only when they get there, it is all rubbish. Either that or they do not fancy it, due to strict upbringing, etcetera. You cannot kid me, sunshine! Come on, fish-to-fish, straight up – did you get any?'

There was a long silence. Far above, a tug hooted.

'It is not why I went,' said the salmon, at last.

'Oh, really?' mocked the skate. 'Oh, well, pardon me, I'm sure, and here was I thinking: poor bugger, every year he trogs off for a touch of your oo-la-la, every year he comes running back to where the good stuff is, well, well, well, just shows you how wrong you can be, stone me, who'd have credited . . .'

And it swam languidly away, derisive laughter bursting from each trailing bubble. The salmon stared after it; eased slowly from bitterness to resignation; and pushed on, gloomily.

'North Sea again, was it?' enquired a pockmarked gudgeon off Gravesend.

'Yes,' replied the salmon, 'and in case you were wondering, I had a really fantastic eight . . .'

'Nothing to do in the evenings, is there?' said the gudgeon. 'As I understand it, the North Sea is bloody dead after six o'clock.'

The salmon chewed its little lip, and breathed in, deeply.

'Have you been recently?' it murmured.

'Me?' enquired the gudgeon. '*Me?* I wouldn't be caught dead up the North Sea! Well,' and here it laughed unpleasantly, 'as a matter of fact that is exactly what I would be. Caught dead. All that salt. I don't know how you *stand* that climate, you're bloody lucky not to end up pickled, no doubt you are currently congratulating yourself on getting back to dear old England in the nick of time?'

'I am a salmon,' snapped the homecomer, 'you ignorant little nerd! I am a sophisticated bleeding international globetrotter, I am equally at home in fresh, salt, or brackish, you name it, I *love* the sea!'

The gudgeon nodded.

'Yes, you'd have to say that, of course,' it said. 'Going back to the same foreign dump year after year, you'd have to say you liked it or people'd think you needed your head looking at. I quite understand, mate.'

Whereupon it deftly dodged the salmon's cumbrous lunge, and skittered away into the enfolding weed.

Is it worth going on? I ask myself, the salmon asked itself.

But it went on, because it was a salmon, and there was nothing else it could do.

'Bring anything back?' called a minnow, off Woolwich. And, without waiting for a reply, continued: 'No, well, you wouldn't really, would you, there's bugger-all there, load of tatty foreign junk, falls to bits on the trip home, I've heard about that, not worth bothering about, must be nice to be back.'

But the salmon did not even pause to reply, nor indeed to think about whether it cared or not, since it was fairly rapidly ceasing to care about anything much. It swam slowly and moodily on, feeling not just the benefits but the very memory of its holiday seep out of its homecoming scales. It passed wearily through the Pool of London, rolled with the sluggish tide through Chelsea Reach, and was just coasting past Fulham when, through what had gradually become a depressed reverie, it heard the faint but penetrating voice of a roach.

'Back off holiday?' enquired the tiny fish, circling the salmon. The salmon ignored it.

'Dogger Bank again, was it?' persisted the roach.

The salmon slowed, and set its imperceptible jaw.

'Don't bother,' it muttered. 'It has already been borne in upon me what a prat I have been in going away. I have already been reliably informed what a marvellous bloody country this is. Better fish than you have already dinned into me the fact that I am over the moon to be home, and what a lucky bastard I am. Thank you very much.'

'I wouldn't say that,' said the roach. 'In fact, it is my considered view, as a roach, that you are a mug to *come* back.'

The salmon backfinned itself to a stop, and cast an eye roachwards.

'What?' it said.

'Where you from?' replied the roach obliquely. 'Where's you know, home?'

'Chertsey,' said the salmon. 'Chertsey is where the family is. Where I start it, anyway,' it amplified. 'Why?'

'Very nice, Chertsey,' said the roach. 'Very smart. Very secluded. Beats me how you find it every year.'

'Trade secret,' said the salmon. 'You have to be a salmon. Being a salmon is the only method of getting from the North Sea to Chertsey, take my word.'

'I believe you,' said the roach. 'You poor sod,' it added.

'I'm sorry?' enquired the salmon.

'Not only very smart,' murmured the roach, almost to itself, 'it is also very clean, Chertsey. You can see your face in it.'

'It is one of its strong points,' acknowledged the salmon.

'Oh,' said the roach, 'is it? Is it really?'

The salmon stared at the roach for a while, holding itself motionless against the running tide.

'Is there something I should know?' it enquired finally.

'It wouldn't make any odds,' answered the roach. 'There is no way of stopping you from going to Chertsey, is there?'

'I am a salmon. There is this inexorable urge.'

'Yes,' nodded the roach, 'there would be.'

And it shot off, leaving the bewildered salmon even more wretched than before. So it gave in to the rhythm of its old genetic song, and swam wearily on, as the Thames grew ever narrower and ever cleaner, and it dragged itself at last under the shadow of Chertsey Bridge, and it thought to itself, miserably: *it is as if I had never been away.*

But it wasn't.

It had never seen a line before, but by some buried atavistic blip, the salmon recognized it. It's always the way, it thought tiredly, you come back off holiday and something's gone wrong with the place. A thousand miles to the North Sea, it reflected, a thousand miles back, what is it all for, why do we bloody bother?

God, it thought, I'm knackered.

And, not ungratefully, it took the hook.

£10.66 and All That

A Dorset wood which was valued at £9 in the Domesday Book is now on the market at £120, 000.

Daily Telegraph

GLOOMINGLY, THE Shaftesbury branch-manager of William & Bastards rubbed a clear patch in the little mullioned window with his smocked elbow, and stared out.

'Cats and dogs,' he muttered.

'What?' said his assistant.

'The rain is coming down,' replied the manager, 'cats and dogs.'

'Bloody portent, that is,' said the assistant. 'There'll be bishops dead all over by tea-time.'

'Not *real* cats and dogs,' said the manager, irritably. 'It is just an expression.'

'It doesn't mean anything,' said his assistant.

The manager rolled his eyes, rooted in his hirsute ear, cracked a hidden nit.

'You cannot expect to know what everything means, these days,' he said. 'The language is in a state of flux. Cats and dogs is probably from the Norman.'

'Why not?' grumbled the assistant. 'Everything else bloody is. I never eat out any more. Time was, you found a maggot on your plate, you stuck an axe in the cook. These days it's more than likely simmered in a cream sauce with a bloody peppercorn on its head.'

The manager sighed.

'Nevertheless,' he said, 'estate agency is nothing if not

adaptable to change. We are at the forefront, Egwyne. We have got to be perceived to be red-hot. Hence smart fashionable expressions, e.g. cats and dogs.'

'What is e.g. when it's at home?' enquired the assistant.

'It's another one,' replied the manager. 'You hear it everywhere.' He peered out again. 'Funny thing about this glass stuff,' he said, 'it makes people's legs go little. That woman from Number Four just went past, her feet were coming out of her knees. Her dog looked more like a bloody lizard.'

'If she finds out it's the glass what's doing it,' said the assistant, 'she could very likely sue us. I reckon we ought to have it took out again, God knows what it's doing to our eyes, they could start going little any minute, why did we have it put in in the first place?'

'It is what is called chic,' said the manager.

His assistant stared at him.

'Do not blame me, Egwyne,' said the manager, looking away, 'this stuff is coming straight down from head office. I am getting memos headed *From the Stool Of The Senior Bastard* informing me they are determined to drag estate agency into the eleventh century. You do not know the half of it, Egwyne. It is a whole new, er, ball game. It is where it's at.'

His assistant sniffed.

'I wouldn't care,' he said, 'we've hardly shifted nothing since we were set up. It may well be estate agency is not a British thing.'

'Concept.'

'What?'

'Never mind. Since you raise the point, Egwyne, the plain fact is it is all a matter of marketing.'

'What is marketing?'

'It is the name of the game. The old days of if you want somewhere to live you go round to the bloke with three chickens and if he doesn't reckon it's a fair price you knock him about a bit are over, Egwyne.'

The shop-bell tinkled. A young couple, entering, shrieked and ran out again. The manager hurried to the open doorway.

'What is it?' cried the young man, backing off. 'Leprosy?

Boils? Ague?'

'Do not be alarmed!' replied the manager. 'It is only a concept. It rings when you open the door.'

His assistant appeared at his shoulder.

'Yes,' he said reassuringly, 'it is a ball game where it's at. Come on in out of the cats and dogs, it's bloody chic in here, e.g.'

Hesitantly, the young couple re-entered.

'We're after a hut,' said the man.

The manager beamed, drew up a pair of stools, flicked an unidentified dropping from one, and motioned his clients seated.

'And what sort of price range are we talking about?' he said.

'About eight bob,' said the husband, 'tops.'

The manager sucked his teeth.

'What have we got in the way of eight-bob huts, Egwyne?' he said.

'There's that rat-riddled old drum we've been trying to shift down by Aelfthryth's Swamp,' said his assistant, 'or possibly in it, by now; you know what it's like with bogs.'

'Rats?' enquired the young woman.

'Not large ones,' said the manager. 'Some of 'em are virtually mice. It's got a lot of roof.'

'It would have to have,' said the young man, 'for eight bob.'

'I'm not saying eight bob,' said the manager, quickly. 'We could certainly knock one-and-threepence off for cash. It's got a door up one end with a brand new string on it,' he added, 'it's got a ladder for climbing up to repair some of the roof it hasn't got, and a nice window without any of that glass what makes your legs shrink.'

'Has it got a floor?' enquired the young man.

'All right, six bob,' said the manager.

'Any land?' said the young man.

'Ah,' said the manager. 'It has got land, hasn't it, Egwyne?'

'No point denying it,' said his assistant. 'They'd notice it straight away, anyhow. You cannot miss it, bloody great forest out back, could be anything in there, goblins, bogeys, trolls, you name it, well, it wouldn't be five bob otherwise, would it?'

'Four and sevenpence,' said the manager. 'It's got a relatively scum-free well, mind.'

'I don't know,' said the young woman, 'we were rather set on . . .'

'Tell you what,' said the manager quickly, 'you could chop the trees down, anything nasty'd soon run out, call it four bob and I'll chuck in Egwyne to come round with his axe, he'll have that lot down in next to no –'

But the shop-bell had tinkled again. Egwyne watched them go, from the window.

'She'll never fancy him now his legs have gone little,' he said. He grinned. 'Serve 'em right, it was a steal at four bob, some people don't know when they're lucky.'

The manager might well have responded, had not the door opened again.

It was a slim young man in a neatly tailored smock, flared, patch pockets, and polychrome embroidery at the scalloped neck. He was clean-shaven, save for a thread of ginger moustache, astonishingly symmetrical for the period, and his hair glinted with polished lard. He had at least four teeth.

'Good morning,' he said. 'Edward the Smart, from head office.'

The manager and his assistant cringed expertly backwards.

'Sir,' they murmured, 'sir.'

Edward the Smart waved the deference away with one heavily ringed hand, while the other raised a large leatherbound book it had been holding and laid it on their table.

'We have noticed up head office,' he said, 'that Shaftesbury is into a disappointing situation tradewise. In short, as of this moment in time, you have shifted sod-all.'

'It is always a bit quiet after a war, Edward the Smart, sir,' mumbled the manager. 'People want to be dead sure the pillaging etcetera has finished before rushing into property.'

'E.g.,' added his assistant, keenly.

'Yes, well, be that as it may,' said the man from head office, 'we have something we wish for you to run up the flagpole.'

The manager narrowed his imperceptible brows.

'Is it a concept?' he asked. 'Is it red-hot and chic?'

Edward the Smart looked at him, and knuckled his moustache smooth.

'It is called advertising,' he said. 'We have just invented it.'

'Is it like cream sauce?' enquired the assistant, eager to commend himself. 'Is it like snails' legs? Is it e.g.?'

Edward the Smart opened the big book. The page was blank.

'This is what we call the *Domesday Book*. It is a property guide. It goes free to everybody earning more than two pounds per annum.'

'The rich get everything,' muttered Egwyne.

'On each page,' continued the man from head office, 'William & Bastards will advertise a desirable property to the discerning buyer. Now, what can we put in from the Shaftesbury branch?'

'We got a four-bob rat-infested drum in the middle of a haunted wood,' said the manager. 'That's about it.'

'Better write down three-and-six,' said his assistant. 'No point misleading anybody.'

Edward the Smart looked at him for a very long time. Finally he said:

'Do you have a written specification of this item?'

The manager produced a crumpled note, licked a cheesecrumb off it, and handed it across. Edward the Smart considered it for a while, hummed a snatch or two of galliard, finally began to write.

'Just in the market,' he said aloud, quill darting, 'a bijou cottage-style residence in the midst of a fine wooded country estate, magnificently located beside a lush water-meadow supporting a truly rich profusion of wild life. The house itself is wholly original and constructed from local materials to blend perfectly with its environment, and requires only a touch of sympathetic decoration to create a magnificent rural retreat that is, nevertheless, being secluded but not isolated, within easy reach of all amenities. The superb woods which go with the property are rich in local legend, and offer a mature aspect from all windows. Due to bereavement, the present titled owners wish to dispose of the property quickly, a factor reflected by the realistic price of only nine pounds. An early inspection is advised.'

Edward the Smart put down his quill.

The manager was whimpering quietly in the corner.

The assistant licked dry lips.

'Nine pounds?' he croaked, finally. *'Nine pounds?'*

Edward the Smart snapped shut his book.

'Yes, I know what you're going to say,' he said, 'but if it *does* turn out to be underpriced and we get a few nibbles, we can always withdraw it, bung it in at auction, and crank it up a bit on the day, could go as high as a tenner. I take it you have a false beard and something to wave?'

And with that, he was gone.

Slowly, the manager pulled himself together and hobbled to the window.

'Tell you a funny thing,' he said, 'his legs haven't gone little. What do you suppose that means?'

The assistant thought for a while.

'That he's Old Nick?' he said.

'E.g.,' replied the manager.

The Hangover in Question

4.17 AM, light from fridge snaps on, reverberates through head like noise, can *hear* pupils contracting, shut fridge door, little polychrome rhomboids continue to kaleidoscope about in brain.

Or I am dead. This is Elysian fridge, I have snuffed it and gone to Kitchen, God's final jest, doomed to an eternity standing on jammy lino in bare feet, unable to find bottle opener, parched for Coke.

Would He be this tough on drinkers? Cannot recall pentateuchal injunctions against alcohol, is there an XIth Commandment somewhere in small print, *Thou shalt not booze*? Are there parables in minor prophet texts, *And Jeroboam came home legless, and fell over the cat, and uttered oaths; and the LORD God brought forth thunderbolts and smote him in that place where he was, saying: Henceforth shall the floor of thy mouth be as a wadi, and thine eyeballs as twin coals, and the fruit of thy loins go about on all fours, even unto the tenth generation?*

Amazing what a few minutes of natural sleep can do for you. Such as maim. Came home at 3.15, not tight, loosened, if anything, one or two joints unbolted, no more than that, perfectly capable of sticking key in letter-box and walking into Christmas tree, got glass ball off ear at only third attempt, negotiated staircase easily as falling over a log, found bedroom door handle well before 3.30, removed clothes with nothing more than minor pause to work out best way of pulling trousers over head, climbed athletically up onto bed, stubbed fag out on clock, sank into oblivion.

Rose from oblivion 4.13, not tea-time already, surely? No,

clock still smouldering, faint smell of plastic molecules reorganising their domestic arrangements.

Tongue lying on mouth-floor like felled cactus.

Got up, carrying head carefully in both hands, groped for dressing-gown, dressing-gown totally incapacitated, arms flapping, belt treble-knotted, dressing-gown obviously just got in from even wilder New Year's Eve party than mine, crawled downstairs together like, like, like – who was it used to sing *Me and My Shadow*, plump man, white tie, face of some kind?

4.20, now, by kitchen clock; brave fridge searchlights again. Guy Gibson's voice crackling on ectoplasmic intercom as we go in low over the bacon, something registers a hit on hand, grab Coke bottle from back of fridge, slam door, and we are away before gunners can even get range.

What hit hand? Hand got egg-white on it. Two possibilities: either I bleed albumen, or else wife still pursuing mad habit, despite previous incidents, of leaving egg-whites in cup after using yolks, standing cup on top shelf, and awaiting results.

Cannot bring self to open fridge again, know what it looks like, seen it before, it looks like giant snail has run amok; not generally known fact that average hen's egg contains up to eighteen miles of mucus if allowed to drip long enough.

Put it behind me, other things on what's left of mind, how, for example, to open Coke bottle? By light chiaroscuring in from street lamp, as in Caravaggio's immortal *Parched Drunk Looking For Coke Bottle Opener*, begin tugging at utensil drawers, forgetting Second Law of Ergodynamics which states that all drawers stick during small hours, also forgetting Third Law of Ergodynamics which states that all drawers *only stick for a bit*.

Said bit having elapsed, all drawers leap from their cavities and vomit cake-cutters, used batteries, bent screwdrivers, half a scissor, corks, spare fuses, knife handles, flea collars, pieces of gas bill, empty Sparklets, flints, two-pin bakelite plugs you brought from your last house just in case, Good Boy drops, cup handles, matchboxes (empty), matchboxes (with screws in; or, after drawer flies open, with screws out), doll's heads, and seventy-one keys you brought from your last house just in case.

No bottle-openers, though.

4.26.

Think.

Have seen John Wayne open bottles with teeth. Or, no doubt, John Wayne's double's teeth. Probably special teeth, though, enamelled steel props built at San Diego Navy Yard. *John Wayne's double lies a-mouldering in the grave, but his teeth go marching on . . .*

Shall not chance own vulnerable choppers, though, last time I chomped an incautious cobnut, mouth resembled tiny Temple of Dagon, crumbling masonry everywhere, crown dust rising, bits of bridge, World War Two fillings – God knows what Coke bottle would do, whole skull might come off.

Ah.

Remember seeing someone open Coke bottle in door jamb.

Ah.

Look at foot.

Foot still hissing slightly, Coke bubbles dying among instep hair. Must be special trick in opening horizontal Coke bottle in door jamb. Must be *two* special tricks, since large sliver of door jamb now lying beside Coked foot.

4.31.

No more Coke in house.

Water, squash, milk, no use, need something aerated, no good simply de-parching tongue, am Very Aware of need to shift something lying sideways across oesophagus. Seem to have swallowed large plank. Could be case for Red Adair, long experience assures me only megacharge of bubbles will do trick, no point ringing Dyno-Rod at 4.33, *You must be joking, squire, couldn't touch anything till February earliest, we're up to here with paperwork, not to mention staff shortages, unofficial strike up Northampton, black ice, Good Friday looming, etc . . .*

If plank *is* lying across oesophagus.

Aorta? Vasa cava inferior? Duodenum? Ventriculus dexter? Pulmo?

Stop, in larder, hand on bicarb packet; reflect.

All down to Jonathan Miller, this. We live in post-*Body In Question Age*. Used to know nothing about what goes on past tonsils. Now know three per cent. Point-three per cent. Know it looks like Rotorua mud-spring, in constant state of peristaltic glug; know about referred pain, i.e. if feel sudden stabbing pain in shin, could mean going deaf. To layman – to 0.3% expert – entire nervous system is result of giant connective cock-up, nothing hurts where it's supposed to, everything where it isn't. If Dalston Junction like that, Central Line tube to Chancery Lane ends up in East Kilbride.

Prior to Miller, all my anatomical information came from Arthur Mee. *Children's Encyclopaedia* used to have big sepia illustrations of human body in section, showing little men in overalls shovelling food into tin boiler (stomach), little men in head with Box Brownies (eyes), little men in lungs with footpumps. Very nice. Liked to think of them all down there, contented work force beavering away; felt like benevolent mill-owner, loyal workers whistling as they shovelled, pumped, treadled, ticked carbohydrates off clipboard check-list, stoked furnaces.

Pleasant, having anthropomorphic view of own insides; every time I ate breakfast, thought of little men in spotless gumboots carrying egg away in buckets.

Impossible, now. Post-Miller, see myself as not even human, merely large biochemical complex or permanent germ-warfare battlefield. A great itinerant skin bag of blood and offal, horribly vulnerable. Never used to worry about smoking, drinking, guzzling, little men would take care of all that, scouring lungs, washing down intestinal tract, buffing liver to spotless health.

4.38.

Bicarb packet still in hand, plank still across throbbing insides. Eyes (not Box Brownies) focus on minuscule print: $NaHCO_3$.

Yes. Could be anything, really, could well combine with whatever I am to produce $SO_9C_4Pb_8Th_2Nb_6H_3Sb_2Zn_7$ . . . without unease, post-Jonathan, bunging assorted valences down into the pulsing tripes, what if wedged-plank-plus-aching-eye-plus-metal-tongue syndrome is actually referral of neurological complaints about dislocated spleen, could be $NaHCO_3$ is worst possible treatment for dislocated spleen, could end up quitting vale of tears on one terminal burp.

Appalling way to go.

Return bicarb to shelf, shut larder door, hobble across floor on Coke-gummy foot, fuses, screws, Good Boy drops sticking to sole, wedged plank grinding in chest cavity, possibly indicating grit behind patella, mastoid sprouting in left ear, onset of silicosis.

4.56.

Shameful, tragic, terrifying how body gets abused, body only thing I have (gave up idea of soul 1967, following TV programme by glib atheist), New Year less than five hours old, good time to make New Year Resolution, must stop punishing tissues, must give up fags, liquor, toast, fatty . . .

Hang on.

Wonder if hair of dog good for wedged oesophagal plank?

Where scotch?

El Sid

In a poll carried out among Spaniards, the British tourist emerged as the most sexless, most tasteless, worst dressed, most stingy, and above all the most boring of all foreign visitors. 'It is almost,' said the poll's organiser, 'as if his behaviour was deliberate.'

Daily Mail

WITH THE July temperature in the high nineties, with the brass sun gonging down from the white noon-day welkin, with the only breeze itself so hot that flies' wings shrivelled in mid-flight, the Hotel Miramar Beach froze.

That is to say, the elegant French stopped dead before the peach foyer mirrors, their preens unfinished; the lissome Scandinavians around the pool paused in the rhythmic insulation of one another's astounding breasts, the coconut oil evaporating on their inert fingers; the cheerful Minnesotans at the bar, poised to buy doubles for everyone, let the wallets drop from their suddenly benumbed hands; and the witty wags from Düsseldorf and Köln found the punch-lines dying on their nerveless lips.

While the only noise to disturb the fraught silence of the huge stucco complex was a low and undulating Iberian moan from a thousand uniformed throats.

For El Sid stood on the blue foyer tiling, the hotel doors swinging shut behind him. True to his legend, he had returned at the same moment, on the same day, to the same spot; El Sid had kept his covenant.

He had come from the North, and he wore the uniform of the North: the electric-blue nylon anorak, wondrously filled with mock-kapok, the bright badge over his heart proclaiming his proud membership of the Durex works team; the off-white teeshirt beneath (the gift of a grateful *Sun*), cunningly worked to show bums of all nations; the QPR knitted cap with its jovially obscene bobble and embroidered misspelled oaths; the genuine ex-Chief Petty Officer's navy shorts, just kissing the tripe-hued knees; the chic mail-order plimsolls, tide-marked with salt lines left by last year's ebbing sweat.

He dropped his two smart chipboard suitcases, and fixed the trembling Hall Porter with an adamantine eye.

'Gatwick!' cried El Sid. 'Don't talk to *me* about bleeding Gatwick!'

The doors sighed shut again. His squire stood beside him, his short rotundity set off to full advantage by an elderly Gannex and floor-length Charlton scarf. He wore a sombrero with a Union Jack on it.

'Don't talk to us about bleeding Gatwick!' he said. 'Eighty-five pee for a pork pie and you have to take your own Cellophane off.'

'Pork brick, more like,' thundered El Sid. He jabbed the Hall Porter's chest with a gnawed forefinger; the man cringed. 'Your *genuine* pork pie was invented, as you may recall, by Lord Pork. Am I right, squire?'

'Definitely. He was gaming up his club. They come to him in the middle and told him his dinner was on the table, and he replied: *Piss off, I am playing brag, bring us a pie!* He'd turn in his wossname if he knew what they was getting away with these days. When I was a boy, you could go to Benghazi and back for eighty-five pee and still have change for a pint of whelks.'

'Or seventeen bob, as it was then called,' said El Sid.

'Or seventeen bob, as it was then called,' said his squire.

'Sometimes,' said El Sid darkly, 'I wonder who won the war.'

He snatched his key from the Hall Porter's hand. In other circumstances, with other guests, the man might have fawned, chatted, joked, hovered for tips; but he had tried that once with El Sid, long ago, and been held for an hour with a meticulous description of how to get to Hornsey from Sudbury Town avoiding the North Circular entirely, and even now would often break out in herpes at the memory.

So El Sid took up his bags, and walked towards the lift; which, at his approach, suddenly spilled its waiting cargo of suntanned Danes and svelte Italians, so that he and his squire rose in solitary comfort.

'They know me here,' murmured El Sid.

They walked into the bar.

El Sid had changed into his leisure clothes, string vest and green eye-shade with the ex-CPO shorts; his squire favoured a Tesco bikini with a Fair Isle slipover.

The bar was crowded: elegant Gucci shapes glided about in the polyglot pre-lunch hum, or waited patiently for their turn to catch the barman's eye.

'Bloody stroll on!' muttered the squire. 'Could take all day.'

But El Sid had set his iron jaw. The glint was in his eye.

'OY!' he bellowed, with such force that, in the trim rock garden beyond the windows, lizards leapt, and shed their tails. 'DOS BROWN ALES, CHOP-CHOP!'

A hundred pairs of Polychromatic lenses swung round so fast, they had scant time to pale; when they did, and the eyes behind made out the epic duo, the mouths beneath fell slack. The ranks opened; El Sid walked majestically through. An American at the bar, whose turn it was, licked his lips quickly and shrilly cried:

'No! No! Allow me!'

El Sid returned a small smile.

'Very generous,' he said. 'We won't say no, will we, squire?'

'We won't say no,' said the squire.

'Two treble Glenlivets,' said El Sid.

They drank them, in the taut silence.

It was El Sid's round.

'If a grasshopper was as big as a man,' he said, 'he could jump over St Paul's Cathedral.'

'There's not many people know that,' said his squire to the American.

The American mopped his forehead.

'Conversely,' said El Sid, 'if a man was as big as a grasshopper, he couldn't jump over bleeding anything.'

'Is it all to do with kinetic energy, El Sid?' asked his squire.

'That comes into it,' replied the hero. 'Course, strong back legs has a part to play as well. Funny things, strong back legs: my brother-in-law Dennis . . .'

'Is that the one from West Hartlepool who married your sister Beryl who used to gut herrings in Yarmouth?'

'Not Yarmouth. Hull. None of my family's ever even bloody *seen* Yarmouth, the nearest they ever got was, what's the name of that place in Norfolk, used to have a very good non-league side, big ginger striker, werl, I *say* striker, he was more of a roving sweeper, when you come right down to . . .'

'I guess I'll take an early lunch,' croaked the American, backing away.

His movement was as a shot fired that precipitates an avalanche. Within seconds, the bar was empty, save for El Sid, his squire, and its overturned chairs.

'Left a lot of nice drinks behind,' said El Sid, bending to sniff an untouched Pernod.

'Not to mention nuts,' murmured his squire.

They rolled, half-cut and singing, into the dining-room, and were shown to a table.

'I'd rather be sitting at that one,' said the squire, jabbing his thumb towards the neighbouring table, 'next to the window.'

'Course you would,' said El Sid. He leaned across, tapped the German's arm. 'I see you're managing to hold them prawns down,' he said pleasantly.

'Excuse me?' said the German.

'My friend here tried the prawns last year,' said El Sid.

'Only once,' said the squire.

'Only once,' said El Sid. 'You wouldn't believe what come up over the next couple of days, would he?'

The squire shook his head.

'It's on account of them breeding in sewage,' said El Sid, 'little bits of it get wedged in their joints. Look at a prawn's knee under the microscope, you can actually make out the . . . bring your drink, Dennis.'

They re-settled themselves.

'That's better,' said the squire. 'Got a view of the sea now.'

El Sid tossed the menu aside.

'I think I'll have eggs, sausage, bacon, fried kidney, tomato, baked beans and double chips,' he said.

'Can they do that here?' asked his squire.

'Definitely. I had it every day last year. The chef kicked up a bit of a barney first day, mind, but I went in there, very friendly, and told him about the time me and Geoff Rymold tried to renew the cylinder head gasket on Geoff's cousin Albert's mate's old Dormobile. So he give in finally, after it started to get dark.'

'You got a way with people,' said the squire reverently.

El Sid's steely eyes gazed out over the sparkling Mediterranean, offering glint for glint.

'They didn't build the Empire on bleeding paella,' he said.

As their last belch echoed titanically through the cringing restaurant, El Sid and his faithful squire wiped their mouths on the tablecloth and strode out into the sunshine.

'There's a nice spot,' said El Sid, pointing to a pair of reclining chairs in the shade beside the diving-board.

'They've got someone's towels on them,' said his squire.

'Oh, have they really?' said El Sid, clomping lithely across and shedding his vest, 'Oh, my goodness! Oh, dear me!'

He sat down on one of the chairs. His squire collapsed into the other.

'Excuse me, please, but you have our chairs taken.'

El Sid squinted up through his eye-shade. Two tall German girls hovered, smiling apologetically.

'Pardon?'

'Our towels,' explained one of the girls, pointing.

'*Your* towels, stone me, I'd never have guessed they was *your* towels!' cried El Sid. 'Knockers like yours –' and here he paused, moulding his own flabby bosom, lest their English be not entirely adequate, '– knockers like yours, I'd have thought you'd have needed something much bigger, know what I mean, squire? Here, what about you two coming down our beach cabana for a bit of a gobble?'

'Don't women run funny?' said his squire, as they watched them flee.

'All they're good for,' said El Sid, mysteriously. 'Fancy a swim?'

His squire sat up.

'Pool's a bit crowded,' he said. 'I wouldn't like to get me hairpiece ducked.'

'Hang on,' said El Sid pushing himself up from his chair.

He walked to the edge of the pool. The sleek international heads glanced up. Above them, El Sid, white, scrawny, magnificent, towered. On his callus-crusted heroic heel, he turned.

'Just going to have a quick dip, squire,' he shouted. 'I'm busting. It must be the vino.'

Bloomers

A West German university lecturer, equipped with a computer and unlimited patience, is ploughing through more than a million words of difficult English prose to produce the first really definitive version of one of the most monumental works of modern fiction – James Joyce's 'Ulysses'.

Daily Telegraph

BY LORRIES along Sir John Rogerson's quay Mr Bloom walked soberly, past Windmill Lane, Leask's the linseed crushers, the postal telegraph office, ping, whirr, clunk. We would draw your attention to the enclosed outstanding telephone account in the sum of £971, 000, 000, 004.02 do not fold staple bend crease stick lick or touch and if paying by bank giro credit please state inside leg measurement when orduring; please state date of bath; police state all previous convictions on separate sheet provided (batteries not included) DO NOT detach, semi-detach, end of terrors, bijou torn house, 3 bed 1 bth 1 ktch dwnstrs clks ample gge spce, patio patio bkrs mn, we have 7, 000, 000, 000, 002 fine examples like these on our flies.

Mr Bloom turned from the morning noise of the quayside and walked through Lime Street, ping, clackety-clack, EC4 OH2 2DG it is essential to write postcode in box provided, provided box is provided, Box will provide, box must NOT exceed 67875000 centimetres overall unless excess postage paid please state excess card number when ogling, John Barleycard, American Excess or other fine cars. And a bottle of Banker's draught for the little woman, please indicate OVERLEAF whether spinster/wife/mistress/other martial state.

Gonna take a centimetre journey, gonna get myself a train, please refer to fully-automated indicator board, the 189.30 am from Peterborough to Irkutsk is now overdue. If overdue 189.30 remains unpaid within SEVEN (7) days to our Peterborough office (if resident in Irkutsk) or Irkborough office (if non-patrial with six or more parents domiciled in Peterkutsk), instrument will be cut off.

Bloom crossed Townsend Street, past Nichols' the undertakers, ping, whizz, This is to inform you that your husband's instrument has been cut off, the hospital deeply regrets any inconvenience caused by the error but, due to sleet on computerised points at Didcot, your current driving licence MUST be forwarded to Swansong unless hat-size smaller than 67$^{1}/_{4}$, or rush me *War and Peas*. If I am not completely delighted and satisfied with this magnificent purchase, I undertake to buy 1888 more classics, please bill me.

Along came bill, an ordinary gay, the Department of Health deeply regrets loss of instrument, please place deceased in box provided, DO NOT FORWARD TO ALHAMBRA STREET, DUNDEE, Ml5 UFO, except between January 18 and March 93 (not Wiltshire rat-payers or if over 650 on April 0), for details please consult local press, ping, clink, bong, do NOT press, stitch, gum, nail, sniff; this form requires two (7) signatures by a bank manacle, justice of the police, parish proust, or Chief Rabbit, and DOES NOT CONSTITUTE A CONTRACT WITHIN THE MOANING OF THE ACT, but see above sub-section 999999.99 (*not available*).

Leopold Bloom strolled out of the post office and turned to the right where a large number of tuckatuckatuckatucka ping PLEASE NOTE that your new National Insurance number is £3.55$^{2}/_{3}$, you must TAKE (not post) it to your nearest gas showroom on or before the last date not specified hereinunder, and POST (not take) it to ONE (ONE) of the registered dealers on the accompanying leaflet (c/455-61, *alternate* Thursdays). THIS OFFER CLOSES ON WEMBLEY 14th! I am over 121.

Will the vehicle be drivelled by (a) insured only? (4) with/without* matching bra (**delete whichever is applicable UNLESS resident in United Kingdom*) or (xviii) if more than 8

O-levels, please STATE whether self-employed, or next-of-kin. NB This offer depends upon availability, plus two bottle-tops, and is NOT open to miners (–).

– Hello, Bloom, where are you off to?

– Hello, M'Coy, ping, whirr, bleep, this is a recorded massage, the speaking cock is not at home as of this moment in time, when the tone sounds would you please Hello, this is the Gobi Hilton fully-automated customer courtesy desk for your delight and convenience thank you for crawling, we have reserved 197 rooms with bath facing the Mediterranean for you and your wine as per your telex, we note that your Donors Club number is This is the Test Match Service, tea-time scone West Englies 859740036 for 56, Current Account 10.43 and forty seconds, Hello, this is a recorded messuage . . .

Mr Bloom passed, dallying, the window of Brown Thomas, silk mercers, drapers, purveyors of fine carpets, ping, thunk, billions (3) of carpets MUST be shifted due to computerising of stock, luxurious deep-pile Axemurderers sought by Interpol computer. Interpolly wants a crackpot, please state your old passport number on SEPARATE ROAD FUND APPLICATION, when ordering new pisspot please list (on blank sheep provided) ALL diseases contracted in past 2 minutes, do you suffer from (g) number plates at 25 miles? (4 *or* 17b) credit accounts at any other stores? (gamma) paying tax at the standard rape?

Mr Bloom crossed over the greystone bridge, feeling the pressure on his bladder, ping, tonk, hum, As we have no record of your existence on our files, your water has been cut off from May 8, backdated to Ramadan, if you wish to be reconnected, report at Catterick 07.00 SHARP, April 3, bringing old dog licence (£25 for colour) with you plus vests, string (2), underpants, wincyette (2), plimsolls, canvas (000000.00), *unless* vehicle is MORE than 50 cwt (2kilos) and/or/but registered PRIOR to the 1972 Road Sidesaddle Act (*repealed*).

Bloom looked in at the butcher's window, noted the purple liver at eightpence a pound, ping, clackety-clackety, You have not converted, we can not process this information, please insert your card a second time, thank you, that is £6.77 a millilitre, 3 francs an ell, 950 lire a rood, more if bloody rood, representing a

724% fall against a bastard of European currencies compared with 1984. Bloody ell, thought Bloom, that's four rods a hectare, two poles a lysander (or some such names as these).

Bloom, not seeing Corny Kelleher, watched the drayman roll the fat vats, ping, buzz, VAT is *not* payable (i.e. *not* payable) on children's seed, mouse clothing, gibbets FOR OWN USE (except early closing day Runcorn & Exmoor Central), clockwork ponds, SECONDHAND bacteria (unless pre-packaged for use NOT before January 1, 1979), wooden tunnels, dependent relatives (tinned), *Dead* Sea scrolls, unknown soldiers (if intended as presents), goal areas, yak droppings, or women exempted from jury service under the 1839 Scottish Peers of the Realm Act (BBC-2, Thursday, *rpt.*) IF YOU HAVE NOT BEEN VACCINATED, your AA number may have changed BUT the membership fee (£7777.77) will be nevertheless automatically debited from your deposit account. DO NOT throw this away, it is NOT an advertisement, the fixed penalty notice is already on its way to you, REMEMBER that failure to comply could mean a *minimum* of three months imprisonment, plus 35p postage & packing (returnable on receipt of counterfoil if HANDED in *personally* at your local Department of Health and Social Security or most large stores within our delivery area).

And, hiccup, Leopold Gloom, reprocess, Leopold Gloom, ping, reprocess, Leopold Gloom, clunk, reprocess, Leopold Gloom . . .

We are instructed to inform you that no Leopold Gloom exists in our records, there is no NI number in that nume, there is no VAT number in that nume, there is no car registration, cat registration, hat registration, hut registration, there is no service guarantee in that gnome, no account, no attached docket, ticket, bucket, pocket, packet, locket, there is no . . .

Person.

He does not exist.

Exits.

Triese – Zurich – Paris – Swansea – Southend – Whitehall, 1979 – 1900000.02

Some Enchanted Evening

8.5
Design by Five
A series of five programmes
4: A Sitting Room for Alan Coren designed by Max Glendenning
ALAN COREN, Editor of Punch, raconteur and wit, wants his sitting room to be a background for lively conversation amongst his journalist and cartoonist friends.

Radio Times

'I NEARLY got the car back this morning,' I began.

They settled in their chairs.

'*This* morning?' enquired a cartoonist.

'Before lunch, as it were?' asked the literary editor.

'Quite,' I riposted, swishing the Hine around its balloon. 'I'm talking about – what? – somewhere between eleven and eleven-thirty.'

Nobody said anything; there were one or two sharp intakes of breath, though.

'Yes,' I continued, 'I went up to Malvern Road, and I nearly got it back. When I say nearly, what I mean is they'd managed to get the bell-housing out, but the part they'd back-ordered from the stores at Brentford hadn't come in.'

'Typical!' said the features editor.

Everyone roared.

'A cog, as I understand it,' I said.

'Haven't they closed off Malvern Road?' asked another cartoonist. 'I only bring the point up because I used to use Malvern Road as a short cut when I was married to my first wife in Elgin

237

Avenue, and in those days – where are we now? 1979? – in those days, when we used to have to visit her mother in the Brompton Hospital with her chest, in those days the best way to cross the Harrow Road was to go down Malvern Road. As it then was. And then last week, when I had to go to Fulham, I suddenly remembered somebody telling me that they'd closed it off.'

'Well, it's not *exactly* closed off,' I countered, quick as a flash.

'More of a temporary detour, perhaps?' offered a senior political correspondent, helping himself to scotch.

'Exactly!' I said. 'You can still get in if you approach it from the Paddington end.'

'Isn't that strange?' said the second cartoonist, quietly.

We leaned forward.

'I never realised,' he said, almost to himself, 'that it had a Paddington end.'

'London's changed so much in the past ten years,' said the literary editor. 'All the one-way systems, those zig-zags near zebra crossings, the treble yellow marks.'

'I've never known what those stand for,' said the first cartoonist. 'Is it no unloading, or no waiting between the times specified?'

A third cartoonist, who up until this moment had not spoken, walked slowly to the window, and looked out towards the darkened garden.

'I don't bloody know,' he said.

Everybody took another drink. Time seemed to stand still.

'So there I was,' I said, when I judged the moment right, 'looking at this bell-housing, and the works foreman came up, and he said: *I was thinking whether we couldn't make do with a cog from a later model, but then I thought, no.*'

The literary editor looked at me. His cigar had gone out.

'He was probably thinking that if he *were* to do that,' he said, 'you'd only have more trouble with it later on.'

I nodded, and drained my glass.

'Those were his very words,' I said.

The editor of a major political weekly, who had bided his time until now, suddenly cleared his throat.

'I had the same trouble with a 1973 Saab,' he said. 'It left all of us on the A226, four miles from the thing.'

'The A20 intersection?' suggested the second cartoonist.

'If that's the one I'm thinking of, yes,' said the editor. 'Of course, when I say the *same* trouble, I suppose what I really mean is similar trouble. The window went up and caught my wife's ear in it.'

There was a long silence.

'I wouldn't call that similar,' said the features editor.

'I wish I'd said that,' said the second cartoonist.

The literary editor smiled a secret, literary smile and said:

'You will –'

The third cartoonist interrupted angrily.

'What I fail to see,' he said, squirting his syphon irritably, 'is why it left *all* of you on the A226.'

'Look,' I said, 'aren't we rather getting away from the point? The point is, I had to walk back from Malvern Road towards Kensal Rise tube station. I bought a ticket to Blackfriars, and . . .'

'No you didn't,' said the first cartoonist.

In the tension, the clock ticked, the central heating bonged a muted bong. Out of the corner of my eye, I saw something walk up the rubber plant.

'What?' I muttered.

'There isn't a Kensal Rise tube station,' said the first cartoonist. 'You may have *walked* to Kensal Rise, I'm not saying you didn't, but once there, you either went into Kensal Green tube station, or –' and here he paused significantly '– Queen's Park.'

'You put *either* in the wrong place,' said the editor of the major political weekly. 'You went *either* into Kensal Green or Queen's Park, is the correct syntax.'

The first cartoonist looked at him.

'Shut your face,' he said.

When the laughter had died down, and we had finished scribbling the *mot* on our dickies, the second cartoonist said:

'On your walk to Kensal Rise, did you pass any women with big knockers?'

I thought for a while. Someone opened another bottle.

'I'm not sure,' I said.

The second cartoonist snorted.

'Calls himself a raconteur,' he said.

'Personally,' said a journalist who up until now had been lying under the drinks cupboard, 'personally, I'm a leg man. That swelling of the calf. Know what I'm driving at?'

The editor of the major political weekly reached for an olive, and knocked over the peanuts.

'What did you expect us to do?' he cried. 'We couldn't just bloody leave her there with her ear jammed in the door.'

The literary editor put an arm around his shoulder, tipping his gin down the editor's lapel.

'Legs, knockers, what does it matter?' said the features editor. 'They're all women in the final analysis, at the end of the day, when you come right down to it. Or am I wrong?'

'Look,' I snapped, opening a second bottle of brandy and pouring a generous treble over my hand, 'whichever way you slice it, there I was on the Bakerloo Line, *but going towards Watford Junction!*'

'Bloody hell!'

'Christ Almighty!'

'You should have been going towards Elephant and Castle,' said the senior political correspondent, through a haze of blown Twiglet dust, 'if you'd bought a ticket to Blackfriars!'

'Exactly my point,' I cried.

The features editor got up slowly, and walked into the wall.

'Do you know,' he said, stanching his left nostril with his tie, 'just how many eligible women there are in the world? Even cutting out South America and those over sixty, it comes to nearly a billion.'

'How much did you earn last year?' replied the first cartoonist.

The editor of the major political weekly dried his eyes.

'If you want my opinion,' he said, 'Saabs is why all those Swedes cut their wrists.'

'Finns,' corrected the third cartoonist.

The editor stared at him.

'Cut their fins?' he said. He reached for the syphon, and filled his shoe. '*Cut their fins?*'

'Come on!' shouted the first cartoonist, leaping up and bunching his fists. 'How much? Six grand? Ten? *Twenty?*'

'What he means,' the literary editor said to the editor of the major political weekly, 'is the Saab is Finnish.'

'Mine bloody is,' said the editor, nodding gloomily. 'Kaput. Up das spout. Chop, chop.'

On the carpet, the features editor crawled slowly towards the door, dragging his empty bottle. My guests stared at him, heads bobbing. I felt their attention slipping away.

'So what I had to do,' I said, loudly, 'was get out at Stonebridge Park, cross over to the other side, and wait for a train going in the opposite direction.'

There heads swung round again. The literary editor was the first to speak.

'There's an olive in my brandy,' he said.

'You were drinking gin,' said the editor of the major political weekly. 'It's all down me. I wouldn't forget a thing like that.'

'Well, then, clever dick,' shouted the literary editor triumphantly, 'why has it gone bloody brown, then?'

'Thirty grand?' screamed the first cartoonist. 'Forty?'

The features editor had reached the corner, and was folded into it.

'On reflection,' he said, largely to a lamp, 'on reflection, I see no reason to exclude South America. They have wonderful women down there, so I understand. Hairy, yes, but not without charm. That brings the total to nearly one and a half billion. Not,' he added, sitting up and looking at me out of one eye, 'that you would have passed many South American women walking to Stonebridge Park.'

'Next time,' said the editor of the major political weekly, 'it's an Allegro for me, and bugger the status.'

The third cartoonist dropped lithely into a heap and crept towards the features editor. He took him by the lapel, with a wet fist.

'He never bloody walked to Stonebridge Park,' he muttered. 'He changed *trains* at Stonebridge Park.'

The features editor sat looking at the third cartoonist for some minutes, the grey sweat gleaming on his forehead like lard on a lightbulb.

'I don't think I feel very well,' he said, at last.

'Here we go,' I quipped. 'Someone pass him the *Radio Times*, will you?'

Moby Junk

Dolphins fear cry of glass fibre whale
The prototype of a mechanical killer whale, designed to frighten dolphins away from Japan's fishing waters, appears to deceive the ocean's most intelligent mammal, when recorded cries of the whale are transmitted from within the equipment.

The Times

CALL ME Ishmael. I think it's a really terrific name, I practise it in front of the mirror a lot, it has, you know, *resonance*.

My publisher came up with it just before I sailed on the *Pequod*, he is a very now person, he is right in there where tomorrow publishing is putting it together.

It isn't Ishmael Anything, or Anything Ishmael, it's a whole new marketing concept, just the one name, like Capucine, Gucci, Regine, all that. It was bound to happen on the book scene sometime, my publisher says, and sometime just blew in.

The book was his idea, too. We met at Jacky's a few months back, and he'd seen this spread I did for *Cosmo* about how you can judge people's libido from how thin their watches are, and he said: 'The next big thing is whales. Did you hear where they're going, what is it, extinct, and everybody who is anybody is out of their skulls with worry, Liz Taylor, Princess Michael, Twiggy, you wouldn't *believe* how much Big People are into whales, I see quartermillion hardback, *minimum*! Do a book, about 10 x 8, something substantial, double page pix. So what am I talking about? I am talking about *Jaws* with *heart*, that's what I'm talking about!'

*

I met Queequeg at the Spouter-Inn. I really dig Nantucket, it's full of very creative persons, top agency men, tax geniuses, ex-Watergate guys who are putting all their stash into decor consultancy, everyone has these weekend places up there; they all hang out at the Spouter-Inn, it has these wonderful polystyrene beams, terrific repro barometers everywhere, a roaring Flamo Fumefree Adjustaflicker fire, and a whole load of marvellous *kitscherei* – Mickey Mouse ice cubes in plastic pineapples, cryogenic swizzle-sticks with little male chauvinist pigs on the end, genuine Gottlieb pin-tables, you really have to see it. Anyhow, I was sitting in the Chappaquiddick Room (they've done it up as a submerged Chevy Impala; one wall is nothing but fog-lights with live guppies in them) when I saw this huge, I mean *huge*, coloured guy, covered in tattoos. I had eighteen shots of him in the Pentax before I even went across to ask if he'd like his Campari freshened.

'Call me Ishmael,' I said.

'Terrific,' he replied. 'Call me Queequeg.'

'Queequeg who?'

'Just Queequeg.'

I reeled!

'You have to be kidding!' I cried. 'You're an author, too?' He shook his head.

'I whale,' he said.

I relaxed.

'An alto player,' I said, 'I should have guessed. With all the rhythm you people have – you know, sometimes I feel maybe slavery wasn't such a bad thing, it taught you pain, it made you respond. Tell me, do you know *Melancholy Baby*?'

He looked at me kind of funny; then he reached behind him and brought out this enormous pole with a terrible barb on one end.

'Jesus!' I cried. 'You play *that*?'

Next morning, when he came to give back my copy of *Giovanni's Room*, he said:

'Look, man, how'd you like to sail on the *Pequod*?'

'The *Pequod*! It's exactly what I've been looking for! But

244

could you swing it?'

'No sweat, man,' said Queequeg. 'We're low on scribes this trip. Lensmen, sound crews, environment freaks, you name it, they're busting out of every goddam hatch; but no scribes. It's killing the Captain. He's very, you know, yesterday; he's really into verbal communication. Let's go and see him.'

'Terrific!' I cried, grasping his hand. And noticing, as I did so, that his tattoos seemed to have vanished.

'Transfers,' explained Queequeg, when I enquired. 'Where's your head at, man? Everybody's into acrylic water-solubles now. It's where being a matelot is. Listen, if I'm gonna go sticking needles into my goddam arm, it sure as hell ain't gonna be ink I'm shooting!'

And here the huge harpoonist laughed his thunderous laugh.

I have to admit my first sight of the *Pequod* was disappointing.

'It has a funnel, for God's sake!' I said to Queequeg. 'It has, like, rigging.'

'Yeah,' said Queequeg. 'That's Ahab, all right.'

'I was hoping for a pool,' I said. 'Do you carry Scalectrix?'

Queequeg shook his enormous head.

'Fridays we fix a sauna up aft,' he said. 'We tap the boiler. But it's pretty, you know, ad hoc.'

We started up the gangplank, towards a squat, swarthy figure standing at the top.

'Who's he?' I whispered.

'Starbuck,' replied Queequeg. 'First mate.'

'*Who* Starbuck?' I enquired anxiously. 'Jack? Warren? Burt?'

'Just Starbuck.'

My heart sank. Maybe I didn't have such a hot publisher, after all.

'Watch him,' muttered Queequeg, 'he's a God-freak. Very heavy.' He raised his voice as we reached the top. 'Morning, Starbuck. This is Ishmael. He's sailing with us.'

'Really?' cried Starbuck, a blaze starting in his piggy eyes. 'How'd you like to go to Guyana?' He shoved a clipboard under my nose. 'If I get fifty-one per cent of the crew to sign, we'll send a deposition to the Captain.' He shoved a pen into my hand.

'It's this really terrific cult, very fundamentalist, you'll love it, they have girls, liquor, the food is out of this world, sucking pig, armadillo on the half-shell, roast –'

'BELAY THERE, STARBUCK!'

Gulls rose, shrieking, at the voice! It rolled across Nantucket Bay like thunder! It froze the blood in my very veins! My head whipped up, in time to see its owner, peg-leg swinging, hurtle along the deck towards us, snatch the clipboard from Starbuck's hand, and send it winging on a spinning arc into the sea.

'THOU SHALT HAVE ONE GOD ONLY!' roared the Captain. His terrible eye rolled upward, and his terrible finger followed. 'I know Him, and He knows me!' His free hand gathered around Starbuck's throat. 'None of your trashy plastic faiths, Mister Mate, none of your Johnny-come-lately evangelistic rubbish, none of –'

'Okay, okay,' here Starbuck, wriggling, spread concessionary hands, 'how about Bali, it's hardly out of our way, there's this Unitarian consciousness-raising group, they believe up to four per cent of the Old Testament, Captain, and if you only saw how some of them dames is built, you'd –'

The Captain flung him aside, and turned his great head to me.

'You must be Captain Ahab,' I said pleasantly. 'I'm sorry, I didn't catch your first name.'

'Just Ahab,' he growled.

'Oh.'

'I'll not be doing,' he bellowed, 'with any of your cheap trashy, TV-dinner-on-your-lap names, with your Kevins and your Craigs, your Melvyns and your Russells, your Jonathans and –'

'I really like your leg,' I said, frantic to stem his rage. 'It's very chic.'

In the long silence, I could hear the creak of something shippy.

'Ah,' said Ahab, at last, and quietly. 'Chic, is it? Trendy, perhaps? *In?*'

'Well,' I said, 'perhaps not *in*, exactly, I mean what is *really* in is prosthetic tibia-plus-whole-foot units in space alloys, just one more wonderful Apollo spin-off, they're so good you can actually wear wedges without tottering, and –'

The breath left my body as Ahab's thick forearm pressed me

against the mast.

'*This* peg,' he growled, his face a millimetre from mine, 'was hand-carved from a sperm-whale's jaw by *craftsmen*! She is a custom leg, a bespoke leg, she is none of your tatty Moon rubbish! That tin trash may do very well for your intergalactic pansy scum with their natty silver suits, I ain't saying it don't, but is it a leg for a seafaring man with a heart full of boiling blood?'

I shook my head vigorously.

'Absolutely not!' I cried. 'No, no, no, that leg is *you*!'

He dropped me, and spun away.

'Cast off for'ard!' roared Captain Ahab. 'Cast off aft!'

I didn't talk to him for the next eight days as the *Pequod* ploughed north to whale-water, but I saw him standing motionless on the bridge, his terrible eye glittering over the doings below as *Vogue* models posed that year's sable anoraks against the davits, and the documentary Arriflexes whirred, and the crew sang shanties into the microphones of a dozen different record labels, and bearded politicians in faded denims told bearded journalists in faded denims of the desperate need to find synthetic substitutes for ambergris.

But on the ninth morning, bored with pounding my IBM, I took the liberty of mounting the bridge.

'I was wondering, Captain,' I said, 'whether you would care for a hand of kaluki? You looked so, I don't know, *solitary*.'

The grey face, with its livid scar, turned slowly from its motionless scanning of the sea.

'Kaluki, is it?' he muttered. 'Or canasta, perhaps? Backgammon, bridge, Cluedo? Scrabble, cribbage, gobs, Up Jenkins, eh, Mister Ishmael, while the cauldrons of hell bubble?'

I sighed.

'I sometimes wonder,' I said, waving a hand towards the activity below, 'how you stand us all.'

Ahab spat fluently.

'I stand 'ee,' he said, 'on account of ye finance the Quest. I put up with the rubbish and the squawking and the posing and the mincing and the natter because it pays the bill. It keeps the *Pequod* afloat. It'll settle the account of Moby Dick!'

'Moby Dick?' I exclaimed. 'Could that be the great white whale who took your leg off at the knee, since when your whole life and being has been committed to his pursuit and destruction, with all the symbolic overtones that that entails?'

'Aye,' said Ahab. 'That's 'im.' He turned his head towards the sea again. 'They wants to be chartered accountants, they wants to live in detached freehold premises, they wants Porsches for the golf clubs and Volvos for the wife, they wants double ovens and video-cassette recorders and solar panels for the swimming pool, they wants Colour Supplements and three weeks on the Costa Smeralda and a Filipino couple in a flat over the garage, they wants quartz-digital this and silicon-chip that and a wafer-thin pocket calculator ye can slip into your flipper to enable 'ee to compute tax-benefits while snorkelling off Grand Bahama – but what is all that to the *real* Quest, eh?'

I cleared my throat.

'I take it,' I said, 'that as far as Saving The Whale is concerned, your wholehearted support cannot fully be –'

'THAR SHE BLOWS!'

Our two heads swivelled simultaneously upward, to where Queequeg hung pointing from the crow's nest. Ahab flicked out his telescope, smacked it against his eye, and staggered.

''Tis him!' he screamed. ''Tis him!'

And it was.

So we crammed on steam, and we crammed on sail, and we crammed on lenses and type-ribbons and microphones and tape-recorders, and we hugged ourselves with excitement for a day and a night, as we tracked the great white whale in its ultimate sprint, with sweating Queequeg crouched in the prow, harpoon in hand (for the Captain would have no truck with pansy guns and newfangled trash); but when the great white whale paused, at last, exhausted, it was Ahab himself who stumped to the bow, and snatched the spear from Queequeg's hand, and Ahab himself, with a terrible cry, who hurled it down to the glistening flanks.

And, therefore, Ahab himself whose foot was caught in the spilling line, and Ahab himself who was plucked from the prow, and Ahab himself who was lashed to his quarry with the kind of irony you normally get only in hand-tooled uniform editions, and Ahab himself who was dragged to the bottom with the ruined whale.

Leaving us on the bobbing *Pequod* with the earnest prayer that his dying ears had never picked up the unmistakable clunk of busted clockwork.

Two Sleepy People, with Nothing to Do

The English are not a sensual nation: puritanism, a cold climate, and an education which frowns on joy have seen to that. They go to bed with each other for various reasons, but only sometimes for the simple pleasure of food. They go there in order to be seen by other people; to have their egos massaged by subservient waiters; to impress the opposite sex with their social adroitness; to get drunk.

Tatler

IT WAS generally agreed to have been the most super wedding one had ever been to.

The bride, of course, looked absolutely stunning.

'Doesn't Lucinda look absolutely stunning?' said her best friend Melissa.

'Ra*ther!*' cried Melissa's husband.

'Jolly stately and serene,' said Melissa, as Lucinda swept past them down the aisle on the arm of the Earl. 'One is rather reminded of old Queen Mary, isn't one?'

'I thought that had three funnels,' said Melissa's husband, frowning.

Rodney-Rodney made a magnificent bridegroom. Scion of the only English family allowed to hyphenate its Christian names (a favour bestowed at Bannockburn when one of Rodney-Rodney's illustrious ancestors had relieved a pustule on Edward II), he was as tall as it is possible to be without arousing genetic suspicion, and slim as a flute. True, his chin fell away sharply from his upper canines, above which, as if in Dame Nature's kindly compensation, his nose sprang out for several overstated inches (he had been known as Beaky-Beaky at Dame Poumfret's Preparatory Academy for the Appallingly Dim, and the name had stuck); but by great good fortune, his bride's county nose was retroussé to the point of invisibility and her chin jutted out so far that her small bust lay in permanent shadow. In short, Lucinda and Rodney-Rodney appeared to complement one another perfectly: when they kissed at the altar, their two profiles meshed as effortlessly as Bentley clutch-plates.

It was, however, the first kiss in which either of them had ever been involved. Throughout her twenty-one years, Lucinda's only romantic attachment had been a heavy crush on Red Rum, while Rodney-Rodney, at twenty-three, had entered into only one non-platonic relationship, with a Fräulein Sharon, to whose discreet Curzon Street premises he would repair every Thursday after the Brigade dinner, to be beaten with a blancoed length of Boer webbing.

But because Lucinda's daddy, the Earl, owned eighty thousand acres of shooting but preferred fishing, whereas Rodney-Rodney's daddy, Charlie-Charlie, owned eighty miles of salmon-river but preferred shooting, their marriage had been a foregone conclusion for some time.

Nevertheless, to say that they were ill-prepared is seriously to underestimate the English upper classes: on the day before the ceremony, Charlie-Charlie took Rodney-Rodney into the library at Toppins, gave him a large brandy, and showed him an illustrated copy of Fernleigh's *Breeding Springers*; and the Countess, for her part, formally handed over to Lucinda the Hapsburg bullet upon which her family's brides had been biting ever since the Thirty Years' War.

At the reception, everybody got wonderfully, wonderfully tight. They danced the Lancers, in which seven shoulders were dislocated, and the Gay Gordons, in which no fewer than thirty-seven people made the same joke about MI5, and an Eightsome Reel, in which no fewer than thirty-seven people made the same joke about Highland underwear, and they played Maim the Staff, in which Rodney-Rodney himself managed to disable two footmen and an under-gardener with Dom Perignon bottles from sixty paces, despite having had his monocle shattered during the Ladies Excuse-me Wall Game.

And at six o'clock, being tired little teddy bears, the happy couple slipped away in Rodney-Rodney's Lagonda across the croquet lawn, and, pausing only to leave the offside front wing on an elderly yew, purred off towards the far Savoy and the first leg of their mooners in Canners.

It was a pleasant suite: by jumping on the bed, Rodney-Rodney found he could bang his head on the ceiling, and Lucinda was ecstatic to find that there was even a tiny, tiny paddling-pool beside the loo so that her rubber duck could float about without getting lonely. She unpacked carefully, put her bullet by the bed, and slid between the sheets, leaving Rodney-Rodney to pad into the bathroom with *Breeding Springers* for a little last-minute revision while she turned the pages of *Tatler*, which was the only reading-matter she ever saw and from which she invariably took her behavioural cues.

It was while she was flicking through the glossy breathlessness in the hope of finding, perhaps, some indication of when the bullet was supposed to be enmouthed, that she suddenly issued a shrill cry. Rodney-Rodney, who had been barking seductively behind the door, dashed out, his long face twisted apprehensively at this new evidence of feminine unpredictability.

'What is it, old stick?' he cried, 'not women's problems?' He raked, gamely, through his sparse garnering of marital notes. 'Should I burp you, or something?'

'Oh, Beaky-Beaky!' cried Lucinda, eyes a-shine. 'Nothing like that! There is a super piece in *Tatler* about how people are supposed to do it!'

'Do what?'

'You know,' murmured Lucinda. 'Thing.'

'*Thing?*' exclaimed Rodney-Rodney, his imperceptible jaw dropping. 'In *Tatters*?'

'Isn't it thrilling?' shouted Lucinda.

'And just in the nick of, er, whateveritis!' cried Rodney-Rodney, jumping up and down. 'Does it tell one how to examine one's feet for hardpad? This book's jolly difficult to follow.'

'There's nothing about that here,' replied Lucinda.

'Apparently one sometimes starts off with food.'

'Hurrah!' shouted Rodney-Rodney, 'I think this ought to be one of those times don't you? One works up a jolly enormous appetite barking, I can tell you! Hardly surprising dogs get right down to it, shoving their beezers in the jellymeat, no knives or forks or anything, one suddenly sees the reason behind it. Let's have some oysters and a duck or two!'

'Right-ho!' shrieked his bride, clapping her hands. 'I say, Beaky-Beaky, I was never allowed to eat in bed were you? Isn't it absolutely super being grown-up? And the other thing about getting food sent up is the waiters will be able to massage our egos!'

Two lines crinkled on Rodney-Rodney's teeny brow.

'What on earth are *those*?' he said. 'I say, I hope it's not that thing they caught little Berkshire doing with Crown Prince Bhunah at Dame Poumfret's. If one went blind, one's hunting career would be utterly ruined!'

'It'll be all right,' said Lucinda confidently. 'There'll be other people watching.'

'What sort of people?'

'It doesn't say. I should think any old people would do. Why don't I order the food while you nip out and whip in a few spectators?'

'*Super!*' cried Rodney-Rodney, slipping into his dressing-gown. 'I say, old thing, is one allowed to drink, too?'

'It says,' replied Lucinda, scanning the page almost without moving her lips, 'that one is supposed to get drunk!'

Rodney-Rodney reeled.

'What bliss!' he shouted. 'Is it any wonder one's parents keep one in the old harry darkers about thing? One would never do anything else!'

When, ten minutes later, he returned, there were five small Japanese businessmen with him. They bowed towards Lucinda.

'Best I could do, I'm afraid,' said Rodney-Rodney. 'They were jabbering in the corridor. They don't seem to speak anything but Jap, but they shot off like grouse when I snapped my fingers. Can't think why. Do you suppose they're prisoners-of-war, or something?'

'Jolly lucky being imprisoned in the Savoy,' said Lucinda.

'Oh, I don't know,' said Rodney-Rodney, 'I bet they have to stick to the set menu. Things like that. Will they do?'

'I should think so,' replied Lucinda, waving the Japanese to sit. 'They only have to watch, after all.'

There was a soft knock on the door, and Rodney-Rodney opened it to admit two waiters pushing a trolley, and a sommelier with a shouldered crate of Bollinger. He shot into bed. They followed with the trolley, served the oysters, eased a cork, and were about to leave, when Rodney-Rodney cried:

'I say, would you mind staying? This is our wedding-night.'

The trio paused; but since Rodney-Rodney's accent was full of money, they stayed, sliding themselves professionally back against the walls. Lucinda, having despatched three bivalves with scarcely a slurp, hurled the shells at the gazing Japs. She hit two.

'I say!' exclaimed her husband. 'That's a bit strong, old girl. Geneva Convention, and all that.'

'One is supposed,' replied Lucinda, passing the magazine across, 'to impress the opposite sex with one's social adroitness.'

'I *see!*' shouted Rodney-Rodney. 'Well, I'm jolly impressed, old girl. I've not seen better chucking from a sitting position since Farty Cork-Snettering laid out the Connaught's maître d' with a chump chop! Still, just to show that one is no mean hand oneself when the social adroitness rosettes are being dished out . . .'

Whereupon Rodney-Rodney sprang lithely from the bed, scattering croquettes, stood on his head in the middle of the room, and downed an entire bottle of champagne without taking it from his inverted lips.

'As performed on Boat Race Night '74!' he shrieked.

The Japanese applauded.

'God,' gasped Rodney-Rodney, when he had removed his head from the waste-bin and allowed a little colour to drain back into his saffron cheeks, 'isn't this the most super fun? Beats being a springer, I can tell you!' He wiped his mouth, while a clench-faced waiter took the waste-bin to the bathroom. 'What do we have to do next?'

There was no reply.

Rodney-Rodney loped erratically to the bed. Lucinda, having

drunk two bottles on her own loyal behalf, lay fast asleep, her head on a duck, her auburn locks fetchingly highlighted by the *sauce de cerises*.

Her husband gazed at her for some time, rocking on his bare heels.

'Was it wonderful for you, too, old thing?' he murmured finally.

Then he sat down sharply on the floor beside her, and opened his third bottle.

Back at the grimy composing-room of *Tatler*, the horny-handed printers toasted their latest brilliant sabotage in Newcastle Brown, and plotted their next. They had been given a riding article to set, explaining how best to present a horse at a 6-foot jump. It would be the work of a moment to make it 16-foot. By such canny sleights, a dropped line here, a transposed word there, it would not be long, surely, before all the ancient lines died out, all the ensigns of privilege were extirpated, and the revolution was quietly ushered in.

The Cricklewood Greats

Why not build film studios there? After all, to many people,
Cricklewood is a vibrant, cosmopolitan, glamorous place.
                                                    Evening Standard

I LOVE this crazy town.

I came here a long time ago, the way a lot of people did who
had stars in their eyes, and it still has the old magic. That
wonderful wacky feeling of waking up in the morning and
knowing that anything could happen, and probably will! Maybe
there'll be a refuse strike, and we'll have to haul our garbage
right over to Dollis Hill, Rovers and Volvos and chirpy little
Hondas with their seats piled high with bulging black plastic
bags, and behind the wheel famous faces from the shoe industry,
from the world of quantity surveying and army surplus, from the
tobacconist profession, driving along just like ordinary men and
women, pulling their weight for the community. Or maybe the
milkman will be out of cherry yoghurt and you'll hear kids'
voices raised above the busy clatter of breaking crockery. It
could be that the traffic lights will blow again, the way they do
in this anything-goes town, at the glittering junction of
Cricklewood Lane and Hendon Way, and the colourful
juggernauts will be backed up as far as Cricklewood Broadway,
many of them hooting. Or I might just take an ordinary thing,
such as a stroll, down to the famous mailbox in West End Lane
and meet one of Cricklewood's real old-timers, like Nat Selby,
say, the former blouse factor now sadly retired, who's been here
so long he'll walk right past me without saying anything. That's
the kind of town Cricklewood is.

I came out here soon after I was married, a green kid from nearly three miles away; that was in the days before there was a flyover at Staples Corner bringing, as it inevitably did, the Edgware Road into the raucous, sizzling, tinsel world of the Twentieth Century. In the old days of which I speak, you could actually drive right past the Staples Mattress Factory itself, look up at the windows, and almost see the people making the interior springing destined to travel from there to countless parts of the Home Counties. Now there is only the flyover: tourists can roar in from Colindale and Burnt Oak right to the very heart of Cricklewood itself, even missing the bus garage at Gladstone Park where the big Number Sixteens turn round in their dozens, under the ever-watchful eyes of top-name Inspectors.

They had the studio system, then. It was run by a handful of moguls who had become legends in their own lifetime. They hadn't always been moguls, most of them had come over here as ragged kids from Poland and Russia and Latvia; they came to this wide open town, and even if they couldn't speak English too well, they knew the studio business. The way it worked was, you would go into one of their famous estate offices, and you would ask if they had any flats at around eight pounds a week, and they would look at you and come out with one of their now-legendary wisecracks, such as 'Flats at around *eight pounds a week*? You're asking me if we've got any *flats* at eight pounds a week. At eight pounds a week, you're asking *me* if we've got any flats?'

And then, just as you were about to apologise and leave, the mogul would riffle through his papers and say: 'How about a studio?'

And you, because you were young and romantic and naïve and remembered Cornel Wilde composing his Unfinished Symphony in a sun-filled atelier, you would turn and cry: 'A studio?'

And the mogul would quip, 'Have *I* got a studio for you!'

And within an hour you would be sitting in your own base-ment bedsitter in Definitely Not Kilburn, hoping someone would come and drive the removal van away from your air-vent and let enough light in for you to swat the rats. It was a large area, Definitely Not Kilburn, a mile or so from downtown Cricklewood; it received its name from estate agents' handouts, and a lot of us lived there, underneath Kilburn High Road. But by the time you realised, it was too late: you had signed the contract; you were bound to the studio for years.

But you made good, in time, because a lot of people did, and if they didn't, you didn't get to hear about it, because Cricklewood wasn't about failure. The ones who didn't make it just quietly packed up and went back to Limerick and Hyderabad and Lower Volta.

And yet, for those who did make it, success often came at incalculable personal cost. I talked, just a day or so ago, to Bernie Schwartz, a man who has been a star for as long as anybody can remember and whose name is a household word wherever pickle-jars are opened; not, of course, that that name was always Bernie Schwartz; he was born humble Tony Curtis, but there was a lot of prejudice in Cricklewood in the early days, and as he so frankly puts it, 'Who'd buy delicatessen from someone called Curtis?'

We were sitting in the manicured grounds of his elegant nearly-detached Brondesbury Hills mansion, beside his pool, and watching his children inflate it from an expensive-looking foot-pump, when I said to him: 'You've come a long way, Bernie, from that one little shop in Fortune Green Road. You now have two little shops in Fortune Green Road. You must be a happy man.'

He smiled, a little wearily.

'*Nihil est ab omni parte beatum*,' he murmured, in the rich Middle Etonian accent of his people, which he has never quite lost. 'Nothing is all good, old sport. It cost me my wife, remember. Ambition is a cruel taskmaster. Putting her in charge of the second shop was a terrible mistake.'

I looked away. I had, of course, heard rumours. In a town like Cricklewood, gossip runs rife; and stars have many enemies.

'I understand,' I said, quietly, 'that she couldn't keep her hands off the stock?'

'It was the pumpernickel that finally got her,' he said, nodding. 'She weighs twenty-eight stone now, you know. She may have to spend the rest of her life at a health farm.'

There are many personal tragedies like that in Cricklewood.

*

As the song says, a million hearts beat quicker there,* and it is a pace to which many of those bright hearts fall victim. Marriages and a Cricklewood career rarely mix: take, for example, the star-cros't, ill-matched Sidney and Doreen Brill, whose tempestuous relationship came to its dreadful but inevitable end in that summer of 1971 that none of us will ever forget.

Sidney, at forty-four, was at the height of his career as a traveller in bathroom sundries. His work naturally took him away from home much of the time, driven on as he was by the dream not only of becoming Area Sales Manager (NW London), but also of earning enough to convert his toolshed into a sauna. Doreen was left alone, drinking advocaat and wondering when he was going to put the shelf up in the kitchen. One evening in late July, after he had returned worn-out in his sleek Mini Clubman, she put that question to him, for the twentieth time. 'I don't bloody know,' he replied; and she hit him with the bottle. It was the end of his career; after the blow, he could never remember how to get out onto the North Circular from Willesden Lane. They were forced to sell Dunscreamin, and moved away. We never heard of them again. Just two more casualties of the battle for wealth and stardom.

But there were heroes, too; and none more worthy of the name than that tiny, courageous, persecuted group who became known as The Cricklewood Ten. Now, two decades on, it is almost impossible to convey the terror that the name of McCarthy could evoke in all but the stoutest breasts. He was nothing much to look at, short, balding, only the tiny paranoid eyes betraying what lay in the addled brain behind, but when his council truck rumbled down the opulent Cricklewood streets every November, and McCarthy would hammer at each pastel door and cry his fearful cry of 'Happy Christmas from the dustmen!', people coughed up. It was more than your life was worth to ignore him; but ten householders did, and paid the dreadful penalty. Pleading the Fifth Amendment, which states that all council dustvans must bear clearly on their doors the legend *No gratuities*, they turned him from their teakette porch extensions, and faced a year not only of boot-crunched geraniums, fish-heads in the hedge, and a

*© Cricklewood Broadway Melody of 1933.

tin-filled front lawn, but also of the opprobrium and ostracism of their colleagues and neighbours who stared bitterly out from their trim John Lewis curtains at the litter-strewn streets and asked one another what the neighbourhood was coming to. Even now, long years afterwards with the old battles fought and won, some simmering rancour remains; only the other day, veteran member of the Ten, Dennis Bagley, told me: 'Hardly a night goes past without old Mrs Simmonds letting her collie widdle on my bumper.'

But if many of the old attitudes haven't changed, Cricklewood itself has. Time and economics have caught it up; the wildness, and the crazy hopes, and the crazier buccaneering are long gone. The days when a raw good-looking kid could blow in from Tipperary and begin digging holes in the hope of making a fortune are past. Big international agglomerates do the road-works, now. The little unostentatious seeming-tatty garment shops where men became legends in their own lifetimes, if only with their tax inspectors, have made way for rank upon rank of anonymous chain-stores. And television, of course, has taken its drear toll of Cricklewood: stroll down the Broadway now, and every third window belongs to a TV-rental company, its glimmering sets stared at by groups of expatriate Provisionals trying to follow the test card.

True, there are still parties where you can get cheddar and pineapple on the same stick, but they don't go on beyond ten pm any more; there are still wacky people doing wacky stunts, but they're not in the same league as the time old Big Bill Hooper came to a Guy Fawkes' celebration in his wife's raincoat; there is still a strange smell at the corner of Fordwych Road, but it doesn't make the headlines any more.

Yet to many of us who remember the great days, Cricklewood remains a very special place, even if, perhaps, the glamour is today compounded largely of nostalgia. There is still that special something in the air, even if we've all come a long and not always happy way from that bright morning long ago when I put my handprint in the fresh cement outside the Ding Dong Chinese Takeaway, and was chased almost to Swiss Cottage by a screaming Mr Ding and a cleaver-waving Mrs Dong.

But what that special something is, who can say? When you begin to analyse it, it just, well, sort of comes apart in your hands, leaving nothing behind.

The Unacknowledged Legislators of NW3

A most attractive low-built Georgian house (c. 1770) close to the heart of Hampstead village, with many literary associations. It is believed John Kates spent time here, and entertained numerous notable poets of the day.

Advertisement in the Observer

OBADIAH CROCKER stood behind his wife, brows clenched, and silently mouthed the words, with considerable difficulty, as she quilled them onto the pasteboard rectangle, her fat tongue curled up over her top lip, tracing her soft moustache with bright dew.

She finished with a flourish, and tucked the quill neatly into her mob-cap.

'There!' she cried.

'NISE ROOM TO LETTE,' read her husband, 'NO BLAKKIES OR IRISH. WULD SUIT POET OR SIMLAR. Is that it?'

'I think it says it all,' said his wife. 'I'll put it in the front window.'

'Hang about,' said Crocker. 'What are blakkies?'

His wife threaded the cord, carefully.

'I'm not sure,' she said, when she had finished. She banged her temple sharply with the heel of her hand to adjust her squint. 'All I know is, you got to avoid them at the top end of the residential market. They widdle in the cupboards. It's a well-known feature of the profession.'

'I wouldn't say our loft was the top end of the residential

262

market,' said Crocker. 'I wouldn't call letting it out a profession. It's not as if it was cordwaining. It's hardly better than dentistry, letting rooms. All you got to do is swat the mice and stand there with your hand out Fridays. What's wrong with the Irish?'

'They're all Papists,' said his wife. 'They keep potatoes under the bed. Anyway, that wall wouldn't stand having a crucifix nailed to it. I'm not lying in bed every night all tensed up, waiting for his crucifix to fall off.'

She picked up the card, and waddled out of the scullery.

'I'm not sure you ought to be letting rooms at all,' shouted Crocker after her, 'with all your peculiar ideas! I'm not certain you're landlady material.'

'I wouldn't have to,' snapped his wife, coming back, 'if you'd learn to make a go of cordwaining.'

'Don't blame me,' retorted Crocker, darkening. 'It's all down to the Prince bloody Regent, is that. Cotton trousers, silk pumps, fur tippets – the bottom's dropped right out of leather.'

'Ha!' cried his wife. 'I suppose you never heard of suitcases? I suppose the word is entirely foreign to you?'

'It's not man's work, suitcases,' muttered her husband. 'Bloody box with a brass hinge on it, I don't call that cord-waining. I don't call that fulfilment. I don't recognise that as adequate recompense for five years' apprenticeship.'

'It's where the future is,' said his wife. She pointed a fat finger at the big black stove. 'See that kettle-lid bobbing up and down? Any day now, they'll be swarming between Stockton and Darlington like flies. The demand for smart luggage will be overwhelming.'

'Carpentry is what I call that,' said her husband.

'It's where the money is,' said his wife, bitterly.

'Why poets?' enquired Crocker, desperate to change the subject. 'Why would our loft suit poets?'

'They like lofts. Or studios, as we call them. Being up the top of things gives them inspiration.'

'Consumption is what it gives 'em,' said her husband. 'You can hear poets three streets away. You wouldn't credit what you can catch off poets. I'd rather have blakkies widdling in the cupboards. I'd rather have potatoes nailed up all over. I don't want some skinny herbert upstairs, honking away all night.' He fell briefly silent, stared at the table, set his jaw. 'That's not why I got married.'

'A poet,' said Mrs Crocker firmly, 'will add *ton*. I should not be so much a landlady as a sponsor of the arts. In France, people like that get famous. They hold salons.'

'It's not hard getting famous in France,' said Crocker. 'There's no standards. If I was to describe the quality of their leatherwork, you'd have a fit. It is an open secret among cordwainers that the outcome of the Battle of Waterloo hung totally upon the differing quality of the footwear. By the time the French Imperial Guard got to the top of their hill, they couldn't bloody move, let alone aim.'

'That's just your opinion.'

'Oh, is it? Just my opinion, is it, clever dick? If it's just my opinion, how come you never hear much about the Napoleon Boot?'

He was still chortling when the front-door knocker shook the little house. His wife bustled to answer it. When she returned, beaming, puffing, fanning herself, a thin young man in a straggled beard stood uncertainly behind her.

'This is Mr John Kates!' cried Mrs Crocker. 'He is a poet!'

Her husband glowered at him, kerchief to his lips.

'You better not breathe in here, mate!' he snapped, after a somewhat muffled fashion. 'We prepare food in here. Also, there's the cat! They got tiny chests, cats: one poetic bloody wheeze and it's goodbye, Raymond.'

'I like cats,' said the poet, gently. 'I've written an ode about them.' He cleared his throat, and Crocker winced horribly. 'Thou wast not born for death, immortal Mog!' declaimed Kates, 'No hungry generations . . .'

'Very nice,' interrupted Crocker. 'What about the consumption?'

His wife withered him with her good eye, the other rolling in glaucous fury.

'Don't you mind him, Mr Kates!' she cried. 'I may bear his name, but it stops there. He is not a person of *ton*. You sit down, and I'll coddle you a nice egg.'

'Oy!' barked Crocker. 'That's my egg.'

'Was,' corrected his wife, removing it from the larder. 'A salon may not be the proper place to bring this up, but nevertheless I would remind some people that they are not in work, whereas other people are bringing in rent regular and need to keep their strength up. Mr Kates is doing a long poem and does not want his energy drained.'

'Best place for it,' muttered Crocker.

'It could turn out an epic,' said the poet, sitting down at the table. 'They can take hours, epics. It's called *On A Chinese Urn*.'

'What's a Chinese urn?' enquired the solicitous Mrs Crocker.

'ABOUT FOUR GROATS A WEEK!' cried her husband. He fell off his chair, rolled on the stone floor, dragged himself upright, wiped his eyes.

'God,' said his wife, 'you're common!'

'Joe Miller,' said Crocker, glaring hard at Kates. 'There was a man. Never had a day's illness in his life.'

Kates, his mouth being full of food, did not reply. But when he had finished, he pushed away his plate, burped decorously into his thin whiskers, put one hand on his breast, threw the other out to arm's length, and cried:

'O what can ail thee, coddled egg?
  Alone and palely loitering?'

Mrs Crocker gasped, and clapped her hands.

'It just sort of come to me,' murmured Kates, blushing. 'They do that, poems. Course, it'll need work.'

He stood up, bowed stiffly, and went out.

'Isn't it wonderful?' sighed his new landlady. 'I shall be known to history as Madame de Crocker, I shouldn't wonder. People a century hence will beat a path to this door and pay up to two bob for a jam tea.'

Her husband ground his teeth.

'I never thought,' he muttered, 'I'd ever hear a wife of mine say hence.'

'Classbound, you are,' said Mrs Crocker. 'Plus no soul to speak of. I may be outgrowing you, Crocker.'

He was still sitting there, trying to think of a suitably caustic reply, when the front door banged, and Kates came back into the scullery. Behind him was a short redfaced man with a cardboard suitcase.

'Madame,' said Kates, and at the word Mrs Crocker's fat heart fluttered visibly beneath her smock, 'may I introduce a notable poet of the day? Byron, I should like to present Mrs Crocker.'

The good lady staggered, and fell back against the Welsh dresser. When the rattle of crockery had died, she said, hoarsely:

'*Lord* Byron?'

Byron pinched his nose, and wiped his thumb on his hat.

'Not entirely,' he replied, 'begob.' He put out his hand. 'Mick Byron. Poet,' he said, 'and wit.'

'First time I seen a poet,' said Obadiah Crocker slowly, 'with a shovel tied to his suitcase. If you can call it a suitcase.'

'Give us a poem, Mick,' said John Kates, nudging his friend.

'*To Mrs Crocker*,' announced Byron, after a moment's brow knitting. 'She walks in beauty, like the newt.'

Mrs Crocker sighed, and beamed.

'It's a bit bloody short,' said her husband.

'I don't do yer long jobs,' said Byron. 'No, what I sez is, get in, do it, get out. What's the pint in hanging about, dat's the philosophy of Mick Byron. Also, tink of what it saves yez in ink alone. Will I be after nipping out and fetching Shelley in, John?'

'Shelley?' enquired Mrs Crocker.

Kates smiled his most melting smile.

'It's such a *big* loft, Madame,' he crooned. 'And, as I am sure so sensitive a lady would be the first to appreciate, poets need the company of other poets. It stimulates us, it inspires us, it enables us to invoke the Muse, does it not, Byron?'

'Oh God, does it ever!' cried Byron. 'Sure, and isn't it meself been stood in me hole, up to me neck in mud, a hundred times, jist crying out for a bit of the ole Muse?' He mopped his huge face with a green spotted handkerchief. 'Oi gets as far as "So, we'll go no more a diggin, so late into the night", and oi stops dead.'

He stumbled out, and came back a moment later with a tall Jamaican.

'May I present,' said John Kates, 'Clyde Shelley?'

'Gimme some skin!' cried Shelley, slapping Crocker's dangling palm. Crocker stared at him.

'What's happened to your face?' he said. 'It seems to have been burnt!'

'How awful!' exclaimed Mrs Crocker. 'You poor thing!'

'Ain't it de troof?' said Shelley. 'Look on mah haid, ye Mighty, an' despair! Heh, heh, heh!'

Mrs Crocker took his two huge hands in hers and squeezed them.

'Well, we'll look after you here, my dear,' she cried. 'You'll all be writing away in next to no time. Think of it, *three* poets under my little roof! Come along, boys, I'll show you to your studio.'

'Great!' said Shelley. 'Where de cupboard, man?'

They filed out of the scullery. Crocker watched them go, in his solitary bitterness. It was, he recognised, their house, now. He had dreamed, once, of becoming a major cordwainer, an innovator, a guildmaster, a teacher; of establishing leather in the vanguard of honoured materials, like gold, like marble, like, indeed, words. There would, perhaps, be a blue plaque outside his house, announcing to the awed and pilgrim world that Obadiah Crocker, master cordwainer, had lived and worked here, once upon a time.

But the world, like his wife, had different priorities. Houses did not list leather associations among their desirable features; there were no laureate cordwainers. You had, in this world, to cut your coat according to your hide, and your losses with it. So Obadiah Crocker sighed, glanced at the singing kettle, and, taking up his wife's discarded quill, began, after a reflective moment or two, to design a cut-price suitcase.

Just a Gasp at Twilight

Joseph Califano Jr, the US Secretary of Health, yesterday called for a global campaign to end cigarette smoking by the year 2015.

Daily Telegraph

IT WAS December 31, 2014; and it was nearly time. My companion and I hobbled out onto the roof terrace, fetched up wheezing against the low balcony wall, and gazed silently out over winter-black London. A mile or so away, the trusty old face of Digital Ben read 11:36.

'Twenty-four minutes,' I said.

'The fags are going out all over Europe,' murmured Watson. He coughed for a while, and I watched the dislodged tiles detach themselves from the nearby roofs and slide into the chill darkness. 'We shall not see them lit again in our lifetime.'

'True, old friend,' I said.

'There is a clean fresh wind blowing across the world,' said Watson, 'sod it.'

I took out a kitchen-roll tube stuffed with Admiral's Greasy Black Shag, and turned it lovingly in my ochre fingers. Watson stared at it for a minute or two, rocking back and forth on his frail heels as he struggled for breath.

'What's a nice chap like you doing with a joint like that?' he said, at last.

'Ah, the old jokes, Watson!' I cried, with such atypical energy that I swear my lungs twanged. 'When shall we look upon their like again?' I hefted the giant fag, and the cold starlight caught the maker's hand-set monogram. 'It was the last one my little

268

man underneath St James's made for me before they took him away. It was his *coup d'adieu*, cobbled cunningly from ten thousand dog-ends, bonded with vintage dottle, the final defiant gesture of a genius, made even as the Health Police hobnails clattered on his cellar steps! I have been saving it for the big occasion. Have you a Vesta?'

Watson reached into his waistcoat pocket, sweating from the effort.

'It could kill us both,' he said.

'Something has to, old friend,' I replied.

'God knows, that's true,' nodded Watson. 'It has long been my philosophy. I once gave up, you know; in 1988. For almost thirty-two minutes. And during all that time, the only thing I could think of was: Suppose I were to be knocked down by a bus? The sacrifice would have been utterly in vain. I am, I think, a connoisseur of irony.'

'I, too,' I said. 'I have toyed with abstinence myself, and felt: Suppose a rabid fox were to fix his fangs in my shin?'

'Suppose thermonuclear war were to break out?'

'Suppose some errant meteorite . . .'

'Exactly,' said Watson.

He lit up, and we choked for a while.

'There aren't many of us left, you know,' hawked Watson, after a bit.

'Tubby Stitchling's wife went last week,' I said.

'Really?'

'Emphysema.'

'Ah. I'd only known her as Mrs Stitchling, I'm afraid. I had a sister-in-law called Pondicherry once, though.'

I stared at him through the encircling fug. It was always possible that smoking induced brain-rot. Over the years, research had indicated that it induced everything, despite some intermittently heartening reports from various tobacco companies that it cured baldness, enhanced virility, prevented foot odour and made you taller.

'I think it must have been a joke of her father's,' continued Watson, after his fit had subsided. 'He was in the FCO, you know. He was a smoker's smoker. Put in for a posting to India solely on account of the stogies.'

'Amazing!'

'They were the world's most advanced smoke. Dark green, as I recall. If you left them out in the sun too long, they could blow your hand off. He was dead in six months.'

'Lungs, eh?'

Watson shook his head.

'Dizzy spell. Got up one morning, lit his first of the day, inhaled, and fell on his borzoi.'

'They're sensitive animals,' I said. 'Easily startled.'

'Had his throat out in a trice,' said Watson. 'A fearfully messy business.'

'I can well imagine,' I said.

'There was tar everywhere.'

'Ah.'

'Smoking tragedies always dogged Tubby's family,' gasped Watson. He watched fallen ash burn through his dickie, waving a thin hand feebly at the spreading char. 'D'you suppose it was some kind of ancient curse?'

'What else could explain it?' I said. I stared into the empty night, and my eyes filled with tears. It was good shag, all right. 'So many dead. Do you remember the night old Bob Crondall bought it?'

'As if it were yesterday, old man. A chap with his experience, an eighty-a-day wallah, you wouldn't have thought he'd have been caught out like that, would you? Pottering down the M4, lights up, fag drops in lap, old Bob gropes frantically at the incinerating crotch, next thing you know he's jumped the reservation and swatted himself against an oncoming juggernaut. They found him in the glove compartment, you know.'

'Fate,' I said. 'If it's got your number on it, old man, there's no point trying to duck.'

'Just a matter of luck,' nodded Watson. 'My wife died peacefully in bed. Went to sleep, never woke up.'

'Wincyette nightie, wasn't it?'

'Right. Went up in a flash. Roman bloody candle.' He laughed, a short wry laugh, and went into spasm. When he'd recovered, he said: 'The ironic thing was, she was trying to give up at the time. She was using one of those filter jobs designed to wean you off the weed. The holder was still clenched between her teeth when they found her. It took three morticians to prise it loose.'

I blew a thick grey doughnut, and watched it dissolve.

'The risks in giving up are enormous,' I said. 'I don't think you ever knew Maurice Arbuckle?'

'Only by reputation,' said Watson.

'He used to get through a hundred a day. Gave up just like that, one morning, and was dead an hour later. Choked to death on a Polo.'

'Good God!'

'Tried to inhale.'

We fell relatively silent; only the faint crepitations beneath our vests, like the sound of distant mopeds, disturbed the night. The far clock said 11:50.

'They never tried to ban Polos,' muttered Watson bitterly, at last. 'You never hear the figures for tooth cancer.'

'Conspiracies,' I said. 'Big business interests, powerful dental lobby, all that.'

Watson sighed; then, faintly, smiled.

'I wonder if old Sam Wellbeloved is looking down and laughing, now,' he murmured.

'Bound to be. Anyone who takes a pinch of snuff and blows himself through a plate glass window on the 8.14 has to be able to see the funny side of things.'

Watson sighed again, a sort of low sad rattle, and leaned over the balcony.

'It was all such fun, old chap,' I said, sensing his mood, 'wasn't it? The cheery smoke-filled parties, the first deep drag of the new dawn, those happy post-coital puffs in the days when we still had the wind? The new brands, the bright ads, the racing-cars and free-fall parachute teams, the vouchers, the gifts? And what shall we do now, old friend?'

There was no reply.

'Watson?' I said.

And then, far off, the great clock struck midnight. I reached out, and prised the smouldering stub from my old companion's rigidifying fingers, and took my final drag. It was what he would have wanted. In my place, he would have done the same.

Sentiment is sentiment; but waste is waste.

T'Curse of T'Pharaohs

A major exhibition of Manchester's Egyptian mummies is to be staged later this month to coincide with an international symposium attended by leading experts. A basement area of the city's museum is being adapted to reflect the atmosphere of an ancient Egyptian tomb.

Daily Mail

THE IRON clang of the museum door reverberated through the dank and dim-lit crypt. The key grated in the ancient lock. The footsteps of the Assistant Curator (Egyptology) rasped even more faintly on the cold flagstones, whispered on the stone stairs, faded altogether, died on the far clunk of the front door shutting. The silence folded in upon itself, save for the faint tracery of rats' feet, pattering in search of crisp shards dropped by the day's school crocodiles, or Marmited crumbs.

The crypt smelt of slow time and dried millegenarian unguents and dusty skin. Along its grey walls, the mummies ranged in their yellowed swaddling, like embossed ghosts, motionless, silent, cold.

And then the clock struck seven.

'. . . so ah loooked 'im straight in t'eye,' said Ackroyd IV, 'ah loooked 'im straight in t'eye, and 'e wur as close to me as ah am to you now, ah loooked 'im straight in t'eye, and do you know what ah said?'

'Course ah bloody know what you said,' muttered Fosdyke III, 'ah been bloody stood standing 'ere next to you for God knows 'ow many 'oondred bloody years. You said . . .'

'Ah loooked 'im straight in t'eye,' went on Ackroyd IV,

ignoring him, 'and ah said: *What's so bloody special about bloody Cairo?'*

'Ah'll bet he didn't know where to loook,' said Grimshawe VI, who never tired of hearing the story; or indeed, of re-telling it.

''E didn't know where to loook,' said Ackroyd IV.

''E must 'ave been completely taken aback,' said Grimshawe VI.

''E wur *completely* taken aback,' said Ackroyd IV, firmly. 'Ah didn't leave it there, neither. Ah said to myself, ah said, ah'm not letting this soft bloody Sootherner off t'hook.'

'You pressed 'ome your advantage, did you, Ackroyd IV?' enquired Grimshawe VI.

'That is *exactly* what ah did!' retorted Ackroyd IV. 'Ah drew meself oop to me full height . . .'

'Bloody 'ell!' moaned Fosdyke III.

'. . . ah drew meself oop to me full height, and ah said: *There's more to do on a wet Thursday night in Alexandria than there is in a whole bloody MONTH in Cairo!'*

'By 'eck!' breathed Grimshawe VI. 'That wur telling 'im!'

''E doesn't mince words, my 'oosband,' said a somewhat shorter mummy from the opposite wall. ''E wur never one to stand by and see Alexandria slandered by some toffee-nosed Cairo snob with a ploomstone in 'is gob oop for t'weekend.'

'And quite right too, Mrs Ackroyd IV,' interjected Mrs Grimshawe VI, beside her. 'It wur a reet fine city, wur Alexandria. It wur known as t'Southport of the East. There wurn't *noothing* you couldn't buy in t'shops.'

'Noothing,' confirmed her neighbour. 'We went down to Cairo once, it wur all roobish in t'stores, ah wun't 'ave poot it on t'mantelpiece if you paid me, would ah, pet?'

'You what?' said Ackroyd IV.

'Ah said we went down to Cairo once, and . . .'

'The beer wur like rat's piss,' said Ackroyd IV.

'Did you complain, Ackroyd IV?' enquired Grimshawe VI.

'Did *ah* complain?' cried Ackroyd IV.

'Did *'e* complain?' cried his wife.

'Ah 'eld it oop t'light,' said Ackroyd IV, 'ah 'eld it oop t'light,

274

and ah loooked 'im straight in t'eye, and 'e wur as close to me as ah am to you now, ah loooked 'im straight in t'eye, and do you know what ah said?'

'You said,' muttered Fosdyke III, savagely, 'that . . .'

''Ere!' shouted Ackroyd IV. 'Who's telling this bloody story, thee or me? Ah loooked 'im straight in t'eye, and ah said: *Ah've seen better beer coom out of our cat!*'

Grimshawe VI gasped.

'Bloody 'ellfire!' he cried. 'That wur telling 'im, Ackroyd IV! What happened then?'

''E hit me,' said Ackroyd IV.

'They used to worship t'cat down there,' explained his wife.

'Right,' confirmed her husband. 'They're all bloody Micks in Cairo.'

'It didn't stop 'em building a damn good sphinx,' said Fosdyke III.

'Who said that?' said Ackroyd IV.

'It wur him,' said Grimshawe VI quickly. 'It wur Fosdyke III. It wurn't me.'

'Yes,' said Ackroyd IV, 'ah thought it wur *'im*. It's joost the sort of stupid bloody remark ah'd 'ave expected from *'im*. 'E wur an emigrant, Fosdyke III, didn't you know?'

'What, a blackie? Well, I'll go to t'foot of our stairs, Ackroyd IV, here's me been propped next to him all these . . .'

'No, no, no!' shouted Ackroyd IV. ''Ave you got cloth bloody ears?'

'As a matter of fact,' murmured Grimshawe VI, 'yes.'

'That wur completely ooncalled for, Ackroyd IV,' snapped Mrs Grimshawe VI, 'soom of us 'as not withstood Time's oonkind ravages as well as oothers.'

Ackroyd IV groaned.

'What ah meant was,' he said, 'that Fosdyke bloody III 'ere couldn't wait to get down to Cairo. Alexandria wurn't good enough for 'im. 'E wur what ah'd call a class traitor, am I right, Grimshawe VI, or am I not?'

'You are that,' replied Grimshawe VI. 'It's *worse* than being a ruddy blackie. It's no woonder 'e likes sphinxes.'

'Sphinxes!' snorted Ackroyd IV. 'Ah wouldn't give you a

thank-you for 'em.'

'Voolgar,' said his wife.

'*And* trendy,' said Mrs Grimshawe VI. 'Call me oon-fashionable if you will, but ah've never been one to go with t'fashion, joost because, and 'ere's the point ah'm making, joost because it *is* t'fashion.'

''Ere, 'ere!' cried Mrs Ackroyd IV.

'We never 'ad no sphinxes in Alexandria,' said her husband, 'but, by 'eck, we 'ad soom memorial benches that ranked with t'finest in t'civilised bloody world!'

'And no cats' feet on 'em, neither!' cried Grimshawe VI.

'Reet! Call us plain, but by God we was honest!' shouted Ackroyd IV. 'Oonlike soom as ah could mention.'

'At least,' said his wife tartly, 'at least when folk went t'theatre in Alexandria, they could oonderstand every word. Give me a well-made play any day of t'week and actors you can 'ear at t'back and you can keep your modernistic roobish, ah've said it before, and ah'll say it again.'

'Well put, moother!' exclaimed Ackroyd IV. ''Ere, Grimshawe VI, tell me one thing, 'ave you ever 'eard a Soothern comic who made you laff?'

'Me?' shrieked Grimshawe VI. '*Me?* Are you asking me if ah ever 'eard a Cairo bloody so-called comic who made me laff? If you want my opinion, they're nobbut a load of pansies!'

'Or worse,' said Ackroyd IV darkly.

'Tell me, Mrs Fosdyke III,' murmured Mrs Grimshawe VI, clearing what was left of her throat carefully, 'do *you* 'ave any opinion upon what we are discussing?'

There was a long, taut silence.

'She never says owt,' said Mrs Ackroyd IV, finally. 'She probably doesn't deign to talk to plain, honest, decent, simple, *oonfashionable* folk.'

'Either that,' said Mrs Grimshawe VI, 'or she's afraid 'er new Soothern accent'll make her a laffing-stock wherever decent folk gather. I'd like to 'ear 'er say *mooshroom.*'

'Either *that*,' broke in her husband, 'or there's nothing in there. They never 'ad t'first idea about embalming in bloody Cairo. If you wanted a proper job done, you 'ad to go oop North, didn't you, Ackroyd IV?'

'You're not wrong. That's where t'real craftsmen wur. Thinking of which, Grimshawe VI, ah'm reet looking forward to this exhibition do they're putting on, aren't you?'

'By goom, ah am an' all!' cried his friend. 'There'll be no end of pooblicity and thee and me'll be reet in t'middle of it. It'll be joost like that Tutenkhamun do they 'ad in Loondon, won't it, Ackroyd IV?'

There was a very long silence. Even the rats were still.

'Loondon?' said Ackroyd IV, at last. 'Where's that?'

The Unnatural History of Selborne

Letter I
TO THE LATE REV. GILBERT WHITE, MA

Dear Sir,

Let me, at the outset of what must, sadly, be a somewhat monological correspondence (you having passed, these two centuries gone, beneath the lucky sod), say that no greater admirer exists of your work than I. During the harsh brickbound years of my urban life, I have turned on occasions without number towards the green solace of *The Natural History of Selborne*; gleaning therefrom, in your meticulous chronicling of moth and toad, stoat and minnow, not merely those moments of peace that go with rural things, but also the thrills that must accompany the observations of your incomparable eye and the wondrously informed speculations of your remarkable brain.

For I have long dreamed of myself becoming a naturalist; and last year the opportunity was afforded me, after nigh on forty London summers, of following your shade a little way along those paths which you so bravely beat two hundred years ago. Employing that shrewd trading sense which is perhaps the only legacy of an urban upbringing, I purchased one of the few tracts of genuine swamp in the New Forest, together with the small cottage sinking picturesquely into it, not so very far from your own beloved Selborne; and it was here that I determined to acquaint myself as intimately as you had done with the flora and fauna of my little square of Matto Grosso.

Since the past few months have been occupied with stopping the property from falling on me, I have only just begun my observations; my first impression is that there are several million species of tree out there, all indistinguishable from one another. They are full of penguins.

I am, etc.

Letter II

Dear Sir,

Or magpies. Upon my small son's having pointed out that penguins do not fly, I purchased an agreeable little volume, *The Observer's Book of Birds*. This gave me great hope of laying down a basis from which to work, since all I know of birds to this date is that sparrows are the ones which are not pigeons, and that neither of them is a starling.

Unfortunately, my hopes were soon dashed. Walking abroad last evening with my little book and a stout stick hewn from one of our English oaks, I found the birds whizzing past me like bullets, at a considerably faster rate than I could turn the pages. So far, I have managed to identify only a pigeon; being dead, it afforded me time to find the page, where I learned that it is larger than a dove. Unfortunately for my records, I had no dove to compare it with, so it may actually be a dove instead of a pigeon. Until I find a dead alternative, either larger or smaller, I shall, I am afraid, be none the wiser. It was covered with insects I was, I must confess, unable to identify, since I can recognise only ants.

A little later, I leaned upon my stout oaken stick to contemplate what might have been a fox, or dog, and it broke. I have no way of knowing for certain, but I think it may not be oak at all. My son, who had been contemplating the book as I lay beneath him in the mire, pointed out that birds could be identified by their song; thus, according to the book, the stonechat goes *whee-chat*, the redstart goes *wee-chit*, and the plover goes *oooi-oooi*. All one has to do, therefore, is listen for something going *wee-chit*, or *oooi-oooi*, or whatever, and pin it down instantly.

It is not easy. This evening, if the book is to be believed, we heard a hoopoe, two puffins, and a bar-tailed godwit. I happened to mention this in our local hostelry later, and an old cowman had to be carried bodily from the cribbage board and revived with quarts of foaming Campari.

I am, etc.

Letter III

Dear Sir,

According to *The Observer's Book of Trees* just purchased, what I had been leaning on was a stick hewn from the common juniper. This is odd, since the common juniper is a bush, whereas ours is ninety feet high and full of spoonbills. Or possibly bats. It may therefore be an uncommon juniper, which does not figure in the index. Could this, Sir, be my first breakthrough as a naturalist? My small daughter afforded me much relaxed laughter by insisting that the tree was a larch! I reminded her that the larch was a fish, but not sternly; she is but six, and easily upset by scorn.

I now know, you would be interested to hear were you not dead, that the animal I observed as I fell was neither fox nor dog, but a weasel. I identified it instantly from my new *Observer's Book of Wild Animals*. Ours is a large specimen, about the size of a child's tricycle, and I have advised the family to keep well away from it.

This evening, my son and I embarked upon a pleasant excursion to collect examples of the wild flowers with which this part of the forest is so abundantly blessed. We collected a daisy, and fifty-nine things that weren't.

I am, etc.

Letter IV

Dear Sir,

My mind is much exercised of late by droppings. In my life so far, spoor has not formed a major ratiocinative component, since in London it will be generally dog, and if it is not dog then little follows from further deliberation but unease. But in the country, the magic of droppings is all about us; sadly, however, one has to pick it up as one goes along, as it were, since – whether from editorial sensitivities or misguided commercial priorities, I know not – there is as yet no *Observer's Book of Droppings*. I have therefore been forced to glean what information I can from the conversation of countrymen, in particular the computer software executive up the hill and the literary agent who is his goodly live-in friendperson, and I am now fairly well versed in recognising the movements of forest animals from their tracks.

I am thus able to impart two pieces of remarkable information that I could not have come by through any other means, viz., there have been sheep on the roof of my car, and the creature that nightly calls *yek-yek-yek* and bites through the wire mesh on the toolshed window is not, as I first thought, a golden eagle, but a bull.

By the by, the daisy turned out to be a wort of some kind, possibly bladder.

I am, etc.

Letter V

Dear Sir,

I strolled down to the Avon banks this morning, since I had heard ospreys in the night and wished to capture them on Polaroid. They had gone, however, and the only sign of life, apart from the odd owl paddling in the reeds, was a solitary fisherman. I pulled on my pipe and enquired in an equable manner whether or not the larch were biting, and he turned and stared at me for a long time.

There is much inbreeding in the country, of course, and I put it down to that.

Walking back to the cottage through the dew-bright fields, I was startled out of my wits by a rabbit which sprang up suddenly and blocked my path. It did not move! It was clearly poised to attack, but I kept my head and hurled my *Observer's Book of Pottery & Porcelain* at it, and it made off. I had purchased the volume in the hope of identifying a great hoard of blue and white fragments I had come upon while looking for my gumboot in our front bog, never imagining for a moment that it should prove so trusty a weapon *in extremis*!

But that, of course, is what one learns in the country: by our wits, by our improvisations, by sharpening our reflexes, do we survive.

I am, etc.

Letter VI

Dear Sir,

Good God, but the stream and the pond teem like no other part of the woodland with Dame Nature's arcane mysteries! You will note that I am uncharacteristically excited; yet why should I not be? For some weeks past, I have been closely observing the larva of the biting-midge *Ceratopogon* (*The Observer's Book of Pond Life*, plate 56), awaiting with almost the excitement of the father itself the final metamorphosis from minuscule egg into winging midge. Last evening, towards dusk, with all the landscape holding, it seemed to me, its breath, the final act of the great drama took the stage: the frail case shook, the thin skin split, and, as my son and I watched spellbound, what should burst from that tiny fecund pod but – a tortoiseshell butterfly!

Who can say what interventions brought on this bizarre genesis? I should deem it evidence of a Divine sense of humour, did the hard scientist in me not instantly cavil: for could it not, perhaps, be due instead to the curious, nay, unique vegetation of my little patch of ground? Diet, after all, can play strange tricks upon the growing insect foetus, and where else on this earth will you find a combination, as I have observed, of Horseshoe Vetch, Charlock, Sea Urchin, Hemlock, Water-Dropwort, Mango, Cat's Ear, Wall Lettuce, Pineapple, Loon, Yam, Nettle-Leaved Selfheal, Cactus, Twayblade, Bougainvillaea, Saxifrage, Breadfruit, and Tundra?

It would not surprise me if this part of the New Forest were capable of supporting anacondas and scorpions. Indeed, last night as I brushed my teeth, I clearly heard what could well have been a tapir rooting around behind the flymo, or vice versa.

Tomorrow, I am determined to purchase *The Observer's Book of Fungi*. I have noticed, in my happy peregrinations, many delicious-looking examples of this nourishing genus; and I do firmly believe, Sir, that with a modicum of good fortune, my little family might well become self-sufficient.

I am, etc.

Divine Sparks

Guardian

G. SCOTT FITZGERALD was born on September 26, 1896, in St Paul, Minnesota, the son of respectable – though not rich – middle-class parents.

Of the ill-starred, wayward, tragic genius who will forever be known as the Electrician Of The Jazz Age, his early life gave little indication. In the fall of 1905, he went to St Paul's Academy, but showed scant interest in the school's wiring system; one of his few extant contemporaries, now Dr Elmo Reeves Jr of Weasel Falls, Mo., recalls him thus: 'I saw him change a light-bulb once, but it was nothing special. He just sort of, well, took the old one out, and then kind of replaced it with a new one. I remember thinking at the time: 'What's so damned hot about that?'

There is practically no juvenilia remaining: in the spring of 1909, Scott fell in love with Eulalia May Ravenal, the first of many Southern belles in his life, and made her a toaster, but it blew up and she lost an ear; and in 1911 he dedicated a plug to

283

Magnolia E. Lee, but she married someone else and lost it. He never really got over these earlier experiences, however, and it could be said that the major work of his maturity was deeply influenced by these first romantic and electrical setbacks. Indeed, the first fridge he ever designed was originally called the Magnoliator De Luxe, before it was withdrawn from the market for blacking out Boston.

In 1916, he went to Princeton, where for the first time he met brilliant young electricians of his own generation to whom he could talk, and who would understand what it was that he was trying to do, particularly young Edwin Wilson, who subsequently became the father of modern air-conditioning. Here, too, Fitzgerald suffered another of those seminal disappointments that were to leave their scars for the rest of his life – he had long dreamed of gaining his letter for football, but his hopes of becoming team electrician were dashed when his first gauche attempt at under-pitch heating resulted in the electrocution of three quarterbacks, two guards, a tackle, and the Princeton coach. That year, they lost to Notre Dame 178–0.

That year, too, the United States entered the Great War, and Fitzgerald enlisted immediately in the 7th Minnesotan Electrical Volunteers. He left Princeton and was sent to Fort Volt, Ga., to learn European wiring codes, but found great difficulty in remembering whether it was the brown that went to the earth terminal or the green, and by the time he had sorted it out, the Armistice had been signed. But though he 'never got over', he did, while stationed at Fort Volt, meet the beautiful daughter of one of the South's oldest families, Zelda Protozoa, with whom he fell deeply in love. On the night of December 11, 1918, he asked her to marry him, and one of the most famous exchanges in twentieth-century conversation then took place; Fitzgerald said, 'The rich are different from you and me,' to which Zelda replied, 'No, they're just different from you.'

Thus cruelly rebuffed, Scott determined to go to New York and earn the million dollars with which he would then return to win Zelda's love. It was 1919, the War was over, jazz had arrived from the Delta, the Volstead Act was in force, the boys came home, the girls bobbed their hair, and everybody sang *Yes We*

Have No Bananas; in short, the stage was set for the biggest, wackiest, wildest spending spree the world had ever known. And all the Jazz Age needed was a good electrician: already, in the thousands of mushrooming speakeasies, gangsters were shooting the wrong people because the light was so lousy; girls in skimpy skirts were going blue every time the central heating went on the blink; and more and more people were singing *Yes We Have No Baaaaaargh*, because that's all they ever heard on juke boxes that were continually blowing fuses.

The time was ripe; it was merely a question of seizing the day. G. Scott Fitzgerald did just that; stunningly good-looking in his brown overalls, never without a full range of insulated screwdrivers and pliers, he took the town by storm. As he wrote in his diary for 1920: 'This year I done real good, 4, 316 new plugs in Manhattan alone.' In June, he appeared in the *Saturday Evening Post* for the first time, rewiring the entire circulation department within the space of a single weekend and putting in an ice-making machine at practically cost.

Word got around. Soon, he had a commission from *Atlantic Monthly* to install automatic garage doors in the loading bay, an offer followed from McGraw Hill for him to do his first full-length insulation, and by the end of the year he was able to take his old Princeton chum Edwin Wilson to the top of the Woolworth Building, look out over the shimmering magical experience that is night-time Manhattan, and say: 'That lift we just come up in, I did the whole damn alarm system, how about *that* for openers?'

By now, Fitzgerald was both rich and famous. That Christmas, he travelled south, secretly fixed the lights on the Protozoa family Christmas tree so that they spelt I LOV YU (it must be remembered he left Princeton early), and asked Zelda once more to marry him. This time, she consented, and on New Year's Day 1921, they travelled north together on the Savannah Limited, a trip marred only by the fact that Scott had his head out of the window the entire journey, trying to figure the best way of electrifying the line. It was Zelda's first intimation of the conflict in him between man and artist, and like any sensitive new bride, she went to the club car and got plastered.

By the time the train pulled into Grand Central, Scott had pleurisy and Zelda had cirrhosis. It was to be the pattern of their subsequent lives, with slight variations; each was terribly jealous of the other, so some of the time he had cirrhosis, and she went out and caught pleurisy, often by dancing in those very fountains where Scott was slaving away, trying to fix the floodlights.

For the work had to go on: Fitzgerald was by this time gripped with the overpowering ambition to realise the dream of the Great American Switch, something where you could come into a room, press a button, and everything would start at once – air-conditioning, lights, garbage disposal, food mixer, coffee grinder, phonograph, cocktail shaker, and libido. This almost monomaniacal pursuit of his dream was further complicated by the Fitzgeralds' visit to Paris in 1924, where Scott ran into Alfred Hemingway who was already building a considerable reputation in fluorescent tubing. Hemingway was not only many of the things Fitzgerald wasn't, he was also many of the things Fitzgerald wished to be – apart from anything else, Hemingway had been with the Italians at the front in 1918 and received a severe shock from a portable espresso machine – and when they all went down to Pamplona together, Fitzgerald found himself utterly outshone: Hemingway was a local folk hero. For El Electrico, as everyone called him, had that year totally revolutionised the Running Of The Bulls by the brilliance of his invention. As the trap flew open at Pamplona Stadium and the six bulls sprang out in pursuit of the little electric matador, Fitzgerald recognised the threat to his reputation, and at once sailed for home.

In 1925, he duly produced what most central generating boards today consider his masterpiece: it is difficult, now, to understand the sort of impact the New York subway made on its first appearance, but G. H. Eliot instantly recognised the brilliance of conception, the economy of execution, the cleanness of line. As he immediately wrote to Scott: 'This is your best work to date. Once I got on, I could not get off again. Terrific, and no smell to speak of.'

But, as so often happens, success itself became its own undoing. Young, rich, internationally acclaimed, Fitzgerald became obsessed with the idea that there was nowhere to go but down. He would never match the perfection of the NY subway. In 1927, he and Zelda went to the Riviera so that he could work on his most ambitious project to date, a wiring diagram of Texas. But things went wrong from the outset; not only was Scott drinking heavily, but Zelda was showing distressing signs of schizophrenia; most Tuesdays she thought she was a cheap wardrobe. Doctors were expensive, especially those prepared to come in and give her two coats of varnish, and Scott soon found the money running out; in 1930, he succumbed to the lure of Hollywood.

It proved the beginning of his end. Like so many brilliant young electricians of The Lost Generation – Wilfred Faulkner, Dorothy Barker, Sam Dos Passos, Gamaliel West – he learned too late that genius and integrity were Hollywood disposables. Time and again, his lighting instructions were ignored, his wind machines re-sited without consultation, his ring-mains tampered with by studio hacks ten years his junior. He made enemies: producers got sick and tired of hearing about the New York subway; actors walked off sets on which Fitzgerald, to humour her, had placed his wife, because they said her doors squeaked; and by 1935, Scott was on two bottles a day, and the scrap heap.

He put Zelda into a nursing home; within six weeks, she was having an affair with a handsome breakfront bookcase from Alabama, and Scott entered the last dark days of his self-pitying decline. He fixed very little, a plug here, a fuse there, one or two small and unimportant generators, green lights on the ends of people's docks.

And then, late in 1939, a chance of redemption seemed to offer itself: he met a young English flashlamp rep, Sharon Grahame, went to live with her, dried out, began teaching her all he knew as if to construct the dream partner – lover, wife, wiring engineer – he had never found, and, most important, began working again. It was his most spectacular oeuvre yet – a scheme for a great transatlantic subway, linking the Bronx with Cockfosters.

It was never finished. On December 11, 1940, while trying to reach a 13-amp fuse which had popped out and rolled under the sideboard, G. Scott Fitzgerald collapsed and died.

For the man who had once lit up an entire generation, only one person appeared at the funeral. She was Dorothy Barker, who stared at the grave and said: 'It's so goddam dark in there.'

It remains his most resonant epitaph.

Diplomacy

*'WINNINGTON ROAD, HAMPSTEAD, N2. Directly opposite
Hampstead Golf Course. A magnificent Georgian-style home
offering a general feeling of such importance that it has been
mistaken many times for an Ambassadorial residence.'*
Advertisement in the Observer

MR HENRY RAPPAPORT OBE sighed his sage Corniche through the
high wrought-iron gates of Casa Nostra, crunching the carriage
drive.

A brick bounced off the bonnet.

He got out, stared at the four-figure dent, winced. Someone
smashed a placard over his head; it settled on his shoulders. He
re-aligned his gold-rimmed glasses, read the upside down
message carefully.

'Steve who?' he said.

'BIKO LIVES!' screamed the crowd. 'BIKO LIVES!'

A tall girl in a SWAPO tee-shirt shook her fist in Mr
Rappaport's trapped face.

'No South African grapes here!' she cried.

'MULDERGATE, MULDERGATE!' howled the crowd.

'Grapes?' said Mr Rappaport. 'Who eats grapes? You swallow
a pip, you could get an appendix. Ask me the last time I had
grapes.'

A large Zulu in an LSE scarf thrust a sheaf of petitions into Mr
Rappaport's hands.

'As the South African ambassador,' he said, 'we call upon you
to . . .'

'*You're* the South African ambassador?' interrupted Mr
Rappaport, beaming. 'Wonderful! Didn't everybody say it was

289

just a matter of time? Didn't *I* say it was just a matter of time? Only wait, I said, let them come and play cricket, how much can it hurt?'

The crowd stopped chanting.

'Not me,' said the Zulu, 'you.'

Mr Rappaport stared at him from the framing poster.

'I'm in blouses,' he said.

'Blouses?'

'All right, a little property as well. Not much. A sideline. These days, you have to diversify. Blouses, I'll admit it, they're not what they were. Young people today, all they want is knitwear. Big loose cardigans, you look like an elephant's backside. You know who I blame? Woody Herman, Buster Keaton; the sloppy look, everybody in secondhand cardigans, tell me how you can make a living in blouses?'

He was alone by now. The crowd, during this melancholy soliloquy, had drifted away. Leaflets littered the manicured lawns, blew against the hybrid teas. Mr Rappaport took off the tattered poster, sighed, walked to his front door. Across it, someone had sprayed KILL CHILE FASCISTS NOW! The red paint was still tacky. Mr Rappaport turned his key in the lock, and went in.

'You're home!' screamed his wife, in the marble hall.

'Definitely,' said Mr Rappaport.

'Don't use the downstairs toilet!'

Mr Rappaport frowned.

'Toilet? It was always a cloakroom. I used to call it a toilet, you went mad. All of a sudden it's a toilet?'

'I'm emotional,' said his wife. As her metallic coiffe quivered, it caught the subdued pelmet lighting, fired sparks.

'And that means I shouldn't use the downstairs toilet?'

'Cloakroom. Ask me why I'm emotional?'

'Why are you emotional?'

'There's a South Moluccan locked in the cloakroom. He's got a gun. He's got the au pair in there with him. He's threatening to kill her.'

'I sympathise,' said Mr Rappaport, hanging up his coat. 'Three mornings running I had a hair in the porridge. I thought the Swiss were supposed to be clean. You go to St Moritz, it's spotless.'

Mrs Rappaport glowered bitterly at her husband.

'When people at the bridge club ask me how come you only got the OBE,' she muttered, 'I'll know what to say. For a genuine knighthood, you need brains.'

'You need raincoats,' said Mr Rappaport. 'When was the last time a prime minister gave a press conference in a blouse? Mind you, if Mrs Thatcher gets in, who knows? I could send her the guipure lace number, in pastel blue. *Lord* Rappaport, possibly.'

His wife followed him into the enormous living room.

'I've got sixty people coming for canasta,' she said. 'Suppose he shoots the girl?'

'You've got a dishwasher,' said Mr Rappaport.

He looked at the Canaletto over the fireplace, the way he did every evening. It had cost eighty thousand. Even if he lived to be a hundred, it still worked out at a fiver a night. Just to look.

'I didn't mean that,' said his wife. 'I meant about the cloak-room.'

'They could use upstairs,' said Mr Rappaport, not turning from the fireplace. 'We got eight.'

'Upstairs is full of Persians,' said his wife.

'They take any amount of wear,' replied her husband. 'Let them walk. What harm can it do?'

'Not carpets,' said his wife. 'Persians. They came this morning. They want visas. They want to go to America, make a new life. They say they won't go away until they get them.'

'You told them I was in blouses?'

'*I* speak Persian?'

Mr Rappaport sighed, walked to the window, gazed out over the swimming pool. As dusk fell, the underwater lights came on.

'You saw the pool?' asked Mr Rappaport.

'I saw,' said his wife. 'It's a vigil. They came in over the back wall.'

'A vigil,' muttered Mr Rappaport. 'You know what I pay in rates?'

'They think we're Japs.'

'Is that any reason to fill my swimming pool with a – a – what?'

'It's supposed to be a whale,' said his wife. 'They say we're killing whales to make unnecessary consumer goods.'

'Do they know how many whales go into the average blouse?' enquired Mr Rappaport heavily.

There was a scream from the hall.

'He's murdering her!' cried Mrs Rappaport. 'Do something.'

Mr Rappaport walked slowly from the room, crossed the hall, tapped on the cloakroom door.

'What do you want?' he said.

'We demand the return of Indonesia!' shrieked the gunman.

'You got it,' said Mr Rappaport.

Slowly, the door opened. A dark face peered around the jamb.

'You mean it?' said the gunman.

'Sure,' said Mr Rappaport. 'Leave me your address, I'll put it in writing.'

'You are formally prepared to give up territorial rights over . . .'

'Absolutely. I'll even throw in an extra pair of pants.'

The gunman left. There was something crestfallen about him. The au pair straightened her sweater.

'Ah weesh to and in mah notice,' she said. 'Ah do not come ere to be lock wiz loony in cloakroom.'

'Toilet,' said Mr Rappaport. He turned, and was about to go back into the living room when a small black man in a morning coat barred his way, clicked heels, and handed him a long yellow envelope. Mr Rappaport bowed slightly, and took it away.

'Well?' enquired his wife.

'We are at war with Togo,' said Mr Rappaport, refolding the note.

'Who's we?'

'You're asking me?' He glanced out into the hall. 'It's a pity he didn't wait. I could have negotiated. Maybe they'd have settled for a shipment of bedjackets at cost. I got a warehouse full. I need the space.'

A window shattered, and the Rappaports wheeled. A face, bearded, crowned with a Basque beret, poked through.

'REMEMBER ETA!' it shrieked, and vanished.

'Etta?' said Mr Rappaport to his wife. 'Didn't she marry your cousin from Leeds?'

'The furrier?'

'Not the furrier, the one with the hip replacement, used to be in mail-order shoes.'

'The midnight-blue Jaguar with the phone?'

'That's him.'

'Muriel was his wife's name. He married a Muriel. She had a birthmark.'

'Then who was Etta?'

'I don't remember.' Mrs Rappaport lit a cigarette. Her mouth was tight. 'If we had a flat overlooking Regent's Park, fourth floor, fifth floor, could they break the windows? Could they put rubber fish in a swimming pool we didn't have? Could they run about declaring war when I've got sixty people coming?'

'I like it here,' said her husband.' I like the neighbourhood. I don't want to move. I got friends here. Who do I know in Regent's Park?'

The doorbell gonged. He went to open it.

'Sam!' cried Mr Rappaport. 'Frances! Come in, friends I'm always glad to see.'

'Who is it?' called Mrs Rappaport from the living room. 'David Owen? Sadat?'

'It's the Sheldons from up the road,' replied her husband, beaming at them. 'So don't stand there, come . . .'

'Cossack!' shouted Mr Sheldon. 'Butcher!'

Mr Rappaport cleared his throat carefully.

'Sam,' he said, 'why are you wearing a prison suit with a number on the pocket? Why are you holding a crust of bread?'

'Ha!' cried Mrs Sheldon. 'Suddenly you don't recognise a political prisoner? Suddenly it's news to you your stinking Siberian labour camps are full of innocent human beings?'

'I'm a symbol, Henry,' said Sam. 'I shaved my head specially.'

'Don't call him Henry!' snapped his wife. 'Soviet pig! Hitler didn't do enough?'

'Frances,' murmured Mr Rappaport, 'it's me. I'm in blouses. We've known each other . . .'

'All these years you were KGB,' muttered Mr Sheldon. 'All these years we never guessed. A viper we nurtured!'

Mr Rappaport shut the door.

'They didn't come in?' enquired his wife.

'Regent's Park,' said her husband, 'is very convenient.'

'And smart,' said Mrs Rappaport quickly.

'First thing tomorrow,' said Mr Rappaport, 'I'll phone the estate agent.'

Say it Again, Sam

Programmes for the FAR EAST – Burma, Brunei, Cambodia, China, Hong Kong, Indonesia, Japan, Korea, Laos, Philippines, Thailand, Vietnam. These quarter hour programmes are entirely in English.
WEDNESDAY: *SAY IT AGAIN – the English you need everyday – demonstrated in the context of scenes from classic films. Stories of love, horror, spying and comic misunderstanding provide a sound basis for learning English.*
BBC's English by Radio

WEARILY – FOR it had been a long hot day at the filing cabinets, the monsoon drumming on the tin roof, the fan on the blink, the flies fat as winging plums – Mr Pham Nik Ding climbed the treadworn wooden steps to his maisonette door at 49 Kipling Crescent, Rangoon. He removed the key from his moist waistcoat pocket, dreaming, as he often did, of the day when it would be cold to his thumb, an English key for an English door in a cool English street. Rillington Place, perhaps, Tobacco Road, Wimpole Street. Somewhere like that.

When he had the English.

Because when he had the English, he would apply for a transfer to the London office, and they would give him a secretary with a big bust, and a vintage car on the company, and he would take his secretary's glasses off and tell her she was beautiful and they would go down to Brighton in his vintage car and eat in one of those smart roadhouses where people in dinner jackets threw custard pies at one another.

He hung up his umbrella, and walked into the kitchen. Mrs

Ding was chopping eels.

'Tennis, anyone?' said her husband.

She put down a twitching head, and looked up.

'You say that every night,' said Mrs Ding. 'What does it mean?'

His brown brow furrowed, bleakly.

'I don't know,' he said. 'This whole thing doesn't add up, Professor. Maybe we're not asking the right questions. Why don't you slip into something a little more comfortable?'

Mrs Ding sighed, and went out. When she came back, she was wearing a bicycle cape and gumboots. Her husband stared at her, chewing his lip.

'There's something terribly, terribly wrong here,' he muttered. 'I can't put my finger on it, but it's just this crazy feeling I have. Call it a hunch.' He lifted the yellow hem. 'This thing is bigger than both of us.'

'But it's comfortable,' said Mrs Ding stubbornly.

Her husband shrugged.

'All right. Let's give it a whirl. It might just work. God knows, we've tried everything else.'

His wife sighed, and squeaked back across the tiling to her chopping-board.

'You have not forgotten,' she said, gouging a tiny brain, 'that Mr Sung is coming to dinner?'

Mr Ding staggered.

'My *boss*?' he shrieked. 'Coming *here*? For *dinner*? But I haven't a thing to wear!'

Mrs Ding threw a grey crab into the stew. It thrashed about briefly, and sank, hissing.

'Wear your grey pinstripe,' she said, 'with the blue tie.'

Her husband shook his head.

'I don't like it,' he said. 'It's too quiet.' He drove his fist into his palm, suddenly. 'This could be my big break, baby! Sung is the one they call Mr Big! We've had our eye on him for some time. He goes right to the top. In many ways, he *is* the Organisation!'

'Tin Toys (Burma) Limited?'

Pham Nik Ding smiled the crooked smile he had been

practising behind the filing cabinet all day.

'They call it that,' he murmured darkly.

'It is its name,' said his wife. 'That's why.'

'Yes!' cried Ding with a short, sharp laugh. 'He's a cunning little devil, your johnny toy manufacturer!'

She pared a writhing squid, deftly.

'And you think Mr Sung will send you to London?'

Ding walked to the little window, his hands behind his back.

'There's a mole in the circus,' he said softly.

'I hope your English will pass muster,' said his wife.

When her husband turned, a moment later, there was a smear of boot-polish across his upper lip, and a carrot between his teeth. He removed the carrot with a flourish.

'If it doesn't,' he snapped, 'I'll get it to pass the mayonnaise, and if it doesn't pass the mayonnaise, I'll get my check. It may not be English, but I'd rather speak Czech than listen to a language that doesn't know the first thing about waiting on tables. And that's another thing, Mrs Teasdale, if I told you you had a beautiful . . .'

The doorbell chimed. Mr Ding stuck the carrot back in his mouth, dropped to a half crouch, and loped to answer it.

'Good evening,' said Mr Sung.

'Good evening?' cried Ding. 'Well, that covers a lot of ground. Say, you cover a lot of ground yourself. You better beat it, I hear they're going to tear you down and put up an office building where you're standing. You can leave in a taxi. If you can't get a taxi you can leave in a huff. If that's too soon, you can leave in a minute and a huff. You know you haven't stopped talking since I came here?'

Mr Sung inclined his bulk more into the light, and stared.

'Is that you, Ding?'

'I don't have a photograph,' said Ding, tapping the carrot, 'but you can have my footprints. They're upstairs in my socks. Come in!'

He stood back, and ushered the bewildered Sung into the tiny hall, bowing low. When he stood erect again, the moustache had gone.

'Perhaps this will refresh your memory!' he cried.

Mr Sung gazed at his perspiring employee for a time.

'Are you perfectly well, Ding?' he enquired finally.

Ding blanched.

'Are you trying to tell me something?' he cried. 'Is it my hands? Are you saying I may never play the violin again?'

Mr Sung cleared his throat, and examined a thumbnail.

'I wonder, Ding,' he murmured, glancing suddenly up, 'do you know what a violin is?'

Ding stared into space for some time, panic rolling his eyes. At last, he shouted:

'I don't have to answer your goddam questions! I demand to see my lawyer! How about a little drink, baby?'

Mr Sung sighed heavily.

'Perhaps a little tea?' he said.

Pham Nik Ding sprang to his feet. He tore off his tie. He ripped open his collar. He hurtled towards the kitchen.

'HOT WATER!' he yelled. 'AND PLENTY OF IT!'

At the bellow, his wife ran to the door, and collided with him. Dried peas lurched from her saucepan, and bounced chattering upon the tiles.

'You crazy little fool, you might have got us both killed!' cried Ding. 'Don't you know what happens when two healthy young people meet?'

Mrs Ding watched the ricocheting peas, her frail shoulders hunched.

'You should not have shouted,' she muttered. 'You startled me. I dropped the chicken.'

'Oh my God!' exclaimed Ding. 'I don't think I can take any more! This used to be a decent town where a guy could settle and raise a family! Where did we go wrong, Mildred?'

'Is something the matter?' enquired Mr Sung, who had risen and started towards the kitchen. Ding stepped smartly in front of him, and put his hands on his employer's plump shoulders.

'I don't think you should go in there, Chuck,' he said, gently but firmly. 'It's – it's – it's your chicken.'

Mr Sung looked at Mrs Ding. Mrs Ding looked away.

'He gets very tired,' she said, in a small voice. 'He works very hard all day, and then he listens to the radio all night. Please try to understand that his –'

Her husband raised his hand.

'It's no good arguing with these earthlings, Vulgan,' he said. 'We have studied their culture and determined that they have hardly reached the stage our forebears knew during the time of Nork the Worm King. Why, they are still using antiquated nuclear weapons, ha-ha-ha!' He turned to the gazing Sung. 'We seek only peace, earthling, but be warned that should it unfortunately prove necessary, we have it in our power to destroy your entire planet.'

Mr Sung picked up his hat.

'My apologies, Mrs Ding,' he said, 'but I have only just this minute remembered a prior engagement.'

'Please,' she said, touching his arm. 'There is still the fish stew. It is very important to him that you stay. He dreams of England.'

Mr Sung hesitated.

'Well –'

'You wouldn't know about England, my little Nicole,' said Ding, his eyes moist, 'the patchwork of green fields, the rooks cawing, the sun setting as the blacksmith trots up to bowl the last over. It may not sound anything special to you, but it's why chaps like me are prepared to jump out of Dakotas into the blackness. I don't say we can stop the Hun here, but we can give him a bloody nose, and that's what counts for the time being, until the Yanks come in and we can open the Second Front and set all Europe free so your kids and mine can sleep peacefully in their little beds again.' He took Mr Sung's fat hand. 'Maybe, when all this is over, I'll take you there.'

'I'll get the stew,' said Mrs Ding.

They sat down, and she began ladling the food into little porcelain bowls; and because Mr Sung was the honoured guest, she gave him the crab. It was a little large for the dish, and its claw hung over the rim, and as she set the dish down in front of Mr Sung, the movement caused the claw to bend slightly. As Mr Sung lifted his spoon, Pham Nik Ding leapt to his feet.

'Stand back, Professor,' he shrieked, 'that thing's alive! It must be some crazy mutation caused by the recent testing of that new atomic device out in the Nevada desert. We have to get the women and kids off the base!'

Whereupon he lunged at the brimming bowl. It slid from his hand. It seemed to stay airborne for a very long time. And when it came down, Mr Sung looked slowly at his lap. His white linen trousers were the colour of eel. The crab slid gently from his steaming thigh. After a silent moment or two, he stood up.

'Thank you for your hospitality, Mrs Ding,' he said. 'But I really must be off.'

He walked, with awkward dignity, to the front door, leaving an oily trail, dotted with small vertebrae. Mrs Ding got up and scurried after him. Her husband fell back into his chair, clutching his breast.

'Mother of mercy,' he moaned, 'is this the end of Rocco?'

At the open door, Mrs Ding wrung her hands.

'Please, esteemed Mr Sung,' she sobbed, 'can you not understand and forgive? Can you not allow him one more chance? This possibility of England, it means so much to him, he studies so hard, I am not asking for myself, I am only –'

She stopped. Mr Sung had turned in the doorway, to face her. A small smile played at his lip, beneath a single raised eyebrow.

'Frankly, my dear,' he said, 'I don't give a damn.'

A Dingley Dell Situation

A good-humoured Christmas Chapter, containing an account of the ongoing marital involvements of the Pickwickians with some remarks about the reliability of the new Saab, a view of the yuletide economy with reference to the good offices of Mrs Margaret Thatcher, a disquisition upon such seasonal benisons as the quality of independent television and the scandal of welfare handouts to Trotskyite malingerers, together with some notes upon the sexual predispositions of Her Majesty's servants, the ubiquitousness of Arabs, the inadequacy of daily help, the tide of blasphemous filth that threatens to engulf us all, and the gratifying buoyancy of the property market.

SHALL WE allow ourselves the authorial licence of remarking that there was a particular spring to the step of Mr Winkle as he leapt from the tasteful leopardette driving seat of his Yule-buffed Peugeot and addressed himself to the wrought-iron intricacies of the Wardle gate?

Certainly, his spirit did not go unobserved by his good lady!

'Why do you not open my door for me, you bastard?' enquired Mrs Winkle. 'Can you not wait to get your hands upon the Wardles' au pair?'

'Shut your face, my dear!' cried Mr Winkle, doubtless distressed that his new executive kar-koat had snagged upon the Wardles' latch, leaving tufts of simulated beaver hanging from the elegant curlicues. 'And as to Miss Elke Lundqvist, let us remember that she is far from home this Christmas and doubtless in need of a little good cheer beneath the traditional mistletoe, or indeed anywhere else. Always provided,' and here the good fellow barked a short laugh that echoed ringingly across the Dingley Dell Development of Homes for the Discriminating Executive, 'she does not have a headache!'

He pressed the doorbell of Los Wardlos, and hardly had the sonorous notes of *Volare* died than the rubicund countenance of Mr Wardle himself appeared, his bright-veined eyes twinkling in the light of the twin carriage-lamps, like very maraschinos.

'Huzzah!' cried Mr Wardle, a punch-clove flying from his shining lip and fixing itself upon Mrs Winkle's cheek like a commando's grapnel. 'Merry Christmas!' He swung wide the neo-Edwardian door. 'It is Kevin and Arabella Winkle, everyone!'

'Aha!' bellowed a cheery and familiar voice from within. 'Surgical stocking and friend!'

How they all laughed at Mr Pickwick's deft quip (for it was, of course, none but he), and clapped their hands, and nudged, and winked! Somehow, Mr Pickwick was always the cynosure of such jocund assemblies, Mr Pickwick with his gravel pits, his elegant Romford casinos, his discreet loan companies, his renowned nationwide Jolly Jiblet takeaway emporia, above all his cheery escort agencies from the august portals of which no Pickwickian had ever been turned away without a sloe-eyed mulatto or big Turk, at practically cost.

The Winkles having by now crossed the threshold, Mrs Wardle herself leapt graciously from the comfortable lap of Mr Tupman, with whom she had been commiserating upon the unfortunate inability of Mrs Tupman to comprehend the manifold pressures exerted upon a man doing his utmost to manufacture chiming dangle-dollies in direct competition with cheap South Korean labour, and advanced upon them, rebuttoning the bodice of her seemly lurex jump-suit as she went.

'Will you take a glass of punch?' she offered, her clear bell-like voice making the Scotcade chandelier tinkle and twinkle in the warm electric firelight. 'It is made from a special recipe Mr Wardle and I brought back from our recent travels in Ibiza.'

'Thank you so much, dear Mrs Wardle,' replied Mr Winkle. 'Mine is a large one.'

'That,' cried a beaming Mr Pickwick, 'is not what I hear!'

How the happy company roared! The welkin rang with a multitude of cries to the effect that Mr Pickwick was a caution, that he would be the death of them, that it was easy to see how he had revolutionised the fast food industry, and so forth; and, indeed, they might have been chuckling still, had Mrs Winkle not chosen to change the subject by declaring her deep sympathy for Mr Pickwick at the tragic news that his dear wife had gone off with a teenage Carib bouncer from one of Mr Pickwick's own fashionable bingo establishments.

But hardly had this intelligence imparted itself upon the rapt company – how news of dear ones flies thick and fast when friends who have not met these twelve months past conjoin around the festive tree – than there came a great clatter-my-batter, a loud fulmunderdiddle, a roaring thunnerkin-bunnerkin from beyond the doors, as of a mountain of tin cans crashing down into the echoing valley beneath, and Mr Alfred Jingle, his auburn wig awry and his lipstick smeared, burst into their midst!

'New Volvo – missed gate – sharp turn – icy patch – bloody Peugeot – written off!' he exclaimed.

What a tumult ensued! What a rush to the door! And what a joyous relief flooded all their hearts upon their perception that it was not their Peugeot which had been reduced to scrap by Mr Jingle's untimely buffet! All hearts, that is, save the one pounding within the breast of the hapless Mr Winkle as that worthy stared, mute, at the pile of dismembered tin which had so lately, and so bravely, borne him thither.

'It is my opinion,' offered Mr Tupman, by way of consolation, 'that you had been better advised to have purchased a Saab. There is in their reinforced body shell a security afforded by none other of my acquaintance.' Here he indicated the outlines of the item in question, just perceptible through the frosty gloaming. 'Not, of course, that I am proud of my selection of a foreign product, but which of us in the wisdom of his years would now purchase the offerings of British Leyland?'

'How everything degenerates about us!' exclaimed Mrs Trundle, dashing a tear from her young and pretty eye with a Wedgwood-pattern Kleenex.

'So true,' nodded her husband. 'Personally, I blame the

blackamoors, do I not?'

'Well said, dear Mr Trundle!' cried Mr Tupman warmly. 'I do not, naturally, have anything to reproach them with personally, and there is no gainsaying the appeal of their piccaninnies, but, surely, to take men so recently descended from the colonial trees and place them in positions of responsibility within our great manufacturing industries is flying in the very face of nature?'

'And furthermore,' declaimed Mr Pickwick, who had joined the outside party with a shrewd view to valuing Mr Winkle's Peugeot for scrap, 'my long and if I may say so successful entrepreneurial career leads me to believe that if the good Lord had wished men to form themselves into unions, He would have placed chimney pots on their heads!' As several of the company applauded this wisdom, he turned to his dimpling neighbour. 'What say you to that, dear Mrs Tupman?'

Mrs Tupman lowered her eyes demurely.

'What I have never been able to understand,' she murmured, 'is how people capable of putting a man on the Moon seem totally unable to stop rice from sticking together.'

It was at this point, as all stood nodding sagely, that the door of Mr Jingle's Volvo opened, and a Fat Boy emerged. Mr Pickwick, by way of enquiry, turned to Mr Jingle, and raised a quizzical eyebrow.

'Reason I bought Volvo,' explained Mr Jingle. 'Saw advertisement – man driving Volvo – late at night – deserted countryside – flagged down by comely young fellow – fellow climbs in – talk about antiques – frightfully cosy – turns out young fellow attracted by Volvo – ideal car for me – rushed out – cash on nail – here we are!'

'Won't you please introduce us?' enquired Mr Wardle.

'‘Ullo,' said the Fat Boy.

'Few words,' explained Mr Jingle. 'Hairdresser – MI5 – nice manners.' He adjusted his hairpiece. 'Promised him trip to France.'

Mr Wardle cleared his throat.

'Shall we go in to dinner?' he said.

And so they did. And what a feast was there! Such avocado soup, such taramasalata, such poppadums, such deliciously thawed ratatouille, and – goes it not without saying? – such poultry! No mundane turkey or downmarket duck at this groaning board, but fashionable goose, the mounds of white fat steaming and quivering on each eager plate, or elegant pigeon, a generous gift from Mr Pickwick's new shoot (acquired by him upon the takeover of an ailing massage-parlour empire), each little bird so well accounted for by the guns of Mr Pickwick's parliamentary acquaintances that the Yuletide dining-room echoed with the crunch of bridgework and the patter of pellets in the finger-bowls!

And the conversation! How the witty perceptions flew hither and yon upon such divers topics as hysterectomy and central heating, the relaxation of exchange controls and the brilliance of Miss Penelope Keith, and with what oohings and aahings and claspings of hands did each of that company greet the news of the other, anent the almost embarrassingly ridiculous prices that the houses of all of them could now command.

Yet what was all this but the joyous gustatory prolegomenon to the entry of the Pudding? The lights went out, the Fat Boy squealed, Mr Pickwick sprang cheerily on Mrs Tupman, and then, her radiant features lit tantalisingly from beneath by the glow of incinerating Spanish brandy, Miss Elke Lundqvist bore in that giant ebon sphere, that stone-ground low-calory pesticide-free masterpiece, that *Sunday Times* Club miracle-offer *pudding*!

How thunderous the applause! How eagerly the nearest men grasped their hostess's plump thigh in gratitude! How maliciously glinted the fair eyes of the ladies in the flickering pudding-light!

But what is this! The ravishing Miss Elke Lundqvist, her thoughts perhaps not there but in that far fjord to which the worthy Mrs Wardle would not let her return this Christmas and where her young friends may even at this moment be rolling ecstatically around their Yuletide sauna, the ravishing but preoccupied Miss Elke Lundqvist has *slipped*!

The pudding flew! The flaming liquor spilled upon the remarkable embonpoint of Miss Elke Lundqvist! And, true to the traditional gallantry of his English stock, the selfless Mr Winkle, until then morosely quiet with his thoughts of broken cars and yet more broken teeth, leapt from his chair and hurled himself upon her, beating with his bare hands the flames which threatened to engulf her bust!

What confusion! What tumultuous cries! What threshings in the dark!

The lights snapped on, and there, supine upon the Casa Pupo rug, smouldering, yes, but otherwise unharmed, Miss Elke Lundqvist lay, muttering those Nordic imprecations, reader, over which both decorousness and monolinguality require us to draw a blessed veil. And beside her, oddly bent, the unnervingly inert form of the evening's hero, Mr Kevin Winkle.

With Mrs Winkle's pastry-fork protruding from his throat.

Talkin' Wid de Lord

THE PROBLEM, as I see it, is not theological at all, but social: when, that is, the Almighty shakes whatever it is I have for a hand (a wing? a flipper? an ectoplasmic pod?), informs me that He is pleased to meet me, and offers me a plate of little sausages on sticks, do I reply: 'I will give thanks unto Thee, for I am fearfully and wonderfully made' or 'I see QPR played another blinder, then?'

If, of course, He would ever say He was pleased to meet me. Leaving aside such metaphysical imponderabilia as whether He already knows me even as I am known, how do we begin to make sensible guesses about divine etiquette? After all, what class is God? Is He a toff? Lower middle? Senior executive? Working? Not – marginally possible – English at all, but someone who will simply click his heels and snap 'Entzückt!' or (shaking His Rastafarian locks) cry 'Gimme some skin!'?

Perhaps He doesn't shake hands at all. Many foreigners (if He will forgive me, and there is every reason to believe that He will, this being a trespass of minor proportions) embrace; Eskimoes rub noses; some Melanesians, according to Margaret Mead, pull one another's ears on meeting. It is possible He does all of these, and more.

Though, on balance of probability, not. With a million people dying every week, there would never be time for anything but the most cursory of greetings: three people every two seconds pouring into Reception from geriatric wards, DC-l0s, Cambodian bunkers, fogbound motorways, imploded tankers, KKK rallies, inept barbershops, East End casinos, potholes, scaffolds, free-fall parachute displays – many of them, too, still somewhat bewildered and in no shape to have their ears pulled by the Almighty.

Unless time is different There, mind. A thousand ages in His sight are, as I understand it, like an evening gone: Crossing Over may well be like going into Italy and suddenly finding small change with 1, 000 written on it. You may get anything up to six eternal months to the hour sterling, Over There.

It's a complicated business, eternity.

I shouldn't have got myself enmeshed in its boggling coils at all, had it not been for Glenda Jackson, Willie Whitelaw, Flora Robson and, of course, Richard Baker. They, and 596 like them, are why I am standing here today, just inside the pearly gates, wondering if I ought to be wearing a dinner jacket. For those six hundred eminences have just presented a petition to the General Synod of the Church of England, asking for the restoration to normal worship of the Book of Common Prayer and the Authorised Version of the Bible, and have thus set a cat among the liturgical pigeons more than likely, as such things traditionally do, to leave the loft full of bloodstained feathers and beak-torn fur.

Now, I must point out immediately (since I have no wish to spend whatever mortal time I have left writing mollifying letters to millions of apoplectic readers whose temple veins begin to throb like lugworms whenever they feel that the Litany is under the cosh) that I care not a whit how people worship, or, indeed, whether they worship at all. With the gas-boiler on the blink and the lawn full of moss and a phone-bill just in that makes the National Debt look like Bob Cratchit's take-home pay after stoppages, I have scant inclination to worry about other people's immortal souls; and in fact should have paid no attention to my own, had it not been for a remark passed on this morning's *Today* programme, while I was shaving, by a hired torpedo sent along by the General Synod to stick up for his employers' desperate tinkerings. 'It's all about,' he murmured, 'finding a comfortable way of talking to God.'

Which, as it was bound to do, left me for some minutes staring, motionless, at that soap-girt face which in the fullness of time, or (who knows?) its shallowness, may, if the General

Synod, Richard Baker, and numerous other unimpeachable authorities are to be credited, be staring at its Maker and murmuring rubbish about how nice it is to be here.

Because how *will* one talk to Him?

The manner will be the least of one's worries. Personally, though I risk offending against Glenda Jackson and incurring the wrath of Willie Whitelaw, I shall probably stick to the vernacular, since I should feel a fool, upon shaking hands/rubbing noses, if I were to say: 'O God our heavenly Father, who by Thy gracious providence dost cause the former and the latter rain to fall upon the earth, that it may bring forth fruit in the use of man, we give Thee humble thanks that it hath pleased Thee. . .' and so on. I do not talk like that, and should anyway have a job sustaining it when the conversation turned to whether He had enjoyed *Annie Hall*.

Which is where we approach the nub: for while the Synod and the Chartists currently lock horns on how God is to be addressed, I am chiefly exercised over the fraught business of what we shall actually talk *about*. What, in short, is He interested in?

I am assuming that He and I will not have a great deal of time together, but at the same time assuming that He will try to get around and have a word with everyone, since He is not called the Lord of Hosts for nothing. I suppose I see the occasion as a sort of huge Divine Garden Party, with the newly dead pouring in constantly through one gate, having a drink and a bridge-roll and a quick chat, and then pouring out again through another, towards some further destination as yet unspecified. We shall all thus have only a very few minutes to make an impression; and if that seems a somewhat worldly and ignoble ambition, I have to say in my defence that that is part of my nature and I do not wish to be fobbed off with a nod and a smile and promptly forgotten by the Almighty. I shall, after all, have waited a long time (the longer, if He will once again forgive me, the better) for this chance, I shall have to have popped my very clogs for the opportunity, and I have no intention of being no more than a brief fuzzed face in the crowd, instantly shoved out of sight again as a mob comes in from the latest Kurdish uprising.

I had, as a matter of fact, a sort of dress rehearsal for it, once, and I do not intend to let the like happen again. I was at a Royal wedding reception, almost certainly through a misaddressed envelope, when HM the Q, such were the peristaltic convulsions of the huge crowd, suddenly appeared in front of me, as in some bizarre Paul Jones. She smiled (radiantly, I believe the word is), and I glanced down deferentially, frantically framing some extraordinarily clever epigram about its being remarkably warm for the time of year, and when I looked up again, she had turned into Bernard Levin. I watched her smile being borne away through the mob with an expression on my own stricken face which led the solicitous Bernard to clutch my forearm and enquire whether I wanted a glass of water.

I have no intention of letting that happen Over There. Much as I should enjoy Bernard's scintillating company for (if Einstein will forgive me this time) the duration, I do not plan to move from the celestial spot until God and I have chewed the fat for an adequate spell.

But how to go about it?

Normal cocktail-party opening gambits are, of course, quite useless. 'Have you ever noticed . . .?' or 'Has it ever struck you as peculiar that . . .?' or 'I bet you didn't realise that . . . ?' are quite obviously out of the question. Indeed, omniscience itself could well prove to be an unclearable hurdle, since it would patently come as no surprise to the Almighty that Clement Freud once held the record of 105 omelettes in half an hour or that the male rabbit, if startled, will eat its own children. Facts are the one thing calculated to make the divine eye glaze and wander.

Likewise, jokes. Bizarre though it may be to ponder it, God has heard something like eighteen million jokes, including over two hundred about a man who went into a chemist's shop. Worse than that, and still more bizarre, is that – omnipotency being the thing it is – He also tells them better than anybody else.

We may well be on safer ground with opinions. Assuming that theologians have got it right in framing the concept of Free Will and weren't just cobbling any old thing together to make some sort of logical sense out of life's contradictory lunacies, I think we may take it that our opinions are our own and have not all been previously covered by God. He may, that is to say, be fascinated by our view that the new Lancia reminds us of the old Fiat, intrigued by our suggestion that it is better, when trying to get to Maidenhead from Barnes, to avoid the M4 altogether, and surprised to learn that we felt *Tinker, Tailor, Soldier, Spy* to be incomprehensible cobblers (enabling us, perhaps, to get in some snappy riposte, such as 'It's all right for you, Almighty, you knew who the mole was all the time, har-har-har!')

Not, mind, that there might not be dire pitfalls even here. We do not, for example, know whether the Almighty Himself holds views; is there any point in having opinions when You are in a position to alter the conditions under which You hold them (if there are any Jesuits out there, my number is ex-directory)? Indeed, especially for those who do not cleave to the Free Will dogma, it may be that the facts *are* God's opinions, i.e., He feels that the tallest mountain in the world should be exactly 29, 002 feet high and that Elton John should go bald, which means that you could be on very unsteady ground if you were to use your precious minutes over the elysial Babycham in saying that, in your opinion, the First World War was a bad thing. He might have enjoyed the Somme enormously, the supernal equivalent of blow-football, and meet your small talk with a very stony eye indeed.

Which, now I come to think further upon it, may well be the reason that Willie and Glenda and Richard and all the rest are in favour of sticking to the frequently unfathomable 1662 version; because when all is said, done, and tastefully interred, would it not be better, at that great encounter in the sky, for me to grasp my Maker firmly by the hand, look unwaveringly into His welcoming eye, and cry, with Psalm 147: 'HE HATH NO PLEASURE IN THE STRENGTH OF AN HORSE: NEITHER DELIGHTETH HE IN ANY MAN'S LEGS?'

Which will not only resonate wonderfully over the surrounding hubbub, but also baffle even Him so effectively that He will still be wondering what it was that that clever little soul meant long after I have passed through the further gate, and gone.

Near Myth

Russian scientists have photographed what they believe are the remains of Atlantis. The Soviet Academy's Institute of Oceanography said that analysis of photographs taken deep in the Atlantic showed what appeared to be the remains of giant stairways and walls midway between Portugal and Madeira.

Daily Telegraph

'IF THAT kid drowns,' said Peleus darkly, looking up from his poolside recliner, 'it'll bloody ruin my holiday. We are not insured against you dunking him.'

Thetis tugged Achilles from the hotel pool, by his heel.

'It'll toughen him up,' she said. 'You don't half go on, sometimes.'

'As King of the Myrmidons,' said her husband, 'I am paid to go on. I got responsibilities. These include making sure there's a next King of the Myrmidons. You do not help matters by chucking my sole heir in the deep end every morning.'

'It'll make him arrowproof,' said Thetis. 'About time we had an arrowproof monarch. It said in the brochure that the Hotel Atlantis offered, and I quote, an Olympic-sized pool guaranteed to render our esteemed guests invulnerable. I wouldn't have come otherwise. I've always avoided Madeira. It's full of mortals this time of year. Common as dirt.'

'You don't want to believe everything you read in brochures,' said Peleus. 'It said this was a family hotel. There's a woman in the suite next door who's come here with a swan. They're not even married. I don't call that a family hotel. I didn't know where to look this morning when he was pecking his cornflakes and touching her up with his wing under the table.'

'He was a shower of gold when he signed in,' said his wife. 'I complained to the manager about the swan business, and he showed me the register. Mr and Mrs Shower Of Gold. He said it wasn't up to him to check credentials. Go and swim in the sea,' she called to Achilles, who was sniffing a waiter who had just turned himself into an asphodel rather than catch a nearby guest's eye, 'it'll tone up your muscles.'

Peleus watched his son toddle off towards the beach.

'There's narwhals out there,' he said, shading his eyes against the Atlantic glint. 'Tritons, sirens, you name it. Half of bloody Loch Ness comes down here for the summer. I hope he'll be all right.'

'Watch it,' snapped Thetis. 'I was a fish once.'

'Don't remind me,' said Peleus bitterly. 'That was the same year you were a flame, a giant crab, and, if my memory serves me right, a small pond. I married a Nereid. That was the deal. If I'd known I was going to end up married to a bloody pond, I'd have gone off with that big Indian bird.'

'I wish you had,' said Thetis. 'It would've served you right. She's been a tortoise for the past ten years.'

'Nothing wrong with tortoises. Bit of lettuce now and again. No trouble.'

A scarlet dragon in the deckchair beside them leaned across.

'It might interest you to know,' said one of its heads, 'that the world rests on the back of a tortoise.'

'Rubbish!' cried Peleus.

'What did he say?' said the dragon's other head.

'He said rubbish.'

'Bloody sauce!' said the second head.

The dragon got up and stomped off, its breath shimmering the seascape.

'What did I tell you?' said Thetis. 'They'll let anyone in here. Chinese, anyone.'

'It's the Teutons I can't stand,' said Peleus. 'I swear they get up two hours early just to grab the best deckchairs. *And* they've brought their own tree.'

'It's called Yggdrasil,' said his wife. 'I saw the label when it came off the roof of their chara.'

'I don't care what it's called,' snapped Peleus, 'they got no business planting it outside our window. I went on the balcony this morning, there was a horse looking at me.'

'It belongs to Odin,' said his wife. 'It roots in the foliage.'

'Very nice,' snorted Peleus heavily. 'Tree with a horse in it, that's what I call a sophisticated religion!'

'I heard that!'

Across the pool, a huge Teuton had risen to his feet. He raised an enormous arm.

'See this hammer?' said Thor.

Peleus looked away.

'If you were half a man,' said Thetis, 'you'd . . .'

'I *am* half a man,' said Peleus. 'One of the troubles, being half god, half mortal. Suppose he thumps the mortal half? I could spend the rest of eternity walking about half-corpse. Ever thought of that?'

Thor sat down again. The Teuton party began to laugh, and throw rocks about: some turned into minor Azores, one or two became Vikings, a small pebble metamorphosed as a fountain and began reciting eddas.

'Flash buggers!' muttered Peleus. 'Sometimes I wonder who won the war.'

'Hallo!' cried Thetis. 'What's up with Achilles?'

The little boy was running up the beach screaming. Peleus leapt to his feet, and ran to gather him up.

'What's happened?' he shouted.

'I saw the whole thing,' said a jellyfish, as a wave deposited him at their feet. 'Chuhinaga, by the way; I handle war, weather and after-sales service in the Solomons. I always come here August. Anyway, I was out there having a bit of a float when suddenly this bloke comes whistling out of the sky, nearly fell on your kid.'

'Icarus,' said a centaur who had been playing French cricket with a group of corn-dollies. 'They're a funny family. His old man's still up there. Blooming nuisance, the pair of 'em. I was at the Club Mediterranée in Crete last year, they fell on my hut.'

'Come on, son,' said Peleus, wiping the boy's tears. 'Let's go and have an early lunch.'

The three Greeks were stopped at the dining-room doors by a short, liveried sphinx.

'Table near the window,' said Peleus.

'What's a Grecian urn?' asked the sphinx, nudging him.

'I've no idea,' said Peleus stonily, 'kindly show us to . . .'

There was a faint pop.

'Hallo,' said Thetis, 'you're a stoat.'

Achilles picked his father up and shook him.

'Dad-dad!' he cried gleefully, 'Dad-dad!'

'What's happened?' squeaked Peleus.

'You don't muck about with me, mate,' said the sphinx sternly. 'I ask a riddle, I expect a bloody answer, chop-chop.'

It snapped a claw grudgingly, and Peleus re-appeared. The trio made their way into the restaurant, found their own table; a leprechaun in a wing collar appeared with menus.

'Nearly everything's off,' said the leprechaun, 'begob.'

'Off?' cried Peleus. 'It's only quarter-past twelve.'

'Don't blame me,' said the leprechaun. 'We had a party of hydras in for the first sitting. Begorrah. Business convention. There was only the dozen of 'em, but sure and wasn't there a hundred and eight heads they was after having on 'em? Bedad.'

Peleus sprang to his feet.

'Don't give me that!' he shouted. 'I am sick to death of this rat-hole! You cannot get in the bloody pool for Wop mermaids, you cannot get a decent chair for all them lousy Norse layabouts, not to mention a balcony with outstanding horse views and people banging anvils half the bloody night, you cannot go in the sea without loonies falling on you, you cannot even close your eyes for a second without immigrant dragons buttonholing you with their half-baked heathen ideas, your so-called highly trained staff, far from attending my every whim as per brochure, prefer to turn guests into stoats at the drop of a handkerchief, the swan next door is never, pardon my French, off the nest so's you can't hear yourself think in our room for the rattling of the furniture, the sauna's been full of griffons singing rugby songs ever since we got here, and now you have the gall to tell me that a party of commercial monsters has come in and eaten everybody's dinner! Let *me* tell *you*, sunshine, I happen to be a demigod with friends in very high places, and I shall not hesitate to . . .'

'Leave it out,' said a heavy voice. 'I've told you once.'

Peleus turned.

Thor was towering beside him.

'I don't talk to navvies,' said Peleus.

Thor sighed, and hit him with his hammer.

Whereupon the swan, who had just come into the restaurant, immediately changed, on seeing a fellow-Greek in trouble, into a large bull. It walked across to Thor, put its huge head down, and tossed him through the wall.

Things screamed.

Thunderbolts began to fly.

A few upper floors collapsed into the garden, causing a number of hysterical bushes to burst into flame and start running about, spreading yet further disorder and destruction, and by the time Thetis and Achilles had dragged the unconscious Peleus out of the disintegrating restaurant, the New Wing (which contained a party of vampires who had been hanging quietly in the wardrobes waiting for nightfall) had begun to burn quite vigorously.

And they only just had time to gain the mountainside behind it before the whole collapsing, blazing, shrieking edifice of the five-star Atlantis began to slide slowly down the hill and into the waiting sea.

The hiss awoke the battered Peleus. He touched his bump. He winced. He gazed at the boiling surface of the sea. He sucked his loosened teeth. He shook his head.

'It's the last time I come here,' he muttered.

Oedipus Bruce

In Australia a recommendation was made recently that incest between a mother and son should no longer be illegal.

ACT ONE

Enter Chorus. They are citizens of Adelaide. They have corks dangling from their hats. They are all dead drunk.

CHORUS   Our mouths are like the inside of an abbo's trousers. We have all been walking through yesterday's lunch. We are as much use as an earwig's tit. What happened to last Wednesday?

Enter Barry, King of Adelaide, on all fours.

CHORUS   Hallo, Bazza, you look like two ton of old fish-heads.

BARRY   I've just been out in the fly box, saying goodbye to breakfast.

CHORUS   It's not like old Bazza to honk the bacon down the pipes after a night on the frosty tubes. Old Bazza has a gut like a ship's boiler. We have seen old Bazza sink ten gallons of Mrs Foster's Finest without threatening the drainage. Old Bazza must be upset about something.

BARRY   Too right! I was reading my horoscope in *Beer Weekly*, and it says where it's bad dos on the family scene this year, my flaming son is gonna flaming kill me, also beer could go up by as much as ten flaming cents a tube!

CHORUS   Stone the crows, Bazza! Ten cents a tube? This could spell the end of flaming civilisation as we flaming know it!

BARRY   Next thing you know, the supermarkets'll be charging corkage on flaming Parozone! I blame the Japs.

CHORUS   Too right. What's this about your son? We didn't know you had a son. We didn't realise you ever went near your old lady. Isn't she the sheila who looks like a '37 Holden pick-up, sounds like a dragsaw, and smells like a dead dingo?

BARRY   Time was. She's past her best now. Still, when a bloke's tied a few on of a Saturday night, it's no worse than cleaning the chimney in your bare feet. That's how we ended up with young Bruce. He's a bright little bastard, can't be more'n ten months old, and he's already been done twice for being in charge of a push-chair while unfit. I'll be sorry to see him go, straight up.

CHORUS   Go? What are you gonna do with him, Bazza?

BARRY   I'm not risking some flaming kid growing up and doing his daddy with a lead sock. I'm gonna drive him out to Broken Hill and nail him to the floor.

CHORUS   Good on yer, Bazza! Trouble with kids today, they need a firm hand. No flaming authority left. No sense of family. Good luck, Bazza, got to rush now or they'll be picking bits of bladder off the ceiling.

Exeunt.

ACT TWO

The outback, near Broken Hill. Enter King Barry, carrying Bruce, and Wayne, a shepherd. They are all drunk.

BARRY   There you go, Wayne, I've tied his flaming feet together, all you have to do is drop him in the sheep dip. Watch how you handle him, he can go off like a flaming mortar when he's had a few, we had to redecorate the entire bungalow once.

WAYNE   Count on me, Bazza, I'll pop him in the dippo when I go to fill up me bottles. I'm expecting a few blokes over this evening for a bit of a blast.

Exit Bazzu. Wayne stands holding the baby for a moment or two, then falls down and begins snoring.

BRUCE   Burp.

Exit Bruce, crawling.

ACT THREE

Twenty years later. During this period, Bruce has been brought up as a sheep by an elderly ram and ewe who found him as a baby. He walks on two legs, but neither he nor his adoptive parents think this in any way odd. This is Australia. Bruce's diet has been grass and sheep dip. He is tall, strong, and permanently drunk, and has picked up a little English from the labels of the beer cans with which the outback is strewn.

It is a hot morning. Bruce is staggering along a dusty track, when he meets another man staggering towards him. The man is Craig, a brewing representative. He is drunk.

CRAIG   Stone the flaming crows, it's Bruce!

BRUCE   You got the wrong bloke, blue. My name's Sixteen
            Fluid Ounces. It was Pull Ring Here for a time, I'll
            give yer that, but it's never been flaming Bruce.

CRAIG   Well take it from me, cobber, it's Bruce now all
            right, they had your picture in *The Daily Beer*, and
            if you want my advice you'll keep away from your
            folks. It says in the paper that as sure as flies lay
            eggs in a wombat's trade-mark, you're gonna fill in
            your old man and marry your old lady!

BRUCE   Yeah, well, the bloke who wrote that never saw my
            old lady. She's got four black hooves and twelve
            nipples, not to mention some bloody peculiar
            personal habits. You'd think twice before jumping
            on a mattress with that.

CRAIG   Don't argue, mate, *The Daily Beer* never lies!

He falls down. Bruce hesitates for a time, then shrugs, sets his shoulders, turns his back resolutely on Broken Hill and takes instead the opposite direction, towards Adelaide.

ACT FOUR

The road near Adelaide. A battered truck is rattling along it, with King Barry at the wheel, lurching in every pot-hole and spilling old beer-cans at every yard. At the top of a little rise stands Bruce, albeit unsteadily. As the truck approaches, he thumbs it down. Barry looks out of the window.

BRUCE   Afternoon, sport. You wouldn't have a tube of Foster's aboard by any chance? I haven't eaten for six weeks.

BARRY   Well, now, blue, that's a very interesting question! A very interesting question indeed. Why not have it engraved on brass and shove it where the moon never shines, har, har, har!

At this, Bruce tears the door off, drags Barry out onto the road, and batters him lifeless with it. He removes eight cans of lager from the body, drains them, belches happily, climbs into the truck, and sets off on a zig-zag course, back towards Adelaide.

ACT FIVE: Scene One

A month later. Adelaide, before the royal palace. It is an attractive wooden bungalow with a pleasing neo-Georgian room-extension in primrose mock-stucco nailed to the front. There are five carriage lamps on the front door, and a gnome holding a sign that reads '38 to 38A Alopecia Avenue'. Enter Bruce, who pushes open the wrought-iron gate and rings a doorbell. The chimes of Viva España die away, the door opens.

BRUCE   Queen Glenda?

GLENDA   That's right. Sorry about the Marigold gloves, sport, I was just worming the cat. What can I do for you?

BRUCE   Promise you won't laugh, Glenda, only I met this sphinx up the road.

GLENDA   I know how it gets sometimes, blue. I usually get pink spiders running over the flaming sideboard.

BRUCE   No, straight up, Glenda, I met this sphinx and it said if I got three riddles right I could come round here and marry you. I didn't have anything else on this morning, so I thought, what the hell, it's better than a poke in the eye with a sharp stick!

Enter Chorus, supporting one another.

CHORUS   He'll be flaming sorry he said that!

Exeunt, on hands and knees.

GLENDA   So you answered the riddle all right, then?

BRUCE   I don't know. The sphinx was legless. It was all he could do to give me your address before he fell over.

GLENDA   I swear they put something in it up the factory. When I was a girl, you could drink thirty-one pints before breakfast.

They marry. The wedding reception goes on for nine weeks. At the end of it, the bungalow has disappeared beneath a pyramid of beer cans. A number of guests are dead.

Scene Two

Some of the cans clatter to the ground. Bruce emerges from the gap, obviously distressed. He has a stick up his nose. Enter Norman, a neighbour. He is drunk.

NORMAN   Stone the flaming crows, Bruce, what's that stick doing up your conk?

BRUCE   I've been trying to poke me flaming eyes out, Norm. I can't seem to get the flaming range. I guess I'll have to wait till I'm flaming sober.

NORMAN   You don't want to go poking yer eyes out, mate. They'll rob you blind up the off-licence. It could cost a flaming bomb! What made you think of it?

BRUCE   I found out Glenda's me mum, Norm. I've only gone and married me flaming mummy!

NORMAN   No cause to pop yer headlights, blue! Mind, I can see it could be a bit awkward. Been a few naughties, have there?

BRUCE   Nothing like that, Norm. Nothing of that order. I haven't been capable, for one thing. Glenda says they put something in up the factory. No, it's giving up the bungalow, Norm. You spend twenty years as a flaming sheep, suddenly you got gas central heating and three flaming low-flush pastel suites, it's not easy to give it all up just like that.

NORMAN   Strikes me you're being a bit previous, cobber. I can't see why you and Glenda can't make a go of it. She's a very nice woman when she's drunk and no beard to speak of.

BRUCE   But it's against the flaming law, Norm!

NORMAN   Then they'll have to flaming change it, mate!

BRUCE   Would they do that, Norm?

NORMAN   Would they . . .? You just come down the pub with me, cobber, we'll wake up the Home Secretary and put it to him straight!

Exeunt. Enter Chorus, dragging one another.

CHORUS   In Australia, all is flaming possible! In Australia, a new world is flaming born! In Australia, I flaming will! In Australia . . .

They collapse. They lie there. They snore.

CURTAIN

Doctor No Will See You Now

CIA agents who lose the qualities that make good spies are retired at fifty under special pensions, according to testimony yesterday before a House Intelligence Sub-Committee. 'A 70-year-old James Bond is kind of hard to imagine,' said Republican Senator Sam Stratton.

Herald Tribune

BOND TENSED in the darkness, and reached for his teeth.

There was something in the room.

You did not train for fifty-three years without developing that imponderable acuity that lay beyond mere observation. Indeed, you found that as the years went by, this sixth sense came, perforce, to replace the others: these days, he could hear dog-whistles, with or without his batteries in.

At least, he assumed they were dog-whistles. Nobody else seemed to hear them.

The teeth fell exactly to hand, there between the senna and the Algipan on his bedside table. He waited a calculated split second for the cement to cleave snugly to his palate. It felt good. It should have: it was made for him by Chas. Fillibee of Albemarle Street, the world's premier fixative man. Senior British agents had been going to Fillibee since before the War; he knew their special requirements. When Witherspoon 004 had gone into the London Clinic to have his prostate done and the KGB had taken the opportunity to lob an Ostachnikov nuclear mortar into his grape-box, the only thing left intact between Baker Street Station and the Euston underpass had been Witherspoon's upper plate.

Very carefully, Bond slid his hand beneath his pillow and

closed it around the ribbed butt of his Walther PPK 9mm Kurz with the custom-enlarged trigger guard by Kinz of Stuttgart which allowed the arthritic knuckle of Bond's forefinger to slide smoothly around the trigger. His other hand took the light switch.

In one smooth, practised move, Bond snapped on the light switch and simultaneously peered around the room.

There was a shadowy, half-familiar figure by the dressing table. Bond fired, twice, the fearful reports cracking back and forth between the walls, and the figure reeled.

'So much,' murmured Bond coolly, 'for Comrade Nevachevski!'

Miss Moneypenny sat up in bed, her grizzled bun unravelling, her elegant muffler in fetching disarray.

'You silly old sod,' she said.

Bond beamed, deafly.

'Yes, wasn't it?' he said. 'Inch or so wide, mind, should've been straight between the eyes, but, my God, he didn't even have time to draw!'

'YOU'VE SHOT YOUR WIG-STAND!' shouted Miss Moneypenny. She stuck an ephedrine inhaler in her left nostril, and sucked noisily.

Bond put on his bi-focals.

'Ah,' he said. He brightened. 'Still a bloody good shot, though, eh?'

'I should cocoa,' said Moneypenny. 'It ricocheted off the hot-water bottle. God alone knows what it's done to your rubber sheet.'

'Bloody hell,' said Bond.

He switched the light out again, and lay back. As always, after untoward events, his wheeze was bad, crackling round the room like crumpling cellophane.

'Shall I rub you in?' murmured Moneypenny softly, from her distant cot.

'Don't start,' said Bond.

Moneypenny sighed. At sixty-eight, it seemed, her virginity was moving slowly but surely beyond threat.

Bond shuffled nonchalantly into M's office and tossed his hat in a neat arc towards the polished antler. The hat fell in the waste-bin. 007 stared at it for a time, and finally decided against picking it up. On the last occasion upon which he had attempted a major stoop, it had taken four osteopaths to unwind him.

'Good morning,' said M, 'if you're from Maintenance, I'd like you to know that the roller towel is getting harder and harder to tug. I don't know what they're doing with them these days. I think they put something in them at the factory. When I was a lad, you could pull them down between thumb and forefinger. Possibly the KGB has a hand in it. Also, I have great difficulty in pulling the soap off that magnetic thingy.'

'It's me, sir,' said Bond, '00 –'

He frowned.

M stared at him glaucously from nonagenarian eyes.

Bond took off his James Lobb galosh, and removed a slip of paper.

'7,' he said. '007.'

M trembled suddenly. He tugged at a drawer, but it did not budge.

'I've got a gun in here somewhere,' he said. 'By God, you'll know it when I find it! You're not 007, you swine, I've known 007 fifty years, he's bright ginger!'

'I shot my wig,' said Bond, gloomily.

M relaxed.

'No good getting angry with a wig,' he said. 'It's only doing its job.'

'You sent for me,' said Bond.

'In the CIA,' murmured M, 'I'd have been retired forty years ago. I would have one of those thermal pools with a thing that makes waves in it. I would have my own genito-urinary man coming in on a weekly basis. A TV hanging from the ceiling, mink linings for the cold snap, a hollow cane with Remy Martin in it, a rare dog.'

'About this job,' said Bond.

M blew his nose, ineptly.

'Usual thing,' he said. 'MIRV-launching Russian satellite has been brought down by a defecting Albanian inter-galactic tail-gunner in the pay of the Irgun Zwei Leomi. As you would expect, it has fallen down inside Vesuvius: crack KGB, CIA, Mafia, Triad, and IRA teams are already racing to the spot. I promised the PM we'd send our best man.'

'Oh, good,' muttered Bond. 'You don't think Snuggley might fit the bill better?'

'003?' said M. 'His leg's gone in for its annual service. No, James, it's you – bags of parachuting, ski-ing, scuba-diving, unarmed combat, all that, right up your street.'

'Quite,' said Bond.

'Pop along and see Charlie in Special Equipment,' said M.

'This,' said Charlie, 'is probably the most advanced truss in the world.'

'It's snug,' said Bond. 'What are all these pockets for?'

'Spare surgical stockings,' said Charlie, ticking off his fingers, 'international pensions book, collapsible alloy crutches, Sanatogen capsules, arch supports, emergency pee bottle, mittens, underwater deaf-aid, thermal liberty bodice, and a handbell in case you fall over somewhere and can't get up.'

'Super,' said Bond.

'Also,' said Charlie, 'we've been over your Morris Traveller and, ha-ha, tarted it up a bit. Apart from the fact that you'll now be able to get it up to fifty-five –'

'Christ!'

'– there's an emergency inertia brake that brings it to a dead stop in the event of the driver having a heart attack, plus two big orange lights on stalks in both wings enabling you to drive it through narrow spaces, a foot-button that throws your window out instantly in the event of nausea, an inflatable antihaemorrhoid ring set in the driver's seat that activates at the first scream, and a 3 x magnifying windshield that enables you to read road signs without getting out of the car.'

'Fantastic,' muttered Bond.

'Good luck, 007,' said Charlie, 'and good hunting!'

He shook Bond's hand, but gently.

Bond nosed forward out of the roundabout, onto the Dover road.

People hooted.

The Traveller lurched forward, stalled, lurched on again. 007 ground into third gear. He glanced in his mirror, for the tenth time. Somebody was following him. They had been following him since Blackheath, almost two hours ago.

At the next traffic light, Bond got out, and walked back.

'I don't sell off the float, grandpa,' said the milkman.

'Why have you been following me?' said Bond levelly.

'I got no option, have I?' said the milkman. 'First off, we're the only two vehicles doing fifteen miles a wossname, second off, every time I bleeding pull out to overtake, you start wandering all over the road.'

'Evasive action,' snapped 007. 'Don't tell me you weren't trying to force me into the ditch. You're with SMERSH, right?'

The milkman took his cap off.

'It says Unigate on here,' he said.

'Ha!' cried Bond, and sprang into a Nakusai karate crouch, his left hand a club, his right fingers a dagger.

The milkman got out and helped him up.

'It's this knee I've got,' said Bond.

'Shouldn't be out, old geezer like you,' said the milkman. 'It's freezing.'

Bond laughed one of his short dry laughs. Once, men had gone white at the very sound.

'Be warm enough, soon, eh? I trust you're bound for Vesuvius?'

The milkman looked at him.

'I got Mafeking Crescent to do, and a bulk yoghurt up the telephone exchange,' he said, 'then I'm off home for *Pebble Mill.*'

'A likely story!' cried Bond. 'What's under that moustache, you Chinese bastard?'

007 made a lightning grab at the milkman's upper lip, misjudged the distance, and caught his forefinger in his opponent's mouth. The milkman closed his teeth on Bond's frail knuckle, and the agent fell back into the road. As he lay there, a bus-driver walked up, stood on him absently, and said to the milkman:

'These bleeding lights have gone green twice, sunshine.'

'Don't blame me,' said the milkman, 'this old bugger stuck his hand in my gob.'

The bus-driver glanced down.

'It's this ten pounds Christmas bonus they're getting,' he said. 'It's driving 'em all barmy. They've been smoking on the downstairs deck all morning.' He bent down, and hauled Bond upright. 'Come on, uncle, I'll see you across to the Whelk & Banjo.'

He took Bond into the public bar, and sat him on a stool, and went out again.

Bond took five pills. His hand was shaking, his heart was pounding, there was a tic in his right eye, and his bronchitis was coming back. He ought to get on, it was four clear days to Naples, given that he refused to drive at night and wanted to pop into the clinic at Vitry-le-François for his monthly check-up.

But, then again, was it worth it? The KGB might hit him, the CIA might shout at him if he couldn't keep up, his surgical skis were as yet untested, and as for swimming the Bay of Naples, he had noticed in himself of late an unsettling tendency to sink. Added to all of which, his SMERSH counterpart was a big Balinese stripper fifty years his junior, and he doubted that his current sexual techniques would persuade her to defect, given that he preferred doing it in his herringbone overcoat these days, apart from the fact that he had last performed a mere eight months before and seriously doubted whether his forces were yet in a position to be remustered.

It wasn't a bad pub, all in all, thought Bond. He could write out a report from here, elaborating a bit. After all, what could they expect for fifty quid a week after stoppages?

The barman looked up at Bond's cough.

'What'll it be?' he said.

'I'll have a small Wincarnis,' said Bond. He took off his balaclava. 'Shaken, not stirred.'

A Small Thing but Minoan

'We can be quite precise about the date. 4, 000 years ago in Crete, during the Middle Minoan Period, linear writing in pen and ink was born.'

Fodor Guide to Crete

AGOROPHON SQUINTED up at the noonday sun. It gonged down out of a brass sky; the arid rock baked; insects gasped, crept slowly for the shade of crevices.

'Beats me why you dragged me all the way out here,' he said irritably. 'Day like this, what you want is your feet in a basin and a bird standing behind you with a large frond.'

'I've got something to show you,' said Memnos. 'It's private.'

Agorophon looked at him.

'It's not that rash again, is it?' he said.

Memnos shook his head. He groped down inside the neckline of his smock, while his friend watched uneasily.

'There you are,' said Memnos, handing him a fragment of dried leaf, 'have a butcher's at that.'

'If it's a scab,' said Agorophon, 'I'm not going near it.'

'It's a leaf,' said Memnos, 'it's got something written on it.'

'*Written* on it?' cried Agorophon. 'How can you chisel a leaf?' But he looked at it.

'You're right,' he said, at last. 'Squiggles. What a miraculous thing Nature is!'

'It's not natural,' replied Memnos. '*I* did it. I did it with ink.'

'Ink?'

'It's something I made from roots.'

'I thought that was gin,' said Agorophon.

329

'Different roots,' said Memnos. 'You don't drink this one.'

'Pity,' said Memnos. 'You can have enough of gin, this weather.'

'You write with it,' said Memnos. 'You dip a twig in it, and write.'

'Get off!' cried Agorophon. He looked at the leaf again. 'All right, what does it say?'

'It says X. P. Memnos, Number 9a, High Street.'

'What's it for?'

Memnos shrugged.

'It's all I could think of. You could give it to people. It's better than carrying a bagful of them stone visiting cards. Also, you can just dash 'em off. Instead of sitting there all day with a mallet.'

'Easier on the thumbs,' said Agorophon, 'I'll give you that.'

Memnos looked away from his friend, out over the broiling landscape, feeling faintly hollow. Disappointed wasn't quite the word. But, then, what was? The Cretan vocabulary was small, detailed, a lot of synonyms for food, weapons, internal organs, not much more. Perhaps it would expand, now, with the tedium of chiselling gone.

'Mind you,' said Agorophon, breaking into his reverie, 'I'll be glad to see the back of cuneiform, I don't mind saying. I could never make head nor tail out of it, it was just triangles. If we'd stuck with hieroglyphs, I could have got somewhere. I could have made something of myself. I used to enjoy reading hieroglyphs, all them little parrots, frogs, titchy houses, all that. I don't know why they gave it up.'

'Progress,' said Memnos.

'Yes, well,' said Agorophon.

Memnos frowned down at his leaf.

'I wonder what I ought to write first?' he murmured.

'Make marvellous betting slips,' said Agorophon.

'Very interesting,' said Old Memnos, looking disparagingly at the leaf. 'When are you going to go out and earn a living?'

'I want to be a writer,' said his son.

'What kind of work is that for a man?' said his mother. She dropped a rabbit's head into the pot, stirred it absently. 'I see them sitting in the square every day, hammering tablets, covered in dust. Labourers is what they are.'

'But this is a very fast system,' protested her son. He dipped his twig in a vial of murky liquid, and dashed off his address, ten times over, on a large piece of goatskin.

'Hang on!' shouted Old Memnos. 'She was making me a vest out of that!'

'It's got our address on it now,' said his son. 'That's another valuable asset.'

'I doubt whether you could market *that*,' said his mother. 'I don't see where there's much call for addressed underwear.'

'If you got run over,' said her son, 'they'd know where to bring you.'

His mother sniffed.

'About the only thing *I* can think of,' she said, 'is shopping lists. With stone shopping lists, time you've chiselled *Two kilograms brussels sprouts*, they've gone out of season.'

'I was planning on something bigger,' said Memnos, as the old hollowness moved through him once more. 'A personal statement, perhaps. Possibly rhyming. About love, or death, or going barmy. Something major.'

'Here!' cried his father. 'What about posters for tourists? They're always coming here from the mainland; we could do posters advertising dancing folklorique up the town hall, souvenir shops where they could get them little minotaurs for holding toothpicks, guided tours of the labyrinth. We could go down to the boats and hand 'em round, we'd get ten per cent off the retailers, we could clean up!'

'It's not exactly what I had in mind,' said his son.

His father glared at him.

'Advertising,' he said, 'that's where the money is!'

'Kids!' said his wife. 'Do they listen?'

He sat under a tree. Flies buzzed around his ink. He chewed his twig for the hundredth time. Around him, the parched ground was strewn with crumpled leaves.

He took a fresh one from his bag, smoothed it out, laid it on the board across his knees. Slowly, tongue curling over his upper lip, he wrote:

'It was a dark and stormy night.'

He stopped.

His mind teemed with shapes, people, mountains, ships, jokes, accidents, names, dreams. They floated about, they interleaved, they fragmented.

He tore up the leaf, and plucked another.

'It was the best of times,' he wrote, 'it was the worst of . . .'

'OY!'

Memnos looked up.

Agorophon was galloping down the hill, scattering goats. He fetched up, breathless.

'Journalism!' he gasped.

'What?'

'Nice big leaf, rhubarb, palm, something like that, bring it out every day, nail it up in the town square, stand a couple of big blokes in front of it with clubs, people want to read it, they have to pay! Main news, discus results, drawings of birds with their skirts up, spot-the-javelin contest, seer forecast, classified ads – how about it?'

Memnos shook his head.

'It would be selling out,' he said.

Agorophon clenched his fists.

'At least,' he muttered, 'it'd be selling.'

'That is not,' murmured Memnos, 'what it's all about.'

'It's what some of it's about, mate,' snapped Agorophon.

It took Memnos several years to sail to the mainland, and hardly a night passed on that terrible voyage when he did not regret his decision to leave Crete, nor long for the old companionship of the simple Cretans who had wanted him to abuse his gift.

And when, at last, he arrived, and sat on the pebbled beach, what, he asked himself, had it all been for?

And then he knew.

He had something to write about now.

When the sack of scribbled leaves was full, he strapped it to a mule, and he trekked into Athens, and –

What did one do with a great poem?

*

He pushed through the hanging beads.

'Is this,' enquired Memnos timidly, 'the registered office of Homer, Homer, Homer, Homer, Homer, Homer & Homer?'

'Yes,' they said.

'I understand,' said Memnos, putting his sack down, 'that you recite great poetry?'

'Sometimes it's great,' said all the Homers, 'sometimes it's not so great. You win a few, you lose a few. Also, it depends how much you can remember. We take it you know about the oral tradition?'

'It's over,' said Memnos, not without a hint of triumph. 'Mine's written down.'

The Homers looked at one another, sharply.

'*Written down?*'

'It's in two parts. One I called *The Odyssey*. The other I called *The Iliad*.'

'Catchy,' said the Homers. 'Could be very big.'

'Also,' said Memnos, 'I can teach you to read it. Then you could read it aloud everywhere, and I would get rich and famous.'

'So teach,' said the Homers.

And he did.

And when he had gone, the seven Homers split the manuscript up into seven parts, and each Homer learned his seventh by heart.

Then they burned the manuscript.

'Tough on the kid,' said the Homers, 'but business is business.'

And This is the Little Appliance

Despite the new Sex Equality laws, most British males will continue to treat their wives as more or less useful objects.
                                                          Time magazine

'COME HOME Friday, didn't I?' said the man in the blue dungarees, fingernailing a speck of nut from his beer-froth, 'and what was there? Pile of washing on the kitchen floor, dinner with the frost still on it, cat's doings in the corner by the telly. I thought, Gawdbleedingblind O'Reilly, it's packed up again!'

'And had it?' enquired the man in the herringbone overcoat, over the rim of his glass.

'Completely,' said the man in the blue dungarees. 'There it was in the corner. I gave it a poke, it just sort of wobbled a bit.'

'You can try kicking 'em,' said the man in the Wimpey jacket. 'It sometimes gets 'em going. Especially on cold mornings.'

The man in the dungarees finished his pint, and sucked the froth from his moustache.

'No,' he said, 'I could tell this was a skilled job. You don't want to go mucking about with 'em when it might be something radical. You could do a hell of a lot of damage. I gave mine a shake a couple of years back, turned out it had dislocated itself going after cobwebs. I put its bloody shoulder out. I didn't get it back for a fortnight. You wouldn't believe the state of my hosiery, time it got started again.'

'So what did you do this time?' asked the man in the herringbone overcoat, returning from the bar with three fresh pints.

The man in the blue dungarees drank a third off, belched, shrugged.

'Had to phone up, didn't I, get a man in. Not easy. He wanted me to bring it to him, first off. All that way, must be two miles, dragging that great big thing.'

'You could give yourself a rupture,' said the man in the herringbone overcoat. 'You could rip a sleeve, dragging.'

'That's what I told him. He come round, finally. Well past dinner-time, I might say. I had to get a pork pie down the wossname, the pub. Anyway, he had a look at it, had a feel underneath, shone his light in, listened with his stethoscope.'

'What was wrong?'

'*Varicose veins*,' said the man in the blue dungarees. 'Can you credit it?'

The other two looked at him, shocked.

'Varicose veins?' said the man in the herringbone overcoat. 'I can't see why that stops 'em cooking. You don't bloody cook with your legs, or am I mistaken?'

'I had the veins go on mine, once,' said the man in the Wimpey jacket. 'I put it right myself. What you do is, you bind the legs up with elastic bandage. Get it anywhere, Boots, anywhere. Did the whole lot for under a quid.'

'I'm not handy that way,' said the man in the blue dungarees. 'I'd probably make a muck of it. Stop its circulation, or sunnink. Legs'd probably fall off, and then where would I be? Eating out of tins, getting a laundry to deliver, it could cost a fortune. Anyway, he said the veins were affecting it all over, it'd have to go away and have 'em done proper.'

'Bloody hell,' said the man in the herringbone overcoat, 'how long will that take?'

The man in the blue dungarees pursed his lips.

'He couldn't say right off,' he said. 'They got work piled up to here, apparently. Might not be able to fit mine in for six months. And once they've got it up on the bench, it could take a fortnight to get it going proper. And *then*,' he added bitterly, 'you got to run 'em in for a bit. Light work only, no standing, no lifting.'

'The state your floors'll be in!' said the man in the Wimpey jacket. 'It don't bear thinking about. Not to mention the other.'

'The other?'

'The ironing. It's got to stand up to iron. I got mine ironing once in the non-standing position when it got water on its knees, you ought to have seen the state of my blue worsted, it had flat sleeves and three bleeding lapels.'

'I know,' said the man in the blue dungarees morosely. 'I said to the bloke, bloody hell, I said, it's only forty-three, you don't expect 'em to start going at forty-three, it ought to have thirty years left in it before a major wossname, overhaul. Rate it's going on, I said, it'll start needing new bits before long. I might have to put a lung in it, or something, and Gawd knows what that could cost.'

The man in the herringbone overcoat shook his head.

'Can't put lungs in,' he said. 'They can get along on one lung – mind you, it slows 'em down getting upstairs with tea, you'll have to reckon on putting the alarm on a good quarter of an hour earlier – but if they both pack up, that's it.'

'I never realised,' said the man in the blue dungarees. 'You see where they put new hearts in and everything, I thought you could just go on replacing with spares.'

'You want to watch yours,' said the man in the Wimpey jacket. 'I hope I'm not speaking out of turn, but I saw it once, cleaning out the coalhouse in the rain. It can ruin 'em, leaving 'em out in the rain. And it was smoking. Combination of rain and smoking, them lungs it's got won't be fit for blowing on your porridge in a year or two.'

The man in the herringbone overcoat nodded.

'You ought to look after it better,' he said. 'It pays off in the end. Stop it smoking, for a start. And if it's got to go out in the rain, you ought to get one of them plastic hoods to tie over it. You can get 'em at Woolies. Five bob, but it's worth it. My old man looked after his a treat, he was a bit of a fanatic really, he used to keep it spotless. Once the dirt gets in the wrinkles, he used to say, they start to go. Do you know, when he popped his clogs, it was still going like the clappers, after nearly eighty years. Someone said I ought to give it to an old folks' home; bugger that, I said, that's got a lot left in it, that has, so I installed it in the attic. It was still doing little jobs, making sandwiches, sewing, till it was nearly ninety. Released mine for all sorts of major work. That's how I got the extension built.'

The man in the blue dungarees sighed.

'They don't make 'em like that no more,' he said. 'Mine had to have glasses before it was thirty. It was either that or put forty-watt bulbs in, and you know how they burn it. It's going to need a deaf aid soon, as well, I'm sick of shouting for the evening paper now it can't hear the whistle over the noise of the eggwhisk. That's four batteries a year, for a start, not to mention initial outlay.'

'British,' said the man in the Wimpey jacket, 'that's the trouble.'

'What?'

'British. Load of bleeding tat. If I had my time over again, I'd get a Jap one. They're beautifully put together. Brother had a Jap, got it out east thirty years ago, it still ties his shoe-laces of a morning.'

'No!'

'Gerroff!'

'Straight up,' said the man in the Wimpey jacket. 'Also makes furniture out of old newspaper. Not to mention bloody accurate. Send it down the shops, it never gets short-changed, never buys the wrong thing, never comes back two minutes late on account of not assessing bus connections efficiently. It's saved him a packet, over the years.'

The man in the blue dungarees leaned forward, slightly uneasily.

'Tell me,' he said, 'this Jap. Does it get, er, headaches?'

'At night, he means,' said the man in the herringbone overcoat.

'I know what he bloody means!' snapped the man in the Wimpey jacket. 'I got a British one, haven't I? No,' he said to the man in the blue dungarees, 'as I understand it, it has never had a headache in its life. Night after night after night, my brother says, it don't suffer from headaches.'

The three of them sat in silence after this, for some time.

'Funny thing about British models,' said the man in the blue dungarees, at last. 'You can't help feeling they got a basic design flaw in 'em somewhere.'

'That's what it is, all right,' said the man in the Wimpey jacket.

Once I Put it Down,
I Could Not Pick it Up Again

A couple of years ago, some organisation calling itself the Encyclopaedia Britannica sent me twenty-three books to review. Like any reviewer faced with such a task, I wasn't able, of course, to read any of them – just snatched a quick look at the titles on the spines and made a few shrewd guesses.

A. ANSTEY

F. Anstey, author of *Vice-Versa*, *The Brass Bottle*, and many other best-sellers, was one of the most famous figures in Victorian London. A. Anstey wasn't. This, indeed, was the nub of his personal disaster, a searing comment on nineteenth-century society, told for the first time in this splendid volume. A. Anstey was constantly being introduced at smart Victorian soirées to people whose instant reaction was 'Not *the* Anstey?' to which he would immediately answer 'No, just *a* Anstey, ha-ha-ha!' This pitiful little quip commended him to no one, and was usually met with a sneering 'You mean *an* Anstey' and a snub. He endured this for eighteen years before finally hanging himself in a rented room just off Lewisham High Street.

ANT BALFE

When General Tom Thumb crowned a successful fairground tour with a command performance in front of Queen Victoria, the seal was set on a midget-vogue of staggering proportions. Country fairs and London theatres alike were filled with talented dwarfs, each tinier than the last. The smallest and indubitably the most adroit of these (he could play Mozart's four horn concertos on a

338

drinking-straw while riding on a stoat) was Ant Balfe, so called because of his incredible diminutiveness. Who knows to what figurative heights he might not have risen, had he not, at his Drury Lane première, been trodden on by an inept autograph-hunter?

BALFOUR·BOTH

A fascinating tale of Georgian surgery, this recounts the earliest known sex-change operation, on the unfortunate Geraldine (née Gerald) Balfour. It seemed successful at first, and the happy Geraldine took to signing herself G. Balfour (Miss), but subsequent developments proved this course to be premature, and soon she was sending letters of complaint to the General Medical Council signed G. Balfour (Both). Eventually, the name was changed by deed poll to Balfour-Both to avoid upsetting pre-permissive sensibilities. Beautifully illustrated.

BOTHA CARTHAGE

An exceptionally well-documented life of Hannibal, whose dying words give the book its intriguing title. His actual words, apparently, were 'Bugga Carthage!' but the publishers, I understand, felt that this might have meant rejection by W. H. Smith, and compromised accordingly.

CARTHUSIANS COCKCROFT

Subtitled 'An Edwardian Tragedy', this bitter book tells the story of Thomas Cockcroft, perhaps the most promising Senior Master in Charterhouse's history. He was due for appointment to the headmastership at the incredibly early age of thirty, when certain facts were made public by a disgruntled porter concerning the intimate teas to which Cockcroft would invite the smaller boys. Inevitably, the yellow press dubbed him Carthusians Cockcroft at his infamous trial (*The Daily Graphic* even tried to christen him Fag Cockcroft, but the multi-entendres were too much for its working-class readership), and upon his release from Brixton, he went off to the Congo to shoot porters. There is a statue of him in Chisholm St Mary, erected in error.

COCKER DAIS

Perhaps the best loved of the East End flyweights, Cocker Dais at one time held the British, British Empire, and European titles. At the peak of his career, he fought an unknown American for the World title, and was knocked out in the second minute of the first round. His pub, *The Cocker Dais*, later became a famous dockside landmark for German bombers.

DAISY EDUCATIONAL

A poignant, heart-warming novel about an elderly school-mistress in a tiny Welsh village. The influence of *How Green Was My Valley* is, of course, observable, but the presence of a black Druid boutique owner gives the book an essentially modern air.

EDWARD EXTRACT

I'm delighted that the publishers have seen fit to reprint this little-known eighteenth-century novel by Tobias Sterne, because it's a narrative gem of the first water. A bawdy, picaresque romp, it tells how postboy Edward Extract makes off with Squire Weasel's buxom daughter Phyllis, loses her to a Turkish mercenary during the Battle of Blenheim, makes his way to Utrecht disguised as an alternative Pope, falls in love with Warty Eva of Bosnia, is press-ganged into the Hungarian navy, loses his leg at Malplaquet, seduces a lady-in-waiting to Queen Anne, becomes a Whig, loses his right arm at Sheriffmuir, gets Gräfin von Immel with child, goes deaf during the siege of Belgrade, abducts a Moorish slavegirl, and returns at last to his native Suffolk, where he knocks out his left eye on a broken wainshaft. Lusty, purgative, rollicking, and highly recommended.

EXTRADITION GARRICK

It is said that when Lord Chief Justice Sir Esmond Garrick (1789–1852) was refused his request to the Brazilian authorities to extradite Bloody Ned Magee on a charge of treason, he sailed personally to São Paulo, strode into the Court of Justice, decapitated the President of the Brazilian Supreme Court, and, turning to the other judges and waving his bloody sabre above his wig, cried: 'I would remind ye that English law is based on precedent, and I have just created one!' Magee was released forthwith, and duly hanged at the notorious Vile Assize of 1828. As Extradition Garrick, Sir Esmond pursued an inflexible hunt for refugee criminals, often giving up his holidays to root about in the stews of Marseilles and Cadiz, heavily disguised, in his inexorable search for what he called 'hanging fodder', frequently bringing them back to England in a gunny-sack. A thundering good read.

GARRISON HALIBUT

I was bored by this long, scholarly thesis on the Minneapolis dry-goods salesman who rose to be the Governor of Minnesota and is chiefly remembered as the initiator of off-street parking.

HALICAR IMPALA

If you like books that take the lid off the motor industry, then this is for you! Spurred on by what they thought was going to be the enormous success of the Ford Edsel, a group of General Motors designers made a survey of what the typical *female* customer wanted in a motor car, and proceeded accordingly. After two years of research and the expenditure of eighty million dollars, the first Halicar Impala was built. The engine started well enough, but at 35 mph the linkage connecting the hair-drier to the eye-level grill snapped, disconnected the telephone, and threw the crib through the windscreen. Upon applying the brakes, the driver inadvertently set the instant heel-bar in motion, and was riveted to the wardrobe by a row of tintacks. A second Impala was never built.

IMPATIENS JINOTEGA

Jose Ortega 'Impatiens' Jinotega was the father of modern bullfighting. Until his appearance in 1919, the average matador took eight hours to kill a bull, and there was only one fight per afternoon. Impatient as his nickname suggests, Jinotega soon saw that strangling was a slow and inept method, and, on his first appearance in the Barcelona ring, he pulled a sword from beneath his cloak, and despatched six fighting bulls in the space of half an hour. This book is a magnificent tribute to a man who died as he would have wished, gored by Ernest Hemingway during a bar-brawl in Pamplona.

JIRASEK LIGHTHOUSES

A penetrating analysis of the great Czech film director, Inry Jirasek, known in the West as Jirasek Lighthouses, after his greatest film, a four-hour satirical study of the life of a solitary wick-trimmer. *Lighthouses* was followed by *An Old Bus*, *Jackets*, and the deeply disturbing *My Bath And Hat*. After vigorous appeals by Ken Tynan, Arnold Wesker, Vanessa Redgrave, George Melly and others, Jirasek was allowed to leave Prague for England. He left London almost immediately for Hollywood, where he now makes half a million dollars a year scripting *I Love Lucy*.

LIGHTING MAXIMILIAN

Sean Kenny's detailed account of his special effects work on the Peter Weiss/Peter Brook production of *The Manic Depression And Concomitant Hallucinations That Led To The Nervous Breakdown Of Emperor Maximilian Of Austro-Hungary As Performed By Members Of The Portuguese World Cup Team*.

MAXIMINUS NAPLES

The first Proconsul of what was, in the second century BC, still Calabrium, Maximinus is chiefly remembered for his habit of throwing political opponents into Vesuvius. His proconsulate was exceptionally stormy, corrupt and inefficient, and in 134 BC, Emperor Tiberius Gracchus demoted him to the proconsulate of Sicilia, where he is chiefly remembered for his habit of throwing political opponents into Etna. His significance is minimal, and my own opinion is that this dreary account was long underdue.

NAPOLEON OZONOLYSIS

The story of how Napoleon Ozonolysis rose from humble origins to become the wealthiest Greek shipowner in the world has, of course, all the fabulous ingredients of legend, and in this frank autobiography (as told to Des Lynam), the amazing tycoon reveals all. Lavishly illustrated with photographs of colonels, the book also contains an extremely useful index of eligible American widows. Just the thing for a Hellenic cruise, or a short piano leg.

P–PLASTERING

I opened this volume with considerable trepidation, believing it to be just another Do-It-Yourself tract. Imagine my delighted surprise to discover that it was in fact a history of stammering! Packed with fascinating information – did you know, for example, that George Washington was unable to enunciate 'teaspoon', or that *K-K-K-Katie* was not written by Gustav Mahler? – the book is a veritable mine of glottal arcana. The appendix on Regency hiccups is on no account to be missed.

PLASTICS RAZIN

If you like escapology as much as I do, then you'll find it hard to resist this vivid biography of The Great Razin (pronounced *Rah'tsin*). Louis Razin's career began astoundingly early: in the last stages of labour, his mother was rushed to hospital in Boston, Mass., by hansom cab, but by the time she arrived on the maternity ward, she was no longer pregnant. Hysterical, she was led back to the waiting cab by her doctor, only to find the infant Louis screaming on the back seat! By the age of fourteen, he was already The Great Razin and Doris (subsequently The Great Razin and Beryl, after Doris had failed to emerge from a cabinet on the stage of the Holborn Empire), and in 1923 he became the first man to escape from a straitjacket on radio. When transatlantic flights became regular with the advent of the Super Clipper, Razin celebrated by eating an entire canteen of airline cutlery, and the nickname stuck. Plastics Razin is buried in Boston Cemetery, probably.

RAZOR SCHURZ

On the afternoon of September 8, 1926, a short, stocky man in a barathea coat and a pearl-grey fedora walked into a garage in South Side Chicago. When he walked out again, four minutes later, he left six men dead behind him, cut to ribbons. That was the beginning of the career of Razor Schurz, dreaded torpedo of the Capone gang and by the time he was finally trapped in an alley beside the Rexo Bowling Palace in Peoria, Illinois, early in 1937, and mown down by the guns of J. Edgar Hoover – or was it the hoovers of J. Edgar Gun? The print in my copy was tiny and execrable – he had accounted for no less than sixty-eight other hoodlums. This book, by the way, is now being made into seven feature films.

SCHÜTZ SPEKE

Schütz speke (sometimes schützspeke) was an entirely new language invented by embittered ex-Esperantist Wilhelm Schütz, and was designed to be the greatest international medium of communication the world had ever known. Unfortunately, the secret died with Schütz, and since this volume is written in it, the publisher's motives escape me. It may be a tax-loss, or something.

SPELMAN TIMMINS

This expensively produced facsimile edition of the diary of a fourteenth-century warlock is not particularly interesting in itself, but it contains some interesting recipes entirely new to me: I would recommend in particular his tasty *langues de crapauds au fin bec*, even if it does, for some mysterious reason, make your face come out in long ginger hair.

TIMOLEON-VIETA

These collected love-letters of young Timoleon, Prince of Tyre, to Vieta, the beautiful fourteen-year-old daughter of a Sidonian lunatic, make poignant reading. The two lovers never touched, and saw one another only briefly, just once, when Timoleon's carriage ran down Vieta's milk-float early in AD 981. Their tender and passionate affair came to an abrupt end when palace Nubians employed by Timoleon's tyrannical father seized the young prince and cut off his allowance.

VIETNAM ZWORYKIN

If, like me, you find the radical-chic posturings of the Zworykin family of New York extremely tiresome – tracts and polemica by Nat 'Cuba' Zworykin, Sharon 'Women's Lib' Zworykin, Chuck 'Legalise Acid' Zworykin, Sigmund 'Environment' Zworykin, and Dustin 'Kill the Pigs' Zworykin have all become best-sellers on both sides of the Atlantic – then this new tirade by the youngest member, Willy 'Vietnam' Zworykin, is not for you, despite its foreword by Gore Vidal, its addendum on Ulster by Edward Kennedy, its footnotes on the poor finish of the Sidewinder missile by Ralph Nader, and its jacket-blurb by Jane Fonda. The fact that the whole text can be pulled out to form a banner may be of interest to bibliophiles.

Publish and be Diblgd!

The Daily Telegraph *recently published a missing chapter, dropped by the author, from* Through The Looking-Glass. *Disappointing in itself, its real revelation was that Lewis Carroll was prepared to cut and change his work to meet objections by illustrators, publishers, printers, and almost anyone else. Which at last explains one of the greatest literary conundrums in the language . . .*

THE JUNIOR porter of Christ Church College, Oxford, came out of his cubby-hole and squinted across the cold cobbled acreage of Tom Quad. The Senior Porter was standing in the fountain, poking a twig up a spout. The Junior Porter trotted across on echoing clogs.

'Where is he this time?' he said.

The Senior Porter removed the twig. He examined the end through sweat-blobbed pince-nez.

'See that?' he said. 'Know what that is? Bleeding caviare, that's what that is. Bleeding sturgeon's eggs rammed up the outlet.'

'Stone me!' cried the Junior Porter. 'What is the eternal mystery of the sturgeon that it will swim thousands of miles upstream from bloody anywhere to lay its eggs?'

The Senior Porter removed the pince-nez, and stared at him.

'God Almighty, Scrimweasel,' he muttered. 'Could it be Mr Darwin was on the right track, after all? Is it true as how you are paid in bananas?'

'I don't follow,' said Scrimweasel, sullenly.

''Course you don't,' said the Senior Porter. He shook his head.

'The eternal mystery to what you are referring concerns the salmon, son. The sturgeon just bleeding lies there, as you'd expect, being a protected species. It just bleeding lies there in the sea, and its eggs come out. They only get up brass bloody spouts as the result of japes on the part of your titled undergraduates, coming home on the outside of two gallons of claret, going "Haw! Haw! Haw!", and poking bloody caviare up brass conduits.'

'Oh,' said Scrimweasel.

'I bin here since 1831,' said the Senior Porter, 'during which time what I have took out of College drains, gullies, bogs, pipes, and students, is nobody's business. There is more to this job than posing for bloody Ackermann, sunshine.'

'Well, then,' countered Scrimweasel, 'if you're so smart, where is Mr Charles Lutwidge Dodgson, then?'

'Smirk at me, lad, I'll knock your 'ead off!' snapped the Senior Porter.

'Sorry,' muttered Scrimweasel. 'I got this note for him, haven't I?'

The Senior Porter consulted an enormous turnip watch. He looked, thought Scrimweasel privately, much like a white rabbit.

'Eleven a.m.,' said the Senior Porter. 'Boar's Hill Junior Girls'll be coming out for 'ockey. You'll find him up the tower with his telescope.'

'Bloody stroll on!' cried Scrimweasel. 'That's two 'undred steps!'

'Take your time,' said the Senior Porter. 'You don't want to come up on him sudden, know what I mean?'

The Junior Porter coughed, discreetly. But the wind snatched it away, so he coughed again, more sharply.

The Senior Lecturer in Mathematics jumped.

'Ha! Ha!' he shrieked. 'Scrimweasel! I was just, er, inspecting the Meadows. There is talk of a by-pass.'

''Course you were, squire,' said the Junior Porter. He held out the note. Dodgson smoothed it against the windblown parapet, and peered.

'Goodness!' he exclaimed. 'It's from Jas. Rumbelow & Sons,

347

Printers. They say that because I agreed to cut my chapter about the wiggy wasp out of my new book, it is now some four pages short, contra to the agreement of the something ultimo hereinunder referred to, and is taking bread out of their mouths!'

'New book?' said Scrimweasel, since some sort of reply seemed called for.

'*Through The Looking-Glass*,' said Dodgson.

Scrimweasel leered horribly.

'Never mind *Through The Looking-Glass*, squire,' he said nudging Dodgson's tea-stained waistcoat evilly, 'what you ought to do is *Through The Telescope*, know what I mean?'

'Do you really think so?' said Dodgson.

'You're a bit of a photographer,' said Scrimweasel, 'catch my drift?'

'Not exactly,' said Dodgson.

'Make a fortune,' said Scrimweasel. 'All this Victorian repression, you could clean up. Forty-eight poses, as seen from top of famous building by genuine connoisseur, sent under plain cover. I would,' he added, putting his small face up against the mathematician's left mutton-chop, 'be prepared to hold the magnesium, for a small consideration.'

'I am afraid,' said Dodgson, simultaneously snapping his hat open and his telescope shut with a single adroit flick, 'I have no time to think about that now. I am already late for poor Mr Rumbelow.'

Whereupon he sprang to the staircase, and clattered out of sight.

Scrimweasel stared after him.

'He's a fool to himself,' he said.

It was not, however, until four more days had passed that Dodgson found himself standing in Ludgate Hill, outside the premises of Jas. Rumbelow. True, he had arrived in London three days earlier, but it had been some time since he had visited the metropolis, and thus had his complicated senses ravished by its promise. Emerging from Paddington Station, he had joined a crocodile of small girls in captivating boaters and in consequence had spent the night accidentally locked in the

Natural History Museum.

The second night, the locking had been somewhat more deliberate; but they had given him a cup of tea in the morning and, it having been explained that he was a famous author and therefore as mad as a hatter, they had returned his possessions to him, including the telescope, and sent him on his way. Unfortunately, he soon after stopped dead in the middle of the Strand to muse upon the madness of hatters, and was knocked over by a brewer's dray; he spent the third night in the London Hospital, but was found the following morning creeping through the fever ward in an attempt to photograph the smaller nurses, and was forcibly discharged.

'Well?' barked Jas. Rumbelow, as the vague figure wandered into the print shop.

'My name,' said Dodgson, 'is Dodgson.'

'How fascinating,' said Rumbelow. 'Well I never. Blow me. There's a thing. Well, Mr Dodgson, it's been a pleasure talking to you, but I have to get on now on account of being four days behind with some bloody –'

'It's him!' cried a compositor suddenly, scattering bright type. 'It's Carroll!'

The staff looked up.

Rumbelow cocked his head, as if downwind of game.

'Carroll?' he said, quietly. 'You said Dodgson.'

'I have,' murmured Dodgson, colouring, 'an assumed name.'

Rumbelow leaned him into the wall.

'I am not bleeding surprised,' he muttered. 'If I was you, I'd change 'em both to Jenkins and emigrate, before the lads get their 'ands on you!'

'I do understand,' said Dodgson, 'I do apologise.'

'Stuck here four days,' cried Rumbelow, 'twiddling our thumbs, orders not touched, contracts going begging, people ringing up about wedding invitations, luggage labels, visiting cards, all nice easy stuff, all turned down, can't touch it, can I? Waiting on Mr Carroll, aren't I?'

'I'm sorry. I was held up.'

'Strung up'd be favourite,' said the compositor.

'Thirty-eight inches short, that book,' said Rumbelow.

'Bloody yard out, this one, Samuel. Calls himself a professional. Bloody yard short.'

Dodgson sighed.

'Well, I suppose it will just have to be a shorter book,' he said, 'that's all. We could have 188 pages instead of 192.'

They stared at him.

'I may have to sit down,' said Rumbelow.

'He's never heard of sections,' said the compositor.

'Don't they teach you nothing at Oxford?' said a tapper.

'They come in sections, books,' said Rumbelow, to Dodgson. 'Never mind pages, mate. They come in bunches of sixteen. How many sixteens in 188?'

'Calls himself a mathematician,' said the compositor.

'Could we not have four blank pages at the end?' enquired Dodgson.

'Oh my God!' said Rumbelow.

'We'd be a laughing-stock,' said the tapper.

'Bugger laughing-stock,' snapped the compositor. 'Any talk of blank pages, I'll have the lads straight out. Wouldn't surprise me if some of the machinery suddenly fell over, neither.'

'Maybe he'd like it done triangular,' said the tapper heavily. 'Nice triangular octavo. Fur endpapers, possibly.'

'Don't joke,' said Rumbelow, 'I remember this ratbag. He's the one what give us that Mouse's Tale in his last book. Bloody wossname, emblematic verse. Started off in fourteen-point, come wiggling down the page unregistered, ended up in bloody diamond-point at the bottom.'

'Never!' cried the compositor. 'Was that *him*? I was here all Whitsun over that. I had to get a draught off the apothecary on the Tuesday, I've never known bowels like it.'

'Oh dear,' said Dodgson, 'what should I do?'

'Bloody write another yard, is what,' said Rumbelow. 'You got twenty minutes. I'm not running into overtime.'

Dodgson blenched.

'One can't just dash it off, you know,' he protested.

'Oh, I see,' said Rumbelow. 'One would prefer to carry one's teeth away in one's hat, would one?'

Dodgson sighed.

'Well, I *do* happen to have a little poem I scribbled on the back of an old charge-sheet I found the other night,' he murmured, 'which I suppose I could pop in at the end of the first chapter. If that would be all right.'

'No problem,' said Rumbelow, 'if it goes to a yard, and no dodgy turns at the end of lines or nothing. Let's have it, then.'

Dodgson groped in his tail-coat pocket, and fished out a crumpled flimsy.

'I don't know how appropriate it is, mind,' he said. 'It's called *JANUARY*.'

'Very nice,' said Rumbelow. 'Straightforward.'

Dodgson cleared his throat.

''Twas chilly, and the slimy roads
Did shine and shimmer in the rain:
All misty were the birds' abodes,
And the cold grassy plain.

Beware of January, my son!
The hoar-frost's bite, the . . .'

'Yes, fine, lovely, terrific!' interrupted Rumbelow. 'We haven't got all bloody day, squire, give it here.'

He snatched the flimsy, and handed it to the tapper, who scuttled off to his stool, closely followed by the compositor.

Dodgson watched them go, nervously.

'Er . . .'

'You still here?' said Rumbelow.

'I was wondering,' murmured Dodgson, 'whether I would see a proof?'

'Do me a favour,' replied Rumbelow. 'We're a week behind as it is.'

'I just thought I'd enquire,' said Dodgson.

Owing to Circumstances Beyond Our Control 1984 Has Been Unavoidably Detained . . .

. . . in which I set out to prove that totalitarianism in Britain could never work. How could it, when nothing else does?

WINSTON SMITH lay on his mean little bed in his mean little room and stared at his mean little telescreen. The screen stared back, blank. Smith eased himself from the side of his mean little blonde, walked across his dun and threadbare carpet, and kicked the silent cathode. A blip lurched unsteadily across it, and disappeared. Smith sighed, and picked up the telephone.

'Would you get me Rentabrother Telehire?' he said.

'They're in the book,' said the operator.

'I haven't got a book,' said Smith. 'They didn't deliver it.'

'It's no good blaming me,' said the operator. 'It's a different department.'

'I'm not blaming you,' said Smith. 'I just thought you might get me the number.'

'I was just going off,' said the operator, 'on account of the snow.'

'It's not snowing,' said Smith.

'Not *now*, it isn't,' said the operator. 'I never said it was snowing *now*.'

'Perhaps I might have a word with the Supervisor,' said Smith.

'She's not here,' said the operator. 'She gets her hair done Fridays.'

'I only need the Rentabrother number,' said Smith, 'perhaps

you could find it for me. You must have a book.'

'I'd have to bend,' said the operator.

'I'd be awfully grateful,' said Smith.

'I've just done me nails.'

'Please,' said Smith.

There was a long pause, during which a woman came on and began ordering chops, and someone gave Smith a snatch of weather forecast for Heligoland. After that, there was a bit of recipe for sausage toad. Eventually, after two further disconnections, the operator came back.

'It's 706544,' she snapped.

Smith put the receiver down, and dialled 706544.

'809113,' shouted a voice, 'Eastasian Cats Home.'

He got a Samoan ironmonger after that, and then a French woman who broke down and screamed. At last 'Rentabrother Telehire,' said a man.

'Winston Smith here,' said Smith, '72a, Osbaldeston Road. I'm afraid my telescreen seems to be out of order.'

'What am I supposed to do?' said the man. 'We're up to our necks.'

'But I'm not being watched,' said Smith. 'Big Brother is supposed to be monitoring me at all times.'

'Ring Big Bleeding Brother, then,' said the man. 'Maybe he's not suffering from staff shortages, seasonal holidays, people off sick. Maybe he's not awaiting deliveries. Not to mention we had a gull get in the stockroom, there's stuff all over, all the labels come off, broken glass. People ringing up all hours of the day and night. You realise this is my tea-time?'

'I'm terribly sorry,' said Smith. 'It's just that . . .'

'Might be able to fit you in Thursday fortnight,' said the man. 'Can't promise nothing, though. Got a screwdriver, have you?'

'I'm not sure,' said Smith.

'Expect bleeding miracles, people,' said the man, and rang off.

Smith put the phone down, and was about to return to the bed when there was a heavy knocking on the door, and before he or the little blonde could move, it burst from its hinges and two enormous constables of the Thought Police hurtled into the room. They recovered, and looked around, and took out notebooks.

'Eric Jervis,' cried the larger of the two, 'we have been monitoring your every action for the past six days, and we have reason to believe that the bicycle standing outside with the worn brake blocks is registered in your name. What have you to say?'

'I'm not Eric Jervis,' said Smith.

They stared at him.

'Here's a turn-up,' said the shorter officer.

'Ask him if he's got any means of identity,' murmured the larger.

'Have you any means of identity?' said the constable.

'I'm waiting for a new identity card,' said Smith. 'It's in the post.'

'I knew he'd say that,' said the larger officer.

'We're right in it now,' said his colleague. 'Think of the paperwork.'

They put their notebooks away.

'You wouldn't know where this Eric Jervis is, by any chance?' said the taller.

'I'm afraid not,' said Smith.

'Who's that on the bed, then?'

'It's certainly not Eric Jervis,' said Smith.

They all looked at the little blonde.

'He's got us there,' said the shorter constable.

'I've just had a thought,' said the taller, 'I don't think people are supposed to, er, do it, are they?'

'Do what?'

'You know, men,' the Thought Policeman looked at his boots, 'and women.'

'I don't see what that's got to do with worn brake blocks,' said his colleague.

They tipped their helmets.

'Mind how you go,' they said.

Smith let them out, and came back into the room.

'I'll just nip down the corner,' he said to the little blonde, 'and pick up an evening paper. Shan't be a tick.'

It was crowded on the street. It was actually the time of the two minutes hate, but half the public telescreens were conked out, and anyway the population was largely drunk, or arguing with one another, or smacking kids round the head, or running to get a bet on, or dragging dogs from lamp-posts, or otherwise pre-occupied, so nobody paid much attention to the suspended telescreens, except for the youths throwing stones at them. Smith edged through, and bought a paper, and opened it.

'COME OFF IT BIG BROTHER!,' screamed the headline, above a story blaming the Government for rising food prices, the shortage of underwear, and the poor showing of the Oceanic football team. It wasn't, Smith knew, the story the Government hacks had given to the printers, but you could never get the printers to listen to anyone, and challenged, they always blamed the shortage of type, claiming that they could only put the words together from the letters available, and who cared, anyhow? The Government, with so much else on its plate, had given up bothering.

It was as Winston Smith turned to go back to his flat, that he felt a frantic plucking at his knee, and heard a soprano scream ring through the street. He looked down, and saw a tiny Youth Spy jumping up and down below him.

'Winston Smith does dirty things up in Fourteen B,' howled the child. 'Come and get him, he's got a nude lady up there.'

The youth spy might have elaborated on these themes, had its mother not reached out and given it a round arm swipe that sent it flying into the gutter: but, even so, the damage had been done, and before Smith had time to protest, he found himself picked up bodily by a brace of uniformed men and slung into the back of a truck which, siren wailing, bore him rapidly through the evening streets towards the fearful pile of the Ministry of Love.

'Smith, W,' barked the uniformed man to whom Smith was manacled, at the desk clerk.

'What's he done?' said the clerk. 'I was just off home.'

'They caught him at a bit of how's your father,' said Smith's captor.

'It's Friday night,' said the desk clerk. 'I go to bingo Fridays.' He turned to Smith. 'Don't let it happen again, lad. You can go blind.'

'I've written him in me book,' said the guard. 'It's no good saying go home. I'd have to tear the page out.' He put his free hand on Smith's arm. 'Sorry about this, son. It'd be different if I had a rubber. We're awaiting deliveries.'

'You'd better take him up to Room 101, then,' said the clerk.

'NOT ROOM 101,' screamed Smith, 'NOT THE TORTURE CHAMBER, PLEASE, I NEVER DID ANYTHING, I HARDLY KNOW THE WOMAN, CAN'T ANYONE HELP ME, DON'T SEND ME UP . . .'

'Stop that,' said the clerk, sharply. 'You'll start the dog off.'

Smith was dragged, shrieking, to the lift.

'Ah, Smith, Winston,' cried the white-coated man at the door of Room 101. 'Won't you come in? Rats I believe, are what you, ha-ha-ha, fear most of all. Big brown rats. Big brown pink-eyed rats . . .'

'NO,' screamed Smith, 'NOT RATS, ANYTHING BUT RATS, NO, NO, NO.'

'. . . rats with long slithery tails, Smith, fat, hungry rats, rats with sharp little . . .'

'Oh, do shut up, Esmond,' interrupted his assistant wearily. 'You know we haven't got any rats. We haven't seen a rat since last December's delivery.'

'No rats?' gasped Smith.

Esmond sighed, and shook his head. Then he suddenly brightened.

'We've got mice though,' he cried. 'Big fat, hungry, pink-eyed . . .'

'I don't mind mice,' said Smith.

They looked at him.

'You're not making our job any easier, you know,' muttered Esmond.

'Try him on toads,' said Esmond's assistant. 'Can't move in the stockroom for toads.'

'That's it!' exclaimed Esmond. 'Toads, Big, fat, slimy . . .'

'I quite like toads,' said Smith.

There was a long pause.

'Spiders?'

'Lovely little things,' said Smith. 'If it's any help, I can't stand moths.'

'Moths,' cried Esmond. 'Where do you think you are, bloody

Harrod's? We can't get moths for love nor money.'

'Comes in here, big as you please, asking for moths,' said Esmond's assistant.

Smith thought for a while.

'I'm not all that keen on stoats,' he said at last.

'At last,' said Esmond. 'I thought we'd be here all night. Give him a stoat, Dennis.'

So they put Winston Smith in Room 101 with a stoat. It was an old stoat, and it just sat on the floor, wheezing, and as far as Smith was concerned, things could have been, all things considered, a lot worse.

Gilded Cage

THE WATERY dawn came up, to little interest. A cassowary honked, half-heartedly; Moskisson's potto squeaked, once; an elderly scorpion broke wind.

They had seen dawns before. There was no point kicking up an atavistic fuss. For one thing, you didn't have to scare breakfast into submission. It came on tin plates.

The lion yawned. Bound to be horse again. Nothing wrong with horse, mind, nice piece of shoulder, can't complain. Slides down a treat, horse.

The only thing was, you couldn't chase a chop. That was the whole trouble with convenience foods. You couldn't bring them down, play with them, scare the life out of them. Be nice, thought the lion wistfully, to hear your breakfast scream a bit, now and again.

He strolled to the bars, looked out.

'Hallo,' he said. 'Here's a do.'

His lioness turned over slowly on her hygienic concrete shelf. Her tail flopped down. She let it swing, idly. Cleaner up here than a tree, she thought, more modern, chamfered for easy maintenance, no moss, insects. And yet.

'What is it?' she said.

'They've duffed up another chimpanzee,' said her mate.

The lioness opened one eye. In the cage across the way, a chimpanzee lay on its back, hands, feet, teeth all clenched in an unmistakable rigor.

'Oh, that,' she murmured. She shut the eye again. 'New frail old chimp horror, anthropoid granny another victim of senseless violence, where will it end, see fabulous free knickers offer page nine.'

'You know who I blame?' said the lion. 'I blame the parents.'

The lioness snored.

At eight o' clock, two keepers came with a black polythene sack and removed the battered corpse.

The lion watched.

The tiger next door came to the front of its cage.

'Keepers won't even bother finding out who did it,' said the tiger. 'Right?'

'What's the point?' said the lion.

'What's the point?'

'Only let 'em off with a bloody caution,' said the lion.

'If that,' said the tiger.

'They'll blame it all on the environment,' said the lion gloomily. 'Am I right?'

'No question,' said the tiger.

'Impersonal high-rise steel cages, parents out picking one another's fleas off all day, lack of properly supervised play areas, catch my drift?'

'Absolutely,' said the tiger. 'Not to mention a cry for help.'

'I'd give 'em bleeding cry for help!' snapped the lion. 'When I was a cub, they'd have got the chop.'

He drew a burnished claw across his throat, as only lions can.

'Bloody good job, too,' said the tiger.

'No messing about,' said the lion, 'eye for an eye, know what I mean?'

'Those were the days,' said the tiger.

At 11.30 am, the lioness jumped down from her shelf.

A keeper let her four cubs in.

She played with them for half an hour.

Then the keeper came and took them out again.

She jumped back up on her shelf, and began to groom.

'I don't call that motherhood,' said the lion.

The lioness shrugged. She rolled on her back, and looked at the ceiling of the cage.

'I ought to get a job,' she said. 'There's more to life than bringing up cubs.'

'You what?' cried the lion. 'A *lioness*? Getting a *job*?'

'While we're at it,' said his mate, 'I think I'll drop the ess. It is discriminatory; it is degrading. Lion, is what I am.'

The lion's claws sprang from their soft sheaths, instinctively.

'What kind of job?' he growled.

'Oh, I dunno,' she said. 'I could roar. I could terrorise visitors. I could attack the keeper.'

'*I* DO THAT!' thundered the lion, with such force that, on the other side of the Zoo, a small herd of antelope woke up, trembled violently, and ran into the wall. 'Any roaring, any terrorising, is down to *me*!'

'I could be just as good,' said the lioness.

'Oh yes! Ha, ha! Oh yes!' muttered the lion. He paced up and down furiously. 'Ha, ha! Oh yes! Very droll. Ha, ha!'

He hurled himself at the bars, and bit them.

'She'll be growing a mane next,' said the tiger next door.

'I blame the Zoo,' said the lion. 'The Zoo does everything for 'em, these days. Food, housing, education, all laid on, know what I mean, whatever happened to self-sufficiency, independence, responsibility?'

'You've been talking to Rhodes Bison,' said the tiger.

'Why not?' said the lion.

'Look at them dingoes,' said the lion, an hour or two later. 'They're at it like knives!'

'When I was young,' said the tiger, 'there was such a thing as courtship.'

'The magic's gone,' muttered the lion. 'I blame the Zoo. No restrictions any more. They used to move in and stop all that. They used to keep 'em apart, except for breeding seasons.'

'Permissiveness,' grunted the tiger.

'Comes back to what I was saying,' said the lion firmly. 'Too much time on their hands, too much done for 'em. In the old days, before the Zoo stepped in and took over everything, they never had no time for all that. Out foraging for food, fighting off enemies, building your own home, competing to survive – it bred a different class, built character, follow me?'

360

'You're talking about the jungle, now,' said the tiger, wistfully.

'Right!' cried the lion. 'Definitely!'

The dingoes shrieked to an umpteenth climax.

'They're like bloody animals,' muttered the lion.

The sparrow zipped through the bars, and landed on the edge of the lion's trough.

'I've just been up the Bird House,' it chirped. 'You wouldn't bloody credit it!'

'What?' said the lion.

'They just took delivery of two gross chrome bells, anodised ladders, mirrors, prefabricated nesting-boxes, you name it.'

'Oh, very nice!' said the lion sarcastically. 'I wonder how much that little lot set the Zoo back?'

'Birds,' twittered the sparrow, 'used to make their own entertainment. There's no end of things you can do with a good pebble, couple of bottle tops, fag-packets, all that. Now they just sit around waiting for the Zoo to provide everything, have you noticed?'

'Have *I* noticed?' cried the lion.

'Has *he* noticed?' said the tiger.

'They'll have Zoo-subsidised tellies next,' said the lion.

'He's not joking,' said the tiger.

The white Range Rover of the Zoo Vet Service rolled past. They watched it turn the bend.

'Elephant,' explained the sparrow. 'Got a bit of colic. I was just round there.'

'*Bit of colic?*' exclaimed the lion. 'Bloody stroll on! What would he do up India?'

'Wouldn't bother about it,' said the tiger, 'would he? More important things to think about. Knocking down trees, leading herds, working out how to get to the graveyard.'

'Stepping on tigers,' said the sparrow.

'Why not?' retorted the tiger. 'Part of life's rich texture. *And* if he did, would I go running to the doctor's? Would I buggery, I'd have a bit of a lick, pull myself together, get on with things, right?'

'You'd probably nip down the village and knock a couple of

tribesmen back,' said the lion dreamily. He ran his purple tongue over his muzzle. 'Set you up a treat, that.'

'Better than free bloody medical treatment, anyway,' said the tiger.

'You know what bothers me more than anything?' said the lion, after a moment or two.

'What's that?' enquired the sparrow.

'It's like this,' said the lion. 'All our offspring are growing up in this mollycoddling bloody environment, right? Everything done for 'em, nothing demanded of 'em, all they got to do if they want anything is ask the Zoo, they get a handout, okay?'

'Get on with it,' muttered the tiger.

'What I'm saying is,' said the lion, 'what I'm saying is, what happens if the Zoo runs out of money? Overspends on services or whatever, and the whole operation starts falling to bits, health service breaks down, cages crumble, keepers pack it in, food gets short, amenities fold up. So there's all the bars fallen off, and there's all these animals wandering about with no one to look after 'em or tell 'em what to do next, and because they've all grown up in the Zoo, would they have any idea of how to fend for themselves?'

'He's a bit of a thinker, this one,' said the sparrow.

'It'd all come back to them, wouldn't it?' said the tiger. 'I mean, it's in the blood. It's *natural*, right?'

The lion shrugged. He looked at his paw, wondering what it would be like to feel grass under it.

'It's only a thought,' he said.

Something About a Soldier

A team of investigators has shown that of all the men who wear regimental ties, six in ten are probably impostors.
                                                    Daily Mirror

THOMAS BREEN laid his green leatherette sample-case carefully in the boot of the company Cortina; shut the lid; locked it. You couldn't be too careful, not with the electric toothbrushes. Valuable items like that, and the country the way it was, no morals any more and much of it black. He crossed the car park, gravel grinding under his brogues, a march step, firm and dependable, can't beat good real leather on your soles, none of your pansy composite, and stepped, smartly, through the saloon lounge door, masculine stride across the figured pile, shoulders fat (but square), belly held in, small smile beneath the smaller moustache, and the wide green gold-striped tie trumpeting on his chest.

'Good morning, sir.'

'It is, indeed! Bright. But not sunny. It'll be taking spin.'

'Sir?'

'The wicket. Bit green after the rain. Taking spin. Definitely. Skittle 'em out by tea. Or soon after.'

'What can I get you, sir?'

'Pink gin. Large.'

Thomas Breen sniffed, twitched his bristles, cleared his throat.

'Ice?'

Short nod, chins interfolding briefly.

'Tight cap this, sir. Can't remember the last time I had to unscrew the pink. Customers don't seem to drink it these days.'

363

'Old habit,' said Breen. He chuckled. 'Medicinal. Not,' he added, leaning slightly towards the barman, humorously, 'that there's much beri-beri round here, eh?'

'Sir?'

Breen slid the bitterness down his throat, and pushed his glass back across the counter.

'Army joke. Same again. Gin for the malaria, Angostura for the beri-beri. That's what we used to say. Bit before your time.'

'I dare say, sir.'

'White man's grave, Burma,' said Breen, allowing his eyes to glaze. 'But a clever little devil, your Jap. Get him in a corner, fights like a rat.'

'Really, sir?'

'Like a ruddy rat. Have something yourself. Yes, many's the time I had to go in with cold steel and finish off some yellow johnny fighting on with half a dozen rounds still in him. Wouldn't lie down.'

'Amazing.'

'Wouldn't lie down. Once – I'm not boring you? – once, down near the Foonsang Delta, rainy season, my chaps were pinned down under a withering –'

Breen's voice frayed, and stopped. Beside him at the bar, a tall bony figure had materialised, grey-suited, with a tangerine rose in his buttonhole, yellow gloves. And a green gold-striped tie. The two men looked at one another, and the pupils ran around their eyes like trapped ants.

'I say!' said Breen.

'Ha, ha!' said the newcomer.

The barman smiled, with all the bonhomie of his calling.

'Here's a turn-up,' he said. 'Same regiment! This gentleman,' he continued, drawing a beer for the newcomer, 'was just telling me about your lot in Burma.'

'Burma?' said the newcomer.

'Only there a week or so,' said Breen quickly. 'Didn't get much chance to meet anyone, ha-ha-ha! Went down with trench foot second week.'

'Trench foot?'

'Mouth. Flown back to Catterick right away.'

'Catterick, eh?'

'Only for the day. Baffled Medical Corps. Didn't see a soul I knew. Driven straight to an isolation unit.'

The new man drank half his beer and put down the glass.

'Never saw Burma,' he said. He took out a handkerchief and mopped his forehead, despite the coolness of the day. Breen unclenched his hands, and licked a bright bead from his moustache.

'Really?' he said. 'Ah, well, they shipped me back there, soon as I'd recovered. Hardly saw anywhere else.'

'Weren't in Libya, then?' said the new man.

'Libya?'

'Or do I mean Palestine? I mean, I do. I say, I reckon the old wicket's due to take a bit of spin this morning, don't you? Not that I think the Australians have sent us much of –'

A third man entered; took off his coat; revealed a wide green gold-striped tie.

'Palestine, did you say?' he asked, looking at them uneasily.

'Libya, actually,' said the second man quickly. 'I was shorter then, of course. Sprang up after I was thirty. Fingleton,' he added desperately, extending a wet hand.

'Breen,' said Breen.

'Wittle,' said the third man.

'Not Charlie Wittle,' said Fingleton, 'by any chance?'

'NO!' shouted Wittle. 'I mean, no. No, they sent *Charlie* Wittle to Libya, I suppose, I mean yes, they did, I remember that on the postings, yes, he went to Libya, and I went to, er, Burma.'

'There's a coincidence!' cried Fingleton. 'Breen here –'

'Just missed you!' exclaimed Breen. 'I remember, it was the day they were flying me home with foot and mouth, and they came in and said, there's a new chap just been sent out, chap called Wittle, pity you've missed him. That's what they said.'

'Breen went back, though,' insisted Fingleton, 'after he was well.'

'I would have been gone by then,' said Wittle, hurling a large Scotch down his gullet, somewhat erratically.

'Yes!' shouted Breen. 'I remember, I got off the plane, and they said, you've just missed Wittle again, he's gone. That's what they said.'

'Did they?' enquired Wittle, staring at him. 'Oh. Yes, well, I got posted back in time for Salerno.'

Breen and Fingleton breathed out. Everyone smiled.

'Parachuted in,' explained Wittle.

Everyone nodded. Fingleton bought another round.

'One of our regulars was at Salerno,' said the barman pleasantly. 'With your lot.' Six eyes fixed on him from the rims of their drinks. 'Major Moult. Often mentions – well, talk of the devil!'

'Breen,' murmured Breen.

'Fingleton.'

'Wittle.'

'Moult.'

'I was telling the gentlemen, Major,' said the barman, taking Moult's pewter tankard from its hook, 'about Salerno.'

'Yes,' said Breen, happily, 'Wittle parachuted in, you know.'

Moult looked at Wittle.

'I didn't know there were any parachute landings at Salerno,' he said.

'Ah, well, you wouldn't, old man,' said Wittle, laughing lightly, despite a shoeful of beer. 'Typical RAF cock-up, ha-ha-ha! Wrong prevailing winds. All baled out over the jolly old target area, and landed forty miles away.'

'I suppose you managed to make your way back to rejoin the regiment, though,' said Fingleton, 'didn't you, Wittle?'

'I would have been out of it by then,' said Moult. 'Got taken prisoner first day, shipped out to Deutschland, chop-chop.'

'Not a POW of the Jerries, were you?' said a new voice.

The four men turned, to find a short wiry man in a camelhair coat and a brown fedora. Between the smooth lapels of the former gleamed two gold bars, on a green ground.

'I escaped almost immediately,' said Moult, very loudly. 'Why did they get you, Mr –'

'Binns. Didn't they get any of the rest of you, then?'

The others shook their heads.

'They got me, all right,' said Binns confidently. 'In Libya.'

'Fingleton was in Libya,' said Wittle.

'Yes,' said Fingleton, 'I came after you were captured. Got sent out from Palestine to replace you. Jerry's got Binns, they said. You'll have to go out to Libya. That's what they said.'

Binns looked at him.

'You sure they said Binns?' he said.

Fingleton eased his tie-knot.

'Er, yes,' he muttered. 'Go out and replace, er, Erasmus Binns.'

A shadow lifted from Binns's face.

'Different chap,' he said. 'I'm *Arthur* Binns. Not, of course,' he added hurriedly, 'that I haven't heard of Erasmus Binns.'

'Have you?' asked Fingleton.

'Of course, he wasn't in Libya at the *exact* same time as I was,' said Binns. 'I think he was in Burma, then.'

'That's it!' cried Fingleton. 'He was in Burma before he went to Libya and got captured and put in a POW camp.'

'After I'd escaped,' said Moult.

'He was probably in Burma about the time you were,' said Fingleton to Breen.

'Just missed him,' said Breen. 'I remember, it was the week I got dysentery, after I got back from Catterick and missed Wittle again. You've just missed Erasmus Binns, they said. As I got off the plane. They've sent him to Libya, they said.'

'Terrible thing, Burmese dysentery.'

'Who said that?' shrieked Breen, knocking over his fourth gin. 'I did.'

The group was joined by a large bald man in a black jacket, set off with green and gold-striped tie. Breen grabbed his sleeve.

'They cocked up my diagnosis!' he shouted. 'What I actually had was phosgene poisoning. Not like you at all. Nothing like it.'

'I wasn't in Burma,' said the bald man carefully.

'None of us were in Palestine,' offered Moult.

'I would have seen you if you had been,' said the bald man. 'I was there for the duration.'

'Fingleton said he'd been in Palestine,' said Breen. 'Didn't you?'

'No! Libya. With the other Wittle, not this one. Erasmus Wittle. If I said Palestine, I meant I'd *passed through it*. At night.

On the train.'

'I recall that train,' said the bald man, licking a dry lip. 'I remember someone saying, Fingleton's on that train. Going to Libya.'

'That's it!' cried Fingleton. 'That's exactly it!'

The bar clock struck three.

'Time please, gentlemen,' said the barman.

The six, as one man, flung themselves at the door, bound for their cars and freedom. Their escape, however, was cut off by a group of four men, waiting quietly outside the saloon bar: two had lost a leg, a third had an empty sleeve pinned across his chest, and was playing *Tipperary*, one-handed, on a harmonica, to the banjo accompaniment of the men on crutches. A fourth man had a white stick in one hand, and a collection box in the other. All wore campaign stars; and wide green gold-striped ties.

Fingleton pulled Breen towards him.

'Look at that,' he muttered. 'Begging!'

'Disgusting!' said Breen. He felt for his car-keys. 'Don't know what the Regiment's coming to.'

A Short History of Insurance

1. THE DAWN OF INSURANCE

It is impossible, naturally, to fix a date for the birth of insurance; but most authorities agree that it was probably discovered by accident, the favoured theory being that our early ancestors found, upon rubbing two sticks together, that their tree burned down.

There are also cave-paintings which show men running after buffalo, and some anthropologists maintain that the men are attempting to interest the buffalo in a policy insuring them against extinction, while the buffalo are running away on the grounds that they already carry enough insurance, but this is at present only informed speculation.

2. INSURANCE IN THE NILE DELTA

Around 5000 BC, the first Egyptian and Mesopotamian settlements were founded. Their inhabitants were roughly divided into two kinds: those who thought that, after death, you came back as a cat; and those who thought you didn't come back at all. As a result of this, life insurance took two forms: the normal With Profits policy, by which the family of the bereaved were guaranteed, on his death, a continuous supply of fish; and, a new invention, an Annuity maturing in old age which provided the insured with gold pots, pans, spoons, etcetera which he could put in his sarcophagus to await his demise, whereupon they would all cross The Great Divide together and he could set up home in some style.

As you know, many of these tombs were subsequently robbed, usually by the families who had only been left fish.

3. THE POLICIES OF THE ALMIGHTY

It was about this time, too, that the Children of Israel first appeared on the insurance scene, introducing the myriad complications that remain to this day and which gave original rise to the All Risks Policy. As you know, the Almighty (in an uncharacteristic lapse from His infinite wisdom) gave an early assurance to His people of overall cover, not realising at the time that they were as accident-prone a race as you could come across in a month of Sundays, all right, Saturdays.

As a consequence, He was constantly intervening in their disordered lives in a desperate running attempt to remain solvent: had Noah's family not had advance warning of unseasonal weather, for example, the compensation would have been astronomical, and who would have thought when assessing the actuarial odds and thereby arriving at a negligible premium, that someone would actually end up in the belly of a whale? Exegeticists who have sought explanations in natural law for the parting of the Red Sea need look no further, once they have totted up the pay-out on forty thousand accidental drownings. The Egyptians, of course, were not covered for the loss of their entire armed forces, and are still, sixty centuries later, trying to catch up. Even now, the Russians will not cover them in the event of TK-47s being taken any nearer than twenty kilometres from deep water.

The result of these early experiences has been, in our day, the Act Of God designation on all insurance policies; which means, roughly, that you cannot be insured for the accidents that are most likely to happen to you. If your ox kicks a hole in your neighbour's Maserati, however, indemnity is instantaneous.

4. THE FIRST GOLDEN AGE

'"The hour of departure has arrived, and we go our ways – I to die, and you to live. Which is the better, God only knows."

And with these words, Socrates bade them remove from him, and they went apart in sorrow and left him. And when a messenger came to tell them that Socrates was dead, they stood about, and many wept, and Glaucus, senior of the disciples and most beloved, uncovered his face at last and said:

370

"One good thing, there's a policy in my name."

And Epidomus said:

"That's better than a poke in the eye with a sharp stick."

But in the late forenoon, Socrates's broker came to Glaucus and said that he was sorry to have to inform him that, Socrates having taken his own life with a draught of hemlock, the policy was null and void. He then referred Glaucus to Section Four, Paragraph Nine.

Whereupon Glaucus turned upon him in rage and argued that Socrates had not committed suicide voluntarily but had been directed to do so by the State.

So the broker referred Glaucus to Section Eight, Paragraph Five.

And Glaucus beat his breast and cried:

"I have sat at that old bugger's feet these thirty years when I could have been out enjoying myself, and I have never understood a bloody word he said, and now you tell me I was on a hiding to nothing, what kind of business are you running here?"

And the broker said:

"Glaucus, in a republic, do we feel it advances the good to allow benefit to accrue to the bad even though the bad are beyond the advantage of the benefit and have therefore endowed the benefit to the good?"

And Glaucus said:

"You know what *you* can do."'

PLATO, Apologia

5. MOTOR INSURANCE IN THE FIRST CENTURY AD

When King Prasutagas died in AD 61, the territory of the Iceni was violently annexed by Rome, and his queen, Boudicca, was raped. Enraged, Boudicca raised the whole of South-East England in revolt against their Roman conquerors, fitted scythe-blades to the wheels of her army's chariots, and drove them through the ranks of her enemies.

Subsequently apprehended and charged with (1) Exceeding XVIII mph in a built-up area, (2) Driving without due care and attention, and (3) Failing to observe the right of way, Boudicca was then issued with some three thousand writs for actual damages by solicitors acting on behalf of the maimed Roman infantry.

Upon contacting her insurance company, she was informed, regretfully, that by making modifications to her vehicles without previously informing the company of her intention to do same, the company had no other course but to declare invalid the Third Party liability. The subsequent proceedings resulted in a bill for damages amounting to £8, 731, 267, a sum utterly beyond the reach of the British, who, then as now, had only the woad they stood up in.

The Romans thought about this for a bit, and decided that their best course of action would be to annihilate the British somewhere between London and Chester.

An interesting sidelight on this affair is that the Romans also learned a lesson from it, which was that the chariot need not be just a way of getting you there and bringing you back, but also a weapon in its own right. Even today, only 19% of pedestrians setting out to cross the Via del Corso get to the other side.

6. 1066: THE GREAT LEAP FORWARD
Insurance came of age on the beach at Hastings, when King Harold, who carried today's equivalent of £100, 000 in Personal Disability insurance, was shot in the eye by a Norman bowman firing through a narrow slit in the defence wall.

His queen immediately contacted the insurance company, enclosing a plan as required by the claim form showing the path of the arrow. The insurers examined the policy for some days and were growing desperate at their inability to find a way of legitimately welshing on the deal when one of their younger colleagues noticed a gap in the defences, which were, of course, Harold's responsibility.

'Here,' he said, 'if that wasn't there, the arrow'd never have got through!'

And thus it was that *loophole* entered the history of insurance, since which time it has gone from strength to strength.

7. THE MODERN ERA
The Modern Era, or Golden Age, of insurance can be said to

have been ushered in by the birth, in 1623, of Josiah Smallprint. Son of a Lincolnshire pharmacist, young Josiah spent his early years amusing himself among his father's alembics and phials. It was thus, on November 18, 1641, that he stumbled upon an ink which could be put onto paper by type, but which remained invisible until the paper was put at the back of a drawer. Upon removing the paper from the drawer and examining it again, the owner found it to carry all sorts of information hitherto unnoticed.

The first example of Josiah's handiwork to be used commercially was the phrase '. . . always provided that a pig flew past at the time the accident occurred'.

There is a statue to Josiah, 1st Baron Smallprint, in the foyer of Policymonger's Hall.

Half a Pound of Tuppenny Vice

*When police raided the Love Inn, where the Cambridge rapist
had been a customer, the owner was alleged to have said:
'There is nothing here. This is just a little family sex shop.'*
Daily Telegraph

ON THE knotty rustic lintel beneath the sign of Ye Olde Curiositie
Shoppe, the little bell tinkled.

Behind the dusty counter on which lay the dismembered cogs
of a cheap Hong Kong dildo into which he was vainly struggling
to fit a new mainspring, the proprietor (*Jas Rumbelow*, ran his
copperplate letterheads, *Purveyor of Fyne Thynges to the Gentrie
since 1926*) looked up over the gold rims of his bifocals. He laid
aside his screwdriver, and beamed.

'Good morning, Mrs Curtoise,' he said.

'Good morning, Mr Rumbelow,' said the customer, a middle-
aged lady in a bottle-green swagger coat, lisle stockings, and a
hat with three petals missing, 'I was just wondering if you had
them gold latex peephole bras and matching suspender belts with
the exposé divided-leg panties showing flags of all nations in
yet?'

Rumbelow shuffled to the back of the shop, bent over, and
shouted down an open trapdoor into the basement.

'Vera, we got any of them Goodnight Las Vegas in a 46?' He
turned, on the half crouch, towards the customer. 'It was a 46,
wasn't it?'

'Yes. And a 52 hip.'

'And a 52 hip!' shouted Rumbelow, into the darkness.

Scuffling came up through the trapdoor, counterpointed with

spasmodic wheezing and the noise of boxes falling. The step-ladder squeaked, and an elderly pink face appeared. A *Penthouse* gatefold was caught in her hairnet by its staple.

'Good morning, Mrs Curtoise.'

'Morning, Mrs Rumbelow. Did you find one?'

Mrs Rumbelow creaked up the last few steps, and into the shop. She shook her head, and the gatefold fluttered to the floor.

'Nearest I come was a 44,' she said, 'but I wouldn't advise it. They give you shocking wind at the best of time, them things. Last thing you want is too small. How about a nice black leather catsuit? I can do that in a 46.'

The customer shook her head.

'Leather doesn't agree with Mr Curtoise,' she said. 'It makes him sneeze in warm weather.'

Rumbelow nodded sympathetically.

'That'll be the tannin,' he said. 'It's like me and rubber, isn't it, Mother?'

'It's like him and rubber,' said his wife. 'We got one of them water-beds off a traveller. A wossname, a sample. Anyway, we filled it off of the upstairs tap, and we got on it, and he was awake all night sneezing, wasn't you? It was like being on the *Titanic*. We was thrown all over the place.'

'I wouldn't have water in the bedroom,' said Mrs Curtoise. 'Call it superstitious, but my old mum used to say "Water in the bedroom, you'll only have girls."'

'I know, I know,' said Mrs Rumbelow. 'I'm the same about lupins.'

'It's a pity about the Goodnight Las Vegas,' said Mrs Curtoise. 'Mr Curtoise'll be ever so disappointed. He put off a Rotary executive meeting specially. I don't know what we'll do tonight, now.'

'There's a new film up the church hall,' said Rumbelow. '*Take Me, I'm Scandinavian And My Old Man's On Nights.*'

'We seen it on holiday,' said Mrs Curtoise. 'It's in black and white.'

'What a liberty!' cried Rumbelow. 'There's no pride in workmanship these days.'

'Young people,' sighed Mrs Rumbelow, 'there's no respect.'

'I blame the bomb,' said Mrs Curtoise.

'The Liberal Democrats,' said Rumbelow, 'wouldn't do any better.'

'They're all as bad as one another,' said Mrs Curtoise.

Mrs Rumbelow looked at her.

'I never realised you was political, Mrs Curtoise,' she said.

Mrs Curtoise sighed.

'You got to be,' she said, 'these days. Well, must be off. There's all Mr Curtoise's tights to iron. He likes a nice crease.'

'He wouldn't be an Area Sales Manager,' said Rumbelow, 'if he didn't.'

'Since you haven't got the Goodnight Las Vegas,' said Mrs Curtoise, 'I'll just take a quarter of aphrodisiac toffees.'

Rumbelow shooed the cat away from the confectionery shelf, took down a large jar, unscrewed it, and shook some of its contents into his scale-pan. He watched the needle carefully, added another sweet, filled a paper bag, and flipped it adroitly.

'When you eat them,' he said, handing the bag over, 'don't forget to take your teeth out. They're like bloody Bostik, pardon my French.'

'I know,' said Mrs Curtoise. 'Mr Curtoise thinks they put something in them.'

'Wouldn't surprise me at all,' said Rumbelow. 'Good day.'

The bell tinkled. Rumbelow watched the door swing shut.

'Good job she never took that catsuit,' he said. 'With her varicose veins, she'd have swelled up something shocking. You'd have to soap her to get her out of it. Like boys' heads in railings.'

'Funny you should say that,' said his wife. 'Only yesterday, man came in, wanted a set of railings to stick his head through. You was out in the smallest room at the time, begging your pardon, Father. So I told him we didn't go in for that sort of thing.'

'Only got so much space, haven't we?' Rumbelow indicated the teetering piles of boxes, the stuffed shelves, the heaps of cellophane-covered books that littered the floor. 'Start catering for all tastes, where will it end? Come in for railings one day, next day it'll be railings *and* small boys already conveniently stuck in 'em.'

'Like that fellow last Tuesday,' said his wife, 'coming in here, big as you please, asking for a packet of Welsh letters. Where do you think you are, I said, Marks and Spencers?'

'Quite right, Mother,' said Rumbelow. 'People today, it's incredible! When my old dad started this business up, you could make a nice little living out of nothing more than a slab of prawns and a half gross of Spanish Fly!'

The bell tinkled again, and a thin fifty-ish man came into the shop, dragging what might have been his misshapen shadow.

'Morning, Mr Collinson,' said Rumbelow. 'What's that you've got there?'

Collinson hoiked the thing up off the floor and draped it over the counter.

'That,' he muttered, and his voice was tense, and his pointing finger shook, '*that* is Miss Mary Wonderful, 38-22-36 When Inflated. Or was.'

'Was?' said Rumbelow.

'Woke up this morning,' said Collinson bitterly, 'and there she was, lying beside me, like a burst inner-tube.'

'Well,' said Rumbelow, 'that's what she, er, was, basically, Mr Collinson.'

Collinson glowered at him.

'That's not what you said when I bloody bought her!' he cried. 'Five-feet-two of delectable rubber pulchritude, you said. Just the companion for those lonely winter evenings, you said.'

'I was reading off the box,' said Rumbelow. 'I don't test 'em all personal.'

'She's perished!' shrieked Collinson. He held up the flaccid corpse, and light shone through its perforated bust. 'My beloved is perished! £14.75, excluding pump, and all I got to show is a load of rubber bands!'

Rumbelow pushed his glasses up onto his forehead and peered at the wreck.

'It looks to me like the dog's been at her,' he said. 'That's never fair wear and tear. You haven't left her lying about, have you?'

'Lying about? LYING ABOUT? What do you take me for? I

went to a grammar school. Women have always been treated with utmost respect on my premises! The dog's never off his chain.'

Rumbelow cleared his throat, awkwardly.

'Mr Collinson,' he said, 'you haven't, as it were, bitten her yourself, have you?'

'Bitten her *myself*?' screamed Collinson. 'I wouldn't take such liberties! I hardly know her. I've only had her out of the box twice, to watch *Upstairs, Downstairs* with me. You can't rush things. Call me old-fashioned, but that's how I am. *And* I want my money back!'

'You could patch her,' offered Mrs Rumbelow, who had come back in to feed the parrot, 'couldn't you?'

'Ho, yes, I should bleedin cocoa!' shouted Collinson. 'Very erotic, that! For them as likes nipping into bed with a second-hand bike, it'd be just the thing!' He gathered up the tattered rubber, and stuffed it under one arm. 'That does it, Rumbelow! I have shopped here man and boy – and, for a brief period, woman and girl – for thirty-two years! But from now on, it's the new supermarket for me!'

The Rumbelows reeled! The Rumbelows paled!

'THE NEW WHAT?' shrieked Mrs Rumbelow.

Collinson cackled nastily.

'You heard!' he said. 'Four floors of arcane delights, wall-to-wall wossname, free films, seductive music as you browse, topless experts to help you with your every enquiry, gratis glossy brochures, cheap travel arranged, money back if not at least partially satisfied – *what do you say to that, you old fleabag?*'

With which Collinson spun on his heel, and strode out, the rubber corpse gesticulating beneath his arm like broken bagpipes.

The Rumbelows stared after him.

'A supermarket!' wailed Mrs Rumbelow. 'All chrome and plastic, cold, impersonal! Cheap, vulgar, American! Nobody giving you the time of day, nobody caring, nobody wanting to know! Where is it all going, Father? What will become of us?'

Rumbelow pressed his face against the window, staring out.

'England, what are you doing to yourself?' he murmured.

The Workers' Bag is Deepest Red

The Scottish coun̶il of the L̶b̶r F̶r̶y today approvea almost unanimously a policy for ̶he compi̶ ̶e nationalisation of the vast privately owned Highland estates and the salmon fisheries if a Labour gove̶nment is returned to po̶er.

The Times

I FOLLOWED the clerk down the eau-de-nil corridor and through ̶ brown door marked FISH DIVISION: ENQUIRIES. Inside, a bald man sat at a steel desk beneath a wall-map of the Highlands pinned with tiny flags and a graph on which a curve plummeted into its lower margin.

'Man here wants to have a go at the salmon,' said the clerk.

The bald man glanced at me over his bifocals.

'Where's your ferret?' he said.

'Ferret?' I said.

'Little bugger with short legs,' said the clerk. 'Can't half run, though.'

'I know what a ferret is,' I said. 'But I'm after salmon. Ferrets go down rabbit holes.'

'Funny place to look for salmon,' said the clerk. 'Still, it takes all sorts, that's what I always say.'

'We can lease you a government ferret,' said the bald man. He reached for a file, wet his thumb, began plucking forms out. 'Need a 121/436/18g, a 72A/ff, and two pound deposit against loss or damage.'

I cleared my throat.

'There seems to be some mistake,' I said. 'You don't catch salmon with ferrets.'

'He's got a point,' said the clerk. 'They go down like stones.'
He indicated the graph. 'Salmon production's been dropping off
sunnink terrible lately.'

'Who told you to use ferrets?' I asked.

The bald man tapped a thick grey-covered book beside his in-
tray.

'Come down from Central Division,' he said.

'We're radicalising,' said the clerk. 'And rationalising.'

'Sounds to me as though they've got their lines crossed
somewhere,' I said.

They looked at me.

'Troublemaker here,' said the bald man.

'There's channels, you know,' said the clerk.

'How you going to catch salmon, then,' said the bald man,
'without a ferret?'

'Flies,' I said.

'Show him out, Sid,' said the bald man.

'I don't understand,' I said.

'We got work to do,' said the bald man, 'without comedians.'

'I'm serious,' I said.

'Pull this one,' said the clerk. 'It's hard enough training ferrets
to jump out of a boat, let alone flies.'

'You'd open your jam jar,' said the bald man, 'and they'd be
off. I know flies.'

'Look,' I said, 'you do it with a rod and line. You tie the fly to
the hook, you cast the line with the rod, you . . .'

'Ah,' said the bald man. He nodded. 'Cross purposes here,
Sidney. I thought he was talking about salmon. It's grouse he's
after.'

'You should've said,' said the clerk, irritably tearing up his
half-filled forms and reaching for a new batch. 'And it's not flies,
it's worms you use for grouse.'

'Don't be ridiculous,' I said, 'how can you catch a grouse with
a worm?'

'Don't ask me,' said the clerk, 'you're supposed to be the
sportsman. We only work here. On attachment.'

'From Swindon,' said the bald man. 'Personally, I prefer
trains. You know where you are with trains.'

'We're working on a pilot project,' said the clerk, 'to put grouse on rails. It's up before the Recommendations & Amendments Committee. It could revolutionise the entire industry.'

'You'd know when they was coming, then,' said the bald man. 'None of this hanging about with a worm on the end of a string. You'd just sit there with your timetable, and soon as the 8.40 grouse showed up, bang!'

'With your stick,' said the clerk. 'Any old stick. Think of the saving!'

'And once you had your rails laid,' said the bald man, 'there's no end to the spin-offs. You could have a dog-track. There's all these hounds we've got, not doing nothing, just walking about and peeing against the van. Train 'em to run after a grouse, you got an entire leisure industry.'

'It seems somewhat less than sporting,' I said.

The bald man looked at the clerk.

'There's your private enterprise talking, Sidney,' he said. 'See what I mean? No grasp of basic concepts.' He turned back to me. 'You don't seem to realise,' he said, 'what the meat industry entails. Mouths to feed, son, mouths to feed. We got an output target of four million grouse this year. Going over to battery production in August. Biggest aluminium shed complex north of Doncaster.'

I sighed.

'Not much sport there, I'm afraid,' I said.

'Don't see why not,' said the clerk. 'You could help with the plucking.'

'It's a far cry from shooting,' I said.

'I thought we was talking about grouse,' said the bald man. 'Not trout.'

'You *shoot* trout?'

He drew a large buff book from a shelf and threw it on the desk.

'Central Division Beige Paper,' he said. 'All in there. Results of the Research Division work-study. They went into the question of how you catch these bleeders when they're only in the air about 1.8 seconds, on average. Tried holding nets over the streams, but they're too sharp. Time you've seen 'em and got your wrists going, they're back in the water again. Only way is to lie on the bank with shotguns, soon as they leap, you're on 'em.'

'And how, exactly,' I said, 'do you bring them in?'

'Retrievers,' said the clerk.

'Oh, come on,' I cried. 'Dogs will never go in after fish!'

'Cats will,' said the bald man.

'Got him there, Harold!' said the clerk. 'He'd never thought of cats.'

'Private enterprise again, Sidney. In blinkers. Hidebound by tradition. Good enough for daudy, it's good enough for me, what? This is 1971, mate!'

'4,' said the clerk.

'1974,' said the bald man.

'And how do you propose,' I said, 'to train cats to swim?'

'Listen,' said the bald man. 'If you can train fleas, we can train bloody cats.'

'I think I'll be going,' I said, and stood up. They stared at my waders. 'For trout,' I explained.

'First good idea you've had,' said the clerk. 'The nettles are terrible.'

'Hallo,' said the bald man, glancing suddenly past us, and pushing his spectacles up his nose, 'the stock's arrived.' He rose.

I followed them to the window. Between the administration building, on the fourth floor of which we stood, and the Amalgamated Ghillie Union tower block opposite, ran a bright tarn that had risen in some now invisible mountain. Beside it, a dump truck was unloading a wriggling pile of small silver fish directly into the hurtling water. Upon entering which, they all turned belly-up. I peered, but we were fifty feet above.

'There's something wrong with those trout,' I said.

'Shows how much *you* know,' said the clerk. 'They're pilchards.'

'Calls himself a sportsman,' said the bald man.

'But pilchards are saltwater fish!' I cried.

'And very popular, too,' said the clerk. 'On toast, with a bit of tomato sauce.'

'But they're all dying!'

'So I should hope,' said the bald man. 'Easy to see he's never tried packing six pilchards in a tin, innit, Sidney?'

'If you did it his way,' said the clerk, 'it'd take six weeks to get the lid on. They hop about like nobody's business, pilchards.'

'Prob'ly never seen a tin,' said the bald man, jabbing a thumb at me. 'His lot prob'ly hunt pilchards on horseback.'

The clerk thought about this for a moment or two.

'Doubt it,' he said at last. 'You'd have a hell of a job aiming.'

The bald man nodded, slowly.

'Common sense, really,' he said.

The Small Gatsby

Conservation, thrift, simplicity, self-containment, a with-drawal from conspicuous consumption and profligate competition, a rejection, indeed, of materialism – this seems to be the President's message. It is a considerable revision of the old American Dream.

US News & World Report

IN MY younger and more vulnerable years my father gave me some advice that I've been turning over in my mind ever since.

'Whenever you feel like criticising anyone,' he told me, 'just remember that all the people in this world haven't had the disadvantages you've had.'

The reason I have been turning this over in my mind ever since is that it makes no goddamned sense to me at all. This may be because I had to leave school in the fourth grade on account of my parents ate my shoes. They had this thing about not eating animals due to where animals was running out, also not eating anything animals ate so that those animals who hadn't run out yet got to eat regular. In consequence, our family ate anything it could swallow, provided animals wouldn't touch it.

Since my father was one of the most influential paupers in our town, the streets was always full of fat animals and thin people. There was no cars. My father saw anyone driving past in an automobile and wasting precious fossil fuels with no thought to the welfare of his fellow man, he'd drag him right out from behind the wheel and kick him senseless.

When I was eighteen, I was sent East. This was because my father suspected I was developing a taste for potatoes which he calculated the world would run out of around AD 3150; so that rather than run the risk of losing the family's good name for austerity and self-denial, they took me down to the station and shipped me to New York second-class freight. True, my mother had softened at the last and pushed into my crate through the air-hole a couple of tasty candles she had kept hidden from my father (who believed that world supplies of wax might not last the century), but beyond that and three dollars I had borrowed from the dog (the only one my father would trust not to buy gasoline when his back was turned), I had nothing in the world.

To cut a long story short, which you have to do these days due to where no novel is allowed to be more than four pages long on account of the trees are running out, I fetched up on Long Island Sound and took a nice hole on the beach at West Egg. West Egg is the somewhat less fashionable half of the Sound; you can look across the water to East Egg and see some very famous heads poking out of the sand – leading environmentalists thinking about the possibility of biodegradable pebbles, leading conservationists working on schemes to harness flatulence, top international paupers with home-made teeth, famous society beachcombers in their seaweed skull-caps – but on the West Egg side there are still people on mains electricity who mix meat with their soya and who, if they don't go so far as actually to own an automobile themselves, certainly know people who own them.

Not that any of this was true of Gatsby.

Gatsby was the most deprived person my side of the Sound, and for all I know anywhere else, too. He had the hole next to mine, and it was just about the worst hole I ever saw. Most nights it fell on him.

Most nights, too, there was a party at Gatsby's hole. Gatsby threw the bleakest parties on the eastern seaboard. There was never anything to eat, and there was even less to drink; there wasn't any music, either, because even if Gatsby could have afforded a needle for a borrowed phonograph, the rigid ethics of the Sound would have prevented him from using it, on account of world supplies of iron was running out.

Everybody came to Gatsby's parties. People would walk from miles away, or if they were coming from East Egg, swim across the Sound: any night, you could see the gleaming lines of home-made flippers drawn up outside Gatsby's hole. But most of the guests never even met their host; they just came because it was a Gatsby party, but they never got around to asking who Gatsby was or where he was, because they never got around to caring.

I used to wonder why Gatsby threw them. I don't think he liked them. He hardly ever went to them himself. I used to see him standing at the edge of the water in his formal pillow case, just staring out across the Sound towards East Egg.

Nobody ever knew how Gatsby had got to be so immensely poor. Some said he had started from very rich beginnings and managed, by investing ineptly, to ruin himself in less than a year. Some said he had started as a bootlegger on the day they repealed the Volstead Act. But it was generally agreed by the hard-faced bright-eyed brittle people who battened onto his hospitality that he had not been broke for very long: sons and daughters of old families who had been destitute for three generations sneered at their host for a *nouveau pauvre* while he stood motionless in the moonlight, gazing silently east.

The only people who never came to his parties that first summer were the Buchanans. Tom and Daisy Buchanan lived right across the Sound from Gatsby's place, in probably the most fashionable hole in all East Egg. Beautiful, idle, penniless, they were each of them descendants of great families who had been on relief since the early seventeenth century, a provenance unscarred by ownership, or waste, or despoliation, or success. Buchanans had been Nothing In The City for as long as anyone could remember, while Daisy's family had been the only people to travel steerage on the *Mayflower*.

Since Daisy was in fact a second cousin of mine, I had been settled in for less than a month when I paddled across to visit them. Their bright laughter tinkled like cut-glass, or broken old jellyjars anyhow, when they saw my log, and I remember blushing and hoping against hope that they would put my ostentation down to boyish inexperience. I'm not sure that they ever did, since they lived their life on a plane beyond my understanding.

The very poor are different from you and me.

They were playing stick with a group of glittering young people as I walked up the beach. Stick was that year's elegant game, a form of polo played without horses, mallets, balls, goals, or jodhpurs. You found a stick and threw it about. It was really keen.

Daisy looked ravishing. From her earliest youth, she had avoided all soaps, shampoos, cosmetics, ornaments, anything, in short, that had come from animals or the earth and was likely to run out sometime, and it was on account of this that her lovely face selected itself from the company of its merely pretty peers like the beacon of its generation; which indeed it was. She put her grey cheek up for me to kiss, and when she laughed she exposed a row of fashionably neglected teeth lovely as datestones, and when she tossed her head in calculated nonchalance, her uneven ringlets slapped lankly against her pimple-peeping neck like cold tagliatelle.

'Nick!' she cried. 'Where have you been keeping yourself?'

'I'm over on West Egg,' I replied. 'I have a hole right next to Gatsby's.'

At Gatsby's name, I felt a ripple shiver the slim body in my arms, right through the gunny sack.

'Gatsby?' she murmured faintly.

'Surely you know him? He throws those fabulous . . .'

'Oh, she knows Gatsby all right!' cried Tom Buchanan suddenly. 'He used to come by here with his begging bowl after he moved in across the Sound. God knows who he was trying to impress with his poverty! I believe he once told Daisy his parents had starved to death. Do you know, Carroway, I think she actually believed him for a while?'

'That was a long time ago, Tom,' whispered Daisy.

'Yes!' shouted Buchanan, his eyes blazing in his grime-caked handsome face. 'And I made a few enquiries and discovered that far from having starved to death, his people actually owned the New Haven & Hartford Railroad and spent half the year on their diesel yacht in Monte Carlo!'

'Diesel!' I exclaimed. 'Europe! Poor Gatsby!'

'*Poor* Gatsby indeed!' thundered Buchanan. 'Rich, ambitious, greedy, wasteful Gatsby, more like! Rotten little parvenu!'

Daisy pulled away from me, and I could see she had been crying. There were deep grooves in her cheeks. I figured it best that I leave. But before straddling my log again, a thought occurred to me.

'He's throwing a party Saturday night,' I called. 'Why not come?'

Daisy nodded her lovely head, so that the encircling flies spun off in crazy pirouettes.

'We'll be there,' she said.

Gatsby could hardly contain himself. When I shouted the news into his hole, he started so violently that it took me best part of an hour to dig him out. It was then that I realised that Daisy Buchanan represented something to Jay Gatsby that I had not even begun to guess at. He took my arm in a rough grip and led me to the water's edge, and pointed out across the Sound.

'Useta be a green light on the end of her, you know, dock,' he muttered.

'Really?'

'No fooling, I swum over and stuck it there myself. So's I could look at where she was nights. It had this, like, eternacell battery, size of your finger, useta glow.' He turned hollow eyes to me. 'I mean, how much goddamn energy can a thing like that use?'

'I've never seen it,' I said.

'That's on account of where they found it, also kicked it in the goddamn sea right after,' he said. 'She sent me this note about what kind of bum uses up the precious resources of Planet Earth sticking green lights on people's premises. She continued only a parvenoo bum, that's what kind of bum. I never saw her again, old sport.'

'I see,' I said.

'Who'd have figured it?' he said quietly, to himself. 'All that godamn fuss about a green light? What is it with poor people, Nick?'

'I have to go and get dirty for your party,' I said.

I never saw him again.

There was a freak tide Saturday evening, and by the time I'd finished baling out my hole and got over to Gatsby's place, the party was over. There was just Gatsby under a sheet with this red stain on it, and a guy with home-made spectacles staring at it. Or near it, anyhow. That's one of the troubles with home-made spectacles.

'Rich son-of-a-bitch,' he said.

'What happened?' I asked.

'Middle of the party, guy busts in, says his name is Wilson and when is Gatsby going to settle his garage bill. Everybody stops suddenly and looks at Gatsby. Daisy Buchanan says there has to be some mistake, Gatsby don't have no automobile. Wilson says for her to stop putting him on, if Gatsby don't have no auto-mobile, what is that interesting green foreign job he drives into Wilson's garage every Friday and fills up with super? Gatsby suddenly screams that Wilson is lying, so Wilson pulls out this large iron item and blows Gatsby away.'

I looked down at the sheeted corpse.

'Someone ought to go see Daisy Buchanan,' I said.

'The Buchanans ain't there,' said the owl-eyed man. 'They shut their hole for the summer. Daisy says the wrong class of people is moving in, next thing it'll be TV and barbecued spare ribs. They went to stay with some people they know on the Bowery.'

Owl-eyes shambled off towards the water, and splashed away. I watched his ripples spread out towards Daisy's lightless dock. Gatsby had come a long way to this dark beach, and his dream must have seemed so close that he could hardly fail to grasp it. He did not know that it was already behind him, somewhere back in that vast obscurity beyond the city, where, one by one, the cars were grinding slowly to a halt.